# DICTIONARY *of Sanskrit* Names

COMPILED BY THE INTEGRAL YOGA INSTITUTE

Integral Yoga® Publications
Yogaville, Virginia

*Books by or about Sri Swami Satchidananda and Integral Yoga*

*Beyond Words*
*Guru and Disciple*
*Integral Yoga Hatha*
*Integral Yoga: The Yoga Sutras of Patanjali*
*Integral Yoga: The Yoga Sutras of Patanjali, Pocket Edition*
*Kailash Journal*
*The Golden Present*
*The Healthy Vegetarian*
*The Living Gita*
*The Master's Touch*
*The Mother is the Baby's First Guru*
*To Know Your Self*
*Peace is Within Our Reach*
*Sri Swami Satchidananda: Apostle of Peace*

*Printed in the United States of America*
*Library of Congress Cataloging-in-Publication Data:*

*Integral Yoga Institute*
*The Dictionary of Sanskrit Names*

*Includes index.*
*1. Names, Sanskrit--Dictionaries. 2. Sanskrit language-Etymology--Names.*
*PK903.D53 1989 491'.2321--dc19*
*CIP 88-26620 ISBN 0-932040-35-7*



*Integral Yoga® Publications*
*Yogaville*
*Buckingham, Virginia 23921 USA*

# *Table of Contents*

OM

Vag-arthav'iva Sampriktau
Vag-artha Pratipattaye
Jagataḥ Pitarau Vande
Pārvatī-Parameśwarau

For the comprehension of words and their meanings,
I salute the Mountain-Daughter (Pārvatī) and
the supreme Lord (Parameśwara), the Parents of the Universe,
who are ever united like words and their meanings.

-Kalidasa

Saccidānanda-Parabrahmaṇe Namah!

To the Supreme Absolute which is Truth-Consciousness-Bliss, salutations!

Saccidānanda-Rūpāya Vyāpine Paramātmane
Namaś Śrī-Guru-Nāthāya Prakāśānanda-Mūrtaye.

Salutations to the illustrious Lordly Guru whose nature
is Truth-Consciousness-Bliss, who is all-pervading, the Supreme Self
and the embodiment of Light and Bliss.

The compound *Sat-Cid-Ānanda*, meaning Truth-Consciousness-Bliss, is one of the main expressions given in Vedānta to indicate the nature of the Absolute (Brahman) and the Self (Ātman).

It is originally found in the Nṛisimha-Tāpinī Upanishad. The first part entitled Pūrvatāpinī reveals thus: "*Saccidānandamayam Param Brahma*: the Supreme Absolute is of the nature of Truth-Consciousness-Bliss." The second part called Uttaratāpinī says: "*Saccidānanda-Pūrṇātmānam*: the Self is filled with Truth-Consciousness-Bliss." Saccidānanda is thus the Swarūpa-lakshaṇa, or indication of the essential nature of Brahman and Ātman.

# *Dedication*

*The Dictionary of Sanskrit Names* is lovingly offered at the Feet of our revered Yoga Master and Guru, H.H. Sri Swami Satchidanandaji Maharaj (Sri Gurudev).

It is through His noble efforts and selfless service that countless seekers worldwide have been awakened to the profound and mystic wisdom of the East, which is expounded in its original language, Sanskrit, and is embodied in the multifarious names and forms that express the One Truth.

Sri Gurudev has inspired us to delve deep into the vast ocean of Sanskrit names to discover the jewel-like treasures hidden within each one.

On behalf of His devotees who have been blessed in receiving one of these names from Him, and in finding their lives transformed, we offer this work in gratitude and humility.

# Foreword

Sanskrit, the most ancient source of Indo-European speech, has been the vehicle of Indian civilization and culture. Written and spoken by the learned and the cultured, it is considered as the most sacred and noble language in India. Sanskrit vocabulary plays a lively part in the daily speech of hundreds of millions of people. Medical, astronomical, mathematical and juridical texts of ancient India are composed in Sanskrit. Besides the immense and significant Vedic literature, which records the profound experiences of the Seers and Sages, Sanskrit has also produced great philosophical, psychological and literary works.

Language is a communication system that relates to intimate connection between *śabda* and *artha*, word and its meaning. The Mīmāmsaka school of Indian philosophy says that the relation between word and its meaning is "inherent" and the Naiyyayika schools say that it is "conventional." In any case, a word has power to convey its meaning, and language is a valuable gift and guide to the study of peoples, cultures, and their thought structures.

The Editors quote the great Sanskrit poet and dramatist, Kalidasa, who opens his poetical work *Raghuvamśa* with a prayer for perfect union of speech and sense:

OM
Vag-arthav'iva Sampriktau
Vag-artha Pratipattaye
Jagataḥ Pitarau Vande
Pārvatī-Parameśwarau

"For the comprehension of words and their meanings,
I salute the Mountain-Daughter (Pārvatī) and
the supreme Lord (Parameśwara), the Parents of the Universe,
who are ever united like words and their meanings."

One cannot be too careful about the usage of words. Only when men know what names and words stand for and use them properly can there be real understanding and communication. Words will be misused and misinterpreted if the meaning is not clear.

The *Dictionary of Sanskrit Names* has collected over two thousand names and words, and presented them with their correct meanings and usage. It lists edifying names and attributes of God and divine personalities, and illustrates them with quotations from primary sources. The work is authoritative and scholarly. There is a felt need for this kind of *Dictionary*. Actually, it is more than a dictionary; it is also a thesaurus. Part II of the work serves this purpose. The Editors, Sri Swami Yogananda, Dr. Lakshmi Barsel and Swami Premananda Ma, deserve warm congratulations on a well-accomplished task.

As practitioners and teachers of Integral Yoga, they have been endeavoring to bring Yoga to the West. The English-speaking world is indebted to their cross-cultural, scholarly efforts for making the wisdom of the East a little more easy of access to the Westerner.

K.L. Seshagiri Rao, Ph.D.
Professor of Religious Studies, University Of Virginia
Chief Editor, *Encyclopedia of Hinduism*
Editor, *World Faiths Insight*

# *Acknowledgements*

The Integral Yoga Institute would like to thank the many devotees whose selfless efforts have borne great fruit in the form of this book:

Sri Swami Yoganandaji for his review and final corrections of the Sanskrit transliterations and definitions, and for the addition of scriptural references and discourses which have transformed this book from a simple dictionary into a spiritual gem.

Lakshmi Barsel, Ph.D., for her final editing and correction of the manuscript and for the Pronunciation Guide. In addition, we are indebted to her for inputing the entire manuscript on computer and for her continual availability as a consultant during production.

Swami Premananda Ma for the initial compilation of this book and for overseeing its production.

Shyamal Ganguly, Ph.D., for his review and initial correction of the Sanskrit transliterations.

Shraddha Boyd, Ranjani Lewis, Mrs. R. Rasiah and Swami Gurucharanananda Ma for their valuable work on the Cross-Reference.

Swami Sharadananda Ma for compiling the Guide and Index to the Cross-Reference, as well as serving as an editorial and production consultant.

Prema Conan for the design, layout and production of the book.

Peter Petronio for the front cover design.

Bhaktan Bennetta for proofreading.

Kumar Shapero for his technical assistance with this desktop-published project.

The numerous karma yogis who served with the Yogic spirit in so many ways.

# *Preface*

Sanskrit is a language specifically developed to bring out various powerful sound vibrations. Every letter in the Sanskrit alphabet has some beautiful, cosmic vibration. That is why each letter can be called a *bījakshara*, or seed word. There are fifty-one letters like that. They are developed that way. This means that the people who were able to meditate well and hear, as well as feel, the various sound vibrations, brought out this alphabet.

Sanskrit is considered to be the most ancient language in the world. There was a language even older than Sanskrit; but more letters were added to it to bring out the entire range of vibrations. That is why it has the name *Samskritam*. Though we call it as Sanskrit in English, it's Sanskrit name is *Samskritam*. It literally means: well (*sam*) made or written (*skritam*).

Sanskrit is mainly used for scriptural purposes (ie, writing of mantras and the verses connected with mantras, and the *Vedas, Upanishads, Bhagavad Gītā, Brahmasūtras* and so on). This is because of its beautiful vibrations. There was a time when it was a spoken language. Slowly people stopped using it for their daily conversation and instead it became what is called *Devabashan*: a divine language. This is similar to Arabic in the Mideast and Latin in the West. In various periods there were different languages used mainly for scriptural purposes because of their beautiful vibrations.

I am especially delighted to see this book, which highlights the depth and beauty of the Sanskrit language, being published in the West. The Sanskrit language, being a perfected one, embodies certain conducive sounds and vibrations that can enrich everyone's life. Even today, when you listen to some of the ancient prayers in temples and shrines, you may not understand all the words, but the prayers are still repeated in those languages because of the beautiful sound vibrations. These special sounds don't belong to any particular culture or country. Sanskrit does not only belong to India. Language belongs to everybody. Just because somebody else found it, doesn't mean that we should not use it. If you are in America and your food comes from an Italian restaurant, should you say you don't want it? We should learn to appreciate what any culture offers if what is offered is good and helpful. Wherever there is good, make use of it. Then you are truly a cultured person. We should really broaden our lives like that. Let us not limit ourselves by country, language or other boundaries.

This book also highlights the importance of names and their vibrations.

Each name has a quality. In addition, the name itself vibrates with that quality. Every word, every name has a vibration of its own. It is not mere sound. So when we name someone, we should see that the name has clean, beautiful vibrations, which will bring out those good qualities. A spiritual seeker should have such a name.

That is the special appeal of this book. Each name listed has a pure vibration and good meaning. If you already have such a name or if you are selecting one, reading about that name will help you live up to that.

My sincere wish and prayer is for every reader to be inspired and uplifted by the purifying vibrations of the Sanskrit language, and thus be filled with peace and joy, love and light. OM Śānti.

Sri Swami Satchidananda
Founder/Sri Gurudev Integral Yoga Institute

# *Introduction*

What is in a name? This is a rhethorical question perhaps; yet many religions and cultures have addressed this question, and entire books have been written on the subject. Languages may differ; philosophies may differ. But all cultures from time immemorial seem to have placed great significance upon, and regard for, names.

In the *Bible*, in Genesis itself, it is said, "God perfects His creation by naming creatures: day, night, heaven, earth, sea...He commands Adam to name each of the animals." Biblical names were often prophetic such as we see in Jacob's naming of Benjamin as "son of my right hand." We also see throughout Genesis that God would change the names of those who became especially devoted to Him, such as Abraham, Jacob, and Sarah. The names have great symbolism and power. "And Jacob said, 'I will not go except Thou bless me.' And God said: 'Thy name shall no more be called Jacob, but Israel (he who strives with God), for thou has striven with God and with man and has prevailed.'" (Genesis 32: 27-29)

Particularly, the name of God is seen to possess a tremendous potency. As God explains to Jacob, "But ask not after My Name, thou art not yet ready to apprehend it."

St. John Chrysostom admonishes, "The Name of Jesus Christ is terrible for demons, passions of the soul, and diseases. Let us adorn and protect ourselves with it." Christ Himself says to His disciples, "Those who believe in my Name shall cast out devils."

In the Hindu tradition, there is also great significance given to names and their meaning, the most important names being those of God Himself. There are thousands of names of God in this religious tradition. These are not different gods, but different qualities and attributes of one omnipotent God.

The names of God are considered so powerful that they themselves are often taken as the foundation for spiritual practice. The Hindu scripture, The *Bhagavatam*, states, "Unknowingly or knowingly the chanting of the Supreme, praiseworthy Name burns away man's sin, even as fire reduces to ashes."

H.H. Sri Swami Sivananda, the great spiritual Master of the Himalayas, spoke continually about the power of God's Name. "All the Divine potencies are hidden in the Lord's Name."

In his book, *Essentials of Hinduism,* Dr. K. Kharmaratnam explains the importance of selecting the proper name for a child. "The name of the Lord is said to be as important as His form. This is why parents often name their child after a Deity (i.e. Kṛishṇa, Rāma, Subrahmaṇya, Saraswatī, etc.) By calling their children many times a day by these names they are unconsciously uttering God's name. The meditation on the Name is calculated to fill the soul with devotion in the same way as the worship of an Image [of God] fills the worshipper's heart."

In the Judeo-Christian and Hindu traditions, we find the belief that the Creation came forth from sound vibration. "In the beginning there was the Word and the Word was with God, and the Word was God." The Hindus speak of the Word or *Vak* as the primeval sound "OM." It was from this cosmic sound vibration that the entire cosmos manifested.

The Sanskrit language is said to have been formulated according to the cosmic vibrations sensed by the ṛishis or sages of yore. The word *Samskritam* literally means: polished, perfect, complete.

Paramahamsa Yogananda, Founder of the Self-Realization Fellowship and one of the first Indian sages to bring Yoga to the West, explained that, "Its (Sanskrit's) alphabetical script is called Devanāgarī, literally 'divine abode.' 'Who knows my grammar knows God!' Pāṇini, great philologist of ancient India, paid tribute to the mathematical and psychological perfection of Sanskrit. He who would track language to its lair must indeed end as omniscient. 'The Sanskrit language', said Sir William Jones, founder of the Asiatic Society, 'whatever be its antiquity, is of a wonderful structure; more perfect than Greek, more copious than Latin, and more exquisitely refined than either.'"

Sri Swami Satchidananda agrees that the Sanskrit language is a perfected one, and as such, embodies highly conducive sounds and vibrations. He discusses the importance of names and their vibrations in the Preface of this book.

A decade under research, this *Dictionary of Sanskrit Names* was compiled by the Integral Yoga Institute, whose Founder is Sri Swami Satchidananda. It is designed to provide an extensive list of ancient, beautiful names with their significance and spiritual resonances. It can also serve as a concise, comprehensive reference dictionary to all persons who read or study works on Eastern spiritual traditions.

A unique and authoritative reference work, the *Dictionary of Sanskrit Names* is especially useful for scholars and researchers in the field of Indian, Hindu, and Buddhist philosophy and literature. It will also be an aid to spiritual aspirants in those traditions and to anyone interested in Hindu history and literature.

The *Dictionary* includes over 2,000 names, defined with commentary. Numerous references to classical scriptures of India are included to help with research and further study. The special qualities implied by each name, such as particular aspects of God, character traits, and spiritual virtues, are highlighted with cross-references to other names having the same quality.

In addition, a list of the many names of each Deity, including Vishṇu, Śiva and the names of Goddesses, generally available separately, are all in this one volume, which has to its advantage an easily readable and enjoyable presentation.

We sincerely hope this *Dictionary* will bring to light the extraordinary timelessness of the Sanskrit language, whose ancient wisdom has so much to offer our modern life.

The Editors

"The great spiritual language of the world."
- Joseph Campbell

# *Pronunciation Guide*

The *Dictionary of Sanskrit Names* is designed primarily for English-speaking people with little or no training in linguistics. For this reason, we have chosen to use a modified version of the standard international system of transliteration for Sanskrit. We use *sh* instead of *ṣ* ; *ṛi* instead of *ṛ*; *m* instead of *ṁ*; and after consonants, *w* instead of *v*. We made these changes so that the transliteration of each name would make it easy for English-speaking readers to pronounce the names correctly at first sight.

The system of transliteration is based on the principle of one symbol (i.e. letter or digraph) for one sound. Therefore, the symbol *c* will always sound like the *ch** in *birch* and **never** the *c* in *cat* or the *c* in *cell.*

The order of the letters in our system of transliteration follows that of the Roman alphabet except that *ā* follows *a*, *ī* follows *i*, *ū* follows *u*, and *ś* follows *s*. All of the other letters with diacritics, such as *ṭ*, *ṇ*, and *ṛ*, are treated like letters without diacritics. For example, given the two words *Kṛishṇa* and *Kriya* the *ṛ* in *Kṛishṇa* will be treated like an *r* without a diacritic and *Kṛishṇa* will occur before *Kriya*. All of the digraphs (e.g. *sh, bh, th,* etc.) will be listed as two letters (e.g. *s* + *h*, *b* + *h*, *t* + *h*) as in an English dictionary, instead of as one letter as they would be in a Sanskrit dictionary.

* The Sanskrit *c*, as in *candra*, is a palatal stop, which does not occur in English. The English *ch* in *birch* or *perch* is the closest English approximation to the Sanskrit sound.

*Vowels:*

| | |
|---|---|
| a | as the *a* in *soda* or the *u* in *but* |
| ā | as the *a* in *father* |
| i | as the *i* in *bit* |
| ī | as the *ee* in *beet* |
| u | as the *u* in *put* |
| ū | as the *oo* in *boot* |
| e | as the *a* in *able* |
| o | as the *o* in *go* |
| ai | as the *ai* in *aisle* or the *i* in *bite* |
| au | as the *ou* in *out* |

*Long Consonants:*

Doubled consonants such as *ll* or *ddh* indicate consonants that are held momentarily before being released.

*Consonants:*

| | |
|---|---|
| k | as the *k* in *skid* |
| kh | as the *k-h* in *black hat* |
| gh | as the *g-h* in *doghouse* |
| ṅ | as the *ng* in *sing* |
| ñ | as the *ñ* in *canyon* |
| c | as the *ch* in *arch* |
| ch | as the *ch-h* in *church-hall* |
| ś | as the *s* in *sure* |
| ṭ, ṭh, ḍ, ḍh, ṇ, sh, ṛ | are pronounced with the tip of the tongue curled back and touching the center of the hard palate. These sounds do not occur in English. |
| t | as the *t* in *street* |
| th | as the *t* in *try* |
| bh | as the *bh* in *abhor* |
| p | as the *p* in *speak* |
| ph | as the *p* in *pop* |
| ḥ | as the *h* in *hum*, except that this sound always occurs at the end of a word |

"Let us behold Thee in all these Names and Forms. Let us serve Thee in all these Names and Forms. Let us ever remember Thee, let us ever sing Thy glories. Let Thy Name be ever on our lips. Let us abide in Thee forever."

-Sri Swami Sivananda

"None can say with finality that He is 'this' and 'nothing else.' He is formless and again He is with forms."

-Sri Ramakrishna Paramahamsa

"My religion consists of a humble admiration of the illimitable Superior who reveals himself in the slight details we are able to perceive in our frail and feeble minds."

-Albert Einstein

"When we are conscious only of the Infinite One, and when our thought is wrapped up in the One (God, Brahma, Truth — It has many names), our whole being is flooded with new life and strength."

-Dr. Rammurti Misra

# PART I:

# DICTIONARY

# *How to Use the Dictionary*

The Dictionary provides an extensive listing of Sanskrit names, their meanings and scriptural references. Its primary purpose is to provide a listing of names and attributes of God, great sages, renowned devotees and Indian cultural heroes, for those seeking inspiring spiritual names. As such, we have intentionally omitted names of demons and less-than-saintly beings.

To find a specific name, look it up alphabetically as you would in any dictionary. The order of the letters follows that of the Roman alphabet, except that ā follows a, ī follows i, ū follows u and ś follows s.

In Part I, you will find the name, meaning and often a scriptural reference. Part II is a Cross-Reference, where you can find all the various names for any particular meaning, listed by subject.

# A

**Abhayan (m), Abhayā (f)** (*a* 'without' + *bhaya* 'fear') 1. The fearless. It is written in the Bṛihad-Āraṇyaka Upanishad, "Fearless indeed is the Absolute." In the Taittirīya Upanishad it is written, "The knower of the Absolute has no fear whatsoever." 2. One who does not produce fear in others.

**Abhū (m)** (*a* 'without' + *bhū* 'to be, exist') 1. The unborn. See the Bhagavad Gītā II:20-1; IV:6; VII: 24,25; IX:11; X:2,3,12. 2. The 437th name of Lord Vishṇu listed in the Vishṇu Sahasranāma. 3. A name of Lord Śiva.

**Acalan (m)** (*a* 'without' + *cala* 'moving') 1. The immovable. See the Bhagavad Gītā II:24,53; VI: 19, 21-22; XII:3; XIV:23. 2. The 745th name of Lord Vishṇu as listed in the Vishṇu Sahasranāma. In his commentary Śrī Saṅkara states, "He who is unshaking from His own nature, power, knowledge and other attributes." 3. Mountain.

**Acalā (f)** (*a* 'without' + *calā* 'moving') 1. The immovable. 2. Mother Earth.

**Acintya (m)** (*a* 'not' + *cintya* 'thought of, thinkable') 1. The unthinkable. See the Bhagavad Gītā II:25; VIII:9, XII:3 and the Māṇḍūkya Upanishad 7. 2. The 832nd name of Lord Vishṇu as listed in the Vishṇu Sahasranāma. In his commentary Śrī Saṅkara states, "He is unthinkable due to His inaccessibility to all means of knowledge, through His witnessing the knower, the knowable, the knowledge and the means of knowledge. He is also called unthinkable due to the impossibility to think of Him as 'this' or 'that,' since He is different from world expansion."

**Acyuta (m)** (*a* 'not' + *cyuta* 'lapsed, fallen') 1. The imperishable or unlapsing. 2. The 100th and the 318th names of Lord Vishṇu as listed in the Vishṇu Sahasranāma. In his commentary Śrī Saṇkara states, "He did not, does not and will not lapse from His own nature and power; He is thus unlapsing. Also (He is unlapsing) because He lacks the six conditions and modifications known as birth, existence, mutation, growth, decay and death." In the Vedas it is written, "He is eternal, auspicious, unlapsing." In the Mahābhārata, the Lord Himself says, "Since I did not lapse previously, I am by that fact the unlapsing."

**Adambha (m), Adambhā (f)** (*a* 'without'+*dambha* 'fraud, deceit') 1. The unpretentious or prideless. 2. A name of Lord Śiva. 3. The second of twenty means to knowledge listed in the Bhagavad Gītā XIII:7.

**Adhiguṇa (m)** (*adhi* 'superior' + *guṇa* 'quality of nature, virtue') Having high virtue or qualities.

**Adhyātman (m)** (*adhi* 'superior + *ātman* 'Self') The Supreme Self. See the Bhagavad Gītā III:30; VII:29; VIII:3; X:32; XI:1; XIII:11.

**Aditi (f)** 1. The boundless. 2. Name of the original Mother of the Gods, spouse of Ṛishi Kaśyapa. 3. The 21st of the 108 names of the Goddess Lakshmī.

**Adrijā (f)** (*adri* 'mountain' + *jā* 'born') 1. The mountain-born. 2. A name of the Goddess Pārvatī, the second daughter of Himavān or Himālaya.

**Adripati (m)** (*adri* 'mountain' + *pati* 'lord') 1. The Lord of the mountains. 2. A name of Himavān or Himālaya.

**Adrirāja (m)** (*adri* 'mountain' + *rāja* 'king') 1. The king of mountains. 2. A name of Himāvan or Himālaya.

**Adwaita (m)** (*a* 'not' + *dwaita* 'dual') The non-dual, meaning "the Truth is One." In the Upanishads it is said: "The Absolute is One and non-dual. There is no diversity whatsoever in It. It should be realized as One alone...This Self is the Absolute."

**Agastya (m)** 1. The mountain-thrower. 2. A celebrated Ṛishi who was born in a jar from Mitra and Varuṇa and who impeded the growth of the Vindhya mountains. He taught Rāma the famous "Hymn to the Sun," *Āditya-Hṛidaya-Stotra*, before Rāvaṇa was killed, and he conquered South India.

**Agni (m)** The (sacred) Fire or Fire-God. After Indra, this God is the most celebrated deity in the Vedas. He is called the "Mouth" of the Gods since He carries to them the offerings of men. He represents the fire of tapas, or austerities, as well as the light of knowledge.

**Ahalyā (f)** (*a* 'not' + *halyā* 'ugly') 1. The unugly, she who is without ugliness. In the Rāmāyaṇa it is written, "She who has no ugliness (*halya*) is known as *Ahalyā*, the unugly." 2. Beauty personified. 3. The first woman created by Brahmā, who married Ṛishi Gautama. She betrayed her husband and was made invisible through his curse. She recovered her form by the grace of Lord Rāma.

**Ahimsā (f)** (*a* 'non' + *himsā* 'injury') 1. The harmless or non-injuring. 2. The wife of Dharma. 3. The third of the twenty means to Knowledge listed in the Bhagavad Gītā XIII:7.

**Aikyan (m), Aikyā (f)** Unity or Oneness. It is written in the Upanishads: "It should be realized as One alone. What sorrow, what delusion for the seer of Oneness?" See Bhagavad Gītā VI: 31; VII:17; XIII:30; XVIII:20.

**Aindrī (f)** 1. She who belongs to the powerful (Lord Indra). 2. The powerful (Goddess). 3. A name of Sacī or Indrāṇī, spouse of Indra.

**Aiśwara (m) [Aiśwaran** in Tamil], **Aiswarī (f)** 1. He/she who belongs to Īśwara, the Lord. 2. The Lordly or sovereign. See the Bhagavad Gītā IX:5; XI:3,8,9.

**Aja (m) [Ajan** in Tamil] (*a* 'non' + *ja* 'born') 1. The unborn or birthless. 2. The 95th, 204th and 521st names of Lord Vishṇu as listed in the Vishṇu Sahasranāma. In his commentary Srī Saṅkara states, "1) Not being born, He is the unborn. In the Ṛigveda it is revealed, 'He has not been born, nor will He be. In the Mahābhārata the Lord says, 'Since I was not, am not and will not be born at any time, I, the inner Self of all beings, am thus known as the unborn.' 2) *Aja* also means the mover, referring to He who enters (*ajati*) the heart, or He who shoots arrows at devils. 3) Again, 'A' is Vishṇu so *Aja* would mean Kāma, or love, born of Vishṇu. Accordingly the Lord says in the Bhagavad Gītā: 'Among letters, I am the letter "A"' (X:33) and also, 'In beings, I am that love which is unopposed to scriptural law' (VII:11)." See the Bhagavad Gītā II:12, 20-1; VI:6; VII:24-5; IX:11; X:3, 12.

**Ajamīl (m)** The name of a devotee mentioned in the Bhāgavata Purāṇa, who attained liberation through chanting the Lord's name.

**Ajara (m)** [Ajaran in Tamil], **Ajarā (f)** (*a* 'not' + *jara* 'wearing out') The ever-youthful, the undecaying. In the Bṛihad-Āraṇyaka Upanishad the Self or the Absolute is described as "unborn, undecaying, immortal, undying and fearless." See the Bhagavad Gītā VII:29; XIV:20.

**Ajaya (m) [Ajayan** in Tamil], **Ajayā (f)** (*a* 'not' + *jaya* 'conquered') The unconquered. In the Muṇḍaka Upanishad it is written: "Truth alone wins, not untruth."

**Ajā (f)** (*a* 'not' + *jā* 'born') Māyā, the veiling power of God.

**Akartā (m)** (*a* 'non' + *kartā* 'doer') 1. The doerless or non-agent. See the Bhagavad Gītā IV:13; V:14; XIII:29; XIV:19; XVIII: 16. 2. Purusha.

**Akāma (m) [Akāman** in Tamil], **Akāmā (f)** (*a* 'without' + *kāma* 'desire') The desireless. In the Bṛihad-Āraṇyaka Upanishad it is written, "The desireless one, freed from desires, whose desire has been attained and consists of the very Self, such a person no longer transmigrates. Being the very Absolute, he is merged in It." See the Bhagavad Gīta II:55,70,71; III:37,39,43; IV:19; V:12,23,26; VI:18,24; VII:11; XV:5; XVI:21-23.

**Akhaṇḍa (m), Akhaṇḍā (f)** (*a* 'without' + *khaṇḍa* 'break') The indivisible; a name for Brahman, the Absolute, which is free from all bhedas or differences, such as Sajātīya, Vijātīya and Sragata. See the Bhagavad Gītā XIII:16, 27, 28.

**Akhilāṇḍeśwarī (f)** (*akhila* 'whole, without supplement' + *aṇḍa* 'egg' + *īśwarī* 'sovereign goddess') The Goddess of the whole egg-universe. This is a name of the Absolute as worshipped in South India. She is the ruling Goddess (*Īśwarī*) of the whole (*akhila*) egg (*aṇḍa*) of the universe, which is conceived as the egg of the Creator Brahmā.

**Akhilātman (m)** (*akhila* 'whole, without supplement' + *ātman* 'true Self') The partless Self. See The Bhagavad Gītā V:19.

**Akilbisha (m)** (*a* 'without' + *kilbisha* 'sin') The sinless. See the Bhagavad Gītā III:13; IV:21; VI:45; XVIII:47.

**Aklishṭa (m), Aklishṭā (f)** (*a* 'non' + *klishṭa* 'afflicted') The unafflicted. He/She who is free from the five "kleshas" or afflictions: ignorance, ego, affinity or attraction, repulsion, and clinging to life.

**Akopa (m)** (*a* 'without' + *kopa* 'anger, fury') 1. The angerless. 2. One of Daśaratha's ministers.

**Akrodha (m)** (*a* 'without' + *krodha* 'anger') The angerless. See the Bhagavad Gītā II:56; III:37; IV:10; V:23,26,28; XVI:2,21,22; XVIII:53.

**Akrūra (m)** [**Akrūran** in Tamil] (*a* 'non' + *krūra* 'cruel, terrible') 1. He who is not cruel. 2. The 915th name of Lord Vishṇu as listed in the Vishṇu Sahasranāma. In his commentary Srī Saṅkara states, "What is called cruelty is that mind peculiarity born of extreme anger, an internal over-excitement accompanied by tenacity. Since the Lord is in a state where all desires have been attained and has verily an absence of desire, He is without anger and therefore without cruelty. He is thus uncruel." 3. The name of Srī Kṛishṇa's paternal uncle.

**Akshara (m)** (*a* 'non' + *kshara* 'transitory') 1. The imperishable. See the Bhagavad Gītā VIII:3, 11,21; XI:18; XII:3. 2. The 17th and 481st names of Lord Vishṇu as listed in the Vishṇu Sahasranāma. In his commentary Srī Saṅkara comments, "He who does not perish is verily the supreme Self called the Imperishable. Truly speaking, He is not distinct from the innermost Consciousness of individuals, as is revealed in the Chāndogya Upanishad, 'Thou art That.' Their difference is simply due to conditioning factors." 3. The primordial sound of the universe, "OM." See the Bhagavad Gītā VIII:13; X:25.

**Akshayan (m), Akshayā (f)** (*a* 'without' + *kshaya* 'depreciation,) 1. The undecaying 2. The everlasting one.

**Amalan (m)** (*a* 'without' + *mala* 'impurity') 1. The immaculate. 2. Free from all defects.

**Amalaratnā (f)** (*amala* 'immaculate' + *ratnā* 'jewel') 1. The immaculate jewel. 2. Crystal.

**Amalā (f)** (*a* 'without' + *mala* 'impurity') 1. The immaculate. 2. Free from all defects. 3. A name of the Goddess Lakshmī.

**Amaleśwarī (f)** (*amala* 'immaculate' + *īśwarī* 'sovereign goddess') The immaculate Goddess.

**Amarabhartā (m)** (*amara* 'immortal' + *bhartā* 'supporter') The supporter of the immortals (Gods); a name of Indra.

**Amaraja (m)** (*amara* 'immortal' + *ja* 'born, caused') Born of the immortals (Gods).

**Amaran (m), Amarā (f)** (*a* 'not' + *mara* 'dying') 1. The immortal or undying. 2. A general name for all the Gods.

**Amaraprabhu (m)** (*amara* 'immortal' + *prabhu* 'lord') 1. The Lord of the immortals (Gods). 2. The 50th name of Lord Vishṇu as listed in the Vishṇu Sahasranāma. See the Bhagavad Gītā X:2; XI:15.

**Amararatna (m), Amararatnā (f)** (*amara* 'immortal' + *ratna* 'jewel') 1. The jewel of the immortals (Gods). 2. Crystal.

**Amararāja (m)** (*amara* 'immortal' + *rāja* 'king') The king of the immortals (Gods); a name of Indra.

**Amarasarit (f)** (*amara* 'immortal' + *sarit* 'river') The river of the immortals (Gods); a name of the Ganges River.

**Amarādhipa (m)** (*amara* 'immortal' + *adhipa* 'ruler, lord') The supreme protector of the immortals (Gods); a name of Lord Siva.

**Amarādri (m)** (*amara* 'immortal' + *adri* 'mountain') The mountain of the immortals (Gods); a name of Mount Meru.

**Amarāvatī (f)** (*amarā* 'immortals' + *vatī* 'abode') The abode of the immortals (Gods); Indra's heavenly residence.

**Amareśa (m)** (*amara* 'immortal' + *īśa* 'lord') The Lord of the immortals (Gods); a name of Lord Siva.

**Ambarīsha (m)** The name of a Rājarshi, an ancestor of Daśaratha and the King of Ayodhyā.

**Ambayā (f)** The Mother.

**Ambā (f)** 1. The Mother. 2. A general name for all the Goddesses. 3. The Bhagavad Gītā. In the Gītā Dhyānam is the verse, "*Amba Twām Anusandadhāmi...,*" "O Mother, I meditate upon Thee..."

**Ambālā (f)** The Mother.

**Ambālikā (f)** 1. The Mother. 2. The Mother of Pāṇḍu and wife of Vicitravīrya in the Mahābhārata.

**Ambālī (f)** The Mother.

**Ambhrina (m)** 1. The powerful. 2. The name of a Ṛishi, who was the father of the Goddess of speech.

**Ambikā (f)** 1. The Mother. 2. A name of the Goddess Pārvatī.

**Ambupati (m)** (*ambu* 'water' + *pati* 'lord') The Lord of the waters; a name of Varuṇa.

**Ameyan (m), Ameyā (f)** (*a* 'not' + *meya* 'measurable') The immeasurable. See the Bhagavad Gītā II:18; X: 40-2.

**Amita (m)** (*a* 'not' + *mita* 'measured') Not measured, the immeasurable.

**Amitābha (m)** (*amita* 'immeasurable' + *ābha* 'luster, light') Having immeasurable splendor.

**Amiti (f)** (*a* 'without' + *miti* 'measure') Boundlessness.

**Ammā (f)** [Tamil] The Mother.

**Amogha (m), Amoghā (f)** (*a* ' without' + *mogha* 'failure') 1. The unfailing. 2. The 110th and 154th names of Lord Vishṇu listed in the Vishṇu Sahasranāma. In his commentary Śrī Saṅkara states, "1) When worshipped, praised or remembered, the Lord bestows all fruits. He does not behave lightly. 2) Also He is unfailing because His will is not untrue."

**Amṛita (m)** (*a* 'without' + *mṛita* 'death') 1. The immortal. 2. Ambrosia, the nectar of immortality. 3. The 119th name of Lord Vishṇu as listed in the Vishṇu Sahasranāma. In his commentary Śrī Śaṅkara states, "He for whom there is no death is the Immortal. In the Bṛihad-Āraṇyaka Upanishad it is written, '(He is) undecaying, immortal.'"

**Amṛitabandhu (m)** (*amṛita* 'immortal' + *bandhu* 'friend, relative') 1. The immortal friend. 2. Friend of immortality, referring to Indra's horse, Uccaiśśravas, which was born along with the nectar of immortality at the churning of the milk ocean. See the Bhagavad Gītā X:27.

**Amṛitamālinī (f)** (*amṛita* 'immortality' + *mālinī* 'garlanded') 1. Immortality garlanded. 2. Having an immortal garland. 3. A name of Goddess Durgā.

**Amṛitavapu (m)** (*amṛita* 'immortal' + *vapu* 'form') 1. Having immortal form or body. 2. The 814th name of Lord Vishṇu as listed in the Vishṇu Sahasranāma. In his commentary Śrī Śaṅkara states, "He whose form or body is devoid of death has an immortal Body."

**Amṛitā (f)** (*a* ' without' + *mṛitā* 'death') 1. The immortal. 2. Ambrosia, the nectar of immortality. 3. The 35th of Goddess Lakshmī's 108 names.

**Amṛitāmśu (m)** (*amṛita* 'immortality, ambrosia' + *amśu* 'ray') 1. Having ambrosial rays. 2. A reference to the moon when it rose from the milk ocean during its churning.

**Amṛiteśa (m)** (*amṛita* 'immortal' + *īśa* 'lord') 1. The Lord of the immortals (Gods). 2. The immortal Lord. 3. A name of Lord Śiva.

**Amśula (m)** [**Amśulan** in Tamil], **Amśulā (f)** The radiant or beaming.

**Amśuman (m)** 1. Possessing radiance or rays. 2. The sun and the moon. 3. The grandson of Sagara, a great king mentioned in the Rāmāyaṇa.

**Amśumatī (f)** Possessing radiance or rays.

**Amśumālī (m)** (*amśu* 'ray' + *mālī* 'garlanded') Garlanded with rays; the sun.

**Anagha (m)** [**Anaghan** in Tamil] (*an* 'without' + *agha* 'misdeed, impurity') 1. The sinless or faultless. See the Bhagavad Gītā IV:14; V:14-15,19; IX:9; XIII:31-2. 2. The 146th and 831st names of Lord Vishṇu as listed in the Vishṇu Sahasranāma. In his commentary Śrī Śaṅkara states, "He of whom there is not the double sin of pain and evil, is the sinless. In the Chāndogya Upanishad it is revealed, 'The Self is untouched by sin.'" 3. A name of Arjuna. See the Bhagavad Gītā III:3; XIV:6; XV:20.

**Anaghā (f)** (*an* 'without' + *aghā* 'misdeed, impurity') 1. The sinless or faultless. 2. The 32nd of the Goddess Lakshmī's 108 names. See the Bhagavad Gītā

IV:14; V:14-5,19; IX:9; XIII: 31-2.

**Anahaṅkārin (m), Anahaṅkārinī (f)** (*an* 'without' + *ahaṅkārin/inī* 'ego') 1. Detached from actions and their fruits, without "doerness." 2. One who does not identify the Self with the non-self. 3. Egoless, selfless. See the Bhagavad Gītā II:71; III:27,28; V:8,9; XII:13; XIII:8, 20-1,29; XIV:19,23; XVIII:16, 17,26,53,58,59.

**Anala (m) [Analan** in Tamil] 1. (*An-ala)* Unlimited. 2. The 293rd and 711th names of Lord Vishṇu as listed in the Vishṇu Sahasranāma. In his commentary Śrī Śaṅkara states, "1) The living soul who receives (*lāti*) the breaths (*anān*) or prāṇas as his Self is '*Ana-la*,' the receiver of breaths. 2) He is also odorless '*A-nala*,' as is said in the Bṛihad-Āraṇyaka Upanishad, 'The Imperishable is odorless, tasteless.' 3) Again, He for whom there is no limitation (*alam*) in power and glory, is '*An-ala*,' the unlimited." 3. (*An-ala*) The insatiable, a name of Agni, the fire-God. He has not (*an*) or never enough (*alam*) fuel to consume, and is thus called "*An-ala*," the insatiable.

**Ananta (m)** (*an* 'without' + *anta* 'limit, end') 1. The infinite or endless. See the Bhagavad Gītā II:12,17,20; X:19,40; XI:16,19, 37,38,47. 2. A name of Śesha, the divine serpent. See the Bhagavad Gītā X:29. 3. The 659th and 886th names of Lord Vishṇu as listed in the Vishṇu Sahasranāma. In his commentary Śrī Śaṅkara states, "Due to His all-pervasiveness, His eternity and His being the Self of all, the Lord is not limited by space, time and objects, He is infinite. The Taittirīya Upanishad reveals Him thus, 'The Absolute is truth, knowledge and infinitude.' And in the Vishṇu Purāṇa it is written, 'The celestial musicians, the nymphs, the accomplished ones, the Kinnaras, Uragas and Cāraṇas, do not reach the end of His attributes, thus the imperishable Lord is called the infinite.'"

**Anantā (f)** (*an* 'without' + *anta* 'limit, end') 1. The infinite or endless. 2. A name of the Goddess Pārvatī.

**Anasūyā (f)** (*an* 'without' + *asūyā* 'displeasure, anger, grudge') 1. She who has transcended envy or jealousy. See the Bhagavad Gītā III:31,32; IX:1; XVIII:67,71. 2. The ideal spouse. 3. The wife of Ṛishi Atri and the mother of Dattātreya.

**Anādi (m)** (*an* 'without' + *adi* 'beginning') 1. The beginningless. 2. The 941st name of Lord Vishṇu as listed in the Vishṇu Sahasranāma. In his commentary Śrī Śaṅkara states, "He of whom there is no beginning or cause, is the Beginningless, being the cause of all." See the Bhagavad Gītā XI:19; XIII:12,31.

**Anāmaya (m), Anāmayā (f)** (*an* 'without' + *āmaya* 'disease') 1. The diseaseless.

2. The troubleless. Śrī Śaṅkara states, "He who is not afflicted by internal or external ills produced by past karma is '*Anāmaya*,' the troubleless." See the Bhagavad Gītā II:51; XIV:6.

**Anāpadā (f)** (*an* 'without' + *āpadā* 'misfortune') Without misfortune or calamity.

**Anāśinī (f), Anāśī (m)** (*an* 'without' + *nāśinī/ī* 'perishing') The indestructible. See the Bhagavad Gītā II:17,18.

**Andhakāri (m)** (*andhaka* 'gloom, n. of a demon' + *ari* 'enemy') The enemy of the demon Andhaka (Gloom); a name of Lord Śiva.

**Aṅgiras (m)** The name of a great Ṛishi, who was one of the seers of the Ṛigveda. His name is mentioned in the Muṇḍaka Upanishad.

**Anila (m)** 1. The beginningless. 2. The unaffected. 3. The undissolved. 4. The 234th and 812th name of Lord Vishṇu listed in the Vishṇu Sahasranāma. In his commentary Śrī Śaṅkara states, "1) Not having come into being, He is *Anila*, the beginningless because of His beginninglessness. 2) He is also *Anila* because He is unaffected by anything. 3) He is undissolved (during Pralaya, or world dissolution). 4) He is devoid of actuation and is thus unactuating. 5) He is the opposite of sleep and ignorance, and is thus non-ignorant because His own nature is ever awakened. 6) Again, He is non-abyssal, that is to say easily accessible to His devotees." 5. A name of Vāyu, God of Air.

**Aniruddha (m)** 1. The unobstructed. 2. The 185th and 638th names of Lord Vishṇu in the Vishṇu Sahasranāma. In his commentary Śrī Śaṅkara states, "1) He is unobstructed by anyone in His manifestations or incarnations. 2) It also refers to the fourth Vyūha, or form, of the Lord." 3. A son of Śrī Kṛishṇa. 4. A name of Lord Śiva.

**Añjali (m), Añjalī (f)** Two hands held with palms together, as in greeting.

**Añjanā (f)** The mother of Hanuman.

**Annadā (f)** (*anna* 'food' + *dā* 'giver') 1. The giver of food. 2. A name of the Goddess Pārvatī or Annapūrṇā.

**Annadāyinī (f)** (*anna* 'food' + *dāyinī* 'giver') The compassionate giver of food.

**Annam (n or f)** 1. Food. 2. Sustenance of life.

**Annapati (m)** (*anna* 'food' + *pati* 'lord') 1. The Lord of food. 2. A name of the sun. 3. A name of fire. 4. A name of Lord Śiva.

**Annapūrṇā (f)** (*anna* 'food' + *pūrṇā* 'full') 1. The nourishing fullness. 2. Filled with food. 3. A name of the Goddess Pārvatī. Śrī Śaṅkara composed the following verses dedicated to Annapūrṇā, which are used currently as a meal prayer:

*Annapūrṇe Sadāpūrṇe*
*Śaṅkara-Prāṇa-Vallabhe,*
*Jñāna-Vairāgya-Siddhyartham*
*Bhikshām Dehi ca Pārvati.*

*Mātā ca Pārvatī Devī*
*Pitā Devo Maheśwaraḥ,*
*Bāndhavāḥ Śiva-Bhaktāha*
*Swadeśo Bhuvana-Trayam.*

O Goddess filled with food, O ever-filled Goddess,
O Beloved of Śaṅkara's (Śiva's) breath,
for the sake of attaining knowledge and dispassion,
grant me alms, O Mountain-Daughter (Pārvatī)!

My Mother is the Mountain-Daughter Goddess (Pārvatī).
My Father is the Divine, the great Lord (Maheśwara).
My relatives are the devotees of Śiva,
and the three worlds are my home (country).

**Antarjyoti (m or f)** (*antar* 'inner' + *jyoti* 'light') The inner light. See the Bhagavad Gītā V:24; XIII:17.

**Antaryāmī (m), Antaryāminī (f)** (*antar* 'inner' + *yāmī/inī* 'guide') The internal ruler. It is written in the Bṛihad-Āraṇyaka Upanishad, "He who, residing in the universe, is internal to the universe, Whom the universe does not know, Whose body is the universe and Who rules the universe from within, He is thy very Self, the internal Ruler (*Antar-Yāmī*), the immortal. Unseen, He is the seer. Unheard, He is the hearer. Unthought, He is the thinker. Unknown, He is the knower. There is no other seer but Him. No other hearer but Him, no other thinker but Him, no other knower but Him. He is thy very Self. The internal ruler (*Antar-Yāmī*), the immortal. What is different from Him is perishable."

**Anyā (f)** The inexhaustible.

**Aparājita (m)** (*a* 'not' + *parājita* 'conquered') 1. The unconquered. 2. The 716th and 862nd names of Lord Vishṇu as listed in the Vishṇu Sahasranāma. In his commentary Śrī Śaṅkara states, "The Lord who is not conquered internally by desires and the rest, and by demons and others externally, is called the unconquered."

**Aparṇā (f)** (*a* 'without' + *parṇā* 'leaf') 1. The leafless. 2. A name of the Goddess Pārvatī. Kālidāsa refers to Her by this name in his poem, "*Kumāra-Sambhava*," in which he describes the austerities that she performed to obtain Lord Śiva as Her spouse: "Living on mere dry leaves is the last limit of austerity, yet She forsook that food. Hence speaking of that lovely-faced Goddess, those who know the past events say 'the Leafless' (*Aparṇā).*"

**Apnavāna (m)** Name of a Ṛishi belonging to Bhṛigu's lineage.

**Aramati (f)** The Goddess of devotion, who protects worshippers and pious acts.

**Araṇyadevī (f)** (*araṇya* 'wilderness, forest' + *devi* 'goddess') The Goddess of the forest.

**Aravinda (m)** A type of day-lotus.

**Aravindāksha (m)** (*aravinda* 'day-lotus' + *aksha* 'eye') 1. The lotus-eyed. 2. The 347th name of Lord Vishṇu as listed in the Vishṇu Sahasranāma. Lord Vishṇu is known for having plucked out His own eye in order to complete His worship service of Lord Śiva with one thousand lotuses, as one lotus was missing. In his commentary Śrī Śaṅkara states, "He whose eyes resemble the lotus, is the lotus-eyed."

**Arcanā (f)** The main part of a pūjā, or worship service, in which one offers flowers at the feet of a Deity or Guru while reciting His or Her holy names. See the Bhagavad Gītā IX: 34; XVIII:65.

**Arga (m)** The name of the Ṛishi who was one of the seers of the Sāmaveda.

**Arhat (m)** 1. The worthy or deserving. 2. The 873rd name of Lord Vishṇu as listed in the Vishṇu Sahasranāma. In his commentary Śrī Śaṅkara states, "The Lord is worthy (Lord fit to be worshipped through formulas of welcome, giving of seat, praise, offering of water for the mouth and water for the feet, chanting of hymns, salutations and other means of worship"). 3. Title of Jains and Buddhists.

**Aripra (m), Ariprā (f)** (*a* 'without' + *ripra* 'impurity, dirt') The spotless or faultless.

**Aripu (m)** (*a* 'without' + *ripu* 'enemy') 1. Without enemy. 2. Not an enemy. See the Bhagavad Gītā VI:5,6.

**Arjuna (m)** 1. The white or clear. In his commentary on the Bhagavad Gītā XVIII:61, Śrī Śaṅkara explains *Arjuna* as "He who is of a clear inner nature, pure-minded. It is said in the Ṛigveda, 'The dark day and the clear (*arjunam*) day.'" 2. Lord Kṛishṇa's disciple in the Bhagavad Gītā, who was a partial incarnation of Indra and the third of the five Pāṇḍava brothers.*

**Arjunī (f)** 1. The white or clear.

**Arka (m)** [in Tamil **Arkan**] 1. The adored or praised. 2. The beaming. 3. The 795th name of Vishṇu as listed in the Vishṇu Sahasranāma. In his commentary Śrī Śaṅkara states, "He is the praised on account of His being fit to be worshipped even by the most worshipful Deities like Brahmā and other Gods." 4. A name of Sūrya, the Sun-God. 5. A name of Agni, the Fire-God.

**Arkinī (f), Arkī (m)** The radiant, beaming, or praising.

**Arugan (m)** A name of Lord Śiva.

**Arula (f)** [Tamil] Grace; filled with grace.

**Aruṇan (m)** 1. The red or rosy. 2. The name of a great sage who was the father of the famous Uddālaka.

**Aruṇā (f)** 1. The red or rosy. 2. The dawn.

**Arundhatī (f)** 1. The name of Ṛishi Vasishṭha's wife, who was formally Brahmā's daughter, Sandhyā. Considered the ideal wife, she is invoked during marriage ceremonies. 2. The tiny star belonging to the Great Bear constellation, which is a symbol of Vasishṭha's wife.

**Aryaman (m)** 1. The possessor of greatness. 2. One of the twelve Ādityas presiding over the sun and the eyes, which is invoked in the Śānti mantra:

*OM Śam no Mitraḥ!*
*Śam Varuṇaḥ!*
*Śam no Bhavatv'Aryamā!*

May Mitra be blissful to us!
May Varuṇa be blissful to us!
May *Aryaman* be blissful to us!

**Asakti (f)** (*a* 'without' + *sakti*'attachment') Non-attachment, which is the thirteenth of the twenty means to knowledge listed in the Bhagavad Gītā XIII:9. In his commentary on this passage Śrī Śaṅkara states, "*Sakti* or

---

* The five Pāṇḍava brothers are Yudhisṭhira, Bhīma, Arjuna, Nakula and Sahadeva.

attachment is nothing but pleasure for sense-objects which are causes of attachment. The absence of such attachment is *Asakti*, non-attachment."

**Asaṅgan (m), Asaṅginī (f)** (*a* 'without' + *saṅga/inī* 'attachment') The unattached. It is written in the Bṛihad-Āraṇyaka Upanishad, "The Self is unattached, for It does not stick to anything." See the Bhagavad Gītā II:48; III:7,9,25; IV:20,23; V:10-12; VI:4; IX:9; XI:55; XII:18; XIII:9; XV:3,5; XVIII:6,9,10,23,26,49.

**Ashāḍha (m)** 1. The invincible. 2. The constellation Cancer. 3. The zodiac sign Cancer.

**Aśoka (m)** (*a* 'without' + *śoka* 'sorrow') 1. He who is without sorrow and without afflictions. It is written in the Chāndogya Upanishad, "The knower of the Self crosses over sorrow." See the Bhagavad Gītā II: 11,14,15,25,30; VI:22,23; XII:17; XVIII: 54, 66. 2. The 336th name of Lord Vishṇu, listed in the Vishṇu Sahasranāma. In his commentary Śrī Śaṅkara states, "He who is untouched by the six waves of hunger and thirst, sorrow and delusion, decay and death, is the sorrowless."

**Aśokā (f)** (*a* 'without' + *śokā* 'sorrow') 1. She who is without sorrow and without afflictions. It is written in the Chāndogya Upanishad, "The knower of the Self crosses over sorrow." 2. The 34th of the Goddess Lakshmī's 108 names. See the Bhagavad Gītā II:11,14,15,25,30; VI:22,23; XII:17; XVIII:54,66.

**Atideva (m)** (*ati* 'beyond' + *deva* 'shining, god') 1. The exceedingly luminous. 2. Surpassing the gods. It is written in the Bṛihad-Āraṇyaka Upanishad, "Even now, whoever knows the Truth as 'I am the Absolute,' that person becomes the all. Even the gods cannot prevent him from doing so, for he becomes their very Self."

**Atirāja [m)** (*ati* 'beyond' + *rāja* 'king') 1. The supreme king. 2. One who is superior to a king.

**Ativiśwa (m)** (*ati* 'beyond' + *viśwa* 'the all, universe') 1. Surpassing all the universe. 2. The name of a muni.

**Atkila (m)** The name of a Ṛishi.

**Atri (m)** 1. The devourer. 2. One of the seven Ṛishis or seers of the Vedas, who was born of Brahmā's mind.

**Avadhūta (m)** 1. He who has shaken off (all attachment). 2. A name of Dattātreya. 2. A name of a sage that taught King Yadu in the Bhāgavata Purāṇa. 3. The highest class of renunciates. 4. In the Avadhūta Upanishad the word *avadhūta* is explained by dividing it into four syllables:

*Aksharatwād-Vareṇyatwād-*
*Dhūta-Samsāra-Bandhanātṇ*
*Tat-Twam-Asy'ādi-Lakshyatwād-*
*Avadhūta Itīryate.*

Due to his imperishableness, his excellence,
his having shaken off the bondage of transmigration,
and his being the aim of "Thou art That" and
other Vedāntic formulas, an *Avadhūta* is thus named.

**Avanipāla (m)** (*avani* 'earth' + *pāla* 'protector') 1. The earth protector. 2. Title for a king. 3. A name used to refer to Śrī Rāma in Kālidāsa's poem "Raghuvamśa."

**Avanīśa (m)** (*avani* 'earth' + *śa* 'lord') 1. The Lord of the earth. 2. Title for a king.

**Avanīśwara (m)** (*avani* 'earth' + *īśwara* 'lord') 1. The Lord of the earth. 2. Title for a king.

**Avanīśwarī (f)** (*avani* 'earth' + *īśwarī* 'sovereign goddess') 1. Queen of the earth. 2. Title for a queen.

**Avarṇa (m), Avarṇā (f)** (*a* 'without' + *varṇa* 'color') 1. The colorless. In the Śwetāśwatara Upanishad IV:1 it is written: "May the One, the Colorless, who creates various colors through His illusive power...may that Divine endow us with an auspicious intelligence!"

**Avatāra (m), Avatāriṇī (f)** 1. An incarnation of God. See the Bhagavad Gītā IV:6-8. 2. The descent.

**Avikāriṇī (f), Avikārī (m)** (*a* 'without' + *vikārī/iṇī* 'change') The immutable, unchanging. See the Bhagavad Gītā II:25.

**Avināśinī (f), Avināśī (m)** (*a* 'without' + *vināśī/inī* 'cessation, destruction') The indestructible. See the Bhagavad Gītā II:17,18.

# Ā

**Ābhā (f)** (*ā* 'quite, entirely' + *bhā* 'brilliant') The luminous.

**Ābhāti (f)** (*ā* 'quite, entirely' + *bhāti* 'beam') The light.

**Ādarśa (m)** (*ā* 'besides, also' + *darśa* 'seeing') 1. Mirror, image, copy. 2. The ideal.

**Ādi (m)** The first or primeval. See The Bhagavad Gītā VIII:28; IX:13; X:2; XV:4.

**Ādideva (m)** (*ādi* 'primeval, first' + deva 'god') 1. The primeval God. 2. The 334th and 490th names of Lord Vishṇu as listed in the Vishṇu Sahasranāma. In his commentary Śrī Śaṅkara states, "1) He is the first Cause through which all beings begin and He is also the Divine. 2) He possesses such qualities like liberality (*dāna*). 3) He possesses such attributes as brilliance (*dyotana*) and others." See the Bhagavad Gītā VII:6; X:12,20; XI:38.

**Ādikavi (m)** (*ādi* 'primeval, first' + *kavi* 'poet'). 1. The first poet. 2. Vālmīki, the author of the Rāmāyaṇa.

**Ādinātha (m)** (*ādi* 'primeval, first' + *nātha* 'master') 1. The primordial master. 2. A name of Lord Śiva.

**Ādirāja (m)** (*ādi* 'primeval, first' + *rāja* 'king') 1. The first king. 2. A name of Manu, the son of Sūrya, the Sun-God.

**Āditya (m)** [in Tamil **Āditya**] 1. The son of Aditi (i.e. the Sun). 2. The 40th and 563rd names of Lord Vishṇu as listed in the Vishṇu Sahasranāma. In his commentary Śrī Śaṅkara states, "1) *Āditya* is the golden being residing in the orb of the sun. 2) It is also Vishṇu among the twelve *Ādityas*, as is said in the Bhagavad Gītā X:21. 3) He is also the consort of the undivided Mother Earth, as is said in the Vedas. 4) It again refers to His dwarf incarnation from Aditi and Kaśyapa. 5) Or it refers to an analogy of the one sun being reflected as many in several water-pots with the one Self being reflected as many in various bodies." Also see the Bhagavad Gītā V:16; VIII:9; XI:12; XIII:33; XV:12.

**Ādyā (f)** 1. The first or primeval (Goddess). 2. Mother Earth. 3. A name of the Goddess Durgā.

**Ākāśa (m), Ākāśā (f)** (*ā* 'entirely' + *kāsa* 'visible') 1. Clear space, sky. 2. The transparent. See the Bhagavad Gītā IX:6; XIII:32.

**Ākūti (f)** (*ā* 'entirely' + *kūti* 'intention') 1. Intention or wish. 2. Daughter of Manu.

**Ānanda (m)** (*ā* 'entirely' + *nanda* 'joyful') 1. The blissful. 2. The 526th and 560th names of Vishṇu listed in the Vishṇu Sahasranāma. In his commentary Śrī Śaṅkara states, "1) He whose own nature is bliss and happiness, is the blissful. 2. Also He is blissful on account of His richness in all glories."

**Ānandabhairava (m)** (*ānanda* 'bliss' + *bhairava* 'fearful') 1. The blissful and fearful. 2. A name of Lord Śiva, who is blissful to His devotees and fearful to others who do not understand Him.

**Ānandabhairavī (f)** (*ānanda* 'bliss' + *bhairavī* 'fearful') 1. The blissful and fearful. 2. A name of the Goddess Kālī.

**Ānandamaya (m)** (*ānanda* 'bliss' + *maya* 'consisting of') 1. Consisting of bliss. 2. The fifth "kośa," or sheath, of the soul in the state of deep sleep, where the individual is very near to pure bliss, though ignorance preponderates.

**Ānandamayī (f)** (*ānanda* 'bliss' + *mayī* 'consisting of') 1. Consisting of bliss. 2. The name of a twentieth century saint.

**Ānandana (m)** The blissful.

**Ānandaprema (m), Ānandapremā (f)** (*ānanda* 'bliss' + *prema* 'divine love') Pure bliss and love.

**Ānandāmṛita (m)** (*ānanda* 'bliss' + *amṛita* 'nectar') 1. The nectar of bliss. 2. Blissful and immortal.

**Ānandinī (f), Ānandī (f)** (*ā* 'entirely' + *nandī/inī* 'joyful') The blissful.

**Ānandita (m), Ānanditā (f)** The delighted.

**Āndāl (f)** [Tamil] A woman saint of South India, who lived in the seventh century A.D.

**Āñjaneya (m)** The son of Añjanā (i.e. Hanuman).

**Āprīta (m), Āprītā (f)** (*ā* 'entirely' + *prītā* 'pleased, glad') The gladdened or joyou

**Āratī (f)** The final waving of lights before an altar in an evening worship service.

**Ārjava (m)** [in Tamil **Ārjavan**], **Ārjavā (f)** 1. The straightforward. 2. The truthful. See the Bhagavad Gītā XIII:7; XVI:1; XVII:14; XVIII:42.

**Ārohī (m), Ārohiṇī (f)** (*ā* 'entirely' + *rohī/iṇī* 'rising') The ascending, climbing. See the Bhagavad Gītā VI: 3-5.

**Ārumugan (m)** [Tamil] The six-faced god, Shaṇmukha.

**Āruṇi (m)** The son of Aruṇa (i.e. the sage Uddālaka).

**Ārya (m)** 1. The noble, great, or excellent. 2. The truthful.

**Āryā (f)** 1. The noble, great, or excellent. 2. The truthful. 3. A name of the Goddess Pārvatī.

**Āryaka (m), Āryakā (f)** 1. The noble, great, or excellent. 2. The truthful.

**Āryakumāra (m)** (*ārya* 'noble' + *kumāra* 'boy') The noble prince or youth.

**Āryamārga (m)** (*ārya* 'noble' + *mārga* 'path') The path of the great or the noble ones.

**Āryamiśra (m)** (*ārya* 'noble' + *miśra* 'mixed') 1. Blended with the great ones. 2. Blended with greatness.

**Āryavan (m), Āryavatī (f)** The possessor of greatness.

**Āśā (f)** Hope.

**Ātmajyoti (m) (f)** (*ātma* 'Self' + *jyoti* 'light') The light of the Self. See the Bhagavad Gītā V:16,24; X:11; XIII:17;33.

**Ātman (m)** The Self. It is revealed in the Bṛihad-Āraṇyaka Upanishad, "The Self should be realized, It should be heard of, reflected on and meditated upon...It should be meditated on as the Self alone, for, everything becomes one in It...This Self is the Absolute." See the Bhagavad Gītā VI:25,29; VII:18; IX:5; X:11,15,20,32; XIII:11,22, 24,29, 31-2; XV:17.

**Ātreya (m)** A descendant of Ṛishi Atri.

# B

**Babhru (m)** 1. The supporter. See the Bhagavad Gītā IX:5; XV:17. 2. The 116th name of Lord Vishṇu as listed in the Vishṇu Sahasranāma. In his commentary Śrī Śaṅkara states, "He who supports the worlds is the Supporter." 3. The tawny-haired; a name of Lord Śiva.

**Badrīnāth (m)** (*badrī* 'name of a temple' + *nātha* 'master') The Lord of the Badrī temple, a place sacred to Lord Vishṇu where the Ṛishis Nara and Nārāyaṇa perform constant tapas or austerities.

**Bahulapremā (f)** (*bahula* 'abundant' + *premā* 'divine love') The great Love.

**Baladeva (m)** (*bala* 'power' + *deva* 'god') 1. The powerful and luminous God. 2. The elder brother of Śrī Kṛishṇa said to have been produced from a white hair of Lord Vishṇu. 3. Another name for Balarāma.

**Baladhara (m)** (*bala* 'power' + *dhara* 'bearer') 1. The bearer of strength. 2. A title of a Brahmin man. 3. A name of Lord Vishṇu. 4. A name of Lord Śiva.

**Balaprada (m), Balapradā (f)** (*bala* 'power' + *prada* 'giving') The giver of strength. Here, the knowledge of the true Self is the "giver of strength." Moreover, such knowledge alone gives real lasting strength since the Self is eternal while all other strengths are perishable.

**Balarāma (m)** (*bala* 'power' + *rāma* 'delightful') 1. The powerful and blissful. 2. The elder brother of Śrī Kṛishṇa, who is an incarnation of Śesha, or Ananta, the great Serpent-God of Lord Vishṇu.

**Balarūpa (m)** (*bala* 'power' + *rūpa* 'form') The image or personification of strength; a name of Lord Śiva.

**Bandhu (m)** 1. Connection, relation. 2. Kinship, kinsman, especially on the mother's side. 3. Friend. See the Bhagavad Gītā V: 29; VI:5,6; IX:18. 4. Husband.

**Bābhravī (f)** Belonging to Babhru (i.e. to Lord Śiva; a name of the Goddess Durgā).

**Bādarāyaṇa (m)** The inhabitant of Badarika Āśrama; a name of Vyāsa, who is so-called because he lived near Badarī in the Himālayas. *Bādarāyaṇa*, or Vyāsa, is known as the illustrious author of the Vedānta-Darśana, (i.e. the Brahma-Sūtras which systematize the Upanishadic teachings on a secure foundation). Below is a verse referring to Vyāsa as *Bādarāyaṇa* :

*Śaṅkaram Śaṅkarācāryam*
*Keśavam Bādarāyaṇam,*
*Sūtra-Bhāshya-Kṛitau Vande*
*Bhagavantau Punaḥ Punaḥ.*

I salute Śaṅkarācāryam, who is Śaṅkara (i.e. Śiva)
and *Bādarāyaṇa* who is Keśava (i.e.Vishṇu),
the fortunate authors of the (Brahma)
Sūtras and their Commentary.

Also see the Bhagavad Gītā X:37; XIII:4.

**Bādari (m)** 1. The inhabitant of Badarī. 2. A name of Vyāsa.

**Bāla (m), Bālā (f)** The child-like. In the Bṛihad-Āraṇyaka Upanishad it is written, "Having learned the Scriptures, one should behave like an innocent child. Having known innocence and scholarship, one becomes meditative (a muni) and a true Brāhmaṇa (i.e. a knower of the Absolute or Brahman).

**Bālikā (f)** Young, childish; a girl.

**Bāladeva (m)** (*bāla* 'youthful' + *deva* 'god') 1. The youthful God. 2. The son of Baladeva.

**Bhadra (m)** [in Tamil **Bhadran**], **Bhadrā (f)** The auspicious. "*Bhadram te*!" meaning: "Auspiciousness unto thee!" This is an expression often used in the Rāmāyaṇa and other epics.

**Bhadrakālī (f)** (*bhadra* 'auspicious' + *kālī* 'the black Goddess') 1. The auspicious Kālī. 2. A name of the Goddess Durgā.

**Bhadramūrti (m)** (*bhadra* 'auspicious' + *mūrti* 'form, image') 1. Having an auspicious form. 2. The expression of auspiciousness.

**Bhadrapriya (m), Bhadrapriyā (f)** (*bhadra* 'auspicious' + *priya* 'beloved') 1. The auspicious and beloved (i.e. God). 2. The beloved of the auspicious.

**Bhaga (m)** 1. The dispenser. 2. A name of Sūrya, the Sun-God.

**Bhagavan (m)** (*bhaga* 'fortune' + *van* 'having') 1. The fortunate. In the Vishṇu Purāṇa two definitions are given for this name, "1) *Bhaga*, the sixfold wealth of the Lord, consists of full sovereignty, virtue, glory, splendor, knowledge and dispassion. 2) He who knows the origin and dissolution of the universe, the coming and going of beings, and also what is knowledge and what is ignorance, He is fit to be called '*Bhagavan.*" 2. Lord. 3. The 558th name of

Lord Vishṇu as listed in the Vishṇu Sahasranāma.

**Bhagavatī (f)** (*bhaga* 'fortune' + *vatī* 'having') 1. The fortunate. 2. A name of the Goddess Lakshmī. 3. A name of the Goddess Pārvati. 4. A name of the Goddess Saraswatī. 5. A name of the Bhagavad Gītā.

**Bhagavatpriya (m)** (*bhagavat* 'fortunate' + *priya* 'beloved') The beloved of the fortunate. See the Bhagavad Gītā VII:17; IX:29; XII:13-20; XVIII: 65,68,69.

**Bhagavatpriyā (f)** (*bhagavat* 'fortunate' + *priyā* 'beloved') 1. The beloved of the fortunate. 2. A name of the Goddess Pārvatī. 3. A name of the Goddess Lakshmī.

**Bhagin (m), Bhagī (m)** The fortunate or glorious.

**Bhagīratha (m)** 1. Having a glorious chariot. 2. The name of a Rājarshi, king and wise man, who was the son of King Dilīpa and ancestor of Rāma. He accomplished a great austerity for the descent of the Goddess Ganges on earth in order to purify the Sāgaras, his 60,000 departed ancestors. See the Rāmāyaṇa for the full story.

**Bhairava (m)** 1. The fear-inspiring. 2. A name of Lord Śiva, who inspires fear in conceited and deluded beings.

**Bhairavī (f)** 1. The fear-inspiring Goddess. 2. The consort of the frightful. 3. A name of the Goddess Durgā. 4. A name of the Goddess Kālī.

**Bhajana (m), Bhajanā (f)** 1. The worshipping. 2. The sharing or partaking (with God). See the Bhagavad Gītā VII:16; IX:14,26,34.

**Bhaktan (m), Bhaktā (f)** 1. The devoted. In the Bhagavad Gītā, Śrī Kṛishṇa speaks of 4 kinds of devotees in chapter VII and then in chapter XII reduces the 4 to 2 kinds: the worshippers of Īśwara or God with form and the worshippers of the non-dual and formless Brahman. See the Bhagavad Gītā VII:16-8; XII; XVIII:54-5. 2. The "partaken (in God)."

**Bhakti (f)** Devotion. See the Bhagavad Gītā VII:17-8; XVIII:54-5.

**Bhaktidāyaka (m), Bhaktidāyinī (f)** (*bhakti* 'devotion' + *dāyaka/ dāyinī* 'giving') The bestower of devotion.

**Bharaṇyu (m)** 1. The supporter, master or protector. 2. A name of fire. 3. A name of the sun. 4. A name of the moon.

**Bharata (m)** [in Tamil **Bharatan**] 1. The supporter. 2. A great monarch of India who was the son of Dushyanta and Śakuntalā and the ancestor of the "Bhāratas" (i.e. the Pāṇḍavas and the Kauravas). See the Mahābhārata of Vyāsa. 3. One of Śrī Rāma's three brothers who ruled the kingdom during Rāma's exile in the forest and out of devotion for his brother placed Rāma's holy sandals on the throne and paid daily homage to them. He is considered a partial incarnation of Lord Vishṇu. 4. The author of the Nāṭya-Śāstra, a treatise on music, dance and singing. 5. A name of Agni, the Fire-god.

**Bharga (m)** 1. The effulgent, effulgence. In the Gayātrī-Mantra of the Ṛigveda the *bharga*, or effulgence, of the sun is viewed as God's effulgence and meditated upon within. 2. A name of Lord Śiva.

**Bhartā (m)** 1. The supporter or sustainer. See the Bhagavad Gītā IX:18; XIII:16,22. 2. The 34th name of Lord Vishṇu listed in the Vishṇu Sahasranāma. In his commentary Śrī Śaṅkara states, "The Lord is called the supporter because He supports the expanded universe as its substratum or supreme ruler." 3. Husband.

**Bhartṛihari (m)** (*bhartṛi* 'supporter' + *hari* 'remover') 1. The supporter and remover. 2. A well-known poet and grammarian of the seventh century A.D., who wrote the "*Vairāgya-śatakam*" (i.e. the "Hundred Verses on Dispassion").

**Bhartrī (f)** 1. The supporter or sustainer. 2. God as Mother.

**Bharu (m)** 1. The Lord or Master. 2. A name of Lord Vishṇu. 3. A name of Lord Śiva.

**Bhava (m)** 1. The existent. See the Bhagavad Gītā II:20. 2. Pure existence. 3. A name of Lord Śiva.

**Bhavaprītā (f)** (*bhava* 'existent' + *prītā* 'beloved') 1. The beloved of the existent (i.e. Śiva). 2. A name of the Goddess Pārvatī.

**Bhavatāriṇī (f)** (*bhava* 'birth' + *tāriṇī* 'savior') 1. The Goddess of the transient world. 2. The savior of rebirth. 3. A name for a scripture, (e.g. the Upanishads, the Bhagavad Gītā).

**Bhavānī (f)** 1. The existent. 2. Pure existence. 3. Goddess of the living world. 4. A name of Pārvatī. Śrī Śaṅkara composed eight beautiful verses to the Goddess Bhavānī with the following refrain:

*Gatis-Twam Gatis-Twam Twam-ekā Bhavāni!*

Thou art the Goal, Thou art the Goal, the only Goal, O Bhavani!

**Bhavāśinī (f)** (*bhava* 'existent' + *aśinī* 'consumer') 1. The destroyer of worldly life or of repeated births. 2. A name of the Goddess Kālī, whose destroying is represented by her garland of skulls. See the Bhagavad Gītā VIII: 15,16,21.

**Bhaveśa (m)** (*bhava* 'worldly life, existence, birth' + *īśa* 'lord') 1. The Lord of the world. See the Bhagavad Gītā VII:13,14,25; IX:8-10; XIII:30; XV:4; XVIII:61. 2. A name of Lord Śiva, since the entire world of diversity and transmigration appears through His illusive power.

**Bhayāpaha (m)** (*bhaya* 'fear' + *apaha* 'removing, destroying') 1. The dispeller of fear. 2. The 935th name of Lord Vishṇu as listed in the Vishṇu Sahasranāma. In his commentary Śrī Śaṅkara states, "Dispelling for men the fear born of transmigration, the Lord is the dispeller of fear. 3. A name of Lord Śiva.

**Bhāgavata (m)** 1. The follower or worshipper of the fortunate. 2. A name for the Bhāgavata Purāṇa. 3. One who advocates the dualistic doctrine of "Catur-Vyūha" (i.e. that the soul has been created by God and is thus an individual self different from the universal One).

**Bhāgavatī (f)** 1. The follower or worshipper of the fortunate. 2. The consort of the fortunate. 3. One who advocates the dualistic doctrine of "Catur-Vyūha" (i.e. that the soul has been created by God and is thus an individual self different from the universal One).

**Bhāgīrathī (f)** 1. The daughter or follower of Bhagīratha. 2. The name given to the Goddess Gaṅgā by Brahmā, the creator, since Bhagīratha also desired children and thus got the Goddess Gaṅgā as his elder daughter. 3. The name of one of the Ganges' three main streams.

**Bhānu (m)** 1. The luminous or shining. It is written in the Upanishads, "As the supreme God shines, so all luminaries shine." See the Bhagavad Gītā V:16; VII:8; VIII:9; X:21,41; XI:12; XIII:17,33; XIV:11; XV:12. 2. The 284th name of Lord Vishṇu listed in the Vishṇu Sahasranāma. 3. A name of Lord Śiva. 4. A name of Sūrya, the Sun-God.

**Bhānumatī (f)** (*bhānu* 'luminous' + *matī* 'possessing') The possessor of luminosity. It is written in the Upanishads, "As the supreme God shines, so all luminaries shine." See the Bhagavad Gītā V:16; VII:8; VIII:9; X:21,41; XI:12; XIII:17,33; XIV:11; XV:12.

**Bhāratī (f)** 1. The Goddess of Bharata's country (i.e. India). 2. A name of the Goddess Saraswatī, Goddess of speech, musical arts and wisdom. 3. One of the ten orders of Sannyāsins traced back to Śrī Śaṅkara. 4. Śaṅkara-*Bhāratī*, meaning the "Speech of Śaṅkara," is a Vedantic work by Śrī Śaṅkara, also called the Vivekacūḍāmaṇi.

**Bhārgava (m)** [in Tamil **Bhārgavan**] 1. The descendant of Bhṛigu. 2. A name of Lord Śiva. 3. A name of Lord Vishṇu's sixth incarnation as Paraśurāma.

**Bhārgavī (f)** 1. The descendant of Bhṛigu. 2. A name of the Goddess Lakshmī. 3. A name of the Goddess Pārvatī. 4. Knowledge of the Self as received by Bhṛigu from his father Varuṇa. See the Taittīriya Upanishad.

**Bhāskara (m)** (*bhās* 'light' + *kara* 'doer') 1. The light-maker. 2. A name of Sūrya, the Sun-God.

**Bhāskarī (f)** (*bhās* 'light' + *karī* 'doer') 1. The light-maker. 2. The 77th of the Goddess Lakshmī's 108 names.

**Bhāsu (m)** The shining (i.e. the sun).

**Bhāvyā (f)** 1. Auspiciousness. 2. A name of the Goddess Durgā.

**Bhedanāśinī (f)** (*bheda* 'difference' + *nāśinī* 'destroyer') The destroyer of difference (i.e. between soul and God). In the Upanishads it is written, "There is no diversity in the Absolute. He who sees diversity in It as it were, goes from death to death...He who worships It as different thinking 'He is one, I am another,' does not know, he is like an animal to the Gods...The knower of the Absolute verily becomes the Absolute." See the Bhagavad Gītā V:16-18, VI:29-31; VII:19; X:11; XIII:2, 16,22,27,30; XV:7; XVIII:20,54,55.

**Bhikshu (m)** 1. The mendicant. 2. A name of Lord Śiva.

**Bhikshukī (f)** The mendicant.

**Bhikshuṇī (f)** The mendicant.

**Bhīma (m)** 1. The fear-inspiring. It is written in the Upanishads, "All this projected universe moves on account of the Supreme Being that is a great terror like an uplifted thunderbolt...From fear of Him fire burns, out of fear the sun shines, out of fear Indra, Vāyu and Yama run...He who creates the slightest difference in the Absolute is smitten with fear. That very Absolute is a terror to the so-called learned man who lacks the unitive outlook." 2. The 357th and 948th names of Lord Vishṇu listed in the Vishṇu Sahasranāma. 3. A name of Lord Śiva. 4. The name of one of the five Pāṇḍava brothers, who is also called "Bhīmasena" (i.e. "having a fearful army" and is a partial incarnation of Vāyu, the Wind-God). See the Bhagavad Gītā XI:20-25.

**Bhīmā (f)** 1. The fear-inspiring. 2. A name of the Goddess Durgā.

**Bhīshma (m)** 1. Frightful, terrifying, dreadful. 2. A name of the great-uncle of the Pāṇḍavas and a leader of the Kuru family, who was a son of Gaṅgā and Śāntanu.

**Bhojarāja (m)** (*bhoja* 'bountiful' + *rāja* 'king') 1. The bountiful king. 2. A king in the Mahābhārata. 3. The name of a scholar that wrote a commentary on the Yoga-Sūtras.

**Bholānātha (m)** A name of Lord Śiva.

**Bhṛigu (m)** 1. The glittering. (See the Bhagavad Gītā X:25.) 2. The name of a Maharshi who was the seer for part of the Ṛigveda and who was the son of Varuṇa, the Water-God and Night-God. 4. The title of the third and last part of the Taittīriya Upanishad.

**Bhuktida (m), Bhuktidā (f),** (*bhukti* 'fruition' + *da/dā* 'giver') 1. The dispenser of the fruits of one's actions. 2. The aspect of God that grants all beings the results of their karma according to past deeds.

**Bhuktidātā (m), Bhuktidātrī (f)** (*bhukti* 'fruition' + *dātā/ dātrī* 'giver') 1. The dispenser of the fruits of one's actions. 2. The aspect of God that grants all beings the results of their karma according to past deeds.

**Bhuktidāyaka (m)** (*bhukti* 'fruition' + *dāyaka* 'giver') 1. The dispenser of the fruits of one's actions. 2. The aspect of God that grants all beings the results of their karma according to past deeds.

**Bhuvanadhara (m)** (*bhuvana* 'world' + *dhara* 'bearer') 1. The world-bearer. 2. A name of Lord Gaṇeśa.

**Bhuvanamātā (f)** (*bhuvana* 'world' + *mātā* 'mother') 1. The Mother of the world or worlds. 2. A name of the Goddess Durgā. 3. A name of various other forms of the Divine Mother.

**Bhuvanapati (m)** (*bhuvana* 'world' + *pati* 'lord') The Lord, master or protector of the worlds.

**Bhuvaneśwara (m)** (*bhuvana* 'world' + *īśwara* 'lord') The Lord of the worlds.

**Bhuvaneśwarī (f)** (*bhuvana* 'world' + *īśwarī* 'sovereign goddess') 1. The sovereign Goddess of the worlds. 2. The last of the Goddess Lakshmi's 108 names.

**Bhūdeva (m)** (*bhū* 'earth' + *deva* 'god') 1. God of the earth, or God on earth. 2. A name of Lord Śiva. 3. A Brāhmaṇa (i.e. knower of the Absolute, or a great man).

**Bhūdevī (f)** (*bhū* 'earth' + *devī* 'goddess') 1. The Goddess of the Earth. 2. A name of the Goddess Lakshmī. 3. Goddess on earth (i.e. a virtuous woman).

**Bhūdhara (m)** (*bhū* 'earth' + *dhara* 'bearer') 1. The earth-bearer. 2. A name of Śrī Kṛishṇa, referring to the time He lifted Govardhana Mount with one finger. 3. A name of Lord Śiva. 4. A name of Lord Vishṇu's serpent, Śesha, who is known to support the fourteen worlds.

**Bhūdhātrī (f)** (*bhū* 'earth' + *dhātrī* 'supporter') 1. The earth-supporter. 2. A name of the Goddess Śakti.

**Bhūman (f)** Immensity or infinitude (i.e. Brahman, or the Absolute). This word occurs in the Chāndogya Upanishad as the culminating revelation of Sanatkumāra to Nārada, where it is written, "Verily, that which is Immensity is bliss. There is no happiness in the small. Immensity alone is bliss...That wherein one sees nothing else, hears nothing else and knows nothing else, that is *Bhuman*, the immensity. But that wherein one sees something else, hears something else and knows something else, is the small. Verily, that which is the immensity is imperishable. As for the small, it is perishable."

**Bhūpati (m)** (*bhū* 'earth' + *pati* 'lord') 1. The Lord, master or protector of the earth. 2. A title used for various gods and kings.

**Bhūtanātha (m)** (*bhūta* 'being' + *nātha* 'lord') 1. The Lord of beings. 2. A name of Lord Śiva.

**Bhūtapati (m)** (*bhūta* 'being' + *pati* 'lord') 1. The Lord of beings. 2. A name of Lord Śiva.

**Bhūteśa (m)** (*bhūta* 'being' + *īśa* 'lord') 1. The Lord of beings. 2. A name of various gods.

**Bhūteśwara (m)** (*bhūta* 'being' + *īśwara* 'lord') The Lord or ruler of beings.

**Bhūti (f)** 1. Prosperity. 2. A name of the Goddess Lakshmī.

**Bimba (m)** 1. The original One. 2. Disc of the moon or sun. 3. Mirror, reflection. 4. Object compared.

**Bimbadhara (m)** (*bimba* 'disc of the moon' + *dhara* 'bearer') The holder of the crescent moon; a name of Lord Śiva.

**Bindu (m)** 1. A dot. 2. The dot on the word "OM," representing the causal state or causal body, as well as the state of deep sleep. 3. The central dot of a yantra.

**Bodhidharma (m)** (*bodhi* 'wisdom' + *dharma* 'spiritual path/duty') 1. One whose spiritual path, or dharma, consists of wisdom. 2. The name of a Buddhist.

**Bodhin (m), Bodhinī (f)** 1. The wise or enlightening. 2. The possessor of knowledge.

**Bodhī (m)** 1. The wise or enlightening. 2. The possessor of knowledge.

**Bodhisattwa (m)** (*bodhi* 'wisdom' + *sattwa* 'essence') 1. The essence of wisdom. 2. One whose mind is enlightened. 3. In Buddhism a saint who out of compassion continually reincarnates to help others reach enlightenment.

**Brahmamayī (f)** (*brahma* 'absolute' + *mayī* 'consisting of') She who consists of the Absolute, the embodiment of the Absolute. It was written in the Muṇḍaka Upanishad, "The knower of the Absolute becomes the very Absolute." See the Bhagavad Gītā IV:10; V:17, 19, 21, 24-6; VI:15, 27, 28; IX:32; XVIII:49-55.

**Brahman (n)** 1. The Absolute, or the absolutely great. See the Bhagavad Gītā II:72; IV:24; V:19, 24-26; VII:7; VIII:3; X:12; XI:18,43; XIII:12-17,30; XIV:26,27; XVII:23; XVIII:54. 2. The formless, nameless, eternal Truth. 3. The 664th name of Vishṇu listed in the Vishṇu Sahasranāma. In his commentary Śrī Śaṅkara states, "On account of His greatness and all-pervasiveness, the Lord is called the Absolute, characterized by Truth and other attributes, as is revealed in the Taittirīya Upanishad, 'The Absolute is Truth, Knowledge and Infinitude.' Likewise, in the Vishṇu Purāṇa it is written, "That which puts an end to limited differences, which is pure existence, beyond the range of words, and knowable as the inner Self, that knowledge is known as the Absolute (*Brahman*).'"

**Brahmaṇya (m)** 1. The benefactor of (earthly) Brahman. See the Bhagavad Gītā IV:8. 2. The 661st name of Lord Vishṇu in the Vishṇu Sahasranāma. Śrī Śaṅkara states in his commentary, "Austerity, Vedas, wise men (Vipras or Brāhmaṇas) and knowledge are known as 'Brahman.' On account of His beneficent nature towards them all, the Lord is called *Brahmaṇya*, the benefactor of (earthly) Brahman."

**Brahmarūpa (m), Brahmarūpiṇī (f)** (*brahma* 'absolute' + *rūpa/rūpiṇī* 'form') The embodiment of the Absolute. In the "Glory of the Gītā" in the Vārāha-Puraṇa, Lord Vishṇu says, "The Gītā is my supreme knowledge, it is the embodiment of the Absolute."

**Brahmā (m)** 1. The Creator; the Great (i.e. the first-born from the great Brahman, or Absolute). He has four faces representing the four Vedas, hence His consort is divine Speech personified as the Goddess Saraswatī. He dwells in *Brahma*-loka or Satya-loka, the highest plane in the sphere of relative existence. 2. The 663rd name of Lord Vishṇu listed in the Vishṇu Sahasranāma. Śrī Śaṅkara states in his commentary, "The Immanent (Vishṇu) who creates all through the person of *Brahmā*, is thus called Himself *Brahmā*, the Creator." See the Bhagavad Gītā VIII:16,17; XI:15.

**Brahmāṇī (f)** The consort of Brahmā (i.e. Saraswatī, Goddess of sacred speech and learning, and of musical art).

**Brāhmī (f)** 1. The consort of Brahmā (i.e Saraswatī, the Goddess of sacred speech and learning, and of musical art). 2. That which pertains to Brahman, or the Absolute, as in the Bhagavad Gītā II:72. 3. A name of the Goddess Pārvatī. 4. A name for all of the Upanishads.

**Bṛihaspati (m)** (*bṛihas* 'speech' + *pati* 'lord') 1. The Lord of the Vedic Word. 2. The name of the Guru of the gods, who is the regent of Jupiter and of Thursday, and who presides over speech and intelligence. He is invoked in the Śānti Mantra:

*OM Śam No Mitraḥ!*
*Śam Varuṇaḥ!*
*Śam No Bhavatw'aryamā!*
*Śam Na Indro Bṛihaspatiḥ!*

OM! May Mitra be blissful to us!
May Varuṇa be blissful to us!
May Aryaman be blissful to us
May Indra and *Bṛihaspati* be blissful to us!

**Buddha (m)** 1. The Awakened. 2. The title given to the founder of Buddhism, who is Lord Vishṇu's ninth incarnation.

# C

**Caitanya (m), Caitanyā (f)** 1. Consciousness. 2. Pure Consciousness, which is the Self. 3. When used as a name by a Brahmacārī, it indicates consciousness associated to sattwaguṇa, pure-mindedness due to continence, service to the Guru, and the repetition of Gāyatrī Mantra.

**Cakrabhṛit (m)** (*cakra* 'wheel, disc' + *bhṛit* 'bearer') 1. The discus-bearer. See the Bhagavad Gītā XVIII:61. 2. A name of Lord Vishṇu referring to Him holding the discus "Sudarśana," the symbol of the swift and shaking mind, or to Him setting samsāra-*cakra* (the wheel of transmigration) in motion.

**Cakrin (m)** 1. The discus-bearer. See the Bhagavad Gītā XVIII:61. 2. A name of Lord Vishṇu referring to Him holding Sudarśana, the discus, the symbol of the swift and shaking mind, or to Him setting the wheel of transmigration, samsāra-cakra in motion.

**Caṇḍālikā (f)** 1. A name of the Goddess Durgā. 2. A name of the Goddess Kālī.

**Caṇḍikā (f)** 1. The fierce Goddess. 2. A name of the Goddess Durgā.

**Candila (m)** A name of Lord Śiva, or Rudra.

**Caṇḍī (f)** 1. The fierce Goddess. 2. A name of the Goddess Durgā. 3. The title given the "Devī-Māhātmya" of the Mārkaṇḍeya Purāṇa.

**Caṇḍīpati (m)** (*Caṇḍī* 'fierce goddess' + *pati* 'lord') The Lord of the fierce Goddess (i.e. Lord Śiva).

**Candrā (f)** 1. The shining (moon). See the Bhagavad Gītā VII:8; VIII:25; X:21; XV:12,13. 2. The 58th of the Goddess Lakshmī's 108 names.

**Candrabhānu (m)** (*candra* 'moon' + *bhānu* 'sun') 1. The moon and sun. 2. A name of a son of Śrī Kṛishṇa.

**Candrabhūti (f)** (*candra* 'moon' + *bhūti* 'power, well-being, fortune') 1. One whose luster or welfare is like the moon. 2. Silvery.

**Candradeva (m)** (*candra* 'moon' + *deva* 'god') The Moon-God. See the Bhagavad Gītā VII:8; X:21; XV:12,13.

**Candraka (m)** Lunar shining.

**Candrakānta (m)** (*candra* 'moon' + *kānta* 'lovely') Lovely as the moon.

**Candrakāntā (f)** (*candra* 'moon' + *kāntā* 'lovely') 1. Lovely as the moon. 2. The daughter of Daksha and the wife of the Moon-God.

**Candrakānti (f)** (*candra* 'moon' + *kānti* 'radiancc') Moonlight.

**Candramaṇi (m)** (*candra* 'moon' + *maṇi* 'gem') The moon-gem, moonstone.

**Candramauli (m)** (*candra* 'moon' + *mauli* 'head, top, diadem') The moon-crested; a name of Lord Śiva.

**Candramālikā (f)** (*candra* 'moon' + *mālikā* 'garlanded') The moon-garlanded.

**Candramukha (m), Candramukhī (f)** (*candra* 'moon' + *mukha/ mukhī* 'face') 1. The moon-faced. 2. A name of Śrī Rāma.

**Candramukuṭa (m)** (*candra* 'moon' + *mukuṭa* 'diadem, crest') The moon-crested; a name of Lord Śiva.

**Candran (m)** 1. The shining (moon). See the Bhagavad Gītā VII:8; VIII:25; X:21; XV:12,13. 2. A name of the Moon-God, the presiding deity of the mind and dwelling place of Pitṛis.

**Candranātha (m)** (*candra* 'moon' + *nātha* 'lord') The Lord or master of the moon; a name of Lord Śiva.

**Candraratna (m), Candraratnā (f)** (*candra* 'moon' + *ratna* 'gem, pearl') The moon-pearl.

**Candrasara (n)** (*candra* 'moon' + *ara* 'fluid') A mythical moon-lake.

**Candrasūrya (m)** (*candra* 'moon' + *Sūrya* 'sun, Sun-God') 1. He whose splendor is like the moon and the sun. 2. He whose eyes shine like the moon and the sun.

**Candraśekhara (m)** (*candra* 'moon' + *śckhara* 'crown, crest, diadem') The moon-crested; a name of Lord Śiva.

**Candravadana (m)** (*candra* 'moon' + *adana* 'mouth, face') 1. The moon-faced. 2. A name of Śrī Rāma.

**Candravadanā (f)** (*candra* 'moon' + *vadanā* 'mouth, face') The moon-faced.

**Candravimala (m), Candravimalā (f)** (*candra* 'moon' + *vimala* 'immaculate') Immaculate as the moon.

**Candrā (f)** The shining (moon). See the Bhagavad Gītā VII:8; VIII:25; X:21; XV:12,13.

**Candrāmśu (m)** (*candra* 'moon' + *amsṛu* 'ray') 1. Moonbeam. 2. The 281st name of Lord Vishṇu listed in the Vishṇu Sahasranāma. Śrī Śaṅkara states in his commentary, "The Lord is called the 'Moonbeam' because His delighting or refreshing nature is similar to moonbeams soothing the mind afflicted by the scorching rays of the heating sun of transmigratory life."

**Candreśwara (m)** (*candra* 'moon' + *īśwara* 'lord') 1. The Moon-God. 2. The Lord of the moon (i.e. Lord Śiva).

**Candrikā (f)** Moonlight.

**Candrila (m)** A name of Lord Śiva, or Lord Rudra.

**Caraka (m)** 1. The wanderer. 2. The name of an ancient physician, author of the Samhitā, a treatise on Ayurvedic medicine.

**Cāmuṇḍā (f), Cāmuṇḍī (f)** 1. The slayer of the demons Caṇḍa and Muṇḍa. 2. A name of the Goddess Durgā, or the Goddess Kālī, in the "Devī-Māhātmya" of the Mārkaṇḍeya-Purāṇa. The slaying of these demons means the removal of rajas and tamas, passion and indolence or ego and ignorance.

**Cārin (m), Cāriṇī (f)** The follower, disciple.

**Cāru (m)** 1. The lovely. 2. The beautiful.

**Cāruhāsa (m), Cāruhāsinī (f)** (*cāru* 'beautiful' + *hāsa/ hāsinī* 'smile') Having a beautiful smile.

**Cāruman (m), Cārumatī (f)** (*cāru* 'beautiful' + *man/matī* 'having') 1. The possessor of beauty. 2. The beautiful. 3. The name of a daughter of Śrī Kṛishṇa.

**Cārurūpa (m), Cārurūpiṇī (f)** (*cāru* 'beautiful' + *rūpa/rūpiṇī* 'form') Having a beautiful form.

**Cāruśīla (m), Cāruśīlā (f)** (*cāru* 'beautiful' + *śīla* 'character, good conduct') Having a beautiful character or nature.

**Cārvī (f)** 1. The lovely. 2. The beautiful.

**Cātaka (m), Cātakī (f)** One who longs for God as the *Cātaka* birds long for the rain-drops upon which they live.

**Cidambara (m)** (*cit* 'knowledge' + *ambara* 'garment') 1. The knowledge-clad. 2. A name of Lord Śiva. 3. The name of a South Indian town where the Lord performed His Tāṇḍava dance.

**Cidambareśa (m)** (*cidambara* 'knowledge-clad, name of a temple' + *īśa* 'lord') 1. The Lord of the *Cidambaram* temple. 2. The knowledge-clad Lord. 3. A name of Lord Śiva.

**Cidghana (m)** (*cit* 'knowledge' + *ghana* 'uninterrupted, whole') The pure or homogeneous consciousness (i.e. the non-dual Truth or Self, the Absolute which is devoid of break and difference).

**Cinmaya (m), Cinmayī (f)** (*cit* 'knowledge' + *maya/ mayī* 'consisting of') 1. The embodiment of knowledge or consciousness. 2. Consisting of knowledge, consciousness. 3. One who has realized the Truth and thus become the very Truth.

**Cintāmaṇi (m), Cintāmaṇī (f)** (*cintā* 'thought' + *maṇi* 'gem') 1. The thought-gem. 2. The name of a fabulous gem yielding its owner all desires. 3. The 20th name of the Goddess Pārvatī, referring to Her granting the boon of knowledge to Her devotees:

*OM! Bhakta-Cintāmaṇyai Namaḥ!*

OM! Salutation to the Thought-Gem of devotees!

**Citrabhānu (m)** (*citra* 'bright' + *bhānu* 'sun, light') The bright light of Sūrya, the Sun-God, or Agni, the Fire-God.

**Citraka (m)** The painter.

**Citran (m)** 1. The bright or variegated. 2. The clear-minded.

**Citrā (f)** 1. The bright or variegated. 2. The clear-minded. 3. The name of one of Arjuna's wives.

**Citrāvasu (m), Citrāvaswī (f)** (*citrā* 'bright' + *vasu/vaswī* 'wealth') Rich in brightness like the stars.

**Cūḍālā (f)** The name of a saintly queen whose story is told in the Yoga-Vāsishṭha.

**Cyavana (m)** The name of a Ṛishi who was the son of Bhṛigu and the father of Aurva.

# D

**Daiva (m), Daivī (f)** The divine (i.e. one who resembles God). See the Bhagavad Gītā XVI: 1-3.

**Daksha (m)** 1. The skillful. 2. The name of a son of Brahmā, who was the father of Satī before She became Pārvatī. He was very skillful in Vedic sacrifices. Lord Śiva destroyed one of his sacrifices when He was not invited. 3. The 423rd and 917th name of Lord Vishṇu listed in the Vishṇu Sahasranāma. In his commentary Śrī Śaṅkara states, "The Lord is called the 'skillful' because He manifests Himself through the form of the universe, or He accomplishes all acts swiftly. The skillful is the manifested, the capable and the one who acts swiftly. These three attributes are established in the Supreme who is thus 'skillful.'" 4. A quality of a Bhakta as described in the Bhagavad Gītā XII:16.

**Dakshajā (f)** (*daksha* 'son of Brahmā' + *jā* 'born, caused') 1. She who is born from Daksha. 2. A name of Satī before she was born to Himavan as Pārvatī.

**Dakshiṇa (m)** The dexterous or skillful.

**Dakshiṇā (f)** 1. The offering or gift. 2. The wife of Yajña, Sacrifice. 3. The south. 4. On the righthand side. 5. Intelligence, right knowledge.

**Dakshiṇāmūrti (m)** (*dakshiṇā* 'right knowledge' + *mūrti* 'form, image') 1. The embodiment of wisdom, or right knowledge. 2. Facing the south. 3. A manifestation of Lord Śiva as the Guru, or spiritual master, who reveals to the four Kumāras the non-duality of the Self and the Absolute through the hand-gesture known as Jñānamudrā or Cinmudrā. In this manifestation He is facing the south, which is the direction of death, so that He can enlighten those who transmigrate with Self-knowledge.

**Damayantī (f)** 1. Subduing, conquering, taming. 2. The name of Nala's wife who was the daughter of Bhīma, the King of Vidarbha.

**Darśana (m)** 1. The vision of God. 2. The realization of Truth.

**Daśabhujā (f)** (*daśa* 'ten' + *bhujā* 'arm') 1. The ten-armed. 2. A name of the Goddess Durgā, or the Goddess Kālī when depicted as holding a sword, disc, mace, arrows, bow, club, spear, missile, skull and conch.

**Daśaharā (f)** (*daśa* 'ten' + *harā* 'remover, destroyer') 1. The remover or destroyer of the ten sins (i.e. those committed by the five sense-organs, such as hearing, seeing, etc., and the five organs of action, such as hands, feet, etc.). 2. A name of the Goddess Ganges. 3. A name of the Goddess Durgā.

**Daśaratha (m)** (*daśa* 'ten' + *ratha* 'chariot') 1. He who has ten chariots. 2. The king of Ayodhyā, who was the father of Śrī Rāma and His three brothers.

**Datta (m), Dattā (f)** That which is given.

**Dattātreya (m)** (*datta* 'given' + *ātreya* 'the son of Atri') 1. The son of Atri received as a gift. 2. The name of a manifestation of Lord Brahmā, Lord Vishṇu and Lord Śiva, who became the son of Ṛishi Atri and his wife Anasūyā. 3. The name of the author of the Avadhūta Gītā, a Vedāntic treatise. See the Purāṇas for his story.

**Dayā (f)** Mercy, compassion. See the Bhagavad Gītā XVI:2.

**Dayālan (m)** [Tamil] The merciful or compassionate.

**Dayāvan (m), Dayāvatī (f)** The merciful or compassionate. See the Bhagavad Gītā X:11.

**Dāmodara (m)** (*dāma* 'cord, band' + *udara* 'belly') 1. He who becomes known by controlling the senses and purifying the mind. 2. The 367th name of Lord Vishṇu as listed in the Vishṇu Sahasranāma. In his commentary Śrī Śaṅkara states, "1) The Lord is called *Dāmodara* because He becomes known through the mind that is perfected (*udarā matiḥ*) by sense-control (*dama*) and other disciplines. It is said in the Mahābhārata, 'On account of sense-control, the Lord is called *Dāmodara*.' 2) Also it is related in the Purāṇas, He is thus called because in His childhood as Kṛishṇa Yaśodā tied Him up with a rope (*dāma*) around His waist (*udara*). 3) Again, as Vyāsa said, 'The worlds are termed *"Dāmas"* and they are inside (*udarāntare*) Him, hence He is called *Dāmodara*.'"

**Dānavan (m), Dānavatī (f)** (*dāna* 'offering, gift' + *van/vatī* 'having') The charitable, or liberal. See the Bhagavad Gītā XVII:20; XVIII:5.

**Dāsa (m), Dāsī (f)** The servant of God. See the Bhagavad Gītā IX:27,28.

**Dātā (m), Dātrī (f)** The giver. See the Bhagavad Gītā XVII: 20; XVIII:5.

**Dehātīta (m)** (*deha* 'body' + *atīta* 'beyond') He who has transcended the body. See the Bhagavad Gītā II:13,20; V:8,9,13; XIV:22,23.

**Deva (m)** 1. The Divine. 2. The shining. 3. God. 4. The 375th name of Lord Vishṇu as listed in the Vishṇu Sahasranāma. In his commentary Śrī Śaṅkara states, "Since He plays through creation, maintenance and dissolution, since He desires to conquer the enemies of the gods, since He functions in all beings and shines as the Self, since He is praised by hymns and reaches everywhere, the Lord is thus called the 'Divine.' It is written in the Śwetāśwatara Upanishad, 'The one God is hidden in all beings.'"

**Devabandhu (m)** (*deva* 'god' + *bandhu* 'friend, relative') The friend of God.

**Devabodha (m)** (*deva* 'god' + *bodha* 'knowledge') He who has the knowledge of God (i.e. who knows his true Self)

**Devadatta (m)** (*deva* 'god' + *datta* 'given') 1. He who is God-given. 2. The name of Arjuna's conch. See the Bhagavad Gītā I:15.

**Devadāsa (m), Devadāsī (f)** (*deva* 'god' + *dāsa/ dāsī* 'servant') The servant of God. See the Bhagavad Gītā III:19, 30-1; V:10-12; IX:26-28; XII: 10-1; XVIII:45,46,56-58,65.

**Devadūta (m), Devadūtī (f)** (*deva* 'god' + *dūta/dūtī* 'messenger) 1. The messenger of God (of the gods). 2. The divine messenger.

**Devahūti (f)** (*deva* 'god' + *hūti* 'sacrifice') 1. The invocation of the gods at the beginning of a Vedic sacrifice. 2. The name of Manu's daughter, who was the wife of Kardama and mother of sage Kapila.

**Devaja (m), Devajā (f)** (*deva* 'god' + *ja* 'born, caused') Born of the gods.

**Devajyoti (m or f)** (*deva* 'god' + *jyoti* 'light') The divine light. See the Bhagavad Gītā V:24; X:11; XI:12; XIII:17,33.

**Devakī (f)** The daughter of Devaka; the name of Śrī Kṛishṇa's mother, the wife of Vasudeva.

**Devakīnandana (m)** (*devakī* 'name of Lord Kṛishṇa's mother + *nandana* 'joy') 1. The joy (i.e. son) of Devakī; a name of Śrī Kṛishṇa. In the Mahābhārata, it is written, "The bright luminaries in the world, the three worlds the protectors, of the worlds, the three Vedas, the three sacred fires, the five oblations and all the gods are nothing but the Son of Devakī (i.e. Śrī Kṛishṇa)." 2. The 989th name of Lord Vishṇu as listed in the Vishṇu Sahasranāma.

**Devalīlā (f)** (*deva* 'god' + *līlā* 'play, sport') Divine play. In the Brahmasūtras, Vyāsa states, "To the Absolute, creation is mere sport." See the Bhagavad Gītā IV:13,14; V:14,15; IX:7-10; XIII:14, 16,29; XIV:3,4; XV:4; XVIII:61.

**Devamaṇi (m)** (*deva* 'god' + *maṇi* 'pearl, gem') 1. The divine gem or jewel. 2. A name of Lord Śiva.

**Devamāyā (f)** (*deva* 'god' + *māyā* 'illusion') The illusionary or illusive power of God.

**Devamuni (m)** (*deva* 'god' + *muni* 'silent meditator') 1. The divine meditator. 2. He who meditates on the Divine. 3. A name for a Ṛishi.

**Devamūrti (m)** (*deva* 'god' + *mūrti* 'image') The image of God.

**Devapati (m)** (*deva* 'god' + *pati* 'lord') 1. The Lord of the gods. See the Bhagavad Gītā X:2. 2. A name of Indra. 3. A name of Bṛihaspati.

**Devapriya (m), Devapriyā (f)** (*deva* 'god' + *priya* 'beloved') The beloved of God. See the Bhagavad Gītā VII:17; IX:29; XII:13-20; XVIII:64, 65,69.

**Devaputra (m)** (*deva* 'god' + *putra* 'son') The son of God.

**Devarata (m)** (*deva* 'god' + *rata* 'delighted') He who is delighted in God. See the Bhagavad Gītā II:55; III:17; V:21,24; VI:8,27,28; X:9; XII:14.

**Devarati (f)** (*deva* 'god' + *rati* 'delight') The delight of God; delighting in God, having one's delight in God.

**Devarāja (m)** (*deva* 'god' + *rāja* 'king') The King of the gods; a name of Indra.

**Devarshi (m)** (*deva* 'god' + *ṛishi* 'seer') 1. The divine seer. 2. The seer of God. 3. The name of a class of Ṛishis who being gods have reached the status of seers of Vedic hymns and mantras (e.g. *Devarshi* Nārada).

**Devarūpa (m), Devarūpā (f), Devarūpiṇī (f)** (*deva* 'god' + *rūpa/ rūpiṇī* 'form') Having a divine form.

**Devasena (m)** (*deva* 'god' + *sena* 'conquering army') 1. The divine commander. 2. A name of Lord Śiva's son, Kārttikeya.

**Devaśakti (m)** (*deva* 'god' + *śakti* 'energy, power') Divine power or energy.

**Devaśrī (m)** (*deva* 'god' + *śrī* 'splendor, beauty') 1. The divine light or splendor. 2. The name of a Ṛishi.

**Devatā (f)** The Deity or Divinity (i.e. the chosen Deity that one worships).

**Devavrata (m)** (*deva* 'god' + *vrata* 'vow') 1. One who takes a divine vow. 2. A name of Bhīshma, who maintained life-long celibacy. See the Bhagavad Gītā IV:28; VI:14; VII:28; IX:14.

**Devāmśa (m)** (*deva* 'god' + *amśa* 'part, portion') 1. A part or portion of God. 2. The incarnation of God. See the Bhagavad Gītā X:41,42; XIII:2; XV:7.

**Devāṅganā (f)** (*deva* 'god' + *aṅganā* 'woman') The divine woman.

**Devānīka (m)** (*deva* 'god' + *anīka* 'front') 1. Divine or celestial host. 2. Divine splendor.

**Devāśis (m)** (*deva* 'god' + *āśis* 'wish') 1. The blessing of God. 2. The desire for God.

**Devātman (m)** (*deva* 'god' + *ātman* ' Self') 1. The divine Self. 2. The Self which is God.

**Devendra (m)** (*deva* 'god' + *indra* 'chief') The chief of the gods (i.e. Indra).

**Deveśa (m)** (*deva* 'god' + *īśa* 'lord') 1. The Lord of the gods. 2. The 492nd name of Lord Vishṇu as listed in the Vishṇu Sahasranāma. 3. Name of Lord Śiva.

**Devī (f)** 1. God in a feminine manifestation as Goddess or Divine Mother, who always symbolizes knowledge of the true Self. Her three main forms are Saraswatī, Lakshmī, and Pārvatī. 2. The 50th, 96th and 102nd of the Goddess Lakshmī's 108 names.

**Devīka (f)** God in a feminine manifestation as Goddess or Divine Mother, who always symbolizes knowledge of the true Self. Her three main forms are Saraswatī, Lakshmī, and Pārvatī.

**Dhairyan (m)** The firm, steady or bold. See the Bhagavad Gītā VI:25; XVI:3; XVIII:33,51.

**Dhairyavan (m), Dhairyavatī (f)** (*dhairya* 'firm, steady' + *van/vatī* 'having') The firm, steady or bold.

**Dhanada (m)** (*dhana* 'wealth' + *da* 'giver') 1. The giver of wealth. 2. A name of Kubera. See the Bhagavad Gītā X:23.

**Dhanadā (f), Dhanadāyinī (f)** (*dhana* 'wealth' + *dā/dāyinī* 'giver') 1. The giver of wealth. 2. A name of the Goddess Lakshmī.

**Dhanalakshmī (f)** (*dhana* 'wealth' + *lakshmī* 'prosperity') The wealth of wealth; the wealthy Lakshmī; a name of the Goddess Lakshmī.

**Dhananetā (m)** (*dhana* 'wealth' + *netā* 'bringer, leader') 1. The bringer or leader of wealth. 2. A title for a king.

**Dhananetrī (f)** (*dhana* 'wealth' + *netrī* 'bringer, leader') The bringer or leader of wealth; a name of the Goddess Lakshmī.

**Dhanapati (m)** (*dhana* 'wealth' + *pati* 'lord') The Lord or master of wealth; a name of Kubera.

**Dhanapāla (m)** (*dhana* 'wealth' + *pāla* 'guardian') 1. The guardian of treasure. 2. A title for a king. 3. A name of Kubera.

**Dhanādhipa (m)** (*dhana* 'wealth' + *adhipa* 'lord') The Lord of wealth; a name of Kubera. See the Bhagavad Gītā X:23.

**Dhaneśa (m)** (*dhana* 'wealth' + *īśa* 'lord') The Lord of wealth; a name of Kubera. See the Bhagavad Gītā X:23.

**Dhaneśwara (m)** (*dhana* 'wealth' + *īśwara* 'lord') 1. The Lord of wealth. 2. The 474th name of Lord Vishṇu listed in the Vishṇu Sahasranāma. 3. A name of Kubera.

**Dhaneśwarī (f)** (*dhana* 'wealth' + *īśwarī* 'sovereign goddess') 1. The sovereign Goddess of wealth. 2. A name of the Goddess Lakshmī. 3. The consort of Kubera.

**Dhanwantari (m)** 1. Moving in a curve. 2. The name of the divine physician produced during the churning of the milk ocean and bearing the nectar of immortality (i.e. amṛita, in a Kamaṇḍalu). He is the originator of Āyur-Veda, or the Science of life.

**Dharaṇī (f)** 1. The supporter 2. A name of the Earth-Goddess.

**Dharaṇīśwara (m)** (*dharan* 'support' + *īśwara* 'lord') 1. The Lord of the Supporter (i.e. of the Earth Goddess). 2. A name of Lord Vishṇu referring to Him supporting the Earth in His serpent form, Śesha.

**Dharā (f)** 1. Support. 2. A name of the Earth-Goddess.

**Dharitrī (f)** 1. The Supporter. 2. A name of the Earth-Goddess.

**Dharma (m)** 1. The support, religious law, virtue, merit, one's righteous action in life. 2. The 403rd name of Lord Vishṇu as listed in the Vishṇu Sahasranāma. In his commentary, Śrī Śaṅkara states, "On account of supporting all beings, the Lord is called *Dharma*, the support. In the Kaṭha Upanishad it is written, "This *Dharma* or principle (i.e. the Self) is subtle."

Again the Lord is thus called because He is worshipped through *Dharmas* or religious duties." See the Bhagavad Gītā II:40; IV:7,8; IX:2,3,30,31; XI:18; XII:20; XIV:27. 3. The God of religious law, virtue, support, who was incarnated as Arjuna's brother, King Yudhishṭhira.

**Dharmabandhu (m)** (*dharma* 'spiritual path, duty' + *bandhu* 'friend, relative') The friend of dharma, or religious law.

**Dharmacakra (m)** (*dharma* 'spiritual path, duty' + *cakra* 'wheel') The wheel of duty. See the Bhagavad Gītā III:16.

**Dharmacāriṇī (f)** (*dharma* 'spiritual path, duty' + *cāriṇī* 'conduct') Having virtuous conduct. See the Bhagavad Gītā IX:31.

**Dharmadeva (m)** (*dharma* 'spiritual path, duty' + *deva* 'god') The God of dharma or justice.

**Dharmanātha (m)** (*dharma* 'spiritual path, duty' + *nātha* 'lord') 1. The Lord of dharma or justice. 2. A name of Yama, God of death. 3. The supreme God, Īśwara.

**Dharmanitya (m), Dharmanityā (f)** (*dharma* 'spiritual path, duty' + *nitya* 'eternal') The ever-virtuous.

**Dharmapatha (m)** (*dharma* 'spiritual path, duty' + *patha* 'path') The path of righteousness or virtue.

**Dharmapara (m), Dharmaparā (f)** (*dharma* 'spiritual path, duty' + *para* 'supreme') He/she for whom virtue (Dharma) is supreme.

**Dharmaputra (m)** (*dharma* 'spiritual path, duty' + *putra* 'son') 1. The son of Dharma. 2. A name of King Yudhishṭhira, who was the brother of Arjuna.

**Dharmarata (m)** (*dharma* 'spiritual path, duty' + *rata* 'delighted') He who delights in virtue (Dharma).

**Dharmaśakti (m)** (*dharma* 'spiritual path, duty' + *śakti* 'energy, power') Having virtuous power, or energy. See the Bhagavad Gītā VII:11.

**Dharmātman (m)** (*dharma* 'spiritual path, duty' + *ātman* 'Self, Soul') Having a virtuous soul. See the Bhagavad Gītā IX:31.

**Dharmiṇī (f)** The virtuous (i.e. she who follows the ordinances of Scriptures).

**Dharmishṭha (m), Dharmishṭhā (f)** The greatly virtuous.

**Dhārmika (m), Dhārmikī (f)** The righteous or virtuous.

**Dhīman (m)** The wise, or intelligent.

**Dhīmatī (f)** The possessor of intelligence.

**Dhīra (m)** 1. The wise or intelligent. 2. The resolute, brave, firm. See the Bhagavad Gītā II:13,15; VI:42; VII:10; XIV:24.

**Dhṛitarāshṭra (m)** (*dhṛita* 'firm' + *rāshṭra* 'empire') 1. Having a firm empire. 2. The eldest son of Vyāsa born blind to Ambikā, Vicitravīrya's widow. He was the brother of Pāṇḍu and Vidura, the husband of Gāndhārī and the father of 100 sons, the Kauravas, among whom Duryodhana was the eldest. His charioteer, Sañjaya, related the Bhagavad Gītā to him along with all that happened during the Mahābhārata war.

**Dhṛitātman (m)** (*dhṛita* 'firm' + *ātman* 'Self, Soul') 1. Having the sustained Self, having a controlled mind. 2. The 160th name of Lord Vishṇu as listed in the Vishṇu Sahasranāma. In his commentary Śrī Śaṅkara states, "He whose Self is sustained through Oneness and freedom from birth and death is the Lord called 'having the sustained Self.'"

**Dhṛiti (f)** 1. Firmness, will-power. See the Bhagavad Gītā VI:25; X:34; XIII:6; XVI:3; XVIII:26, 33-35,51. 2. The wife of the God Dharma.

**Dhruva (m)** 1. The firm, permanent. 2. The 388th name of Lord Vishṇu as listed in the Vishṇu Sahasranāma. In his commentary, Śrī Śaṅkara states, "On account of His imperishableness, the Lord is called the 'firm.'" See the Bhagavad Gītā XII:3. 3. The name of Manu's grandson who through the grace of God became the polar star known as Dhruva Nakshatra.

**Dhūmāvatī (f)** (*dhūmā* 'smoke' + *vatī* 'having') 1. The possessor of smoke. 2. The name of a place of pilgrimage connected with the Divine Mother.

**Dhyānapara (m)** (*dhyāna* 'meditation' + *para* 'intent on, engaged in') Intent on meditation.

**Dhyānarata (m)** (*dhyāna* 'meditation' + *rata* 'delighted') He who is delighted through or in meditation. See the Bhagavad Gītā II:53,66; VI:3, 19,24-28; X:8,9; XII:8; XIII:24; XVIII:52.

**Dhyānavan (m), Dhyānavatī (f)** (*dhyāna* 'meditation' + *van/vatī* 'having') The meditative.

**Dhyānavrata (m)** (*dhyāna* 'meditation' + *vrata* 'vow') He whose vow consists of meditation. See the Bhagavad Gītā II:53,66; VI:3,19,24-28; X:8,9; XII:8; XIII:24; XVIII:52.

**Dhyāyinī (f)** The meditative.

**Dilīpa (m)** The name of a king who was the ancestor of Śrī Rāma and father of Bhagīratha. He is the subject of the first two chapters of Kālidāsa's poem "Raghuvamśa."

**Dinabhartā (m)** (*dina* 'day' + *bhartā* 'master') 1. The master of the day. 2. A name of Sūrya, the Sun-God.

**Dinakara (m)** (*dina* 'day' + *kara* 'maker') 1. The day-maker. 2. A name of Sūrya, the Sun-God.

**Dinakartā (m), Dinkartrī (f)** (*dina* 'day' + *kartā /kartrī* 'maker') 1. The day-maker. 2. A name of Sūrya, the Sun-God.

**Dinamaṇi (m)** (*dina* 'day' + *maṇi* 'pearl, gem') 1. The jewel of the day. 2. A name of Sūrya, the Sun-God.

**Dinanātha (m)** (*dina* 'day' + *nātha* 'lord') 1. The Lord of the day. 2. A name of Sūrya, the Sun-God.

**Dinapati (m)** (*dina* 'day' + *pati* 'lord') 1. The Lord of the day. 2. A name of Sūrya, the Sun-God.

**Dinarāja (m)** (*dina* 'day' + *rāja* 'king') 1. The king of the day. 2. A name of Sūrya, the Sun-God.

**Dinādhīśa (m)** (*dina* 'day' + *adhīśa* 'lord') 1. The Lord of the day. 2. A name of Sūrya, the Sun-God.

**Dineśa (m)** (*dina* 'day' + *īśa* 'lord') 1. The Lord of the day. 2. A name of Sūrya, the Sun-God.

**Dineśwara (m)** (*dina* 'day' + *īśwara* 'lord') 1. The Lord of the day. 2. A name of Sūrya, the Sun-God.

**Divākara (m)** (*diva* 'day' + *kara* 'maker') 1. The day-maker. 2. A name of Sūrya, the Sun-God.

**Divamaṇi (m)** (*diva* 'day' + *maṇi* 'pearl, gem') 1. The jewel of the day. 2. A name of Sūrya, the Sun-God.

**Divyajyoti (f)** (*divya* 'divine' + *jyoti* 'light') The divine light.

**Divyamati (f)** (*divya* 'divine' + *mati* 'thought') The divine thought.

**Divyaśakti (f)** (*divya* 'divine' + *śakti* 'energy, power') Having divine power, energy.

**Divyā (f)** The Divine.

**Dīkshā (f)** 1. Initiation. 2. The wife of the God Soma.

**Dīkshiṇī (f), Dīkshita (m)** The consecrated or initiated.

**Dīnabandhu (m)** (*dīna* 'afflicted' + *bandhu* 'friend, relative') The friend of the afflicted.

**Dīpa (m), Dīpikā (f)** Lamp, lantern, beacon. Illuminating.

**Draupadī (f)** The daughter of King Drupada; the name of the wife of the five Pāṇḍava brothers.

**Dṛiśāna (m)** 1. The seer, or discerner. 2. Name of a Ṛishi. 3. Title of a wise Brāhmaṇa.

**Drona (m)** 1. The bucket-born. 2. The name of the military preceptor of the Kauravas and the Pāṇḍavas, who is said to have been generated by Ṛishi Bharadwāja in a bucket. He was the husband of Kṛipī and the father of Aśwatthāman. The seventh book in the Mahābhārata is named after him.

**Drupada (m)** The name of a king who was the father of Dhṛishṭadyumna, Śikhaṇḍin and Draupadī.

**Druti (f)** The melting.

**Durlabha (m)** 1. The one who is hard to obtain (i.e. God). 2. The 777th name of Lord Vishṇu as listed in the Vishṇu Sahasranāma. In his commentary Śrī Śaṅkara states, "The Lord is thus called because He is attained through a devotion that is hard to obtain. Vyāsa relates, 'Devotion to Kṛishṇa arises for men whose sins are destroyed through austerities, knowledge and Samādhi accomplished in a thousand previous births." See the Bhagavad Gītā II:29; V:23,25; VI:22-3, 33-36, 42, 45; VII:3, 13-4, 19, 24-5; VIII:14, 22; IX:3, 23-4; XI:52-4; XII:5; XV:10-1; XVIII:36-7.

**Durāsada (m)** 1. The one who is hard to approach. 2. A name of Lord Śiva, who is nirguṇa, or attributeless, and thus hard to approach.

**Durgā (f)** 1. The one who is hard to attain. 2. A name of Lord Śiva's consort, who represents Self-knowledge, which is difficult to attain.

**Durvāsa (m)** 1. The badly clad. 2. A manifestation of Lord Śiva born as the son of Atri and Anasūyā and known for his irascibility and for testing spiritual vows. Once, while bathing in the Ganges, he became naked and was saved from dishonor by a piece of Draupadī's garment. He therefore granted her the boon of ever increasing her folds of cloth. Later, she was saved from dishonor by this boon when Duryodhana tried to pull off her sari.

**Dyotana (m), Dyotanī (f)** The enlightening through knowledge.

**Dyumaṇi (m)** (*dyu* 'sky' + *maṇi* 'pearl, gem') 1. The sky-jewel. 2. A name of Sūrya, the Sun-God.

**Dyuti (f), Dyutiman (m)** The luminous through knowledge.

# E

**Eka (m)** 1. The One. 2. The 725th name of Lord Vishṇu as listed in the Vishṇu Sahasranāma. In his commentary Śrī Śaṅkara states, "The Lord is One on account of His complete freedom from all differences, generic, extrinsic and intrinsic, as it is written in the Chāndogya Upanishad, 'The Absolute is verily One and non-dual.'" It is written in the Bṛihad-Āraṇyaka Upanishad, "There is no diversity whatsoever in the Absolute...It should be realized as Oneness alone...There is not that second thing separate from It which It can see...There is no other witness but That..." See the Bhagavad Gītā VI:22,25,26,31; VII:7,17,19; VIII: 22; IX:15; X:8; XI:7,13,43; XIII:16,27,30,33; XIV:27; XVIII:20,66.

**Ekabhakta (m)** (*eka* 'one' + *bhakta* 'devoted') Devoted to the One. See the Bhagavad Gītā VII:17; VIII:22; IX:22,34; XI:54,55; XII:13-20; XIII:10; XVIII:54,55.

**Ekabhakti (f)** (*eka* 'one' + *bhakti* 'devotion') She whose devotion is in the One. See the Bhagavad Gītā VII:17; VIII:22; IX:22,34; XI:54,55; XII:13-20; XIII:10; XVIII:54,55.

**Ekabuddhi (m or f)** (*eka* 'one' + *buddhi* 'intellect') He/she whose intelligence rests in the One. See the Bhagavad Gītā V:17; XVIII:20.

**Ekadanta (m)** (*eka* 'one' + *danta* 'tooth') 1. The one-toothed. 2. Having one tusk; a name of Lord Gaṇeśa, who is said to have broken one of his tusks to write the Mahābhārata.

**Ekadṛiś (m)** (*eka* 'one' + *driś* 'eye, sight') 1. The one-eyed (i.e. having the one eye of knowledge). See the Bhagavad Gītā XI:8; XIII:34; XV:10-1. 2. The seer of oneness. 3. The one consciousness. 4. A name of Lord Śiva referring to His having the third eye of knowledge on His forehead, with which He consumed Kāmadeva, or Cupid.

**Ekajyoti (m or f)** (*eka* 'one' + *jyoti* 'light') 1. The one light. 2. A name of Lord Śiva. See the Bhagavad Gītā V:24; XIII:17,33.

**Ekaliṅga (m)** (*eka* 'one' + *liṅga* 'sacred cylindrical stone') The symbol of oneness (i.e. the sacred stone, the *liṅgam*, is connected with Lord Śiva and represents oneness and formlessness).

**Ekalocana (m)** (*eka* 'one' + *locana* 'eye') 1. The one-eyed. 2. A name of Lord Śiva referring to His having the third eye of knowledge on His forehead, with which He consumed Kāmadeva, or Cupid.

**Ekalū (m)** The name of a Ṛishi.

**Ekamati (m or f)** (*eka* 'one' + *mati* 'thought') 1. He/she whose thought rests in the One. 2. Having only one thought. See the Bhagavad Gītā VI:24-5.

**Ekanayana (m)** (*eka* 'one' + *nayana* 'eye') 1. The one-eyed. 2. A name of Lord Śiva referring to His having the third eye of knowledge on His forehead, with which He consumed Kāmadeva, or Cupid.

**Ekanātha (m)** (*eka* 'one' + *nātha* 'lord') 1. The one Lord. 2. Having one Lord. See the Bhagavad Gītā VI:22,25-6,31; VII:7,17,19; VIII:22; IX:15; X:8; XI:7,13,43; XIII:16,27,30,33; XIV:27; XVIII: 20,66.

**Ekanāyaka (m)** (*eka* 'one' + *nāyaka* 'ruler') 1. The one ruler or leader. 2. Having only one guide or master.

**Ekanetra (m)** (*eka* 'one' + *netra* 'eye') 1. The one-eyed. 2. A name of Lord Śiva referring to His having the third eye of knowledge on His forehead, with which He consumed Kāmadeva, or Cupid.

**Ekapara (m), Ekaparā (f)** (*eka* 'one' + *para* 'devoted; supreme') 1. Devoted to the One. 2. One for whom the One (God) is supreme. See the Bhagavad Gītā IV:39; V:17; VI:14,20,25,31; IX:15,27, 34; X:9; XI: 55; XII:6; XIII:30; XVIII:57,66.

**Ekapurusha (m)** (*eka* 'one' + *purusha* 'Being, Spirit') The One (Supreme) Being. See the Bhagavad Gītā VII:7; VIII:20-22; XIII:22; XV:4,17-19.

**Ekarada (m)** (*eka* 'one' + *rada* 'tooth') 1. The one-toothed. 2. Having one tusk; a name of Lord Gaṇeśa, who is said to have broken one of his tusks to write the Mahābhārata.

**Ekarasa (m)** (*eka* 'one' + *rasa* 'essence') The one essence of truth.

**Ekarasā (f)** (*eka* 'one' + *rasā* 'delight') 1. The one bliss. 2. The 33rd name of the Goddess Lalitā as listed in the Lalitā Triśatī. In his commentary Śrī Śaṅkara states, " 1) The Taittirīya Upanishad relates the following:

*Yad-Vai Tat-Sukṛitam*
*Raso Vai Saḥ*
*Rasam Hy'evāyam Labdhwānandī*
*Bhavati.*

That which is known as the Self-Creator
is verily the Source of Bliss;

For one becomes blissful by coming in
contact with that Source of Bliss.

2) Among the nine sentiments or *Navarasas*, She is the one sentiment (*Ekarasā*), love or Śṛiṅgāra. 3) *Eka* means the supreme Lord, and She is the object of His intense love. 4) Also, She has deep love toward Her husband. 5) Again, *Rasa* means sweetness, one of the six tastes, which is agreeable to sattwic people. As She is Consciousness, limited by Māyā which is primarily sattwic in nature, She likes sweetness, as is said in the Bhagavad Gītā XVII:8."

**Ekarata (m)** (*eka* 'one' + *rata* 'delighted') Delighted in the One. See the Bhagavad Gītā II:55; III:17; V:24: VI:8; X:9.

**Ekarati (f)** (*eka* 'one' + *rati* 'delight, pleasure') She whose delight is in the One.

**Ekarshi (m)** (*eka* 'one' + *ṛishi* 'seer') 1. The one seer. 2. The solitary traveler. 3. A name of Sūrya, the Sun-God in the Īśā Upanishad. 4. The name of a Ṛishi.

**Ekasatī (f)** (*eka* 'one' + *satī* 'existence') 1. The one existence. 2. The daughter of Daksha, who was Lord Śiva's consort and who burned her body when Her Lord was shown disrespect by Her father. Later she was reborn as Pārvatī, the daughter of Himavan or Himālaya. 3. The only Satī or faithful wife.

**Ekatā (f)** (*eka* 'one' + *tā* 'in the state of) The oneness.

**Ekavrata (m)** (*eka* 'one' + *rata* 'vow, obedience, mode of life') 1. He who observes one vow. 2. He who takes food once a day. See the Bhagavad Gītā VII:28; IX:14.

**Ekāgratā (f)** (*eka* 'one' + *agra* 'point' + *tā* 'in the state of') One-pointedness. See the Bhagavad Gītā II:53; VI:12,19,24-5.

**Ekāksha (m)** (*eka* 'one' + *aksha* 'eye') 1. The one-eyed. 2. A name of Lord Śiva referring to His having the third eye of knowledge on His forehead, with which He consumed Kāmadeva, or Cupid.

**Ekānta (m), Ekāntinī (f)** (*eka* 'one' + *anta/tinī* 'end') 1. Having one end or aim. 2. He/she whose end is Oneness. See the Bhagavad Gītā VI:31; VII:18.

**Ekārāma (m)** (*eka* 'one' + *ārāma* 'enjoyment') 1. He whose delight is in the One. 2. Having only one delight. See the Bhagavad Gītā II:55; III:17; V:24; X:9.

**Ekāśraya (m), Ekāśrayā (f)** (*eka* 'one' + *āśrayā* 'refuge') 1. He/she whose refuge is in the One. 2. Having only one refuge. See the Bhagavad Gītā XVIII:62,66.

**Ekātman (m)** (*eka* 'one' + *ātman* 'Self') 1. The one Self. 2. The 965th name of Lord Vishṇu listed in the Vishṇu Sahasranāma. In his commentary Śrī Śaṅkara states, "The Lord is One on account of His complete freedom from all differences, generic, extrinsic and intrinsic, as it is written in the Chāndogya Upanishad, 'The Absolute is verily One and non-dual.'" It is written in the Bṛihad-Āraṇyaka Upanishad, "There is no diversity whatsoever in the Absolute...It should be realized as Oneness alone...There is not that second thing separate from It which It can see...There is no other witness but That..." See the Bhagavad Gītā VI:22,25-6,31; VII:7,17,19; VIII:22; IX:15; X:8; XI:7,13, 43; XIII:16,27,30,33; XIV:27; XVIII:20,66.

# G

**Gajamukha (m)** (*gaja* 'elephant' + *mukha* 'face') 1. The elephant-faced. 2. A name of Lord Gaṇeśa. His human body with an elephant head represents the oneness or non-duality of the Self and the Absolute.

**Gajavadana (m)** (*gaja* 'elephant' + *vadana* 'face') 1. The elephant-faced. 2. A name of Lord Gaṇeśa. His human body with an elephant head represents the oneness or non-duality of the Self and the Absolute.

**Gajavaktra (m)** (*gaja* 'elephant' + *vaktra* 'face') 1. The elephant-faced. 2. A name of Lord Gaṇeśa. His human body with an elephant head represents the oneness or non-duality of the Self and the Absolute.

**Gajānana (m)** (*gaja* 'elephant' + *anana* 'face') 1. The elephant-faced. 2. A name of Lord Gaṇeśa. His human body with an elephant head represents the oneness or non-duality of the Self and the Absolute.

**Gajendra (m)** (*gaja* 'elephant' + *indra* 'chief') 1. Chief of the elephants; one of the four elephants guarding the quarters.

**Gaṇanātha (m)** (*Gaṇa* 'troop of demi-gods attending Lord Śiva' + *nātha* 'lord') 1. Lord of the Gaṇa troop (i.e. demi-gods attending Lord Śiva). 2. A name of Lord Śiva. 3. A name of Lord Gaṇeśa.

**Gaṇapati (m)** (*Gaṇa* 'troop of demi-gods attending Lord Śiva' + *pati* 'lord') 1. Lord of the Gaṇa troop (i.e. demi-gods attending Lord Śiva). 2. A name of Lord Śiva. 3. A name of Lord Gaṇeśa.

**Gandhadhāra (m)** (*gandha* 'fragrance' + *dhāra* 'bearing') 1. Having a divine fragrance. 2. A name of Lord Śiva, which refers to His subtleness which is all-pervading like the fragrance that permeates sandalwood.

**Gandhakālī (f)** 1. The fragrant. 2. The name of Vyāsa's mother, Satyavatī, which was given to her because once she conceived her son Vyāsa, she always smelled fragrant.

**Gandharva (m)** 1. The fragrant. 2. The name of the celestial musicians. See the Bhagavad Gītā X:26.

**Gandhasāra (m)** (*gandha* 'fragrance' + *sāra* 'essence') The fragrant essence (i.e. sandalwood and jasmine).

**Gandhi (m)** 1. The fragrant. 2. The name of a saintly 20th century Indian leader who applied Ahimsa, or non-injury, in political life. He was also known as Mahātma *Gandhi.* [see **Mahātman**]

**Gandhinī (f)** The fragrant.

**Gaṇeśa (m)** (*Gaṇa* 'demi-gods' + *īśa* 'lord') 1. The Lord of the Gaṇa troop (i.e. demi-gods attending Lord Śiva). 2. The main name for Lord Śiva and Goddess Pārvatī's son, who is the remover of all obstacles, the bestower of success and the God of Wisdom. He is worshipped first in religious rituals. He presides over the Gaṇas, a troop of demi-gods that attends Lord Śiva. He has two wives, Siddhi (Accomplishment) and Buddhi (intelligence). He has a human body with an elephant head, which represents the oneness or non-duality of the Self and the Absolute, and one tusk, which again symbolizes oneness. He rides on a mouse which is symbolic of cleverness. He wrote the 100,000 verses of the Mahābhārata under Vyāsa's dictation. He represents the syllable "OM" and the four Vedas. His tales are told in the Purāṇas. He is praised in the Yajurveda and one of the Upanishads of Atharvaveda bears His name, Gaṇapati.

**Gaṅgā (f)** 1. The one who goes swiftly. 2. The river Ganges as Goddess. She is the eldest daughter of Himavan and hence the sister of the Goddess Pārvatī or Umā. She was the wife of King Śāntanu and mother of Bhīshma. She is said to flow from Lord Vishṇu's toe. She is pure knowledge personified. As a celestial river, She is the Milky Way. Because of Bhagīratha's austerities She descended on earth to purify the ashes of his 60,000 Sāgara ancestors and is thereby called "Bhāgīrathī." To protect mankind from such heavy descent, Lord Śiva received the divine *Gaṅgā* on His head, from which comes the sanctity of Her waters. On Her way to earth She flooded King Jahnu's sacrificial ground. Jahnu drank all its waters and allowed the holy river to flow out through his ears. She is thus called Jāhnavī, the daughter of Jahnu. She is the Mother of Lord Śiva's son Kārttikeya. See the Bhagavad Gītā X:31.

**Gaṅgābhṛit (m)** (*gaṅgā* 'the river Ganges' + *bhṛit* 'bearer') 1. The bearer of the Ganges. 2. A name of Lord Śiva, referring to the Ganges flowing from His head.

**Gaṅgādhara (m)** (*gaṅgā* 'the river Ganges' + *dhara* 'bearing') 1. The bearer of the Ganges. 2. The 24th name of Lord Śiva as listed in His 108 names.

**Gaṅgāsuta (m)** (*gaṅgā* 'the River Ganges' + *suta* 'son') 1. The son of the Goddess Ganges. 2. An name of Bhīshma. 3. A name of Kārttikeya.

**Garga (m)** The name of a Ṛishi who was one of the seers of the Ṛigveda.

**Garuḍa (m)** 1. The devourer. 2. The name of the divine and powerful eagle who serves Lord Vishṇu as His vehicle. He is the son of Kaśyapa and Vinatā. See the Bhagavad Gītā X:30. 3. Winged sounds, a name for the Vedic hymns which lift one higher and higher and which are symbolized by *Garuḍa.*

**Gauraṅga (m)** The name of a great devotee of Lord Kṛishṇa who lived in the 15th century.

**Gaurī (f)** 1. The shining or brilliant. 2. The fair-skinned maiden. 3. A name of Lord Śiva's consort, the Goddess Pārvatī.

**Gaurīnātha (m)** (*Gaurī* 'n. of Goddess Pārvatī' + *nātha* 'lord') The Lord of Gaurī (i.e. of Goddess Pārvatī); a name of Lord Śiva.

**Gaurīpati (m)** (*Gaurī* 'n. of Goddess Pārvatī' + *pati* 'lord') The Lord of Gaurī (i.e. of Goddess Pārvatī); a name of Lord Śiva.

**Gaurīśa (m)** (*Gaurī* 'n. of Goddess Pārvatī' + *īśa* 'lord') The Lord of Gaurī (i.e. of Goddess Pārvatī); a name of Lord Śiva.

**Gaurītanaya (m)** (*Gaurī* 'n. of Goddess Pārvatī' + *tanaya* 'son') The son of Gaurī (i.e. of Goddess Pārvatī); a name of Lord Gaṇeśa.

**Gautama (m)** 1. The descendant of the Ṛishi Gotama. 2. The name of the Buddha. 3. The name of several wise men.

**Gayati (m)** A name of Śrī Kṛishṇa.

**Gayā (f)** The name of a holy city in India, which is connected with the Ṛishi Gaya.

**Gāndhārī (f)** The princess of Gāndhāra kingdom, who was the daughter of King Subala and the wife of King Dhṛitarāshtra. Because Dhṛitarāshṭra was blind, Gāndhārī bandaged her own eyes as not to excel her husband. Through the grace of Lord Śiva and Vyāsa, she bore a hundred sons, the Kauravas.

**Gāṇḍīva (m)** The name of Arjuna's bow given to him after his encounter with Lord Śiva.

**Gārgī (f)** The name of a learned woman who questioned Yājnavalkya in Bṛihad-Āraṇyaka Upanishad and was instructed on the Aksharam, or the "Imperishable."

**Gāthaka (m)** The singer of the Purāṇas.

**Gāyatrī (f)** 1. The Savior of the organs. 2. The name of the celebrated mantra of the Ṛigveda imparted to the Brāhmaṇas at the time of their initiation into

Brahmacarya at the age of eight. It is considered, along with the syllable "OM" as the greatest among all the Vedic hymns or prayers and is recited daily by Brāhmaṇas at dawn, noon and dusk. It is addressed to the Sun-God as a form of the divine light. Its seer was Viśwāmitra. It is personified as the Mother of the Vedas (Chandasām Mātā) and protects those who recite it. See the Bhagavad Gītā X:35.

**Ghṛiṇin (m)** 1. The compassionate. 2. The name of one of Kṛishṇa's brothers.

**Giri (m)** 1. He who is like a mountain. 2. One of the ten orders of Sannyāsins founded by Śrī Śaṅkara. The members of this order add the word "*Giri* " to their names.

**Giribandhu (m)** (*giri* 'mountain' + *bandhu* 'friend, relative') 1. The friend of the mountains. 2. A name of Lord Śiva.

**Giribāndhava (m)** (*giri* 'mountain' + *bāndhava* 'friend, relative') 1. The friend of the mountains. 2. A name of Lord Śiva.

**Giribhū (f)** (*giri* 'mountain' + *bhū* 'to be born') 1. The mountain-born. 2. A name of the Goddess Pārvatī indicating that she is the daughter of Himavan or Himālaya.

**Giridhara (m)** (*giri* 'mountain' + *dhara* 'bearer') 1. The Mountain-supporter. 2. A name of Śrī Kṛishṇa referring to the time that He lifted up Mount Govardhana with one finger and held it for seven days to shelter the cowherds from a storm of rain sent by Indra to test Śrī Kṛishṇa's divinity.

**Giridhava (m)** (*giri* 'mountain' + *dhava* 'lord, man, husband') 1. The Lord of the mountains. 2. A name of Lord Śiva.

**Giriduhitā (f)** (*giri* 'mountain' + *duhitā* 'daughter') 1. The mountain-daughter. 2. A name of the Goddess Pārvatī as the daughter of Himavan.

**Girijā (f)** (*giri* 'mountain' + *jā* 'born') 1. The mountain-born. 2. A name of the Goddess Pārvatī as the daughter of Himavan.

**Girijādhava (m)** (*girijā* 'mountain-born' + *dhava* 'lord, man, husband') The Lord of the mountain-born (i.e. of the Goddess Pārvatī); a name of Lord Śiva.

**Girinandinī (f)** (*giri* 'mountain' + *nandinī* 'joy') 1. The joy of the mountains. 2. A name of the Goddess Pārvatī as the daughter of Himavan.

**Giripati (m)** (*giri* 'mountain' + *pati* 'lord') 1. The Lord of the mountains. 2. A name of Lord Śiva. 3. A name of Himavan.

**Girirāja (m)** (*giri* 'mountain' + *rāja* 'king') 1. The king of the mountains. 2. A name of Himavan.

**Girisutā (m)** (*giri* 'mountain' + *sutā* 'daughter') 1. The mountain-daughter. 2. A name of Goddess Pārvatī as the daughter of Himavan.

**Girīndra (m)** (*giri* 'mountain' + *indra* 'chief') 1. The chief of the mountains. 2. A name of Himavan or Himālaya.

**Girīśa (m)** (*giri* 'mountain' + *īsa* 'lord') 1. The mountain-Lord. 2. The 56th name of Lord Śiva's 108 names. It refers to His being the Lord of outer Mount Kailāsa in the Himālayas or the inner Kailāsa that is the space within the heart lotus.

**Giriśwara (m)** (*giri* 'mountain' + *īśwara* 'lord') 1. The mountain-Lord. 2. A name of Lord Śiva

**Gīrdevī (f)** (*gīr* 'voice, speech' + *devī* 'goddess') 1. The Goddess of speech. 2. A name of the Goddess Saraswatī.

**Gītā (f)** 1. The song (of God). 2. The teachings of Śrī Kṛishṇa to Arjuna set in 700 verses by Vyāsa in the Mahābhārata. Along with the Upanishads and the Brahmasūtras, it forms the triple authority of India's spiritual heritage. In his commentary on the Gītā, Śrī Śaṅkara says, "The Gītā treatise is a compendium on the essence of the meaning of all the Vedas, and its significance is difficult to understand...Its aim is the highest good, a complete cessation of transmigration and of its cause (ignorance)."

**Gītāpriyā (f)** (*Gītā* 'n. of a scripture' + *priyā* 'devoted to') Fond of, or delighting in the Bhagavad Gītā.

**Godāvarī (f)** The name of one of India's seven holy rivers. It is related in the Pūjās:

> *Gaṅge ca Yamune cai'va Godāvari Saraswati,*
> *Narmade Sindhu Kāveri Jale'smin Sannidhim Kuru.*
>
> O Gaṅgā, O Yamunā, O *Godāvarī*, O Saraswatī,
> O Narmadā, O Sindhu, O Kāverī, may your presence
> come into this water.

**Gokuleśa (m)** (*gokula* 'herd of cattle' + *īśa* 'lord') 1. The Lord of Gokula village. 2. A name of Śrī Kṛishṇa.

**Gopāla (m)** 1. The cowherd boy; a name of Śrī Kṛishṇa. 2. The earth protector;

a name of Lord Vishṇu.

**Gopī (f)** 1. Cowherdess. 2. The name of Śrī Kṛishṇa's devotees said to be the incarnations of Ṛishis.

**Gopījana (m)** The beloved of the Gopīs; a name of Śrī Kṛishṇa.

**Gopīkā (f)** 1. Cowherdess. 2. The name of Śrī Kṛishṇa's devotees said to be the incarnations of Ṛishis.

**Gopīnātha (m)** (*Gopī* 'cowherdess' + *nātha* 'lord') The Lord of the Gopīs; a name of Śrī Kṛishṇa.

**Gopīśwara (m)** (*Gopī* 'cowherdess' + *īśwara* 'lord') The sovereign Lord of the Gopīs; a name of Śrī Kṛishṇa.

**Goptā (m)** 1. The Protector. 2. The 496th and 593rd name of Lord Vishṇu as listed in the Vishṇu Sahasranāma. In his commentary Śrī Śaṅkara states, "He is called 'Goptā' either because He protects all beings and all worlds or because He conceals Himself through His own power of illusion." See the Bhagavad Gītā XI:18.

**Govardhana (m)** The name of a celebrated hill lifted up by Śrī Kṛishṇa with one finger and held for seven days to shelter the cowherds from a storm of rain sent by Indra to test Śrī Kṛishṇa's divinity.

**Govinda (m)** 1. He who is known through the Scriptures. 2. The 187th and 539th names of Lord Vishṇu as listed in the Vishṇu Sahasranāma. In his commentary Śrī Śaṅkara states, "The Lord is called '*Govinda*' 1) because He rescued the earth which was carried away by a demon, 2) because He has lordship over the cows, 3) because He confers speech, or 4) because He is knowable throught Vedāntic Scriptures."

**Guha (m)** 1. The concealer. 2. The unmanifested one. 3. The 383rd name of Lord Vishṇu as listed in the Vishṇu Sahasranāma. In his commentary Śrī Śaṅkara states, "He who conceals or veils His own nature through His illusive power is the Concealer, as is said by the Lord in the Gītā, 'Veiled by the power of illusion, I am not manifest to all' (VII:25)." 4. A name of Kārttikeya, Lord Śiva's son.

**Guhapriyā (f)** (*Guha* 'the concealer' + *priyā* 'beloved') 1. The beloved of Guha. 2. A name of Indra's daughter. 3. She who is fond of the hidden Self (i.e. God).

**Guheśwara (m)** (*guhā* 'cavity' + *īśwara* 'lord') The Lord of the (heart) cavity. See the Bhagavad Gītā XIII:17; XVIII:61.

**Guhyapati (m)** (*guhya* 'secret' + *pati* 'lord') The Lord of the secret (i.e. referring to God revealing the secret knowledge of His true Self in the Upanishads).

**Guṇadhara (m)** (*guṇa* 'quality of nature, virtue' + *dhara* 'bearer') The possessor of virtues (i.e. the sattwa-guṇa). See the Bhagavad Gītā XVI:1-3.

**Guṇanidhi (m)** (*guṇa* 'quality of nature, virtue' + *nidhi* 'treasure') 1. The treasure of virtues (i.e. the sattwa-guṇa). 2. A name of Lord Śiva.

**Guṇaratnā (f)** (*guṇa* 'quality of nature, virtue' + *ratnā* 'gem, pearl') The pearl or gem of virtues.

**Guṇarāśi (m)** (*guṇa* 'quality of nature, virtue' + *rasi* 'heap') 1. The heap of virtues. 2. A name of Lord Śiva.

**Guṇasampat (f)** (*guṇa* 'quality of nature, virtue' + *sampat* 'wealth') The wealth of virtues. See the Bhagavad Gītā XVI: 1-3.

**Guṇasamudra (m)** (*guṇa* 'quality of nature, virtue' + *samudra* 'celestial waters, ocean') The ocean of virtues.

**Guṇasāgara (m)** (*guṇa* 'quality of nature, virtue' + *sagara* 'ocean') The ocean of virtues.

**Guṇavan (m), Guṇavatī (f)** (*guṇa* 'quality of nature, virtue' + *van/vatī* 'having') The possessor of virtues.

**Guṇākara (m)** (*guṇa* 'quality of nature, virtue' + *akara* 'mine') 1. The mine of virtues (i.e. the sattwa-guṇa). 2. A name of Lord Śiva.

**Guṇālaya (m)** (*guṇa* 'quality of nature, virtue' + *ālaya* 'abode') The abode of virtues.

**Guṇārāma (m)** (*guṇa* 'quality of nature, virtue' + *ārāma* 'enjoyment') The pleasure-grove of virtues (i.e. the sattwa-guṇa).

**Guṇātīta (m)** (*guṇa* 'quality of nature, virtue' + *atīta* 'gone beyond') He who has gone beyond the three binding qualities of nature (i.e. sattwa, rajas and tamas). See the Bhagavad Gītā XIV:17-26.

**Gupti (f)** The preserving or protecting.

**Gurubhāva (m)** (*guru* 'spiritual teacher' + *bhāva* 'he who feels/ thinks about') He whose feelings or thoughts are in the Guru.

**Gurudāsa (m), Gurudāsī (f)** (*guru* 'spiritual teacher' + *dās/ dāsī* 'servant') The servant of the Guru. See the Bhagavad Gītā IV:34; XIII:7; XVII:14.

**Guruprem (m), Gurupremā (f)** (*guru* 'spiritual teacher' + *prem/premā* 'divine love') 1. He who has divine love for the Guru. 2. The divine love of the Guru.

**Gurupriyā (f)** (*guru* 'spiritual teacher' + *priyā* 'beloved') The beloved of the Guru.

**Gurusevaka (m), Gurusevinī (f)** (*guru* 'spiritual teacher' + *sevaka/ vinī* 'servant') The servant of the Guru. See the Bhagavad Gītā IV:34; XIII:7; XVIII:14.

# H

**Haima (m)** 1. The golden. 2. A name of Lord Śiva.

**Haimavatī (f)** (*haima* 'golden' + *vatī* 'having') 1. The golden. 2. The daughter of Himavan; a name of the Goddess Pārvatī. This name occurs in the Kena Upanishad where Umā Haimavatī (Pārvatī) is depicted as the personification of pure knowledge and hence as the most beautiful of women. In these passages she imparts knowledge to Indra. In his commentary on the Kena Upanishad, Śrī Śaṅkara states, "Being ever near to the truth of Lord Śiva, Pārvatī has the knowledge of the truth and thus shines as though wearing ornaments of gold."

**Haṃsan (m), Haṃsā (f)** 1. The swan, which is either a symbol of those able to discern between the Self and the non-Self, the Real and the Unreal, or the vehicle of Brahmā and His consort Saraswatī, which in this case represents knowledge. 2. The dispeller of transmigration. 3. The 191st name of Vishṇu as listed in the Vishṇu Sahasranāma. In his commentary Śrī Śaṅkara states, "The Lord is called *Hamsa* as He dispels (hanti) the fear of transmigration (samsāra-bhaya) for those who meditate upon the oneness of 'I am He' (*aham saḥ*). He is also thus called as He moves in all bodies. It is written in the Kaṭha Upanishad, '*Hamsaḥ śuci-shat,*' 'As the moving sun, He dwells in the pure heaven.'" 4. The mover. 5. The sun. 6. Vital breath (i.e. prāṇa).

**Haṃsavāhanā (f)** (*hamsa* 'swan' + *vāhanā* 'riding, vehicle') 1. She who rides a swan, or she whose vehicle is a swan. 2. The 110th name of the Goddess Lalitā as listed in the Brahmāṇḍa- Purāṇa. 4. A name of Saraswatī, Goddess of wisdom.

**Hanuman (m)** 1. He whose (left) jaw is (slightly broken). 2. The name of Śrī Rāma's devotee who was the son of Vāyu, the Wind-God. He was a divine and powerful monkey who was a model of obedience and alertness. He received this name as a child when mistaking the sun for an orange, he tried to catch it and fell down on his left jaw.

**Hara (m)** 1. The ravishing (of the mind). 2. The destroyer (of transmigration). 3. A name of Lord Śiva.

**Harapriyā (f)** (*hara* 'n. of Lord Śiva' + *priyā* 'beloved') 1. The beloved of Lord Hara. 2. The 104th name of the Goddess Lalitā as listed in the Brahmāṇḍa-Purāṇa. 3. A name of the Goddess Pārvatī.

**Harasakha (m)** (*hara* 'n. of Lord Śiva' + *sakha* 'friend') 1. The friend of Lord Hara (i.e. of Lord Śiva). 2. A name of Kubera, Lord of wealth, who lives on

Mount Kailāsa.

**Harādri (m)** (*hara* 'n. of Lord Śiva' + *adri* 'mountain') The mountain of Lord Hara (i.e. Mount Kailāsa, the abode of Lord Śiva).

**Hari (m)** 1. The remover. 2. The 650th name of Lord Vishṇu as listed in the Vishṇu Sahasranāma. In his commentary, Śrī Śaṅkara states, "He who removes the sins of men through mere remembrance of Him and who equally removes transmigration along with its cause (i.e. ignorance) is the remover." In the Mahābhārata, it is written:

*Harāmy'agham Ca Smartṛīnām*
*Havir-Bhāgam Kratushw'aham,*
*Varṇaś-Ca Me Harid-Ve'ti*
*Tasmādd'harir Aham Smṛitaḥ.*

I remove the sins of those who remember Me,
I take My share of oblations in sacrifices,
And My complexion is blue,
Hence I am known as *Hari.*

**Hariharan (m)** (*hari* 'n. of Lord Vishṇu' + *haran* 'n. of Lord Śiva') 1. One God formed by Lord *Hari* (i.e. Vishṇu) and Lord *Hara* (i.e. Śiva). This manifestation of God occurred when Lord Vishṇu and Lord Śiva appeared as a single form to stop their followers from quarrelling. See the Purāṇas. 2. The son of Lord Śiva and Mohinī, who is a female manifestation of Lord Vishṇu.

**Hariṇī (f)** 1. The golden. 2. A female deer. 3. One of the four kinds of beautiful women. 4. The 83rd of the Goddess Lakshmī's 108 names.

**Hari OM** (*hariḥ* 'n. of Lord Vishṇu' + *OM* 'primordial sound') 1. "Hari is OM." 2. A universal mantra containing the cosmic vibration.

**Hariścandra (m)** (*hariḥ* 'n. of Lord Vishṇu' + *candra* 'shining moon') 1. He who has golden splendor. 2. The name of a pious and truthful king.

**Harshaṇī (f)** 1. She who gladdens. 2. The 175th name of the Goddess Lalitā as listed in the Brahmāṇḍa-Purāṇa. In his commentary, Śrī Śaṅkara states, "She is the giver of all happiness."

**Hayagrīva (m)** (*haya* 'horse' + *grīva* 'neck') 1. The horse-necked. 2. A name of Lord Vishṇu who assumed the head of a horse and recovered the Vedas stolen by two demons.

**Hākinī (f)** 1. The cutting Goddess. 2. The 165th name of the Goddess Lalitā as listed in the Brahmāṇḍa-Purāṇa. In his commentary Śrī Śaṅkara states, "She cuts across birth and death."

**Heramba (m)** A name of Śrī Gaṇeśa.

**Heruka (m)** A name of Śrī Gaṇeśa.

**Himavan (m)** (*hima* 'snow' + *van* 'having') 1. Snowy. 2. A name of Himālaya.

**Himādri (m)** (*hima* 'snow' + *adri* 'mountain') 1. The snowy mountain. 2. A name of Himālaya.

**Himālaya (m)** (*hima* 'snow' + *ālaya* 'abode') 1. The abode of snow. 2. The king of mountains and father of the Goddesses Gaṅgā and Pārvatī.

**Hiraṇya (m)** The golden.

**Hiraṇyagarbha (m)** (*hiraṇya* 'golden' + *garbha* 'embryo') 1. The golden embryo. 2. The 70th and 411th names of Lord Vishṇu as listed in the Vishṇu Sahasranāma. In his commentary Śrī Śaṅkara states, "Because He dwells within the golden egg-universe, the Creator Brahmā is called Hiraṇyagarbha, and the Lord Vishṇu is His very Self. The universe having the form of a golden egg and being the cause of Brahmā's birth, sprang from Lord Vishṇu's energy, and the Lord is its womb." 3. The name given to the Self as being present in the universal subtle body. 4. The original teacher of Yoga who lived long before Patañjali.

**Hotā (m)** 1. The sacrificer. 2. The first of the four officiating priests at a Vedic sacrifice, who invokes the gods at the beginning.

**Hṛidayan (m)** The heart, the seat of emotions and mental activity. The Chāndogya Upanishad gives the etymology of *Hṛidaya,* as follows:

*Hṛidy'ayam-Iti Tasmādd'Hṛidayam.*

This (*ayam*) Self is in the heart (*hṛidi*)
whence the word '*Hṛidayam*' for the heart.

See the Bhagavad Gītā IV:42; VI:21; VIII:12; XV:15; XVIII:61.

**Hṛidya (m), Hṛidyā (f)** 1. Being in the heart, innermost. 2. Dear to the heart, beloved. 3. Pleasant, charming, cordial, hearty.

**Hṛishṭi (f)** Joy or delight. See the Bhagavad Gītā II:55; III:17; V:21-24; X:9.

**Hrīman (m), Hrīmatī (f)** The modest.

# I

**Idaspati (m)** (*idas* 'libation' + *pati* 'lord') 1. The Lord of libations. 2. A name of Pūshan. 3. A name of Bṛihaspati. 4. A name of Lord Vishṇu.

**Indirā (f)** 1. The beautiful or splendid. 2. The 62nd of the Goddess Lakshmī's 108 names.

**Indīvariṇī (f)** The blue lotus.

**Indra (m)** 1. The powerful or mighty. 2. The name of the chief of the gods. He, along with the Fire-God, Agni, is much praised in the Vedas. Holder of the thunderbolt, *Indra* presides over rain. He is the symbol of strength, particularly strength to grasp with the hands. In the Kena Upanishad, it is written that *Indra* excelled over all the gods except Brahmā, Vishṇu and Śiva since He first heard of the Absolute from Umā Haimavatī (i.e. the Goddess Pārvatī). In the Chāndogya Upanishad Prajāpati teaches Him knowledge of the Self after He observed Brahmacarya for 101 years. As all the major gods, *Indra* is an aspect of the Absolute. Accordingly, in some of the Upanishads the Absolute is named "*Indra*." See the Bṛihad-Āraṇyaka Upanishad and the Aitareya Upanishad.

**Indrāṇī (f)** The consort of Indra.

**Indrāvaraja (m)** (*indra* 'chief' + *avaraja* 'younger') 1. The younger brother of Indra. 2. The name of Lord Vishṇu in His dwarf incarnation.

**Indubhṛit (m)** (*indu* 'moon' + *bhṛit* 'bearer') 1. The bearer of the (crescent) moon. 2. A name of Lord Śiva, referring to Him wearing the crescent moon on His forehead. In this case, since the moon presides over the mind, it symbolizes Lord Śiva's perfect mind control.

**Induja (m)** (*indu* 'moon' + *ja* 'born') 1. Born of the moon. 2. Mercury.

**Indujanaka (m)** (*indu* 'moon' + *janaka* 'begetter') 1. The begetter of the moon. 2. A name of the milk ocean from which the moon arose when the gods and demons churned it.

**Indukirīṭa (m)** (*indu* 'moon' + *kirīṭa* 'diadem') 1. The moon-crested. 2. A name of Lord Śiva.

**Indumaṇi (m)** (*indu* 'moon' + *maṇi* 'gem, pearl') The moonstone or moon-jewel.

**Irā (f)** 1. The earth. 2. A name of the Goddess Saraswatī, Goddess of wisdom.

**Ireśa (m)** (*irā* 'earth, Goddess Saraswatī' + *īśa* 'lord') 1. Lord of the earth (i.e. Lord Vishṇu). 2. Lord of speech (i.e. Lord Brahmā).

**Irimbithi (m)** The name of a Ṛishi who was the seer for part of the Ṛigveda.

**Irya (m)** 1. The powerful or energetic. 2. A name of Sūrya, the Sun-God.

**Ishma (m)** 1. The spring. 2. Cupid.

**Ishṭan (m)** 1. The beloved. 2. The worshipped, a name applying to all forms of God. 3. The 308th name of Lord Vishṇu as listed in the Vishṇu Sahasranāma. In his commentary, Śrī Śaṅkara states, 'The Lord is dear or beloved through His nature of supreme bliss. It means also He is worshipped through sacrifices."

**Ishṭā (f)** 1. The beloved. 2. The worshipped, a name applying to all forms of the Divine.

**Ishṭi (f)** 1. The seeking or seeker. 2. The worshipping or worshipper.

**Ishṭin (m), Ishṭinī (f)** The sacrificer or worshipper.

**Ishya (m)** The spring.

# Ī

**Īḍitā (m), Īḍitrī (f)** The praiser or worshipper (of God).

**Īḍitā (f)** 1. The praised. 2. The 51st name of the Goddess Lalitā as listed in the Brahmāṇḍa-Purāṇa. In his commentary Śrī Śaṅkara states, "The root *Īḍ* means 'to praise.' Thus (*Īḍitā*) means She is the object of praise by Scriptures."

**Īḍitri (f)** [See **Īḍitā**]

**Īkshitrī (f)** 1. She who sees, watches. 2. The 48th name of Lalitā as listed in the Brahmāṇḍa-Purāṇa. In his commentary Śrī Śaṅkara states, "She, as a Witness, is unconcerned and actionless."

**Īpsita (m)** The desired.

**Īra (m)** The Wind God, Vāyu.

**Īraja (m)** (*īra* 'wind, Wind-God' + *ja* 'born') Born of the wind; a name of Hanuman.

**Īraputra (m)** (*īra* 'wind, Wind-God' + *putra* 'son') The son of the wind; a name of Hanuman.

**Īshwa (m)** The spiritual teacher.

**Īśa (m)** 1. The Lord or ruler. 2. The first of the ten major Upanishads taught to Vedānta students. It begins with the words "*Īśā Vāsyam idam sarvam...*" "All this universe should be covered by the Lord..."

**Īśā (f)** 1. The ruling Goddess. 2. A name of the Goddess Durgā.

**Īśāna (m)** 1. The Lord or ruler. 2. The 65th name of Lord Vishṇu as listed in the Vishṇu Sahasranāma. In his commentary Śrī Śaṅkara states, "Because He is the ruler of all beings, the Lord is called *Īśāna*." 3. A name of Lord Śīva referring to one of His eight forms and connected with air.

**Īśānī (f)** 1. The ruling Goddess. 2. A name of the Goddess Durgā.

**Īśitrī (f)** 1. The directing force. 2. The 42nd name of the Goddess Lalitā as listed in Brahmāṇḍa-Purāṇa. In his commentary Śrī Śaṅkara states, "*Icchati* means 'She who wills or plans.' *Īshte* means 'She who directs.' As She does both, She is called *Īśitrī* (i.e. 'She who directs everything according to a plan.')."

**Iśwara (m)** 1. The Lord or ruler. 2. The 37th and 74th name of Lord Vishṇu as listed in the Vishṇu Sahasranāma. In his commentary Śrī Śaṅkara states, "The Lord is called *Īśwara* as His sovereignty is unlimited, and as He is all-powerful." 3. A name of Lord Śiva. See the Bhagavad Gītā XV:17; and the Yogasūtras I:24-26.

**Iśwarakoṭi (m or f)** (*īśwara* 'lord' + *koti* 'excellence') The excellence of the Lord.

**Iśwarī (f)** 1. The sovereign Goddess. 2. A name of the Goddess Saraswatī. 3. A name of the Goddess Lakshmī. 4. A name of the Goddess Pārvatī.

# J

**Jagadambā (f)** (*jagat* 'all that moves, universe' + *ambā* 'mother') 1. The Mother of the universe. 2. A name of the Goddess Durgā.

**Jagadambikā (f)** (*jagat* 'all that moves, universe' + *ambikā* 'mother') 1. The Mother of the universe. 2. A name of the Goddess Durgā.

**Jagaddhara (m)** 1. (*jagat* 'all that moves, universe' + *dhara* 'supporter, bearer') The supporter of the universe; a name of Lord Vishṇu. 2. (*jagat* 'all that moves, universe' + *hara* 'destroyer') The destroyer of the universe; a name of Lord Śiva.

**Jagaddhātā (m), Jagaddhātrī (f)** (*jagat* 'all that moves, universe' + *dhātā/dhātrī* 'supporter') Supporter of the universe. See the Bhagavad Gītā IX:17.

**Jagadīśa (m)** (*jagat* 'all that moves, universe' + *īśa* 'lord') 1. The Lord of the universe. 2. A name of Lord Vishṇu. 3. A name of Lord Śiva.

**Jagadīśitā (m)** (*jagat* 'all that moves, universe' + *īśitā* 'master') 1. Master of the universe. 2. A name of Lord Śiva.

**Jagadīśwara (m)** (*jagat* 'all that moves' + *īśwara* 'lord') 1. The Lord of the universe. 2. A name of Lord Vishṇu. 3. A name of Lord Śiva.

**Jagadīśwarī (f)** (*jagat* 'all that moves' + *īśwarī* 'sovereign goddess') 1. The sovereign Goddess of the universe. 2. A name of Devī, the Divine Mother.

**Jagadvandya (m)** (*jagat* 'all that moves, universe' + *vandya* 'worthy of worship') 1. He who is worthy to be worshipped by the universe. 2. A name of Śrī Kṛishṇa. See the Bhagavad Gītā XI:43.

**Jagadvahā (f)** (*jagat* 'all that moves, universe' + *vahā* 'bearer') 1. The bearer (i.e. as in 'being with child' and also as in 'carrying') of the universe. 2. A name of the Earth-Goddess.

**Jagajjananī (f)** (*jagat* 'all that moves, universe' + *jananī* 'mother, producer') 1. The Mother or producer of the universe. 2. A name of Devī, the Divine Mother.

**Jaganmātā (f)** (*jagat* 'all that moves, universe' + *mātā* 'mother') 1. The Mother of the universe. 2. A name of Devī, the Divine Mother. See the Bhagavad Gītā IX:10.

**Jagannātha (m)** (*jagat* 'all that moves' + *nātha* 'master') 1. The Lord or master of the universe. 2. A name of Lord Vishṇu as worshipped at Purī.

**Jagatkartā (m)** (*jagat* 'all that moves, universe + *kartā* 'creator') 1. The creator of the universe. 2. A name of Lord Brahmā.

**Jagatpati (m)** (*jagat* 'all that moves, universe' + *pati* 'lord') 1. The Lord of the universe. 2. A name of Lord Vishṇu. 3. A name of Lord Śiva.

**Jagatprabhu (m)** (*jagat* 'all that moves, universe' + *prabhu* 'lord') 1. The Lord or master of the universe. 2. A name of Lord Vishṇu. 2. A name of Lord Śiva.

**Jagatprakāśa (m)** (*jagat* 'all that moves' + *prakāśa* 'light') The light of the universe. See the Bhagavad Gītā XI:122; XIII:17,33; XV:12.

**Jagatprīti (m)** (*jagat* 'all that moves' + *prīti* 'joy, delight') 1. The joy of the universe. 2. A name of Lord Śiva.

**Jahnu (m)** 1. The name of a king whose sacrificial grounds were flooded by the River Ganges on her way down from heaven. 2. The disintegrator. 3. The 244th name of Lord Vishṇu as listed in the Vishṇu Sahasranāma. In his commentary Śrī Śaṅkara states, "He who withdraws men during the cosmic dissolution is the 'disintegrator.' Also it means the Lord excludes ignorant men from attaining the supreme Goal, and leads His devotees towards It." See the Bhagavad Gītā II:28; VII: 23-25; VIII:18,19; IX:3,7,11,13,19,29; X:9-11, 34.

**Jaladhi (m)** (*jala* 'water' + *dhi* 'receptacle) The water receptacle (i.e. the ocean).

**Janaka (m)** 1. The begetter, father. 2. The name of a great king and realized soul, who was the father of Sītā. Once while *Janaka* was ploughing the ground for a sacrifice, a little girl sprang from the furrow he had just made. He took her as his daughter, calling her Sītā, 'the furrow.' See the Bhagavad Gītā III:20; IV:20.

**Jananī (f)** 1. She who gives birth, the Mother. 2. A name of Devī, the Divine Mother. See the Bhagavad Gītā III:27; IX:8,10; XIII:29.

**Janapriya (m)** (*jana* 'mankind, people' + *priya* 'beloved') 1. The beloved of mankind. 2. A name of Lord Śiva.

**Janārdana (m)** (*jana* 'mankind, people' + *ardana* 'tormenting') 1. The chastiser of (wicked) men. 2. The requested by men. 3. The 126th name of Lord Vishṇu as listed in the Vishṇu Sahasranāma. In his commentary Śrī Śaṅkara states, "The Lord is called '*Janārdana* ' as He punishes wicked men and sends them to hell and other painful conditions. It also means He is requested by men for the human goal such as the attainment of prosperity and salvation." See the Bhagavad Gītā VIII:15-16; IX:24,25,29,30,31; XVI:16,19,20. 4. A name of Śrī Kṛishṇa. See the Bhagavad Gītā I:36.

**Jaṭādhara (m)** (*jaṭā* 'matted locks' + *dhara* 'bearer') He who wears matted locks; a name of Lord Śiva.

**Jaṭin (m)** He who has matted locks; a name of Lord Śiva. The matted locks are associated with asceticism, and in the case of Lord Śiva they served as a receptacle for the Ganges' fall from heaven, which would have otherwise destroyed the world. The Goddess Gaṅgā could not find her way out of the Lord's hair and remained there for many years until He allowed her to flow through the Himālayas.

**Jayan (m)** 1. The victorious. See the Yogasūtras II:41; III:47,48. 2. The 509th name of Lord Vishṇu as listed in the Vishṇu Sahasranāma. In his commentary Śrī Śaṅkara states, "He who wins all beings is the Victorious." See the Bhagavad Gītā X:36. 3. A name given to the Mahābhārata since it opens with this word.

**Jayadeva (m)** (*jaya* 'victorious' + *deva* 'god') 1. The victorious God. 2. The name of the author of the "Gītagovinda."

**Jayadevī (f)** (*jaya* 'victorious' + *devī* 'goddess') The victorious Goddess.

**Jayalakshmī (f)** (*jaya* 'victorious' + *Lakshmī* 'goddess of wealth') The victorious Goddess of wealth; a name of the Goddess Lakshmī, the consort of Lord Vishṇu.

**Jayanta (m)** 1. The victorious, the conquering. 2. The 798th name of Lord Vishṇu as listed in the Vishṇu Sahasranāma. In his commentary Śrī Śaṅkara states, "This name means 'He who conquers His enemies through superiority is the conqueror' or 'the Lord is the cause of victory.'"

**Jayantī (f)** The victorious, the conquering; a name of the Goddess Durgā.

**Jayaśrī (f)** 1. (*jaya* 'victorious' + *śrī* 'all splendor and glory') The victorious and glorious Goddess. 2. A name of the Goddess Lakshmī, who is also known by the name of "Śrī."

**Jayā (f)** 1. The victorious. 2. A name of Devī, the Divine Mother. 3. The 94th of the Goddess Lakshmī's 108 names.

**Jayeśwara (m)** (*jaya* 'victorious' + *īśwara* 'lord') 1. The victorious Lord. 2. A name of Lord Śiva.

**Jayeśwarī (f)** (*jaya* 'victorious' + *īśwarī* 'sovereign goddess') 1. The victorious Goddess. 2. A name of the Divine Mother, Devī.

**Jābāli (m)** The name of a Brahmarshi who was the counsellor of King Daśaratha and the author of a law-book. He tried to convince Śrī Rāma to return to Ayodhyā from the forest by using an atheistic argument but failed. See the Rāmāyaṇa II:109.

**Jāhnavī (f)** The daughter of Jahnu; a name of the Goddess Gaṅgā (i.e. the Ganges River). On Her way down from heaven the Ganges flooded King Jahnu's sacrificial ground. He drank all its waters and allowed the holy river to flow out through his ears. For this reason the Ganges was given this name. See the Bhagavad Gītā X:31.

**Jānakī (f)** 1. The daughter of Janaka. 2. A name of Sītā, the wife of Śrī Rāma. Once while Janaka was ploughing the ground for a sacrifice, a little girl sprang from the furrow he had just made. He took her as his daughter, calling her Sītā, 'the furrow.'

**Jātavedas (m)** (*jāta* 'all that is born' + *vedas* 'he who knows') 1. The knower of all that is born. 2. The enlightened; a name of Agni, the Fire-God.

**Jātavedasī (f)** The consort of Jātavedas, the Fire-Goddess; a name of Agni's consort who is said to be the oblation formula "Swāhā!" uttered in a Vedic sacrifice.

**Jetā (m), Jetrī (f)** 1. The victorious or triumphant. 2. The 148th name of Lord Vishṇu as listed in the Vishṇu Sahasranāma. In his commentary Śrī Śaṅkara states, "As He surpasses all beings naturally, the Lord is thus called 'the Victorious.'"

**Jina (m)** The victorious. (A name commonly used by Buddhists and Jains.)

**Jishṇu (m)** 1. The victorious. 2. A name of Sūrya, the Sun-God. 3. A name of Lord Vishṇu. 4. A name of Indra. 5. A name of Arjuna.

**Jitendriya (m)** (*jita* 'conquered' + *indriya* 'senses') He who has conquered the senses. See the Bhagavad Gītā II: 14, 15, 58, 60-1, 64, 68; III: 16, 34, 41; IV: 39; V: 7, 21-24, 27, 28; VI: 4, 6-8, 12, 24; VIII: 12; XII: 4; XIII: 7, 8; XV: 11; XVIII: 33, 49, 51. See the Yoga Sūtras II: 41; III: 47.

**Jiti (f)** Gaining victory.

**Jīvada (m)** (*jīva* 'life' + *da* 'give') The life-giver. (A name given to physicians.)

**Jīvadātā (m), Jīvadātrī (f)** (*jīva* 'life' + *dātā/ dātrī* 'giver') The life-giver.

**Jīvakan (m), Jīvikā (f)** The living (individual soul). See the Bhagavad Gītā VII:5,9; XV:7.

**Jīvana (m)** 1. The vivifying or enlivening. 2. The 930th name of Lord Vishṇu as listed in the Vishṇu Sahasranāma. In his commentary Śrī Śaṅkara states, "As enlivening all creatures through the form of Prāṇa or vital energy, the Lord is called the 'Enlivener.'" 3. A name of Sūrya, the Sun-God. 4. A name of Vāyu, the Wind-God. 5. A name of Śiva.

**Jīvanī (f)** 1. The vivifying or enlivening. 2. A name of Devī, the Divine Mother.

**Jñānadeva (m)** (*jñāna* 'wisdom' + *deva* 'god') 1. God of wisdom. 2. The name of a Yogī who lived in the 13th century A.D. and who wrote a commentary on the Bhagavad Gītā, entitled the "Jñāneśwarī."

**Jñānaketu (m)** (*jñāna* 'wisdom' + *ketu* 'light, form') Light of wisdom. See the Bhagavad Gītā XIII:7-11.

**Jñānam (m), Jñānā (f)** Knowledge or wisdom. In the Taittirīya Upanishad it is written, "The Absolute is truth, knowledge and infinitude." See the Bhagavad Gītā III: 3; IV: 19, 23, 28, 33-39, 42; V: 16-7; VI: 8, 21; VII: 2, 17-9, 34; IX: 1; X: 11, 32, 38; XIII: 2,7-11, 17-8, 34; XIV: 1, 2, 11, 19; XV: 10, 19-20; XVI: 1; XVIII: 20-22, 42, 50, 55, 63, 70.

**Jñānamūrti (m)** (*jñāna* 'wisdom' + *mūrti* 'form, image') The embodiment of wisdom. See the Bhagavad Gītā II: 54-72.

**Jñānaprabhā (f)** (*jñāna* 'wisdom' + *prabhā* 'light') Light of wisdom. See the Bhagavad Gītā V: 16; X: 11.

**Jñānarūpa (m), Jñānarūpiṇī (f)** (*jñāna* 'wisdom' + *rūpa/rūpiṇī* 'form') The embodiment of wisdom. See the Bhagavad Gītā II:54-72; XIII:7-11.

**Jñānā (f)** See **Jñānām.**

**Joshṭā (m), Joshṭrī (f)** The loving or cherishing.

**Joṭin (m)** 1. The ascetic. 2. A name of Lord Śiva.

**Jyoti (m or f)** 1. The Light. Śrī Śaṅkara composed the following two ślokas dedicated to the Light:

*Antarjyotir-Bahirjyotiḥ,*
*Pratyagjyotiḥ Parātparaḥ!*
*Jyotirjyotis Swayamjyotir-*
*Ātmajyotiś Śivo'smy'aham!*

*Ātmajyotir-Manojyotir-*
*Jyotiś-Cakshushā Paśyati.*
*Sābāhyābhyantara-Jyotiḥ*
*Sa Jyotiḥ Śiva Ucyate.*

Inner Light, Outer Light,
Inward Light, Higher than the Highest!
Light of Lights, Light in Itself,
Light of the Self, That Auspiciousness (Śiva) am I!

Light of the Self, Light of the Mind,
Light which sees through the Eyes.
that Inner and Outer Light is
what is said to be Śiva (Auspiciousness).

2. The 877th name of Lord Vishṇu as listed in the Vishṇu Sahasranāma. In his commentary Śrī Śaṅkara states, "He who shines by Himself alone is called the light." See the Bhagavad Gītā V:24; XIII:17; XV:12.

# K

**Kadamba (m), Kadambī (f)** An orange flower.

**Kadhi (m)** (*kam* 'water' + *dhi* 'receptacle') 1. The water receptacle. 2. The ocean.

**Kailāsa (m)** 1. The crystalline (mountain). 2. The name of the abode of Lord Śiva in the Himālayas.

**Kairavan (m)** The name of a white lotus which blooms at night.

**Kairavī (f)** Moonlight.

**Kaivalya (m)** [in Tamil **Kaivalyan**], **Kaivalyā (f)** 1. Absoluteness, aloneness, the separation of the Purusha and Prakṛiti. See the Yogasūtras II:25; III:50,55; IV:26,34. 2. In Vedānta, the realization of the Self which dissolves Prakṛiti and leaves no duality behind.

**Kakanda (m)** 1. The golden. 2. The name of a king.

**Kakshīvat (m)** The name of a Rishi who was one of the seers of the Ṛigveda.

**Kakubha (m)** The excelling.

**Kakuda (m)** The highest.

**Kalā (f)** 1. The Goddess of fine arts, which number 64. 2. One-sixteenth of the moon.

**Kalādhara (m)** (*kalā* 'one-sixteenth of the moon' + *dhara* 'bearer') The bearer of the crescent moon; a name of Lord Śiva referring to his control of the mind.

**Kalāmālā (f)** (*kalā* 'the fine arts' + *mālā* 'garland') The garland of the fine arts.

**Kalānidhi (m)** (*kalā* 'one-sixteenth of the moon' + *nidhi* 'receptacle') Receptacle or treasure of the moon's sixteen phases; a name of the Moon-God.

**Kalāvan (m)** (*kalā* 'one-sixteenth of the moon, the fine arts' + *van* 'having') 1. Having sixteen phases (i.e. the moon). 2. Having the 64 fine arts. 3. Having the crescent moon; a name of Lord Śiva.

**Kalāvatī (f)** (*kalā* 'one-sixteenth of the moon, the fine arts' + *vatī* 'having') 1. Having sixteen phases (i.e. the moon). 2. Having the 64 fine arts. 3. Having the crescent moon. 4. The 6th name of the Goddess Lalitā as listed in the Brahmāṇḍa-Purāṇa. In his commentary Śrī Śaṅkara states, "*Kalā* means organs like head and hands, or the 64 arts, or digits of the moon. She possesses these to facilitate the meditation of Her devotees."

**Kalmali (m)** The dispeller of darkness.

**Kalya (m)** The healthy.

**Kalyā (f)** 1. She who is the object of meditation. 2. The 146th name of Goddess Lalitā's 300 names as listed in the Brahmāṇḍa-Purāṇa. In his commentary Śrī Śaṅkara states, "She is fit to be meditated upon because She is the most supreme Goddess."

**Kalyāṇa (m)** 1. The beautiful. 2. The auspicious. 3. The blessed.

**Kalyāṇasundaram (m)** (*kalyāṇa*' beautiful, auspicious, blessed' + *sundaram* 'beautiful') The beautiful and blessed.

**Kalyāṇavartman [m]** (*kalyāṇa* 'beautiful, auspicious, blessed' + *vartman* 'path') 1. He who follows the auspicious or noble path. 2. The name of a king.

**Kalyāṇī (f)** 1. The beautiful. 2. The auspicious. 3. The blessed. 4. The blissful. 5. The second name of Goddess Lalitā's 300 names as listed in the Brahmāṇḍa-Purāṇa. In his commentary Śrī Śaṅkara states, "*Kalyāṇam* means ānanda or bliss. She possesses this. A series of the different forms of bliss ranging from earthly sovereignty to absolute bliss are enumerated in the Taittirīya Upanishad...Hence the word *Kalyāṇa* denotes the bliss in different degrees possessed by all the created forms in which She dwells, and which represent Her various limiting vehicles. Just as the sun reflected in the water of a pot is limited by the pot, so also the Absolute when He shines through created forms is limited by them. This form of limitation is called Upādhi. She Herself exists in all these various limited states of unity and diversity. When She is reflected in Māyā, She is known as Īśwara (i.e. Her integral form). When reflected in the mind, She is known as Jīva (i.e. Her individual form). This shows She has the same attributes and definition as the Supreme, the Absolute who is described in the Bṛihad-Āraṇyaka Upanishad as 'Vijñānam-Ānandam', 'pure consciousness and bliss.'"

**Kamala (m)** [in Tamil **Kamalan**] 1. One who is like a lotus. 2. A name of Lord Brahmā.

**Kamalabandhu (m)** (*kamala* 'lotus' + *bandhu* 'friend') The friend of the lotus; a name of Sūrya, the Sun-God.

**Kamalabāndhava (m)** (*kamala* 'lotus' + *bāndhava* 'friend') The friend of the lotus; a name of Sūrya, the Sun-God.

**Kamalalocana (m)** (*kamala* 'lotus' + *locana* 'eye') The lotus-eyed, a name of Lord Vishṇu.

**Kamalalocanā (f)** (*kamala* 'lotus' + *locanā* 'eye') The lotus-eyed, a name of Devī.

**Kamalanayana (m)** (*kamala* 'lotus' + *nayana* 'eye') The lotus-eyed, a name of Lord Vishṇu.

**Kamalanayanā (f)** (*kamala* 'lotus' + *nayanā* 'eye') The lotus-eyed, a name of Devī.

**Kamalanābha (m)** (*kamala* 'lotus' + *nābha* 'navel, center') 1. Lotus-navel; a name of Lord Vishnu which refers to the whole universe springing from His navel as if it were a lotus with the Creator Brahmā seated on it. 2. Lotus-centered. 3. A name of Lord Vishṇu which refers to His dwelling in the heart lotus of all beings.

**Kamalanetra (m)** (*kamala* 'lotus' + *netra* 'eye') The Lotus-eyed, a name of Lord Vishṇu.

**Kamalā (f)** 1. Lotus 2. The 26th of the Goddess Lakshmī's 108 names, referring to her depicted as sitting on a lotus or with a lotus in her hand.

**Kamalākānta (m)** (*kamalā* 'lotus, the Goddess Lakshmī' + *kānta* 'beloved') 1. The beloved of Kamalā (i.e. the Goddess Lakshmī) 2. A name of Lord Vishṇu. 3. The name of a Bengali mystical poet.

**Kamalāksha (m)** (*kamala* 'lotus' + *aksha* 'eye') The lotus-eyed, a name of Lord Vishṇu.

**Kamalākshī (f)** (*kamala* 'lotus' + *akshī* 'eye') 1. The lotus-eyed. 2. The 7th name of Goddess Lalitā's 300 names as listed in the Brahmāṇḍa-Purāṇa. In his commentary Śrī Śaṅkara states, "1) Her two eyes are like the lotus. 2) *Kamalā* means *Lakshmī*, wealth. *Akshī* or the 'eye' signifies knowledge as the eye is the major agency through which it is acquired. So the name means that She is the object of the wealth of such knowledge. 3) Her mere glance will confer great powers, (i.e. She has eyes which are the source of good things, both worldly and other-worldly)."

**Kamalālayā (f)** (*kamala* 'lotus' + *ālayā* 'abode, seat') 1. Abiding in the lotus. 2. A name of the Goddess Lakshmī referring to her rising from the milk ocean on a lotus. This incident symbolizes the awakening of Self-knowledge after hard and long spiritual practices.

**Kamalekshaṇa (m)** (*kamala* 'lotus' + *īkshaṇa* 'eye') The lotus-eyed, a name of Lord Vishṇu.

**Kamalekshaṇā (f)** (*kamala* 'lotus' + *īkshaṇā* 'eye') The lotus-eyed, a name of Devī.

**Kamalinī (f)** The day-lotus.

**Kamalīkā (f)** The little lotus.

**Kamalodbhava (m)** (*kamala* 'lotus' + *udbhava* 'born') 1. The lotus-born. 2. A name of the Creator Brahmā, who is represented as seated on the lotus of creation springing from Lord Vishṇu's navel. See the Bhagavad Gītā XI:15.

**Kamanīyā (f)** 1. The desirable or endearing. 2. The 5th name of Goddess Lalitā's 300 names as listed in the Brahmāṇḍa-Purāṇa. In his commentary Śrī Śaṅkara states, "1) She is most endearing. Since She is of the form of ultimate Bliss, She is the dearest...Since bliss is pleasing, it is desired by all. 2) Similarly, She is *Kamanīyā* because She grants appropriate rewards to worshippers who, enveloped in Māyā, offer worship with love and devotion to deities dear to their heart. 3) She is also dear to Jñānīs or sages because She has the beautiful form of solidified Bliss."

**Kana (m)** The youthful.

**Kanakāpīda (m)** The name of an attendant of Lord Skanda.

**Kanala (m)** [in Tamil **Kanalan**], **Kanalā (f)** The shining.

**Kandalāyana (m)** The name of an ancient sage.

**Kandarpamathana (m)** (*kandarpa* 'cupid' + *mathana* 'destroyer') The destroyer of Cupid; a name of Lord Śiva.

**Kaṇḍānaka (m)** The name of an attendant of Lord Śiva.

**Kañja (m)** (*kam* 'water' + *ja* 'born') 1. The water-born. 2. A name of a lotus. 3. The nectar of immortality born from the milk ocean. 4. The Creator Brahmā seated on Lord Vishṇu's lotus-navel, Himself lying on the milk ocean.

**Kañjalocanā (f)** (*kañja* 'lotus' + *locanā* 'eye') 1. The lotus-eyed. 2. The 16th of Goddess Lalitā's 300 names as listed in the Brahmāṇḍa-Purāṇa. In his commentary Śrī Śaṅkara states, "*Kañja*, or water-born, means a lotus. The name means She has eyes like lotus petals. *Kañja* also means Brahmāṇḍa, or the egg-universe of Brahmā. Thus a look of Her eye created millions of

Brahmāṇḍas, hence She is *Kañjalocanā.* "

**Kañjanābha (m)** (*kañja* 'lotus' + *nābha* 'navel, center') He who has a lotus-navel; a name of Lord Vishṇu.

**Kañjara (m)** A name of the Creator Brahmā.

**Kañjavadana (m), Kañjavadanā (f)** (*kañja* 'lotus' + *vadana* 'face') The lotus-faced.

**Kañjāra (m)** A name of the Creator Brahmā.

**Kannan (m)** [Tamil] A name of Śrī Kṛishṇa.

**Kannapan (m)** The name of a hunter who devoutly worshipped Lord Śiva, offering his eye to God.

**Kanva (m)** The name of a Ṛishi who was one of the seers of the Ṛigveda and was a descendant of Kaśyapa and the foster-father of Śakuntalā.

**Kanyā (f)** 1. The younger. 2. The daughter. 3. A name of the Goddess Durgā, represented as a virgin girl.

**Kanyāratnā (f)** (*kanyā* 'maiden' + *ratnā* 'jewel) The maiden jewel.

**Kapardin (m)** 1. Having matted locks. 2. The 8th of Lord Śiva's 108 names.

**Kapardinī (f)** 1. Having matted locks. 2. A name of the Goddess Kālī.

**Kapila (m)** 1. The tawny. 2. A name of Lord Vishṇu. 3. A name of Lord Brahmā. 4. The name of the author of the Sāṅkhya Darśana. See the Bhagavad Gītā X:26; XVIII:19.

**Kapiladeva (m)** (*kapila* 'tawny' + *deva* 'god') 1. The tawny God. 2. The name of the author of a Smṛiti text.

**Kapiladhārā (f)** (*kapila* 'tawny' + *dhārā* 'stream') Having a tawny stream; a name of the Goddess Gangā (i.e. the holy River Ganges).

**Kapilarudra (m)** (*kapila* 'tawny' + *rudra* 'destroyer') 1. The tawny Rudra (i.e. Lord Śiva). 2. The name of a poet.

**Kapiprabhu (m)** (*kapi* 'monkey' + *prabhu* 'lord') 1. The Lord of the monkeys. 2. A name of Śrī Rāma.

**Kapiratha (m)** (*kapi* 'monkey' + *ratha* 'chariot') 1. He who has the monkeys as a chariot. 2. A name of Śrī Rāma.

**Karāṭa (m)** A name of Lord Gaṇeśa.

**Kardama (m)** 1. The shadow. 2. The name of the first among the Prajāpatis, or the progenitors. He is said to be born from Brahmā's shadow. He was the husband of Manu's daughter Devahūti and the father of Kapila.

**Karmanda (m)** The name of the author of the Bhikshu-sūtras.

**Karṇa (m)** A name of the son of Kuntī and Sūrya, the Sun-God, and thus the elder brother of the five Pāṇḍavas.

**Karṇapitā (m)** (*karṇa* 'man's name' + *pitā* 'father') 1. Karṇa's father; a name of Sūrya, the Sun-God.

**Karṇikācala (m)** (*karṇikā* 'central' + *acala* 'mountain') The central mountain; a name of Mount Meru.

**Karuṇā (f)** 1. Compassion. See the Bhagavad Gītā X:11; XII:13; XVI:2. 2. The 39th of the Goddess Lakshmī's 108 names.

**Karuṇāvatī (f)** (*karuṇā* 'compassion' + *vatī* ' having') Compassionate.

**Karvarī (f)** A name of the Goddess Durgā.

**Kaśyapa (m)** The name of a great Ṛishi who was the son of Marīci, the husband of Aditi and the father of Lord Vishṇu in His dwarf incarnation. He is called Prajāpati, 'the progenitor of beings.'

**Kata (m)** The name of a sage.

**Kausalyā (f)** The name of Śrī Rāma's mother who was the wife of King Daśaratha.

**Kauśika (m)** 1. The son of Kuśika. 2. A name of King Viśwāmitra who was born as a Kshatriya and raised to a Brahmarshi through his great power of asceticism. He is the seer of the Gāyatrī Mantra.

**Kauśikapriya (m)** (*kauśika* 'son of Kusika' + *priya* 'beloved') Beloved of *Kauśika* (i.e. of Viśwāmitra); a name of Śrī Rāma who was given divine weapons and mantras by Ṛishi Viśwāmitra.

**Kauśikī (f)** A name of the Goddess Durgā.

**Kaustubha (m)** The jewel of the milk ocean (i.e. the fabulous jewel which came out of the churning of the milk ocean and which became the ornament of Lord Vishṇu's chest). This represents pure consciousness shining in all luminous manifestations.

**Kavacin (m)** 1. Having an armor, which is the name of Lord Śiva. 2. The 33rd name of Lord Śiva's 108 names.

**Kavela (n)** The lotus.

**Kavi (m)** 1. Poet, sage, seer. 2. The 132nd name of Lord Vishṇu as listed in the Vishṇu Sahasranāma. In his commentary Śrī Śaṅkara states, "*Kavi* means 'far-seeing,' 'seer of All,' in accordance with the Bṛihad-Āraṇyaka Upanishad, 'There is no other seer but Him,' and with the Īśā Upanishad, 'He is the Seer (*Kavi*), the Ruler of the mind.'" See the Bhagavad Gītā VIII:9; X:37. 3. A name of several Gods. 4. A name of Vālmīki. 5. A name of Uśanā, the teacher of the Asuras.

**Kavitā (f)** Poetry.

**Kavīndra (m)** (*kavi* 'poet' + *indra* 'chief') The chief of poets; a name of Vālmīki.

**Kavīndu (m)** (*kavi* 'poet' + *indu* 'moon') The moon of poets; a name of Vālmīki.

**Kavīśwara (m)** (*kavi* 'poet' + *īśwara* 'lord') The lord of poets; a name of Vālmīki.

**Kālabhairava (m)** (*kāla* 'dark' + *bhairava* 'fearful') 1. The dark and fearful. 2. One of the eight 'Bhairava' forms of Lord Śiva.

**Kālabhairavī (f)** (*kāla* 'dark blue, black' + *bhairavī* 'fearful') The dark and fearful.

**Kālabhaksha (m)** (*kāla* 'time' + *bhaksha* 'devour') The time-devourer; a name of Lord Śiva.

**Kālaghāta (m)** (*kāla* 'time' + *ghāta* 'slayer') The time-slayer; a name of Lord Śiva.

**Kālahantrī (f)** (*kāla* 'time' + *hantrī* 'slayer') The time-slayer. The 142nd name of the Goddess Lalitā as listed in the Brahmāṇḍa-Purāṇa.

**Kālakhaṇḍa (m)** A name of Arjuna.

**Kālakaṇṭha (m)** (*kāla* 'dark blue, black' + *kaṇṭha* 'throat') The dark-throated or the blue-throated; a name of Lord Śiva which refers to His blue throat, which became this color when He drank the deadly poison that came out during the churning of the milk ocean.

**Kālakaṇṭhī (f)** (*kāla* 'dark blue, black' + *kaṇṭhī* 'throat') Consort of the blue-throated; a name of the Goddess Pārvatī.

**Kālakarṇī (f)** A name of the Goddess Lakshmī.

**Kālakuñja (m)** A name of Lord Vishṇu.

**Kālanātha (m)** (*kāla* 'time' + *nātha* 'master') The master of time; a name of Lord Śiva.

**Kālidāsa (m)** (*kālī* 'a name of the Goddess Durgā' + *dāsa* 'servant') 1. The servant of Kālī. 2. The name of a famous poet who wrote several dramas and poems, such the "Śakuntalā," the "Raghu-vamśa" and the "Kumāra-sambhava."

**Kālindī (f)** The name of a wife of Śrī Kṛishṇa, who was the daughter of Sūrya, the Sun-God.

**Kālī (f)** 1. She who is black. 2. A name of the Goddess Durgā.

**Kālīvilāsin (m)** (*kālī* 'a name of the Goddess Durgā' + *vilāsin* 'delight, husband') The husband of the Goddess Kālī; a name of Lord Śiva.

**Kāma (m)** 1. Desire or love. 2. The 297th name of Lord Vishṇu as listed in the Vishṇu Sahasranāma. In his commentary Śrī Śaṅkara states, "He who is desired by the seekers of the four human goals (dharma, artha, *kāma*, moksha) is called *Kāma*."

**Kāmadeva (m)** (*kāma* 'desire' + *deva* 'god') 1. The God of desire or love. 2. The 651st name of Lord Vishṇu as listed in the Vishṇu Sahasranāma. In his commentary Śrī Śaṅkara states, "He who is desired by the seekers of the four human goals starting with *dharma* is called *Kāmadeva*." 3. The name of Cupid, who was burnt by a look of Lord Śiva's third eye of knowledge.

**Kāmanda (m)** The name of a Ṛishi.

**Kāmapāla (m)** (*kāma* 'desire' +*pāla* 'fulfiller') 1. The fulfiller of desires. 2. The 652nd name of Lord Vishṇu as listed in the Vishṇu Sahasranāma. In his commentary, Śrī Śaṅkara states, "He who fulfills the desires of the entitled desirers is the fulfiller of desires." See the Bhagavad Gītā VII:22.

**Kāmavīrya (m)** (*kāma* 'desire' + *vīrya* 'strength, vigor') 1. Vigorous at will. 2. A name of Garuḍa, the vehicle of Lord Vishṇu.

**Kāmākshī (f)** (*kāma* 'desire' + *akshī* 'eye') 1. Having loving eyes. 2. A name of the Goddess Pārvatī as worshipped in Kañcipuram, South India. 3. The 28th of the Goddess Lakshmī's 108 names.

**Kāmāri (m)** (*kāma* 'desire' + *ari* 'enemy') The enemy of desire; a name of Lord Śiva, referring to His turning of Cupid to ash with a look from His third eye of Knowledge. See the Bhagavad Gītā IV:19, 37.

**Kāmbojinī (f)** Born or coming from *Kamboja*; the name of an attendant of Devī, or the Divine Mother.

**Kāmeśa (m)** (*kāma* 'desire' + *īśa* 'lord') 1. The Lord or master of desire. 2. A name of Lord Śiva which may either mean He fulfills all desires or that He controls Cupid.

**Kāmeśī (f)** (*kāma* 'desire' + *īśī* 'sovereign goddess') 1. The sovereign Goddess of desires. 2. The 143rd name of the Goddess Lalitā as listed in the Brahmāṇḍa-Purāṇa. In his commentary Śrī Śaṅkara states, "She goads one to desires. Kāma means 'objects of desire.' The root *'Īs'* means 'to direct.' She directs one according to his past actions."

**Kāmeśwara (m)** (*kāma* 'desire' + *īśwara* 'lord') 1. The Lord or master of desire. 2. A name of Lord Śiva which may either mean He fulfills all desires or that He controls Cupid.

**Kāmeśwarī (f)** (*kāma* 'desire' + *īśwarī* 'sovereign') 1. The sovereign Goddess of desires. 2. The sovereign Goddess of Kāmadeva. 3. The 258th name of the Goddess Lalitā as listed in the Brahmāṇḍa-Purāṇa. In his commentary Śrī Śaṅkara states, "She is worshipped by Kāmadeva or Manmatha in the form of Kādi-Vidyā (i.e. Śrī-Vidyā, the fifteen-lettered mantra beginning with 'KA')."

**Kāñcī (f)** The name of a holy city in South India where Goddess Pārvatī is worshipped as "Kāmākshī."

**Kānta (m)** 1. The beloved, or the lovely. 2. The 296th and 654th name of Lord Vishṇu as listed in the Vishṇu Sahasranāma. In his commentary Śrī Śaṅkara states, "He who is extremely handsome and who moves in most handsome bodies is the beloved or lovely. It may also mean He puts an end (*anta*) even to Brahmā (called "*Ka* ") at the end of a cosmic cycle of age."

**Kāntā (f)** 1. The brilliant or lustrous. 2. The 154th name of the Goddess Lalitā as listed in the Brahmāṇḍa-Purāṇa. In his commentary Śrī Śaṅkara states, "The root '*Kan*,' from which this name is derived, means 'brilliance, luster.' Hence, Kāntā means 'most bewitching, lustrous.' It may also mean that She has the form of Madanagopāla or Śrī Kṛishṇa, as revealed in the Tripurā-Tāpiny'Upanishad: 'The primordial Lalitā sometimes assumes the male form of Kṛishṇa, and bewitches the universe with Her enchanting music of the flute.'"

**Kāntāravāsinī (f)** (*kāntāra* 'great forest' + *vāsinī* 'dweller') 1. The forest-dweller. 2. A name of the Goddess Durgā.

**Kānti (f)** 1. The lovely. 2. A name of the Goddess Lakshmī. 3. A name of the Goddess Durgā.

**Kāntimatī (f)** (*kānti* 'lovely' + *matī* 'having') Having loveliness.

**Kārayitrī (f)** 1. The causative. 2. The 19th name of the Goddess Lalitā as listed in the Brahmāṇḍa-Purāṇa. In his commentary Śrī Śaṅkara states, "She is the commanding power. Certain terminations in Sanskrit grammar as 'lin,' 'lot,' and 'tavya' functions indicate mandates. As these mandates are mere words, they are inert and cannot themselves enforce their meaning...Behind these mandates, She, as the presiding awareness of these words or Vedas, is their enforcing or motivating power. In respect of the performance of these authoritative mandates, therefore, She is *Kārayitrī*, the causative, as is written in the Kaushītaki Upanishad, '*Esha hy'eva sādhu karma kārayati*,' 'He alone makes one perform good actions,' and He is nothing but Her, the supreme Goddess.'"

**Kārpaṇī (f)** Gladness or happiness.

**Kārshṇi (m)** The descendant of Śrī Kṛishṇa.

**Kārtika (m), Kārttikeya (m)** 1. The son of the six Pleiads (i.e. Krittikās). 2. One of the names of Lord Śiva's son who is also known as Kumāra, Muruga, Skanda, Subrahmanya, etc. The gods asked Lord Śiva to produce a son who would be able to kill a powerful demon. Thus Lord Śiva sent His energy first into the Fire-God Agni, then into the Goddess Gaṅgā and finally into a thicket of reeds where the six Pleiades became his foster-mothers. According to many traditions this son remained a Brahmacārī. He is identified with Brahmā's son Sanatkumāra. The Skanda Purāṇa bears his name. See the Bhagavad Gītā X:24.

**Kāru (m)** 1. The singer or poet. 2. The maker. 3. A name of the universal architect, Viśwakarmā.

**Kāshṭhā (f)** The culmination. In the Kaṭha Upanishad Yama says to Naciketā:

*Purushān'na Param Kiñcit-*
*Sā Kāshṭha Sā Parā Gatiḥ.*

There is nothing higher than Purusha or Spirit.
He is the culmination; He is the highest goal.

**Kāśī (f)** 1. The shining. 2. A name of the holy city of Benares.

**Kāśīnātha (m)** (*kāśī* 'shining' + *nātha* 'master') 1. The master of the shining city. 2. A name of Lord Śiva as the patron of Benares.

**Kāśīśa (m)** (*kāśī* 'shining' + *īśa* 'lord') The Lord of the shining city; a name of Lord Śiva as the patron of Benares.

**Kāśīśwara (m)** (*kāśī* shining' + *īśwara* 'lord') The Lord of the shining city; a name of Lord Śiva as the patron of Benares.

**Kāśīśwarī (f)** (*kāśī* 'shining' + *īśwarī* 'sovereign goddess') The sovereign Goddess of the shining city. A name of the Goddess Pārvatī or Annapūrṇā.

**Kātyāyanī (f)** 1. A name of the Goddess Durgā. 2. The name of Yājñavalkya's second wife.

**Kāverī (f)** The name of one of the seven holy rivers of India. It is the holy river of Tamil Nadu, South India.

**Kāvyalolā (f)** (*kāvya* 'poetry' + *lolā* 'fond of') 1. Fond of poetry. 2. The 242nd name of the Goddess Lalitā as listed in the Brahmāṇḍa-Purāṇa. In his commentary Śrī Śaṅkara states, "She is interested in or connected with the expressed meaning and secondary meaning of the epics written by such poets as Vālmīki and Vedavyāsa. Also, She is fond of hymns of praise authored by learned poets, which contain figures of speech and suggested meanings."

**Keśava (m)** 1. The beautiful-haired. 2. A name of Śrī Kṛishṇa. 3. The 23rd and the 648th names of Lord Vishṇu as listed in the Vishṇu Sahasranāma. In his commentary Śrī Śaṅkara gives four definitions for this name, "1) He whose hair is beautiful and praised is *Keśava*, 2) He who controls Brahmā (*ka*), Vishṇu (*a*) and Śiva (*īśa*) is Keśava (*ka* + *a* + *īśa*), 3) He who killed the demon Keśi is called *Keśava*, or again 4) He who owns the rays of the sun and other luminaries is *Keśava*."

**Kevala (m)** [in Tamil **Kevalan**], **Kevalinī (f)** 1. The alone. 2. The one. 3. The absolute.

**Khadyotana (m)** (*kha* 'sky, space' + *dyotana* 'illuminator') 1. The sky-illuminator. 2. A name of Sūrya, the Sun-God.

**Khaga (m)** (*kha* ' sky, space' + *ga* 'to go') 1. Moving in space. 2. A name of the divine eagle Garuḍa.

**Khajit (m)** (*kha* 'sky, space' + *jit* 'conqueror') 1. The conqueror of heaven. 2. The name of a Buddha.

**Khakāminī (f)** (*kha* 'sky, space' + *kāminī* 'desiring') 1. Desiring or loving the sky. 2. A name of the Goddess Durgā.

**Khakuntala (m)** (*kha* 'sky, space' + *kuntala* 'hair') He whose hair is the sky; a name of Lord Śiva.

**Khāpagā (f)** (*kha* 'sky, space' + *āpagā* 'river') The heavenly stream; a name of the Goddess Gaṅgā.

**Khidira (m)** An ascetic.

**Kilakila (m)** The sound of joy; a name of Lord Śiva.

**Kirātī (f)** 1. A name of the Goddess Durgā. 2. A name of the Goddess Gaṅgā.

**Kiśora (m)** The youthful.

**Kiśorī (f)** 1. The youthful. 2. A name of Kumārī.

**Kīlāla (m)** Ambrosia.

**Kīrin (m)** The praiser, poet.

**Kīrti (f)** 1. Fame, glory. See the Bhagavad Gītā X:34. 2. The wife of Dharma, virtue.

**Kodaṇḍa (m), Kodaṇḍin (m)** 1. He who has a bow. In the Muṇḍaka Upanishad there is a simile for a bow: "OM is the bow, the individual self is the arrow and the Absolute is said to be the target." 2. A name of Lord Śiva. 3. A name of Śrī Rāma.

**Kolambī (f)** The lute of Lord Śiva.

**Koṇavādin (m)** A name of Lord Śiva.

**Kṛipaṇyu (m)** The praiser of God.

**Kṛipā (f)** Mercy, compassion, grace.

**Kṛipādharā (f)** (*kṛipā* 'compassion, mercy' + *dharā* 'bearer') The bearer of mercy or compassion.

**Kṛipālu (m)** (*kṛipā* 'compassion, mercy' + *ālu* 'having the disposition of') The compassionate, merciful. See the Bhagavad Gītā X:11.

**Kṛipāmayī (f)** (*kṛipa* 'compassion, mercy' + *mayī* 'full of') Full of compassion (i.e. compassionate, merciful).

**Kṛipāparā (f)** (*kṛipā* 'compassion, mercy' + *aparā* 'unrivalled') Having unrivalled mercy or compassion.

**Kṛipāsāgara (m)** (*kṛipā* 'compassion, mercy' + *sāgara* 'ocean') The ocean of mercy or compassion.

**Kṛishkara (m)** (*kṛish* 'carry away' + *kara* 'doer, maker') 1. The withdrawer. 2. A name of Lord Śiva referring to His dissolving the whole universe at the end of a cosmic cycle.

**Kṛishṇa (m)** 1. One whose nature is truth and bliss. 2. Black, dark-colored. 3. The name of Lord Vishṇu's eighth incarnation. Śrī Kṛishṇa is well-known for delivering the famous Bhagavad Gītā to Arjuna on the battlefield in 5000 B.C. on the eve of the present Kaliyuga, or dark age. 3. The 58th name of Lord Vishṇu as listed in the Vishṇu Sahasranāma. In his commentary, Śrī Śaṅkara states, "'*Krish* ' means 'truth' and '*na* ' means 'bliss,' hence '*Kṛishṇa* ' means 'He whose nature is truth and bliss.' Again, He is called '*Kṛishṇa*' on account of His dark complexion." In his commentary on the Bhagavad Gītā, Śrī Śaṅkara further states, "The Lord is called *Kṛishṇa* as He removes sin and other defects from His devotees."

**Kṛishṇā (f)** 1. Black, dark-colored. 2. A name of the Goddess Kālī.

**Kṛishṇabandhu (m)** (*kṛishṇa* 'incarnation of Lord Vishṇu' + *bandhu* 'friend') Friend of Śrī Kṛishṇa.

**Kṛishṇajanaka (m)** (*kṛishṇa* 'incarnation of Lord Vishṇu' + *janaka* 'begetter') The begetter or father of Śrī Kṛishṇa; a name of Vasudeva.

**Kṛishṇanetra (m)** (*kṛishṇa* 'black' + *netra* 'eye') The black-eyed; a name of Lord Śiva.

**Kṛishṇāgata (m)** (*kṛishṇa* 'incarnation of Lord Vishṇu' + *agata* 'attained') He who has attained Śrī Kṛishṇa. See the Bhagavad Gītā IV:10; XIV:2.

**Kṛiśāṅga (m)** (*kṛiśa* 'thin' + *aṅga* 'limb') 1. The thin-bodied. 2. A name of Lord Śiva referring to His subtleness beyond the range of senses.

**Kṛiśodarī (f)** (*kṛiśa* 'thin' + *udarī* 'belly, waist') 1. The slender-waisted Goddess. 2. A name of the Goddess Kālī.

**Kṛitadharma (m)** (*krita* 'what is done' + *dharma* 'duty') Having accomplished duty. See the Bhagavad Gītā XV:20.

**Kṛitajña (m)** (*kṛita* 'what is done' + *jña* 'knower') 1. The knower of what is done. 2. The 82nd and 532nd names of Lord Vishṇu as listed in the Vishṇu Sahasranāma. In his commentary Śrī Śaṅkara states, "He who knows the virtuous and unvirtuous action done by living beings is the Knower of what is done. It also means the Lord gives liberation to those who offer Him even so little as a leaf or a flower. Again, it means the Lord is both the created universe and its Knower or Self."

**Kṛitakara (m)** (*kṛita* 'accomplished' + *kara* 'doer, accomplisher') 1. The accomplished accomplisher. 2. A name of Lord Śiva. See the Bhagavad Gītā XV:20.

**Kṛitaprajña (m)** (*kṛita* 'accomplished' + *prajña* 'wisdom, knowledge') He who has accomplished wisdom. See the Bhagavad Gītā II:55-72.

**Kṛitatīrtha (m)** (*kṛita* 'accomplished' + *tīrtha* 'pilgrimage') He who has accomplished a pilgrimage.

**Kṛitnu (m)** 1. The skillful. 2. The name of a Ṛishi.

**Kṛittivāsa (m)** (*kṛitti* 'skin' + *vāsa* 'wearing') 1. Clad in (tiger or elephant) skin. 2. The 62nd name of Lord Śiva's 108 names. The tiger represents lust, and the elephant pride, both of which Lord Śiva has conquered.

**Krivi (m)** A name of Lord Rudra (i.e. Lord Śiva).

**Kriyā (f)** 1. Religious or purified action. See the Yogasūtras II:1, where tapas, swādhyāya and Īśwara-praṇidhāna are spoken of as Kriya-Yoga. 2. A name of the Goddess Durgā as Kriyāśakti, or the power of action.

**Kshamā (f)** 1. Patience or forbearance. 2. A name of the Earth-Goddess. See the Bhagavad Gītā X:4; XVI:3.

**Kubera (m)** Lord over divine treasures through Lord Śiva's grace. He is therefore known as "the Lord of Divine Treasure. His abode is near Lord Śiva on Mount Kailāsa.

**Kuberabandhu (m)** (*kubera* 'lord of the divine treasure' + *bandhu* 'friend') 1. Friend of Kubera. 2. A name of Lord Śiva referring to His conferring lordship over His treasure to Kubera for his great devotion.

**Kuberabāndhava (m)** (*kubera* 'lord of the divine treasure' + *bāndhava* 'friend') 1. Friend of Kubera. 2. A name of Lord Śiva referring to His conferring lordship over His treasure to Kubera for his great devotion.

**Kuberagiri (m)** (*kubera* 'lord of the divine treasure' + *giri* 'mountain') Kubera's mountain (i.e. Mount Kailāsa where Kubera has his abode near Lord Śiva).

**Kuberācala (m)** (*kubera* 'lord of the divine treasure' + *acala* 'steady, mountain') Kubera's mountain (i.e. Mount Kailāsa where Kubera has his abode near Lord Śiva).

**Kucela (m)** (*ku* 'badly' +*cela* 'clothed') The name of a very poor yet good childhood friend and devotee of Śrī Kṛishṇa. By his devotion, Kucela received the boon of wealth from Srī Kṛishṇa.

**Kuhāvatī (f)** (*kuhā* 'name of a plant' + *vatī* 'having') A name of the Goddess Durgā.

**Kumāra (m)** 1. The youthful. 2. A name of Lord Śiva's son who is also known as Kārttikeya or Muruga. See the Bhagavad Gītā X:24. 3. A name for Lord Brahmā's four sons who renounced the world and learned the Truth in silence from the Guru Dakshiṇāmūrti.

**Kumārī (f)** 1. The youthful. 2. A name of the Goddess Durgā.

**Kumbharī (f)** A name of the Goddess Durgā.

**Kumuda (m)** (*ku* 'earth' + *muda* 'delight') 1. The Earth's delighter. 2. The 589th and 807th name of Lord Vishṇu as listed in the Vishṇu Sahasranāma. In his commentary Śrī Śaṅkara states, "He who delights in the earth is *Kumuda*, or He who makes the earth rejoice by relieving her of her burden." 3. The white night lotus.

**Kumudinī (f)**The white night lotus.

**Kuṇḍalinī (f)** 1. Having coils. 2. The name of a form of the Divine Mother or Śakti said to be coiled like a serpent at the base of the spinal cord.

**Kundara (m)** 1. The bestower of a jasmine-like reward. 2. The 808th name of Lord Vishṇu as listed in the Vishṇu Sahasranāma. In his commentary Śrī Śaṅkara states, "The Lord who bestows or receives fruits as pure as the jasmine flower (*kunda*), is named *Kundara*. It also means that in the form of a boar He tore (*dārayām-āsa*) the earth (*kum*) for slaying the demon Hirāṇyāksha.

**Kundinī (f)** Jasmine-like.

**Kuñjala (m)** The name of an attendant of Lord Skanda.

**Kuñjavihārin (m)** (*kuñja* 'thicket' + *vihārin* 'delighting in') 1. He who sports in the forest. 2. A name of Śrī Kṛishṇa.

**Kuntī (f)** The name assumed by Prithā when she was adopted by King Kuntibhoja. Through the blessing of Ṛishi Durvāsa, she could have children by any God she could invoke. She thus gave birth to Karṇa by the Sun-God. When she married King Pāṇḍu, who through a curse could not approach her, she gave birth to Yudhishṭhira, Bhīma and Arjuna by the Gods Dharma, Vāyu and Indra, respectively.

**Kuraṅgākshī (f)** (*kuraṅga* 'antelope, gazelle' + *akshī* 'eye') The fawn-eyed.

**Kuruṇḍi (m)** The name of an ancient Ṛishi.

**Kuśala (m), Kuśalā (f)** 1. The skillful or clever (i.e. even-minded). This name is derived from the Bhagavad Gītā II:50 where it is written, "*Yogaḥ karmasu kauśalam*," "Skillfulness, or perfection, in action is Yoga." In this case the word *kauśalam* refers to the state of being skillful. This state of skillfulness is called Karma Yoga, or detachment from the fruits of all actions, past and present. Thus to be skillful in action does not mean being a good or perfect worker but rather, being detached. 2. Happy, healthy, prosperous.

**Kuśalin (m), Kuśalinī (f)** Having skillfulness or happiness. (See **Kuśala**)

**Kuśīvaśa (m)** (*kuśī/kuśa* 'son of Śrī Rāma' + *vaśa* 'control') Having Kuśa, the son of Śrī Rāma, under control; a name of Vālmīki.

**Kusuma (m), Kusumā (f)** Flower-like, or blossom-like.

# L

**Labhyā (f)** 1. The accessible, or the obtainable. 2. The 78th name of the Goddess Lalitā as listed in the Brahmāṇḍa-Purāṇa. In his commentary Śrī Śaṅkara states, "While in the world of transmigration, She is masked by the limiting power of ignorance, yet She can be realized as her reflection in the plane of infinite knowledge, which is the inner instrument perfected by hearing about, reflection on and deep meditation upon the Self or Absolute. Being eternal, the Absolute is ever with us. Yet, like the necklace on one's own neck which, when forgotten, is taken as lost, and when remembered, it is there, She, while apparently lost to us while in ignorance, is ever with us and accessible."

**Lajjā (f)** 1. Modesty. 2. The wife of the God Dharma and the Mother of humility.

**Lakshmaṇa (m)** 1. Having (auspicious) marks. 2. The name of Śrī Rāma's brother, who was himself a partial incarnation of Lord Vishṇu born to King Daśaratha's wife Sumitrā along with his twin brother Śatrughna, but while Śatrughna attached himself to Bharata, Lakshmaṇa was fully devoted to Śrī Rāma.

**Lakshmī (f)** 1. Having good marks or good forture. 2. The beautiful. 3. The Goddess of wealth and prosperity, the consort of Lord Vishṇu, who came out of the milk ocean when churned by the gods and demons. She represents divine wealth and Ātma-Vidyā, or Self- knowledge, as well as all beauty, light and splendor. This is the 18th of the Goddess Lakshmī's 108 names.

**Lakshya (m)** [in Tamil **Lakshyan**] 1. The aim or goal. 2. The implied meaning of scriptural words.

**Lalitā (f)** 1. The lovely, gentle and innocent. 2. A name of the Goddess Durgā. 3. The 62nd name of the Goddess Lalitā as listed in the Brahmāṇḍa-Purāṇa. In his commentary, Śrī Śaṅkara states, "She is immensely beautiful. Being the Goddess Tripurāsundarī, She is peerless Beauty. There is none equal to Her in beauty."

**Lalitāmbikā (f)** (*lalitā* 'lovely, gentle, innocent' + *ambikā* 'mother') 1. The lovely and gentle Divine Mother. 2. A name of the Goddess Durgā.

**Lambana (m)** 1. He upon whom all depend. 2. A name of Lord Śiva.

**Latā (f)** 1. Creeper-like (i.e. a slender, graceful woman). 2. She who clings to God.

**Latikā (f)** 1. Creeper-like (i.e. a slender, graceful woman). 2. She who clings to God.

**Lavaṇa (m)** 1. Beautiful or lovely. See the Yogasūtras II:47. 2. The saline. 3. A name of the ocean.

**Lāvaṇyā (f)** Beauty or loveliness. See the Yogasūtras II:47.

**Līlā (f)** 1. Divine play. This word occurs in the Brahmasūtras when Vyāsa says, "To God, creation is a mere pastime or play." 2. The name of a queen who was enlightened by the Goddess Saraswatī. See the Yoga-Vāśishṭha.

**Līlāmayī (f)** (*līlā* 'divine play' + *mayī* 'full of') Full of divine play; beautiful.

**Līlāvatī (f)** (*līlā* 'divine play' + *vatī* 'having') 1. She who is but a manifestation of divine play. 2. Having beauty.

**Lola (m)** 1. Moving to and fro. 2. A name of Śrī Kṛishṇa as a flute player.

# M

**Madānāśinī (f)** (*madā* 'pride' + *nāśini* 'destroyer') 1. The destroyer of pride. 2. A name of the Divine Mother.

**Madhura (m)** Honeyed or sweet.

**Madhusūdana (m)** (*madhu* 'name of a demon' + *sūdana* 'slayer') 1. The slayer of the demon Madhu. 2. The 73rd name of Lord Vishṇu as listed in the Vishṇu Sahasranāma. Madhu (*tamas*) and Kaitabha (*rajas*) were two demons who stole the Vedas from Lord Brahmā and were killed by Lord Vishṇu. 3. A name of Śrī Kṛishṇa.

**Mahanīya (m)** The glorious or praiseworthy.

**Maharshi (m)** (*maha* 'great' + *ṛishi* 'seer') 1. The great seer. 2. A name of God, meaning Īśwara who sees the whole Vedic lore. 3. One who has realized the supreme Self.

**Mahatī (f)** She who is great.

**Mahābala (m)** (*mahā* 'great' + *bala* 'powerful') 1. The highly powerful. 2. The Almighty. 3. The 172nd name of Lord Vishṇu as listed in the Vishṇu Sahasranāma. In his commentary Śrī Śaṅkara states, "As He is stronger than the strongest, the Lord is called the Almighty." See the Bhagavad Gītā VII: 11.

**Mahādeva (m)** (*mahā* 'great' + *deva* 'god') 1. The great God. 2. The last of Lord Śiva's 108 names. 3. The 491st name of Lord Vishṇu as listed in the Vishṇu Sahasranāma. In his commentary Śrī Śaṅkara states: "As He is great and divine through His nature of Consciousness, the Lord is called the great God. The Atharvaśira Upanishad says, 'Since He is glorified in the great sovereignty of the Yoga of Self-knowledge after having renounced all thoughts, therefore the fortunate Lord is called the great God.'"

**Mahādevī (f)** (*mahā* 'great' + *devī* 'goddess') 1. The great Goddess. 2. A name of the Goddess Pārvatī. 3. A name of the Goddess Lakshmī.

**Mahājit (m)** (*mahā* 'great' + *jit* 'conquering') 1. The great conqueror. 2. A name of Garuḍa.

**Mahākāla (m)** (*mahā* 'great' + *kāla* 'time') Time as the great destroyer; a name of Lord Śiva as world annihilator.

**Mahākālī (f)** (*mahā* 'great' + *kālī* 'dark, black) 1. The great Black Goddess; a name of the Goddess Kālī. 2. The 105th of the Goddess Lakshmī's 108 names.

**Mahākānta (m)** (*mahā* 'great' + *kānta* 'pleasing') 1. The greatly pleasing. 2. A name of Lord Śiva.

**Mahālakshmī (f)** (*mahā* 'great' + *lakshmī* 'goddess of wealth and beauty') The great Goddess of wealth and beauty.

**Mahān (m)** 1. The Great One. 2. The 842nd name of Lord Vishṇu as listed in the Vishṇu Sahasranāma. In his commentary Śrī Śaṅkara states, "Since even by argumentation it is impossible to speak of Him as possessing any properties because of His freedom from attributes such as sound, His utmost subtlety and His eternal purity and omnipresence, the Lord is therefore really the Great One, as said by the sage Āpastamba: 'He is soundless, bodiless and touchless, great and pure.'" 3. In the Bṛihad-Āraṇyaka Upanishad, sage Yājñavalkya speaks of the greatness of the Self to King Janaka thus:

*Virajaḥ Para Ākāśad-*
*Aja Ātmā Mahān Dhruvaḥ.*

Taintless, higher than space and
birthless, the Self is great and eternal.

In the Kaṭha Upanishad, Lord Yama also says to young Naciketā:

*Aṇor-Aṇīyān Mahato Mahīyān*
*Ātmāasya Jantor-Nihito Guhāyām.*

Subtler than the subtle and greater than the great,
the Self is lodged in the (heart) cave of every creature.

*Mahāntam Vibhum-Ātmānam*
*Matwā Dhīro Na Śocati.*

Having meditated on the Self as great and
pervasive, a wise man does not grieve.

In the Śwetāśwatara Upanishad the Ṛishi Śwetāśwatara says:

*Mahān Prabhur-Vai Purushaḥ...*

Great, almighty indeed is the Purusha...

4. A name of Lord Śiva.

**Mahānaṭa (m)** (*mahā* 'great' + *naṭa* 'dancer') The great actor or dancer; a name of Lord Śiva.

**Mahāpūjya (m)** (*mahā* 'great' + *pūjya* 'worshipful') The great or most worshipful. See the Bhagavad Gītā XI:43.

**Mahārāj(a) (m)** (*maha* 'great' + *rāja* 'king') The great king. See the Bhagavad Gītā X:27.

**Mahārājñī (f)** (*mahā* 'great' + *rājñī* 'queen') The great queen.

**Mahārānī (f)** (*mahā* 'great' + *rānī* 'queen') The great queen.

**Mahārūpa (m)** (*mahā* 'great' + *rūpa* 'form') Having a mighty form; a name of Lord Śiva.

**Mahāsattwa (m)** (*mahā* 'great' + *sattwa* 'having a tranquil mind') The great-minded.

**Mahāśakti (m) (f)** (*mahā* 'great' + *śakti* 'energy, power') 1. Having great power. 2. A name of the Divine Mother. 3. The 175th name of Lord Vishṇu as listed in the Vishṇu Sahasranāma.

**Mahātman (m)** (*mahā* 'great' + *ātman* 'Self, mind') 1. The great Self; a name of God appearing in the Bhagavad Gītā XI:12,20. 2. The great-minded; a name for sages appearing in the Bhagavad Gītā VII:19; VIII:15; IX: 13.

**Mahāvīra (m)** (*mahā* 'great' + *vīra* 'virility, strength') 1. The great hero. 2. A name of Lord Vishṇu. 3. A name of Garuḍa. 4. A name of Hanuman for having jumped over the ocean and put fire to Rāvaṇa's city in Śrī Laṅkā.

**Mahendra (m)** (*mahā* 'great' + *indra* 'chief') 1. The great Indra; a name of Indra. 2. The Great and Powerful One. The 268th name of Lord Vishṇu as listed in the Vishṇu Sahasranāma. In his commentary Śrī Śaṅkara states, "The Lord is called *Mahendra* as He is the Lord even of lords."

**Mahendrāṇī (f)** (*mahā* 'great' + *indrāṇī* 'consort of the chief') The great consort of Indra; a name of Śacī.

**Maheśa (m)** (*mahā* 'great' + *īśa* lord') The great Lord; a name of Lord Śiva.

**Maheśwara (m)** (*mahā* 'great' + *īśwara* 'lord, ruler') 1. The great Lord. 2. The 2nd among Lord Śiva's 108 names. 3. A name of Lord Vishṇu. See the

Bhagavad Gītā V:29, IX:11, X:3, XIII:22.

**Maheśwarī (f)** (*mahā* 'great' + *īśwarī* 'sovereign goddess') The great sovereign Goddess; a name of the Goddess Durgā.

**Mahinasa (m)** A name of Lord Śiva.

**Mahishamardinī (f)** (*mahisha* 'name of a demon + *mardinī* 'destroyer, crusher') The destroyer or crusher of the demon Mahisha; a name of the Goddess Durgā.

**Mahita (m), Mahitā (f)** The honored or celebrated.

**Mahī (f)** The great; a name of the Earth-Goddess.

**Mahīdhara (m)** (*mahī* 'earth-goddess' + *dhara* 'bearer') 1. The earth-bearer. 2. The 317th and 369th name of Lord Vishṇu as listed in the Vishṇu Sahasranāma. In his commentary Śrī Śaṅkara states, "(This name) means (either) through the form of mountains, the Lord bears the earth, or He accepts worship (Pūjā)."

**Mahīnātha (m)** (*mahī* 'earth-goddess' + *nātha* 'lord, master') 1. The Lord of the earth. 2. A name of Lord Vishṇu.

**Mahīpāla (m)** (*mahī* 'earth-goddess' + *pāla* 'protector') 1. The earth-protector. 2. A name of a king.

**Mahīsura (m)** (*mahī* 'earth-goddess' + *sura* 'god') 1. The earthly god. 2. A general name for Brāhmaṇas, or wise men.

**Mahīyā (f)** Joyousness or happiness.

**Mahodāra (m)** (*mahā* 'great' + *udāra* 'high') The great and high.

**Maidhāva (m)** The son of the wise (i.e. of a Medhavin).

**Maithilī (m)** The Princess of Mithilā; a name of Sītā, who was the daughter of King Janaka of Mithilā.

**Maitreya (m)** 1. The friendly. 2. Name of a sage who, though instructed by Parāśara, went to Lord Śiva for receiving direct knowledge of Truth. This teaching is revealed in the Maitreya Upanishad of the Sāmaveda, which is one among the seventeen Sannyāsa Upanishads.

**Maitreyī (f)** 1. The friendly. 2. The name of the more spiritual of the sage

Yājñavalkya's two wives. He taught her Self-knowledge before he entered into Sannyāsa. In the Bṛihad-Āraṇyaka Upanishad he says to her, "It is not for the sake of all, my dear Maitreyī, that all is loved, but for the sake of the Self (Ātman). The Self should be heard, reflected and deeply meditated upon, then one becomes all."

**Maitrī (f)** Friendliness or benevolence. See the Yogasūtras I:33.

**Manāvī (f)** Manu's wife.

**Manāyu (m)** The devoted.

**Mandayantī (f)** 1. Delighting or rejoicing. 2. A name of the Goddess Durgā.

**Mandākinī (f)** 1. Flowing slowly. 2. The name of an arm of the holy Ganges in the Himālayas. 3. Also the name of the heavenly Ganges, the Milky Way.

**Mandāra (m)** 1. The coral tree. 2. One of the five celestial wish-fulfilling trees.

**Mandodarī (f)** (*manda* 'slight' + *udarī* 'bellied') The name of Rāvaṇa's wife, who was a chaste woman. She advised Rāvaṇa to deliver Sītā, but he refused.

**Mandu (m)** The joyous.

**Maṅgalā (f)** 1. The auspicious. 2. A name of the Goddess Pārvatī. 3. The 95th of the Goddess Lakshmī's 108 names.

**Maṇi (m), Maṇī (f)** Jewel or pearl.

**Manīshā (f)** 1. Desire, wish. 2. Intelligence, understanding. 3. A thought, idea.

**Manīshin (m), Manīshiṇī (f)** Learned, intelligent, clever, thoughtful, prudent. See the Bhagavad Gītā II:51, XVIII:5.

**Mañjarī (f)** Cluster of blossoms.

**Mañju (m)** 1. Beautiful. 2. Sweet.

**Mañjula (m), Mañjulā (f)** 1. Beautiful. 2. Sweet.

**Mañjuman (m), Mañjumatī (f)** (*mañju* 'beautiful, sweet' + *man/matī* 'having') Having beauty.

**Manohara (m)** (*manaḥ* 'mind' + *hara* 'ravisher') 1. The mind-ravisher, or mind-captivator. 2. The 461st name of Lord Vishṇu as listed in the Vishṇu

Sahasranāma. In his commentary Śrī Śaṅkara states, "Due to His nature of infinite bliss, the Lord capitvates the mind. In the Chāndogya Upanishad the sage Sanatkumāra says, 'That which is great or infinite is Bliss. There is no bliss in the finite.'"

**Manohariṇī (f), Manoharī (f)** (*manaḥ* 'mind' + *harī/hariṇī* 'ravisher') 1. The mind-ravisher, or mind-captivator. 2. A name for the Divine Mother.

**Manoramā (f)** (*manaḥ* 'mind' + *ramā* 'delight') Pleasing or delightful to the mind.

**Manthāna (m)** 1. The shaker of the universe. 2. A name of Lord Śiva as dissolving the universe at the end of a cosmic cycle.

**Mantra (m)** (*man* 'thought' + *tra* 'save') 1. The saving thought. When split into *man* and *tra*, this name is explained in the following manner: *"Mananāt-trāyate iti Mantraḥ,"* "By whose thinking one is saved, that is *mantra*, the saving thought." 2. The 280th name of Lord Vishṇu as listed in the Vishṇu Sahasranāma. In his commentary Śrī Śaṅkara states, "The Lord is the *Mantra* characterized by the Ṛigveda, the Yajurveda and the Sāmaveda. He is also thus called on account of being knowable through Vedic *mantras*." See the Bhagavad Gītā IX:16, X:25.

**Mantriṇī (f), Mantrī (m)** 1. The knower of mantras. 2. The wise, eloquent, or counselling.

**Manu (m)** 1. The thinking or wise. 2. The son of the Sun-God, Sūrya. He is considered the father of the human race. There are fourteen *Manus* associated with each creation or cosmic cycle. The *Manu* of the present creation is the 7th, named Vaivaswata, "the Sun-born." He was the first king and ancestor of Śrī Rāma at Ayodhyā. He gave a famous treatise on Dharma or Law. In the Vedas it is written, "Whatever has been spoken by *Manu* is a curative medicine." In the Bhagavad Gītā *Manu* is mentioned as a link in the transmission of Yoga. See IV:1. 3. The 52nd name of Lord Vishṇu as listed in the Vishṇu Sahasranāma. In his commentary Śrī Śaṅkara states, "Because of thinking, the Lord is called *Manu,* the Thinker. In the Bṛihad-Āraṇyaka it is revealed, 'There is no other Thinker but Him.' It also means a mantra of that name, or *Manu,* the progenitor, as a form of the Lord."

**Mardinī (f)** 1. The destroying. 2. A name of the Goddess Durgā.

**Marīci (m)** 1. A ray of light. 2. One of the seven Ṛishis created by Brahmā and represented in the Great Bear. 3. The 189th name of Lord Vishṇu as listed in the Vishṇu Sahasranāma. In his commentary Śrī Śaṅkara states, "Being the Effulgence even of the effulgent, the Lord is *Marīci*, the Luminous One, as said in the Bhagavad Gītā: 'I am the Effulgence of the effulgent.'(VII:9;

X:36)" See also the Bhagavad Gītā X:21.

**Maruta (m)** Flashing or shining; a name of Vāyu, the Wind-God.

**Mati (f)** 1. Spiritual thought. 2. The wife of Viveka or Discrimination.

**Maunī (m)** The silent or thoughtful. See the Bhagavad Gītā X:38; XII:19; XVII:16.

**Mādhavan (m)** 1. The Lord of the Goddess Lakshmī. 2. The Lord of knowledge. 3. The 72nd, 167th and 735th names of Lord Vishṇu as listed in the Vishṇu Sahasranāma. In his commentary Śrī Śaṅkara states, "He who is the Lord (*dhava*) of Lakshmī is *Mādhava*. The Lord is also called *Mādhava* as He is knowable through the Honey Knowledge (*Madhu-Vidyā*) of the Chāndogya and the Bṛihad-Āraṇyaka Upanishads. Also He who is the Lord (*dhava*) of knowledge (*mā*) is *Madhava*. Again, it may mean the descendant of Madhu (i.e. Śrī Kṛishṇa)."

**Mādhavī (f)** 1. Honeyed. 2. Spring flower. 3. Mother Earth. 4. A name of the Goddess Durgā.

**Mādhurī (f)** Honeyed, or sweet.

**Mādrī (f)** 1. The name of King Pāṇḍu's second wife who was the mother of Nakula and Sahadeva by the two Aświn deities. 2. The name of a wife of Śrī Kṛishṇa.

**Mājī (f)** (short for *Mātājī* 'respected Mother') The Mother.

**Mālatī (f)** The jasmine blossoming in the evening.

**Mālā (f)** 1. Garland of flowers. 2. A rosary.

**Mālikā (f)** Jasmine.

**Mālinī (f)** Having a garland.

**Mālya (m)** Worthy to be garlanded.

**Mānasaprema (m)** (*mānasa* 'mental' + *prema* 'divine love') A mind filled with divine love.

**Mānasā (f)** The mental or spiritual; a name of the Goddess Pārvatī.

**Mānikya (m)** Like a jewel.

**Mānyavatī (f)** Honorable; the name of a princess.

**Mārgabandhu (m)** (*mārga* 'path' + *bandhu* 'friend') Friend of the path.

**Mārgapālī (f)** (*mārga* 'path' + *pālī* 'protector') Protector of the path.

**Mārgavaṭī (f)** (*mārga* 'path' + *vaṭī* 'protecting') Protector of the path; the name of a Goddess protecting travelers.

**Mārkaṇḍeya (m)** 1. The son of the sage Mṛikaṇḍu. 2. The name of an ancient sage, narrator of a Purāṇa named after him. He was saved from Yama, the God of Death, through his devotion to Lord Śiva who kicked Yama's chest with His foot.

**Mārtaṇḍan (m)** The son of Mṛitaṇḍa; a name of the Sun-God, Sūrya, referring to His birth from a seemingly dead egg.

**Mārulā (f)** The name of a poetess.

**Mātā (f)** The Mother. See the Bhagavad Gītā IX:17.

**Mātājī (f)** (*mātā* 'mother' + *jī* 'respected') Respected Mother.

**Māyā (f)** The illusory power of God.

**Māyāpati (m)** (*māyā* 'illusion' + *pati* 'lord') 1. The Lord of illusion. 2. A name of Lord Vishṇu. See the Bhagavad Gītā IV:6; VII:13,14; VIII:20; IX:7-10; XVIII:61.

**Māyāvin (m)** (*māyā* 'illusion' + *vin* 'possessing') 1. The possessor or master of illusion. 2. A name of Lord Vishṇu. See the Bhagavad Gītā IV:6; VII:13,14; VIII:20; IX:7-10; XVIII:61.

**Medhā (f)** Mental power, memory, intelligence, wisdom, the power to retain what has been heard or learned, especially in reference to Self-Knowledge. See the Bhagavad Gītā X:34.

**Medhāvin (m)** (*medhā* 'mental power' + *vin* 'possessing') 1. Having mental power or wisdom. 2. The 77th name of Lord Vishṇu as listed in the Vishṇu Sahasranāma. In his commentary Śrī Śaṅkara states, "Having the capacity to retain many treatises, the Lord is called *Medhāvin.*" See the Bhagavad Gītā XVIII:10.

**Medhāvinī (f), Medhāvatī (f)** (*medhā* 'mental power' + *vinī/vatī* 'possessing') 1. Having mental power or wisdom. 2. A name of the Goddess Saraswatī. See the Bhagavad Gītā XVIII:10.

**Medhira (m)** The intelligent or wise.

**Menakā (f)** A name of Himavan's wife, the mother of the Goddess Pārvatī.

**Menā (f)** A name of Himavan's wife, the mother of the Goddess Pārvatī.

**Menādhava (m)** (*menā* 'mother of the Goddess Pārvatī' + *dhava* 'husband, lord') *Menā*'s husband or Lord (i.e. Himavan).

**Menājā (f)** (*menā* 'mother of the Goddess Parvati' + *jā* 'born') She who is born of *Menā*; a name of the Goddess Pārvatī.

**Milīmilin (m)** A name of Lord Śiva taken from a mantra that repeats the word *mili*.

**Mitra (m)** 1. The friend. 2. One of the twelve Ādityas or solar deities, presiding over exhalation and the day, who is invoked in the famous Śānti Mantra: *"OM Śam no Mitraḥ, Śam Varuṇaḥ..."* "May *Mitra* be blissful to us! May Varuṇa be blissful to us..."

**Mīnākshī (f)** (*mīna* 'fish' + *akshī* 'eye') Fish-eyed; a name of the Goddess Pārvatī as worshipped at Madurai.

**Mīrā (f)** The name of a princess who lived in the 16th century. She was a great devotee of Śrī Kṛishṇa and singer of devotional songs.

**Mīrābai (f)** The name of a princess who lived in the 16th century. She was a great devotee of Śrī Kṛishṇa and singer of devotional songs.

**Mohan (m)** 1. The deluder, bewilderer, infatuater. 2. A name of Lord Śiva referring to His power of illusion.

**Mohanāśin (m), Mohanāśinī (f)** (*moha* 'delusion' + *naśin* 'destroyer') The destroyer of illusion. See the Bhagavad Gītā V:16; X:11.

**Mohinī (f)** 1. The enchantress. 2. A feminine form assumed by Lord Vishṇu.

**Moksha (m)** Liberation (from rebirth), which is only obtained by knowledge of the true Self. See the Bhagavad Gītā II:72; IV:16; V:28; IX:1,28; XIII: 34; XVI:5; XVIII:30,66.

**Mokshapriya (m), Mokshapriyā (f)** (*moksha* 'liberation' + *priya* 'dear, beloved') He or she for whom liberation is dear. See the *Moksha-parāyaṇaḥ* in the

Bhagavad Gītā V:28.

**Mūrti (m) (f)** The image or form of God.

**Mṛiḍa (m)** 1. Compassionate, merciful. 2. The 88th of Lord Śiva's 108 names.

**Mṛiḍapriyā (f)** (*mrida* 'compassionate' + *priyā* 'beloved') The beloved of the compassionate; a name of the Goddess Pārvatī.

**Mṛiḍā (f)** 1. Compassionate, merciful. 2. A name of the Goddess Pārvatī.

**Mṛiḍānī (f)** 1. The consort of the compassionate. 2. A name of the Goddess Pārvatī.

**Mṛiḍī (f)** 1. Compassionate, merciful. 2. A name of the Goddess Pārvatī.

**Mṛigī (f)** 1. Like a doe, or female antelope. 2. A name of Rādhā.

**Mṛigīpati (m)** (*mṛigi* 'like a doe' + *pati* 'lord') 1. Lord of the one like a doe. 2. A name of Śrī Kṛishṇa.

**Mṛitsnā (f)** Fragrant like the earth.

**Mukta (m)** [in Tamil **Muktan**] The liberated (from rebirth). See the Bhagavad Gītā V:28; IX:28; XII:15.

**Muktā (f)** 1. The liberated. 2. Pearl.

**Muktādevī (f)** (*muktā* 'pearl' + *devī* 'goddess') 1. The pearl-like Goddess. 2. The Goddess of liberation.

**Mukti (f)** Liberation (from rebirth).

**Muktida (m)** (*mukti* 'liberation' + *da* 'give') The giver or bestower of liberation. 2. A name of Śrī Kṛishṇa.

**Muktidāyaka (m)** (*mukti* 'liberation' + *dāyaka* 'giver') 1. The giver or bestower of liberation. 2. A name of Śrī Kṛishṇa. See the Bhagavad Gītā XII:7.

**Muktidāyinī (f)** (*mukti* 'liberation' + *dāyinī* 'giver') 1. The giver or bestower of liberation. 2. A name of any manifestation of God as the Divine Mother.

**Muktidevī (f)** (*mukti* 'liberation' + *devī* 'goddess') Goddess of liberation.

**Mukunda (m)** (*mukun* 'liberation' + *da* 'giver') 1. The giver of liberation. 2. The

515th name of Lord Vishṇu as listed in the Vishṇu Sahasranāma.

**Mukundadāsa (m)** (*mukunda* 'giver of liberation' + *dāsa* 'servant') The servant of the giver of liberation (i.e. Lord Vishṇu).

**Mukundapriyā (f)** (*mukunda* 'giver of liberation' + *priyā* 'beloved') Beloved of the giver of liberation (i.e. Lord Vishṇu); a name of the Goddess Lakshmī.

**Mumukshā (f)** The desire of liberation, which is the fourth among the four spiritual means in Vedānta. See the Bhagavad Gītā IV:15; V:28; XV:4; XVII:25; XVIII:30.

**Mumukshu (m)** He who yearns for liberation. In his Vivekacūḍāmaṇi, Śrī Śaṅkara defines this yearning in the following passage:

*Ahaṅkārādi-dehāntān*
*Bandhān-ajñāna-kalpitān*
*Swa-Swarūpāvabodhena*
*Moktum-icchā Mumukshutā.*

*Mumukshutā* is the desire to free oneself from
the bonds created by ignorance, beginning
from ego and ending with the body,
through knowledge of one's real nature.

Śrī Śaṅkara considers the yearning for release and dispassion as the main qualifications of the four spiritual means.

**Muni (m)** 1. He who reflects on teaching dealing with Truth. 2. Sage. See the Bhagavad Gītā II:56, 69; V:6,28; VI:3; X:37; XIV:1.

**Munīndra (m)** (*muni* 'sage' + *indra* 'chief') 1. Chief of the sages. 2. A name of Lord Śiva.

**Munīśa (m)** (*muni* 'sage' + *īśa* 'lord') 1. Lord of the sages. 2. A name of Vālmīki.

**Munīśwara (m)** (*muni* 'sage' + *īśwara* 'lord') 1. Lord of the sages. 2. A name of Lord Vishṇu.

**Muñjakeśa (m)** (*muñja* 'kind of grass' + *keśa* 'hair') 1. The muñja-grass-haired. Muṅja is a special grass worn as a girdle by holy men as a mark of tapas, or austerity. 2. A name of Lord Śiva. 3. A name of Lord Vishṇu.

**Muralī (m)** 1. The flute. 2. A name of Śrī Kṛishṇa as the flute- player, the flute being a symbol for the ideal devotee who becomes empty or pure, thus being a perfectly tuned instrument in God's hands.

**Muralīdhara (m)** (*muralī* 'flute' + *dhara* 'bearer') 1. The flute-bearer. 2. A name of Śrī Kṛishṇa. In the Kṛishṇa Upanishad it is revealed: *Vamśas-tu Bhagavān Rudraḥ...*""His flute is verily the fortunate Rudra..." Śrī Kṛishṇa plays the flute which is a symbol of "OM," as a call to spiritual souls to reunite with Him or realize their true Self.

**Murāri (m)** (*mura* 'destroyer, name of a demon' + *ari* 'enemy') The enemy of the Demon Mura, who was killed by Śrī Kṛishṇa; a name of Śrī Kṛishṇa.

**Muruga (m)** The son of Lord Śiva who is also known as Kārttikeya or Kumāra.

**Mūkāmbikā (f)** (*mūka* 'speech-impaired' + *ambikā* 'mother') Mother of the speech-impaired. Through Her grace a speech-impaired person became a poet. 2. A name of the Goddess Kāmākshī or Pārvatī as worshipped in Kāncīpuram.

**Mūrti (m)** Divine form, embodiment.

# N

**Naciketā (m)** [in Tamil **Naciketān**] The name of the grandson of Uddālaka, who was a young and famous Brahmacārī noted for his great determination in the pursuit of knowledge and spoken of in the Kaṭha Upanishad. He was sent to Yama, the God of Death, by his angry father. After he waited for three days at Yama's door, Yama gave him three boons: one to regain his father's affection, another to learn of the sacred fire leading to heaven, and the third to know the true Self. After tempting him with all possible wealth and enjoyment, Yama taught him the full knowledge of the Self. Thus *Naciketān* stands as the ideal seeker of Truth.

**Nadīnātha (m)** (*nadī* 'river' + *nātha* 'lord') The lord of rivers; a name of the ocean.

**Nadīpati (m)** (*nadī* 'river' + *pati* 'lord') The lord of rivers; a name of the ocean.

**Nadīśa (m)** (*nadī* 'river' + *īśa* 'lord') The lord of rivers; a name for the ocean.

**Nagapati (m)** (*naga* 'unmoving, mountain' + *pati* 'lord') The lord of the mountains; a name of Himavan.

**Nagarāja (m)** (*naga* 'unmoving, mountain' + *rāja* 'king') The king of mountains; a name of Himavan.

**Nagādhipa (m)** (*naga* 'unmoving, mountain' + *adhipa* 'overlord') The overlord of the mountains; a name of Himavan.

**Nagādhirāja (m)** (*naga* 'unmoving, mountain' + *adhirāja* 'paramount king') The paramount king of the mountains; a name of Himavan.

**Nagendra (m)** (*naga* 'unmoving, mountain' + *indra* 'chief') The chief of the mountains; a name of Himavan.

**Nageśwara (m)** (*naga* 'unmoving, mountain' + *īśwara* 'lord') The lord of the mountains; a name of Himavan.

**Nakshatra (m or n)** A heavenly body or star.

**Nakula (m)** 1. A mongoose. 2. The name of the Pāṇḍava brother who was the twin brother of Sahadeva by the two Aświns deities through Mādrī. 3. A name of Lord Śiva who, like the mongoose, is immune from the venom of serpents.

**Nalinī (f)** 1. She who is like the lotus. 2. The gentle one.

**Namasya (m), Namasyā (f)** 1. The worshipful, worthy of salutation. 2. The worshipping, saluting.

**Nambudiri (m)** The name of a South Indian tradition of Brāhmaṇas.

**Nanda (m)** 1. The joyous. 2. The name of Śrī Kṛishṇa's foster father. 3. The 528th name of Lord Vishṇu as listed in the Vishṇu Sahasranāma. In his commentary, Śrī Śaṅkara states, "Being rich with all wealths, the Lord is called *Nanda*."

**Nandi (m)** 1. The happy or joyful. 2. The name of Lord Śiva's bull, representative of Dharma. 3. A name of Lord Vishṇu expressing His blissful nature. 4. A name of Lord Śiva expressing His blissful nature.

**Nandinī (f)** 1. Having or enjoying bliss. 2. A name of Vasishṭha's cow of plenty. 3. A name of the Goddess Durgā. 4. A name of the Goddess Gangā.

**Nandirudra (m)** (*nandi* 'joyous' + *rudra* 'roaring, terrific') The joyful Rudra; a name of Lord Śiva.

**Nandī (m)** 1. The happy or joyful. 2. The name of Lord Śiva's bull, representative of Dharma. 3. A name of Lord Vishṇu expressing His blissful nature. 4. A name of Lord Śiva expressing His blissful nature.

**Nandīśwara (m)** (*nandi* 'joyous' +*īśwara* 'lord') The Lord of Nandi; a name of Lord Śiva.

**Nara (m)** 1. Self, man, leader. 2. The 246th name of Lord Vishṇu as listed in the Vishṇu Sahasranāma. In his commentary Śrī Śaṅkara quotes Vyāsa, "The supreme Self, the Eternal, who leads (nayati) all, is called *Nara*, the leader." 3. The name of a divine ascetic who with Nārāyaṇa is worshipped in Bādrināth and said to be reborn as Arjuna and Śrī Kṛishṇa.

**Narahari (m)** (*nara* 'man' + *hari* 'tawny, lion') 1. Man-lion. 2. A name of Lord Vishṇu referring to His fourth incarnation.

**Narapriya (m)** (*nara* 'man' + *priya* 'beloved') 1. The beloved of mankind. 2. The favorable to mankind.

**Narasimhan (m)** (*nara* 'man' + *simha* 'lion') 1. The Man-Lion. 2. The name of Lord Vishṇu's fourth incarnation. There was a demon king by the name of Hiraṇyakaśipu whose son, Prahlāda, was a great devotee of Lord Vishṇu. His son's devotion so enraged Hiraṇyakaśipu that he tried to kill the boy. Lord

Vishṇu protected Prahlāda and then took the form of a man-lion and killed the demon who was invincible to Gods, men and beasts. Another story of *Narasimhan* exists in Śrī Śaṅkara's biography. It is reported that once Śrī Śaṅkara was about to have his head chopped off by a fierce opponent. His disciple, Padmapāda, who lived far from the scene of the impending execution, suddenly saw the whole incident. As Padmapāda had attained perfection in the worship of Lord *Narasimhan,* he identified himself with that form of God and destroyed his master's opponent just as Lord *Narasimhan* had destroyed the evil Hiraṇyakaśipu.

**Naravīra (m)** (*nara* 'man' + *vīra* 'hero') 1. A heroic man. 2. Hero among men.

**Narādhāra (m)** (*nara* 'man' + *ādhāra* 'supporter') 1. The supporter of mankind. 2. A name of Lord Śiva.

**Narendra (m)** (*nara* 'man' + *indra* 'chief') The chief of mankind.

**Nareśa (m)** (*nara* 'man + *īśa* 'lord') The Lord of mankind.

**Nareśwara (m)** (*nara* 'man' + *īśwara* lord') The Lord of mankind.

**Narmadā (f)** She who gives pleasure; the name of the fifth of the seven holy rivers invoked during the sipping of water in a pūjā.

**Narmadeśwara (m)** (*narmadā* 'name of a river' + *īśwara* 'lord') The Lord of the river Narmadā; a name of Lord Śiva who is associated with the holy river Narmadā.

**Narya (m)** 1. The powerful, heroic. 2. Manly, human.

**Naṭana (m)** Dancing; a name of Lord Śiva referring to His fivefold dance which creates, preserves, destroys, veils and blesses.

**Naṭarāja (m)** (*naṭa* 'dancer' + *rāja* 'king') The king of dancers; a name of Lord Śiva referring to His dancing form.

**Naṭavara (m)** (*naṭa* 'dancer' + *vara* 'best') The best of dancers; a name of Lord Śiva referring to His dancing form.

**Naṭeśa (m)** (*naṭa* 'dancer' + *īśa* 'lord') The Lord of dancers; a name of Lord Śiva referring to His dancing form.

**Naṭeśwara (m)** (*naṭa* 'dancer' + *īśwara* 'lord') The Lord of dancers; a name of Lord Śiva referring to His dancing form.

**Naṭeśwarī (f)** The consort of Naṭeśwara (i.e. Lord Śiva); a name of the Goddess Pārvatī.

**Nati (f)** Bowing or humble.

**Navīna (m), Navīnā (f)** Youthful.

**Nābha (m)** 1. The (heart) center. 2. A name of Lord Śiva referring to His residing in the lotus heart.

**Nābhasa (m), Nābhasī (f)** The celestial.

**Nādabindu (m)** (*nāda* 'sound' + *bindu* 'dot') 1. The sound and the dot. 2. The name of the crescent and the dot (ṁ) written over the Sanskrit monosyllable "OM" which represent its manifested and unmanifested name and form. The crescent or *nāda* also represents the roof of the palate above which the dot or *bindu* is hummed or nasalized while repreating the Praṇava. 3. The name of a minor Upanishad.

**Nāgarāja (m)** (*nāga* 'serpent' + *rāja* 'king') 1. The king of serpents. 2. A name of Lord Vishṇu's divine serpent Ananta or Śesha. 3. A name of Lord Śiva who wears serpents as a mark of immortality.

**Nāgāri (m)** (*nāga* 'serpent' + *ari* 'enemy') 1. The enemy of serpents. 2. A name of Lord Vishṇu's divine vehicle, the eagle Garuḍa.

**Nāgendra (m)** (*nāga* 'serpent' + *indra* 'king') 1. The chief of serpents. 2. A name of Lord Vishṇu's divine serpent Ananta or Śesha. 3. A name of Lord Śiva who wears serpents as a mark of immortality.

**Nāgeśa (m)** (*nāga* 'serpent' + *īśa* 'lord ') 1. The Lord of serpents. 2. A name of Lord Vishṇu's divine serpent Ananta or Śesha. 3. A name of Lord Śiva who wears serpents as a mark of immortality. 4. A name of Maharshi Patañjali who is an incarnation of Śesha.

**Nāgeśwarī (f)** (*nāga* 'serpent' + *īśwarī* 'sovereign goddess') The Goddess of serpents; a name of the Goddess Manasā, sister of Ananta or Śesha, who protects mankind from the venom of serpents.

**Nākanadī (f)** (*nāka* 'heaven' + *nadī* 'river') The celestial or heavenly river; a name of the Holy Ganges as the Milky Way.

**Nākanātha (m)** (*nāka* 'heaven' + *nātha* 'lord') The Lord of heaven; a name of Indra.

**Nākapati (m)** (*nāka* 'heaven' + *pati* 'lord') The Lord of heaven; a name of Indra.

**Nākādhipa (m)** (*nāka* 'heaven' + *adhipa* 'overlord') The overlord of heaven; a name of Indra.

**Nākeśa (m)** (*nāka* 'heaven' + *īśa* 'lord') The Lord of heaven; a name of Indra.

**Nākeśwara (m)** (*nāka* 'heaven' + *īśwara* 'lord') The Lord of heaven; a name of Indra.

**Nākin (m), Nākinī (f)** One who dwells in heaven.

**Nārada (m)** 1. The son of Brahmā. 2. The name of the great Devarshi or divine seer. He is a messenger between Gods and men and a devotee of Lord Vishṇu. He is the seer of several hymns of the Rigveda, and is believed to have composed several works, including the Bhakti-Sūtras. He wanders playing the Vīṇā. In the Chāndogya Upanishad, *Nārada* is taught knowledge of the Infinite by the revered Sanatkumāra, another son of Brahmā. By a gradual process the Guru Sanatkumāra leads his disciple *Nārada* from coarse levels to subtler and subtler ones, until they reach the highest level of infinitude and immensity named "Bhūman." Two of the famous passages from the Chāndogya Upanishad that recount these teachings are as follows: "The knower of the Self crosses over sorrow" and "That which is verily infinite, is alone Bliss. There is no bliss in the finite." Praised as the jewel of wandering monks, *Nārada* becomes the teacher of Śaunaka and other Maharshis in the *Nārada*-Parivrājaka Upanishad of the Atharvaveda, which is an extensive teaching on Sannyāsa. Also see the Bhagavad Gītā X:13,26.

**Nārāṇi (f), Nārāṇī (f)** [Tamil] 1. The consort of Lord Nārāyaṇa (i.e. Lord Vishṇu). 2. A name of the Goddess Lakshmī.

**Nārāyaṇa (m)** (*nāra* 'products of the Self' + *āyaṇa* 'abode') 1. The abode of beings. 2. The 245th name of Lord Vishṇu as listed in the Vishṇu Sahasranāma. In his commentary Śrī Śaṅkara states: "'*Nara*' means Ātman or the Self. Space and other effects that proceed from It are called *Nāras*, the products of *Nara*. The Lord spreads these effects and as their cause, pervades them. These products of *Nara* are therefore His abode (*ayanam*), and He is thus called *Nārāyaṇa*, the Abode of His own products. In the *Mahā-Nārāyaṇa* Upanishad it is written, 'The whole universe, whatever is seen or heard inside and outside, having pervaded all that, the Lord *Nārāyaṇa* stands.' In the Mahābhārata it is written, 'Sages know as *Nāras* the principles born from *Nara* or God. As these are His abode, He is thus named *Nārāyaṇa*, the Abode of the *Nāras*.' The Lord is also thus called because He is the abode of living beings (*nāras, jīvas*) during world dissolution...Another definition is given by Manu, 'The waters are called *Nāras*, waters which are verily born from *Nara* or God.

Since they were originally His abode, He is therefore called *Nārāyaṇa*, the Abode of the *Nāras* or waters.' Finally, a fourth definition is offered in the Narasimha Purāṇa, 'Namo *Nārāyaṇāya*! Salutation unto *Nārāyaṇa*! This is the mantra meant for the destruction of the deadly poison of transmigration. This do I proclaim very loudly with uplifted hands. Let the renouncing strivers (Yatis or Sannyāsins) of pure minds and subdued passions listen!'"

**Nārāyaṇī (f)** The consort of Nārāyaṇa (i.e. of Lord Vishṇu); a name of the Goddess Lakshmī.

**Nārī (f)** 1. Woman. 2. The name of a daughter of Mount Meru.

**Nārya (m)** 1. The powerful, heroic. 2. Manly, human.

**Nātha (m)** The Lord or ruler. This name of God is explained in different passages by Śrī Śaṅkara as, sought, shining, blessing and ruling.

**Nāṭyapriya (m)** (*nāṭya* 'dancing' + *priya* 'fond of, beloved') Fond of dancing; a name of Lord Śiva.

**Nāyaka (m)** The (spiritual) guide.

**Netā (m)** 1. Leader, guide. 2. The 222nd name of Lord Vishṇu as listed in the Vishṇu Sahasranāma. In his commentary, Śrī Śaṅkara states, "As regulating the machine of the universe, the Lord is called the leader."

**Netra (m)** 1. Leader, guide. 2. A name for the eyes as they lead beings.

**Netrī (f)** 1. Leader, guide. 2. A name of the Goddess Lakshmī.

**Nidhruvi (m)** 1. Ever-faithful, constant. 2. A name of a Ṛishi who was a descendant of Ṛishi Kaśyapa and one of the seers of the Ṛigveda.

**Nikhileśwara (m)** (*nikhila* 'entire, all' + *īśwara* 'lord') The sovereign Lord of all.

**Nikhileswarī (f)** (*nikhila* 'entire, all' + *īswarī* 'sovereign goddess') The sovereign Goddess of all.

**Niraghan (m), Niraghā (f)** (*niḥ* 'without' + *agha* 'sin') Sinless, faultless.

**Nirahaṅkāra (m)** (*niḥ* 'without' + *ahaṅkāra* 'ego') Egoless, without the notion of being the doer.

**Nirañjana (m)** (*niḥ* 'without' + *añjana* 'black substance') 1. Spot-less, pure. 2. A name of Lord Śiva, which occurs in the following passage of the Śwetāśwatara

Upanishad:

*Nishkalam Nishkriyam Śāntam*
*Niravadyam Nirañjanam...*

Partless, actionless, peaceful,
faultless, spotless...

3. A name for a sage, which occurs in the following passage in the Muṇḍaka Upanishad:

*Nirañjanaḥ Paramam Sāmyam-upaiti.*

The spotless one attains the supreme sameness (of Brahman).

**Nirañjanā (f)** (*niḥ* 'without' + *añjanā* 'black substance') 1. Spotless, pure. 2. A name of the Goddess Durgā. 3. A name of the day of the full moon.

**Nirantara (m), Nirantarā (f)** (*niḥ* 'without' + *antara* 'interval, difference') 1. Undifferentiated, uninterrupted. 2. Without interior, as said in the Bṛihad-Āraṇyaka Upanishad:

*Ayam-Ātmānantaro'bāhyaḥ...*

This Self is without interior or exterior...

**Nirapāya (m)** (*niḥ* 'without' + *pāya* 'end, decay') Imperishable. See the Bhagavad Gītā II:17.

**Nirargala (m), Nirargalā (f)** (*niḥ* 'without' + *argala* 'obstacle') Unimpeded.

**Niravadhi (m)** (*niḥ* 'without' + *avadhi* 'limit') Endless, limitless.

**Nirābādha (m)** (*niḥ* 'without' + *ādbādha* 'trouble, pain, harm') The troubleless, painless or harmless.

**Nirādhāra (m), Nirādhārī (f)** (*niḥ* 'without' + *ādhara* 'support') Without support, independent.

**Nirākula (m)** (*niḥ* 'not' + *ākula* 'confused, perplexed') Unconfused, unaffected. See the Bhagavad Gītā XIV:2.

**Nirālamba (m)** (*niḥ* 'without' + *ālamba* 'support') Without support, independent. This name occurs in the following śloka:

*Namaḥ Śivāya Gurave*
*Saccidānanda-Mūrtaye,*
*Nish-prapañcāya Śāntāya*
*Nir-ālambāya Tejase!*

Salutation to the Auspicious, the Master,
the Image of Truth-Knowledge-Bliss,
the Omnipresent, the Peaceful,
the Independent, the Effulgent!

**Nirbhava (m)** (*niḥ* 'without' + *bhava* 'birth') Birthless. See the Bhagavad Gītā II:20; XIV:2.

**Nirbhaya (m)** (*niḥ* 'without' + *bhaya* 'fear') Fearless. The following passage occurs in the Bṛihad-Āraṇyaka Upanishad:

*Abhayam Vai Brahma*
*Abhayam Hi Vai Brahma Bhavati*
*Ya Evam Veda.*

Fearless indeed is Brahman.
The fearless Brahman verily does
one become who knows (the Self) thus.

**Nirbheda (m), Nirbhedā (f), Nirbhedinī (f)** (*niḥ* 'without' + *bheda* 'difference') Without separation or differentiation. See the Bhagavad Gītā XIII:16; XVIII:20.

**Nirdosha (m)** (*niḥ* 'without' + *dosha* 'defect') 1. Without defect, faultless. 2. A name of Śiva. See the Bhagavad Gītā V:15,19; IX:29.

**Nirguṇa (m), Nirguṇā (f)** (*niḥ* 'without' + *guṇa* 'attribute, fetter') 1. The attributeless, fetterless. 2. The 840th name of Lord Vishṇu as listed in the Vishṇu Sahasranāma. In his commentary Śrī Śaṅkara states, "Being truly devoid of attributes, the Lord is called the attributeless. In the Śwetāśwatara Upanishad it is written, 'He is the witness, the pure consciousness, the single and the attributeless.'" See the Bhagavad Gītā XIII:14, 31; XIV:19-26.

**Nirlepa (m)** (*niḥ* 'without' + *lepa* 'stain') 1. Stainless. 2. A name of Lord Śiva. See the Bhagavad Gītā III:28; IV:14,22; V:7,10; IX:9; XIII: 31-2; XVIII:17.

**Nirlobha (m)** (*niḥ* 'without' + *lobha* 'greed') Without greed. See the Bhagavad Gītā XVI:21-2.

**Nirmada (m)** (*niḥ* 'without' + *mada* 'passion, pride') Passionless, prideless.

**Nirmalā (f)** (*niḥ* 'without' + *malā* 'stain') 1. Immaculate. 2. One who is free from the thirteen impurities: rāga (attraction), dwesha (repulsion), kāma (desire), krodha (anger), lobha (greed), moha (delusion), madā (passion), mātsarya (envy), īrshya (spite), asūyā (jealousy), dambha (ostentation), darpa (arrogance), ahaṅkāra (I-ness or doer-ness).

**Nirmama (m)** (*niḥ* 'without' + *mama* 'mine') Without mineness. See the Bhagavad Gītā II:71; III:30; XII:13; XVIII:53.

**Nirmoha (m)** (*niḥ* 'without' + *moha* 'delusion') 1. Free from illusion, undeluded. 2. A name of Lord Śiva. See the Bhagavad Gītā II:13; IV:35; V:20; VII:28; VIII:27; XV:5.

**Nirmohinī (f)** (*niḥ* 'without' + *mohinī* 'deluded') Free from illusion, undeluded. See the Bhagavad Gītā II:13; IV:35; V:20; VII:28; VIII:27; XV:5.

**Nirnāśa (m), Nirnāśinī (f)** (*niḥ*' without + *nāśa/nāśinī* 'death') Deathless. See the Bhagavad Gītā II:17-21; VIII:20; IX:31; XIII:25,27.

**Nirodha (m)** Restraint. See the Yogasūtras I:2,51; III:9.

**Niruddha (m)** Self-restrained.See the Bhagavad Gītā VI:12,20; VIII:12.

**Niruja (m)** Diseaseless, healthy.

**Nirvāṇa (m) (n)** 1. Bliss, liberation. 2. The 577th name of Lord Vishṇu as listed in the Vishṇu Sahasranāma. In his commentary Śrī Śaṅkara states, "Having the nature of supreme Bliss characterized by the cessation of all pain, the Lord is called *Nirvāṇam.*" See the Bhagavad Gītā II: 72; V: 24-6; VI: 15.

**Nirvikalpa (m)** (*niḥ* 'without' + *vikalpa* 'doubt') Without thought. In his Dṛig-Dṛiśya-Viveka, Śrī Bhāratī Tīrtha describes *Nirvikalpa* Samādhi thus:

*Swānubhūti-Rasāveśād*
*Dṛiśya-Śabdāv'upekshya Tu,*
*Nirvikalpas Samādhis Syān'*
*Nivāta-Sthita-Dīpa-Vat.*

Due to absorption in the bliss of Self-realization,
disregarding objects and sounds,
the non-thinking (*Nirvikalpa*) Samādhi occurs,
similar to a lamp in a windless place.

See the Bhagavad Gītā V:17, 19, 24; VI: 19, 25.

**Nirvikāra (m)** (*niḥ* 'without' + *vikāra* 'change, variation') Unchanging. See the Bhagavad Gītā II: 25.

**Nishkalaṅka (m)** (*niḥ* 'without' + *kalaṅka* 'stain') 1. Without stain, faultless. 2. A name of Lord Śiva.

**Nishkāma (m)** (*niḥ* 'without' + *kāma* 'desire') The desireless. See the Bhagavad Gītā II: 55-6, 70-1; III: 18, 37-43; IV: 14, 19, 21; V: 3, 12, 22-3, 26, 28; VI: 10, 18, 24; XII: 17; XIV: 22; XV: 5; XVI: 21-4; XVII: 11, 17; XVIII: 49, 53-4.

**Nishkāmukā (f)** (*niḥ* 'not' + *kāmukā* 'desirous') The desireless. See the Bhagavad Gītā II: 55-6, 70-1; III: 18, 37-43; IV: 14, 19, 21; V: 3, 12, 22-3, 26, 28; VI: 10, 18, 24; XII: 17; XIV: 22; XV: 5; XVI: 21-4; XVII: 11, 17; XVIII: 49, 53-4.

**Nishkāraṇa (m)** (*niḥ* 'without' + *kāraṇa* 'cause') The causeless. The following passage occurs in the Śwetāśwatara Upanishad:

*Ya Īse'sya Jagato Nityam-Eva*
*Nānyo Hetur-Vidyata Īśanāya.*

There is no other Cause than the Lord
for the eternal Lordship of this universe.

Lord Yama says in the Kaṭha Upanishad:

*Na Jāyate Mriyate Vā Vipaścin'*
*Nāyam Kutaścin'na Babhūva Kaścit.*

The Conscious One is neither born nor does It die.
It did not come from anything nor did anything come from It.

In his Brahmasūtras Vyāsa states:

*Nātmāśruter-Nityatwāc'ca Tābhyaḥ.*

The soul has no (cause), for the Upanishads
do not teach this and its eternity is known from them.

See the Bhagavad Gītā II: 20; XIII: 12.

**Nishpāra (m)** (*niḥ* 'without' + *pāra* 'limit') The boundless. See the Bhagavad Gītā VI:28.

**Nishṭhā (f)** 1. The highest abode. The 583rd name of Lord Vishṇu as listed in the Vishṇu Sahasranāma. In his commentary Śrī Śaṅkara states, "The Lord is called *Nishtha,* the highest abode, as in Him alone abide (*tishṭhanti*) highly (*nitarām*) all beings during world dissolution." 2. Firm devotion. In his Brahmasūtras Vyāsa states, "Liberation is taught to one firmly devoted to Truth (*Tan'nishṭha*)." Firm devotion is also mentioned regarding the Guru in the Muṇḍaka Upanishad:

*Tad-Vijñānārtham Sa Gurum-Evābhigacchet*
*Samitpāṇiś Śrotriyam Brahma-Nishṭham.*

To know that Truth, with sacrificial offerings in hand,
one should approach a Guru only, versed in the Vedas
and firmly devoted to Brahman.

3. Culmination. In the Bhagavad Gītā (XVIII:50), The Lord calls the attainment of Brahman as, "*Nishṭhā Jñānasya Yā Parā,*" "the supreme culmination of knowledge," and He briefly expounds the means to its attainment up to verse 55.

**Niścalā (f)** (*niḥ* 'without' + *calā* 'moving') The unwavering, unshaking. See the Bhagavad Gītā II: 24, 41, 53; V: 18-20; VI: 13, 19-26; X: 7; XIV: 23; XVIII: 33.

**Nistula (m)** (*niḥ* 'without' + *tula* 'equality') Without equal, incomparable. See the Bhagavad Gītā VI: 22; VII: 2, 7; XI: 43.

**Nitai (m)** [Bengali] Name of Gauraṅga's disciple.

**Niṭalāksha (m)** (*niṭala* 'forehead' + *aksha* 'eye') One who has an eye on the forehead; a name of Lord Śiva, referring to His having an eye on His forehead. This third eye of Lord Śiva represents the fire of knowledge, with which He reduced Kāmadeva, or Cupid, to ashes. See the Bhagavad Gītā IV: 19, 37; V: 27; VIII: 10, 12; X: 11; XI: 8; XIII: 34; XV: 10.

**Niṭalekshaṇa (m)** (*niṭala* 'forehead' + *īkshaṇa* 'eye') One who has an eye on the forehead; a name of Lord Śiva, referring to His having an eye on His forehead. This third eye of Lord Śiva represents the fire of knowledge, with which He reduced Kāmadeva, or Cupid, to ashes. See the Bhagavad Gītā IV:19, 37; V:27; VIII:10, 12; X:11; XI:8; XIII:34; XV:10.

**Nityan (m)** The eternal. See the Bhagavad Gītā II:17-21, 24; VIII:20-1; X:2-3, 12-3; XIII:12; XV:7.

**Nityā (f)** 1. The eternal. See the Bhagavad Gītā II:17-21, 24; VIII:20-1; X:2-3,

12-3; XIII:12; XV:7. 2. A name of the Goddess Durgā.

**Nivṛitti (f)** (*ni* 'non' + *vṛitti* 'activity') Non-activity, renunciation. In his commentary on the Bhagavad Gītā Śrī Śaṅkara states:

*Dwividho hi Vedo'kto Dharmaḥ*
*Pravṛitti-lakshaṇo Nivṛitti-lakshaṇaś-ca*
*Jagatas sthiti-kāraṇam.*

Verily, the twofold Dharma (duty) declared
in the Vedas, as characterized by action
(Pravṛitti) and by renunciation (*Nivṛitti*), is
the cause of the world stability.

The Ācārya further describes the path of renunciation or *Nivṛitti*-Mārga as being characterized by knowledge (Jñāna) and dispassion (Vairāgya). Thus by action or Karma Yoga one's mind is purified and by renunciation or Jñāna Yoga one is enlightened and liberated. See the Bhagavad Gītā II:39; III:3,17-8; V:13; VI:3,10, 24-5; XII:16; XIV:25; XV:4-6; XVIII:30,49 and the Yogasūtras IV:25,30.

**Nīlagala (m)** (*nīla* 'blue' + *gala* 'neck, throat') The blue-throated or blue-necked; a name of Lord Śiva whose throat became dark-blue when He drank a deadly poison and retained it in His throat. This happened when the gods and demons were churning the milk ocean to gain the nectar of Immortality. In the course of the churning, the serpent Vāsuki, who was serving as a rope, emitted a deadly venom threatening to destroy the whole universe. Out of compassion Lord Śiva drank the poison. Churning the milk ocean represents Sādhana (i.e. spiritual practice performed to achieve liberation, and the poison represents the obstacles which one has to face and which can be overcome through the Lord's grace). See the Bhagavad Gītā XVIII:36-39.

**Nīlagrīva (m)** (*nīla* 'blue' + *grīva* 'neck, throat') The blue-throated or blue-necked; a name of Lord Śiva. [See **Nīlagala**]

**Nīlakaṇṭha (m)** (*nīla* 'blue' + *kaṇṭha* 'throat') The blue-throated; a name of Lord Śiva. [See **Nīlagala**]

**Nīrajāksha (m), Nīrajākshī (f)** (*nīraja* 'lotus' + *aksha/akshī* 'eye') The lotus-eye

**Nīti (f)** 1. Wisdom personified 2. Discretion. 3. Practical morality.

**Nītiman (m)** (*nīti* 'wisdom personified' + man 'having') One whose conduct is based on wisdom. See the Bhagavad Gītā X:38; XVI:23-4; XVIII:78.

# O

**Ojasīna (m), Ojasīnā (f)** Having *ojas*—a type of vital energy (prāṇa-balam) and mental strength which is produced when the retas (semen) flows upwards instead of downwards.

**Ojaswan (m), Ojaswatī (f)** (*ojāḥ* 'vital energy, mental strength' + *van/vatī* 'having') Having *ojas*—a type of vital energy (*prāṇa-balam*) and mental strength which is produced when the retas (semen) flows upwards instead of downwards.

**Ojaswin (m)** (*ojāḥ* 'vital energy, mental strength' + *vin* 'having') 1. Having *ojas*—a type of vital energy (*prāṇa-balam*) and mental strength which is produced when the retas (semen) flows upwards instead of downwards. 2. A name of Lord Śiva.

**Ojaswinī (f)** (*ojāḥ* 'vital energy, mental strength' + *vinī* 'having') Having ojas—a type of vital energy (prāṇa-balam) and mental strength.

**Ojasya (m), Ojasyā (f)** Having *ojās*—a type of vital energy (prāṇa-balam) and mental strength which is produced when the retas (semen) flows upwards instead of downwards.

**Ojās (m)** One who has *ojas* -- a type of vital energy (prāṇa-balam) and mental strength which is produced when the retas (semen) flows upwards instead of downwards. See the Bhagavad Gītā VII:11; XV:13; XVIII:33.

**Ojman (m)** Having *ojas*—a type of vital energy (prāṇa-balam) and mental strength which is produced when the retas (semen) flows upwards instead of downwards.

**Ojobalā (f)** (*ojaḥ* 'vital energy, mental strength' + *balā* 'powerful') 1. She who is powerful from ojas—a type of vital energy (prāṇa-balam) and mental strength. 2. The name of a goddess associated with the Bodhi Tree in Buddhism.

**Ojopati (m)** (*ojaḥ* 'vital energy, mental strength' + *pati* 'lord') 1. The lord of ojas—a type of vital energy (prāṇa-balam) and mental strength which is produced when the retas (semen) flows upwards instead of downwards. 2. The name of a god associated with the Bodhi Tree in Buddhism.

**Oman (m), Omā (f)** 1. Friend. 2. Protector.

**Omātrā (f)** 1. Friend. 2. Protector.

**Omkāra (m)** (*OM* 'name and symbol of the Absolute' + *kāra* 'word') The word, syllable or sound *OM*, which names and represents Brahman or the Absolute. The syllable *OM* is the most sacred word of the Vedas. It came from the throat of Brahmā. Its Vedāntic philosophy is revealed in the famous Māṇḍūkya Upanishad and expounded by the great Gauḍapāda in his Kārikās. In the Kaṭha Upanishad, Yama says to Naciketā, "I tell you briefly of that Goal which all the Vedas in one voice propound, of which all the austerities speak, and wishing for which people practise Brahmacarya: it is this, viz. *OM*...This support is the best; it is the conditioned as well as the unconditioned Brahman. Meditating on this support, one becomes glorified in the sphere of Brahman." An inspiring verse in praise of *OM* is as follows:

*Omkāram Nigamai'ka-Vedyam-Aniśam*
*Vedānta-Tattwāspadam*
*Co'tpatti-Sthiti-Nāśa-Hetum-Amalam*
*Viśwasya Viśwātmakam,*
*Viśwa-Trāṇa-Parāyaṇam*
*Śruti-Śatais Samprocyamānam Vibhum*
*Satya-Jñānam-Ananta-Mūtim-Amalam*
*Śuddhātmakam Tam Bhaje.*

I always worship the sacred Word *OM* which is solely
knowable through Scriptures, which is eternal and
the Seat of Vedāntic Truth, which is the spotless
cause of the appearance, maintenance and disappearance
of the universe, the Self of all, the saving and
supreme destination of all, the All-pervading proclaimed by
hundreds of Vedic Scriptures, the pure image of Truth,
Knowledge and Infinity, and which is pure by nature.

See the Bhagavad Gītā VIII:13; IX:17; X:25; XVII:23-4.

**Oshadhipati (m)** (*oshadhi* 'herb' + *pati* 'lord') 1. The lord of herbs. 2. A name of the Moon-God. See the Bhagavad Gītā XV:13.

# P

**Padmadhāriṇī (f)** (*padma* 'lotus' + *dhāriṇī* 'holder') 1. The lotus-holder. 2. A name of the Goddess Lakshmī.

**Padmaja (m)** (*padma* 'lotus' + *ja* 'born') 1. The lotus-born. 2. A name of Lord Brahmā as born from and seated on the lotus-navel of Lord Vishṇu. See the Bhagavad-Gita XI:15.

**Padmamukhī (f)** (*padma* 'lotus' + *mukhī* 'face') The lotus-faced, the 96th of the Goddess Lakshmī's 108 names.

**Padmanābha (m)** (*padma* 'lotus' + *nābha* 'navel') 1. The lotus-naveled. 2. The 49th, 196th and 346th name of Lord Vishṇu as listed in the Vishṇu Sahasranāma. In his commentary Śrī Śaṅkara states, "1) The Lord within whose navel stands the lotus symbolizing the cause of all the universe, is called the Lotus-Naveled. In a Vedic text it is written, 'In the navel of the birthless (Lord Vishṇu) all this is established.' 2) The Lord is also thus called on account of His well-rounded navel resembling a lotus. 3) Again, He is called thusly on account of His shining in the middle of the heart-lotus, or 4) because He stands in the pericarp of the lotus universe."

**Padmapāda (m)** (*padma* 'lotus' + *pāda* 'foot') 1. The lotus-footed. 2. The name of Śrī Śaṅkara's first and foremost disciple also known as Sanandana and considered as a partial incarnation of Lord Nārāyaṇa. In a biography of Śrī Śaṅkara, Śrī Vidyāraṇya Swāmī states, "...Moved by deep affection for the devoted disciple, Śrī Śaṅkara taught him his commentaries three times, revealing the highest Truth of the Vedas. This made the other disciples rather jealous of him. So in order to convince them of his inherent superiority, Śaṅkara one day called *Padmapāda* who was then standing on the opposite bank of the Ganges, to come to him immediately. Thereupon, when *Padmapāda* stepped into the Ganges with the conviction that devotion to the Feet of the Guru, which had enabled him to go across the ocean of transmigration, would surely not fail him in crossing this river, the holy Ganges brought out lotuses to support him wherever he placed his feet on her waters. When at last he reached his teacher after crossing the river in this incredible manner, Śaṅkara clasped him to his breast with overwhelming love and wonder, and gave him the name of *Padmapāda*, the Lotus-Footed."

**Padmaśrī (f)** (*padma* 'lotus' + *śrī* 'beauty') 1. Having the beauty of a lotus. 2. The Goddess *Śrī* (i.e. Lakshmī, seated on a lotus). 3. The Goddess *Śrī* (i.e. Lakshmī, holding lotuses).

**Padmavatī (f)** (*padma* 'lotus' + *vatī* 'having') 1. Having or holding lotuses. 2. A name of the Goddess Lakshmī.

**Padmā (f)** 1. The lotus-hued. 2. The 11th of the Goddess Lakshmī's 108 names. Having arisen from the milk ocean seated on a lotus and holding lotuses, the Goddess Lakshmi is thus associated and identified with the lotus flower, the symbol for the cause of the universe as well as the lotus-heart which is the seat of meditation.

**Padmākshī (f)** (*padma* 'lotus' + *akshī* 'eye') The lotus-eyed; the 43rd of the Goddess Lakshmī's 108 names.

**Padmālaya (m)** (*padma* 'lotus' + *ālaya* 'dweller') 1. The lotus-dweller. 2. A name of Lord Brahmā. See the Bhagavad-Gītā XI:15.

**Padmālayā (f)** (*padma* 'lotus' + *ālayā* 'dweller') The lotus-dweller; the 10th of the Goddess Lakshmī's 108 names.

**Padmāvatī (f)** (*padmā* 'lotus' + *vatī* 'having') Having or holding lotuses; a name of the Goddess Lakshmī.

**Padminī (f)** 1. Lotus-like. 2. Having lotuses. 3. The 51st of the Goddess Lakshmī's 108 names.

**Pakshin (m)** 1. Winged. 2. A name of the mythical bird Garuḍa, the vehicle of Lord Vishṇu. See the Bhagavad Gītā X:30. 3. A name of Lord Śiva referring to His having the two wings of the Ṛigveda and the Sāmaveda, the Yajurveda being the Lord's head. In the Taittirīya Upanishad it is stated, *"Tasya Yajur-eva Śirah, Ṛig-dakshiṇaḥ Pakshaḥ, Sāmo'ttaraḥ Pakshaḥ."* "Of Him, the Yajur-mantras are the head, the Ṛig-mantras are the right side, and the Sāma-mantras are the left side." 4. A name of the Self or Purusha, which is spoken of as a bird (*Pakshī*) in His association with the subtle body. In the Bṛihad-Āraṇyaka Upanishad, it is written, *"Puras Sa Pakshī Bhūtwā, Puraḥ Purusha Āviśat."* "Having first become a bird (the subtle body), that Purusha entered the bodies."

**Paṇḍita (m)** The learned or wise, the scholar, one who has acquired knowledge (*Paṇḍā*) from the Guru and the Scriptures. The need of true scholarship is declared in the Bṛihad-Āraṇyaka Upanishad thus:

*Tasmād Brāhamaṇaḥ Pāṇḍityam nirvidya*
*Bālyena tishṭhāset Bālyam ca Pāṇḍityam*
*ca nirvidya atha Muniḥ....*

Having known all about scholarship *(Pāṇḍityam),*
the Brāhmaṇa should try to live upon that strength

which comes of knowledge. Having known all about this strength and scholarship, he becomes meditative...

See the Bhagavad Gītā II:11; IV:19; V:18.

**Paṅkaja (m), Paṅkajā (f)** 1. Mud-born 2. Lotus.

**Paṅkajaja (m)** (*paṅkaja* 'lotus' + *ja* 'born') 1. Lotus-born. 2. Name of Lord Brahmā.

**Paṅkajanetra (m), Paṅkajanetrī (f)** (*paṅkaja* 'lotus' + *netra/ī* 'eye') 1. The lotus-eyed. 2. A name of Lord Vishṇu.

**Paṅkajāksha (m)** (*paṅkaja* 'mud-born, lotus' + *aksha* 'eye') 1. The lotus-eyed. 2. A name of Lord Vishṇu.

**Paṅkajākshī (f)** (*paṅkaja* 'mud-born, lotus' + *akshī* 'eye') The lotus-eyed.

**Para (m), Parā (f)** The supreme. See the Bhagavad Gītā II:59; III:42-3; V:16; VIII:10,20,22, 28; X:12; XI:37; XIII:12,22; XIV:19.

**Paradhāman (m)** (*para* 'supreme' + *dhāman* 'abode') The supreme abode of Lord Vishṇu, which is not different from the All-prevading Lord Himself. See the Bhagavad Gītā VIII:21; X:12; XI:38; XV:6.

**Parama (m)** [in Tamil **Paraman**], **Paramā (f), Paramikā (f)** The supreme, the highest. See the Bhagavad Gītā VIII:3,8,21; X:12, XI:18; XV:6.

**Paramātman (m)** (*parama* 'supreme' + *ātman* 'Self, Soul') 1. The supreme Self. 2. The 11th name of Lord Vishṇu as listed in the Vishṇu Sahasranāma. In his commentary Śrī Śaṅkara states, "That which is the Supreme and the Self is called *Paramātman*. He is distinct from cause and effect, and is by nature eternal, pure, conscious and free." See the Bhagavad Gītā VI:7; XIII:22,31; XV:17.

**Paramātmikā (f)** (*parama* 'supreme' + *ātmikā* 'nature') She whose nature is the Supreme; the 8th of the 108 names of the Goddess Lakshmī, who is the embodiment of Brahman's supreme Light. See the Bhagavad Gītā VI:7; XIII:22,31; XV:17.

**Parameshṭhin (m)** (*parame* 'in the Supreme' + *sthin* 'established') 1. Established in the Highest or Supreme. 2. A name of Lord Brahmā which indicates that He is the first-born of the Supreme and He dwells in the highest plane known as Brahmaloka or Satyaloka. 3. The 419th name of Lord Vishṇu as listed in the Vishṇu Sahasranāma. In his commentary Śrī Śaṅkara states, "The Lord whose nature is to abide *(sthātum)* in His own supreme *(parame)* glory, in the space of the heart, is called *Parameshṭhin* or 'Dwelling in the Supreme.' It is said in the Mantravarṇa, "The *Parameshṭhin* shines supremely.'" 4. A name of Lord Śiva.

**Parameśa (m)** (*parama* 'supreme' + *iśa* 'lord') 1. The supreme Lord. 2. A name of Lord Vishṇu.

**Parameśwara (m)** (*parama* 'supreme' + *iśwara* 'lord') 1. The supreme Lord. 2. The 377th name of Lord Vishṇu as listed in the Vishṇu Sahasranāma. In his commentary Śrī Śaṅkara states, "The Lord who is the Supreme and has a lordly nature is called *Parameśwara*, the supreme Lord." See the Bhagavad Gītā XI:3; XIII:27. 3. A name of Lord Śiva.

**Parameśwarī (m)** (*parama* 'supreme' + *īśwarī* 'sovereign goddess') 1. The supreme sovereign Goddess. 2. A name of the Goddess Durgā or Pārvatī.

**Paramodāra (m)** (*parama* 'supreme' + *udāra* 'great') The supremely great or generous.

**Paraśakti (f)** (*para* 'supreme' + *śakti* 'power, energy') 1. The supreme power. In the Śwetāśwatara Upanishad it is written, *"Parāsya Śaktir-vividhai'va śrūyate,"* "God's supreme power alone is heard (in the Vedas) to be various." See the Bhagavad Gītā IV:6; VII:14; IX:5,7-10,13; X:7; XI:5; XIV:3-4; XVIII:61. 2. God's power personified as a Goddess.

**Paraśurāma (m)** (*paraśu* 'ax' + *rāma* 'delight, name of a Divine Incarnation') Rāma with an ax; the name of Lord Vishṇu's sixth incarnation (before Śrī Rāma), who destroyed the warrior caste about to overpower the priestly caste. He was the son of Jamadagni and Reṇukā.

**Parāśara (m)** The destroyer; the name of the grandson of Vasishṭha and the father of Vyāsa, who was one of the seers of the Ṛigveda. In the Mahābhārata it is said that while the sage *Parāśara* was crossing the River Yamunā, he was attracted to a ferry-girl. He won her confidence by promising her an ever sweet fragrance that would replace the odor of fish and by telling her that she would remain a virgin even though she would bear an illustrious son. She was Satyavatī and her son became the great Vyāsa, a partial incarnation of Lord Vishṇu. *Parāśara*, being a great astrologer, knew that a child, conceived at a particular moment in time, would be born the greatest man of the age, a ray of Lord Vishṇu Himself.

**Parātpara (m)** (*parāt* 'than the highest' + *para* 'higher') Higher than the highest (i.e. than Prakṛiti). See the Bhagavad Gītā VII:7,13-4; VIII:20; IX:7-11; XI:43; XV:16-8.

**Pareshṭi (m)** (*para* 'supreme' + *ishṭi* 'sacrifice') Having the highest sacrifice or worship; a name of the Absolute.

**Pareśa (m)** (*para* 'supreme' + *iśa* 'lord') The supreme Lord. [See **Parameśwara**]

**Parivrājaka (m)** (*pari* 'about' + *vrājaka* 'wandering') The wanderer, itinerant. A name for the Paramahamsa Sannyāsins who wander from place to place for eight months of the year. In the Nārada-*Parivrājaka* Upanishad it is said, "*Swaswarūpajñaḥ Parivrāṭ,*" "The knower of one's own true Self is the wandering monk." See the Bhagavad Gītā II:64,71; XII:19.

**Parjanya (m)** 1. The Rain-God; a name of Indra referring to His presiding over the rain. 2. The 810th name of Lord Vishṇu as listed in the Vishṇu Sahasranāma. In his commentary Śrī Śaṅkara states, "The Lord who, like a rain-cloud *(parjanya),* extinguishes the threefold pain (Ādhyātmic, Ādhibhautic and Ādhidaivic) is called *Parjanya*, 'the Rain-God.' He is also thus called because He showers all objects of desire." See the Bhagavad Gītā III:14.

**Paśupati (m)** (*paśu* 'cattle' + *pati* 'lord') The Lord of creatures; a name of Lord Śiva.

**Pati (m)** Lord, master or ruler.

**Patitapāvana (m)** (*patita* 'fallen' + *pāvana* 'purifier') 1. The purifier of the fallen. 2. A name of Śrī Rāma. See the Bhagavad Gītā XII:7.

**Patnī (f)** Sovereign ruler, wife.

**Pavana (m)** 1. The purifying; a name of the Wind-God, Vāyu. 2. The 291st and 811th name of Lord Vishṇu as listed in the Vishṇu Sahasranāma. In his commentary Śrī Śaṅkara states, "He who purifies is called the Purifier, in accordance with the Lord's words in the Bhagavad Gītā (X:31), '*Pavanaḥ Pavatām-asmi,*' 'The Purifier of Purifiers I am' (i.e. the Wind-God Vāyu). It also means the Lord purifies by mere remembrance of Him."

**Pavitra (m)** 1. The pure. 2. The purifier. 3. The 63rd name of Lord Vishṇu as listed in the Vishṇu Sahasranāma. In his commentary Śrī Śaṅkara states, "The Ṛishi by whom one is purified or the Deity who purifies is a form of the Lord called '*Pavitra...*' It also means, He protects (*trāyate*) from the thunderbolt (*pavi*)." See the Bhagavad Gītā IV:38; IX:2,17; X:12.

**Payaspati (m)** (*payaḥ* 'milk, vital fluid' + *pati* 'lord') The Lord of milk; a name of Lord Vishṇu referring to His resting on the milk ocean while reclining on the divine serpent Śesha or Ananta.

**Pāla (m)** Guardian, protector.

**Pālaka (m)** Guardian, protector.

**Pālita (m)** The guarded or protected.

**Pāmsula (m)** 1. A name of Lord Śiva. 2. The staff and symbol of Lord Śiva, which is crossed at the upper end with transverse pieces representing the breast-bone and adjoining ribs and surmounted by a skull.

**Pāṇḍuranga (m)** (*pāṇḍu* 'whitish' + *raṅga* 'color') 1. Having a whitish hue. 2. The name of an incarnation of Lord Vishṇu or of Śrī Kṛishṇa who visited the city of Pandharpur in Deccan and blessed the Brāhmaṇa Puṇḍarīka for his great filial piety. He is also known as Viṭṭhala and is represented as standing on a brick with His arms akimbo.

**Pāpahara (m), Pāpaharaṇa (m)** (*pāpa* 'sin' + *hara/ṇa* 'remover') 1. The remover or destroyer of sins. 2. A name of Lord Śiva. 3. A name of Lord Vishṇu. See the Bhagavad Gītā IV:36; IX:30-2; XVIII:58, 66.

**Pārijāta (m)** The celestial coral tree, which is one of the five celestial trees fulfilling all desires and was produced at the churning of the milk ocean.

**Pārvatī (f)** The mountain-daughter; a name of Lord Śiva's consort who was reborn to Parvata or Himavan and Menā after she burnt herself to death when Lord Śiva was not invited to her former father Daksha's sacrifice.

**Pāśahantā (m), Pāśahantrī (f)** (*pāśa* 'bond' + *hantā/hantrī* 'destroyer') The bond-destroyer. See the Bhagavad Gītā II:39; III:31; IV:14,41; V:12; IX:9,28; XVIII:58.

**Pāṭalā (f)** 1. Red, pink. 2. A name of the Goddess Durgā who is described as being lustrous like the red flowers of the pomegranate.

**Pāvaka (m)** 1. Bright, pure, shining. 2. Purifying. 3. A name of the Fire-God, Agni. [See **Agni**] See also the Bhagavad Gītā X:23.

**Pāvana (m)** The Cause of blowing. The 292nd name of Lord Vishṇu as listed in the Vishṇu Sahasranāma. In his commentary Śrī Śaṅkara states, "He who causes blowing (*pāvayati)* is *Pāvana,* 'the Cause of blowing,' in accordance with the Taittirīya Upanishad saying: *'Bhīshāmād Vātaḥ pavate,'* 'Through fear of Him the wind blows.'"

**Pinākī (m)** The wielder of the bow; the fourth of Lord Śiva's 108 names. Lord Śiva's bow is also called *Pināka.* In the Rāmāyaṇa this bow is said to consist of the Vedas, and since the essence of the Vedas is the sacred syllable "OM," this bow may also represent the syllable "OM." In the Muṇḍaka Upanishad it is said:

> *Praṇavo Dhanuś Śaro hy'Ātmā*
> *Brahma tal'Lakshyam-ucyate.*
>
> The Praṇava (OM) is the bow, the (individual) Self
> is verily the arrow and Brahman is called its target.

**Piṇḍāra (m)** Religious mendicant.

**Pītavāsas (m)** (*pīta* 'yellow' + *vāsas* 'garment, dress') 1. The yellow-dressed or golden-dressed. 2. A name of Lord Vishṇu. 3. A name of Śrī Kṛishṇa. It is said that "the dark body of the Lord shines through the thin golden cloth just as the divine Truth shines through the sacred words of the Vedas."

**Pītāmbara (m)** (*pīta* 'yellow' + *ambara* 'garment') 1. The yellow or golden-dressed. 2. A name of Lord Vishṇu. 3. A name of Śrī Kṛishṇa. It is said that "the dark body of the Lord shines through the thin golden cloth just as the divine Truth shines through the sacred words of the Vedas."

**Prabhava (m)** 1. The origin or birth-place. 2. The 35th name of Lord Vishṇu as listed in the Vishṇu Sahasranāma. In his commentary Śrī Śaṅkara states, "As that from which the great elements come forth, the Lord is called the Origin. He is also thus called because He is of superior origin." See the Bhagavad Gītā IV:9; VII:6; IX:18; X:2,8.

**Prabhā (f)** 1. The light. See the Bhagavad Gītā V:16; VII: 8; VIII:9; X:11,21; XI:12; XIII:17,33; XV:12. 2. The effulgent rays surrounding the head of Lord Naṭarāja. 3. The 56th of the Goddess Lakshmī's 108 names.

**Prabhākara (m)** (*prabhā* 'light' + *kara* 'maker') 1. The light-maker. 2. A name of Sūrya, the Sun-God.

**Prabhāvan (m)** (*prabhā* 'light' + *van* 'having') Having light, luminous.

**Prabhāvana (m)** (*pra* 'forth' + *bhāvana* 'producing') The creator.

**Prabhāvatī (f)** (*prabha* 'light' + *vati* 'having') 1. Having light, luminous. 2. A name of the consort of Sūrya, the Sun-God.

**Prabhu (m)** 1. The Almighty; Lord or master. 2. The 36th and 299th name of Lord Vishṇu as listed in the Vishṇu Sahasranāma. In his commentary, Śrī Śaṅkara states, "Having surpassing might in all actions, the Lord is called

*Prabhu*, the Almighty. He is also thus called because He exists pre-eminently." See the Bhagavad Gītā V:14; IX:18,24; XI:4.

**Pradīpa (m)** The lamp-like, luminous or radiant. The Bhagavad-Gītā (X:11) compares Knowledge to a lamp removing the darkness of ignorance. Śrī Śaṅkara's comments on this passage are as follows: "The lamp of Knowledge has the form of discerning thought, is fed by the oil of pure devotion, fanned by the breeze of deep meditation upon the Lord and furnished with the wick of wisdom, perfected by means of Brahmacarya and other disciplines. It is held in the dispassionate internal organ, is placed in the wind-sheltered recess of the mind withdrawn from sense-objects and untainted by love and hate, and is shining with the Light of integral vision engendered by the constant practice of concentration and meditation."

**Prahlādan (m)** (*pra* 'forth' + *hlāda* 'rejoicing') 1. The joyful. See the Bhagavad Gītā X:30 2. The name of a great devotee of Lord Vishṇu, who was also the son of the king of demons, Hiraṇyakaśipu. His father, who was unassailable by gods, men, and animals, was so angered by his son's devotion that he tried to kill him, but Lord Vishṇu, taking the form of a Man-Lion came to his rescue and slayed his demon father.

**Prajāpati (m)** (*prajā* 'creatures' + *pati* 'lord') 1. The Lord of creatures. 2. A name of Lord Brahmā and of His ten mind-born sons, who were the progenitors of all beings. 3. A name of Kaśyapa. 4. The 69th and 197th names of Lord Vishṇu as listed in the Vishṇu Sahasranāma. In his commentary, Śrī Śaṅkara states, "Through His lordliness, the Lord is called *Prajāpati*, the Lord of all creatures or beings, which also means that He is the Father of all creatures." 5. The 53rd of Lord Śiva's 108 names.

**Prajāpāla (m)** (*prajā* 'creatures' + *pāla* 'protector') 1. The protector or guardian of creatures. 2. A name of Śrī Kṛishṇa.

**Prajeśa (m)** (*prajā* 'creatures' + *īśa* 'lord') 1. The Lord of creatures. 2. A name of Lord Brahmā and of His ten mind-born sons, who were the progenitors of all beings. 3. A name of Lord Śiva.

**Prajeśwara (m)** (*prajā* 'creatures' + *īśwara* 'lord') 1. The Lord of creatures. 2. A name of Lord Brahmā and of His ten mind-born sons, who were the progenitors of all beings. 3. A name of Lord Śiva.

**Prajña (m)** The wise, or supremely wise. See the Bhagavad Gītā II:11,54-72; XVII:14 and the Yogasūtras I:20,48; III:5.

**Prajñā (f)** 1. The wise, or supremely wise. See the Bhagavad Gītā II:11,54-72; XVII:14 and the Yogasūtras I:20,48; III:5. 2. Wisdom, knowledge personified as the Goddess Saraswatī.

**Prakāśa (m), Prakāśinī (f)** (*pra* 'forth' + *kāśa* 'shining') Luminous, shining forth. In his commentary of Śrī Śaṅkara's hymn to Dakshiṇāmūrti, Śrī Sureśwarācārya concludes with the following verse,

*Prakāśātmikayā Śaktyā*
*Prakāśānām Prabhākaraḥ,*
*Prakāśayati yo Viśwam*
*Prakāśo'yam Prakāśatām!*

The Light-Maker of luminaries
Who by His self-luminous power
illuminates the universe.
May this Light shine forth!

**Pramodana (m)** 1. The joyful, delightful. 2. The 525th name of Lord Vishṇu as listed in the Vishṇu Sahasranāma. In his commentary Śrī Śaṅkara states, "Ever enjoying the immortal nectar of His own Self, the Lord rejoices. It also means, He confers bliss to those who meditate on Him."

**Pramodinī (f)** The joyful, delightful.

**Praṇava (m)** 1. Praise or salutation (i.e. the syllable "OM"). 2. The 409th and 957th name of Lord Vishṇu as listed in the Vishṇu Sahasranāma. In his commentary Śrī Śaṅkara states, "The Lord who is praised (*praṇauti)* is called *Praṇava* or praise. It is written in the Vedas, 'The Lord of beings created the three worlds from which were born Fire, Wind and Sun. The three Vedas were born from them. From the three Vedas were born the words Bhuḥ, Bhuvaḥ and Swaḥ. From these the three letters A, U, and M were born. He joined these three letters together. That is this 'OM.' Therefore one praises *(praṇauti)* Him by saying 'OM.' Also, the Lord who is saluted *(praṇamyate)* is called *Praṇava*, salutation. Sanatkumāra states, 'As the Vedas salute (*praṇamanti*) Him, He is named *Praṇava*.' The name *'Praṇava'* is the syllable "OM" expressive of the supreme Self. Through a figurative identity with that, the Lord is called *Praṇava* (i.e. 'OM')." See the Bhagavad Gītā VII:8; VIII:13; IX:17; X:25 and the Yogasūtras I:27. [See **Omkara**]

**Praṇaya (m)** (Spiritual) leader.

**Prapatti (f)** Surrender of devotion. See the Bhagavad Gītā XV:4.

**Prasannā (f)** Pure, serene, gracious. See the Bhagavad-Gītā II: 64-5; XVIII:54.

**Prasavitrī (f)** The Mother.

**Prasāda (m), Prasādinī (f)** 1. Purity, serenity, grace. 2. A gift from God. 3. The remnants of food offerings made to the Lord and to the Guru, which represent a form of grace in which their devotees partake. See the Bhagavad Gītā II:64-5; XVII:16; XVIII:37, 56, 58, 62, 73 and the Yogasūtras I:33,47.

**Praśānta (m)** Calmed. See the Bhagavad Gītā VI:14,27; XVIII:53.

**Praśānti (f)** Supreme peace. See the Bhagavad Gītā II:70-1; IV:39; V:12,29; VI:15; IX:31; XII:12; XVI:2; XVIII:62.

**Pratāpa (m)** Glory; a name of Lord Śiva.

**Pratimā (f)** The image or symbol of God. See the Bhagavad Gītā X:17, 21-38, 41.

**Pratīka (m)** The image or symbol of God. See the Bhagavad Gītā X:17,21-38,41. In his Brahma-Sūtras, Vyāsa says that the symbol should be seen as God and not God as the symbol since God as such is nameless and formless. In other words, the symbol should be raised to God's level while God Himself should not be lowered or limited to the level of a mere symbol. Vyāsa states, *"Na Pratīke Na Hi Saḥ...Brahma-Dṛishṭir-Utkar-shāt,"* "One ought not to meditate on the Self in a symbol since He is not a symbol...The symbol is to be viewed as God, on account of its consequent exaltation." (IV,i:4,5)

**Pravrāj (m), Pravrājaka (m)** 1. The wanderer, itinerant. 2. A name for Sannyāsins who wander from place to place for eight months of the year. In the Nārada-*Parivrājaka* Upanishad it is said, "The knower of one's own true Self is the wandering monk." See the Bhagavad Gītā II:64,71; XII:19.

**Prājña (m)** 1. The wise, or supremely wise. See the Bhagavad Gītā II:11,54-72; XVII:14 and the Yogasūtras I:20,48; III:5. 2. The Self associated with the state of deep sleep.

**Prāṇa (m)** (*pra* 'forth' + *ana* 'breathing') 1. Life-force or life-breath. 2. The 67th, 320th and 407th names of Lord Vishṇu as listed in the Vishṇu Sahasranāma. In his commentary Śrī Śaṅkara states, "That which breathes forth (*prāṇiti)* is *Prāṇa*, the Knower of the field (i.e. the individual Self) or the supreme Self. It is written in the Kena Upanishad, 'He is the Prāṇa of prāṇa.' This name also means the main life (*Mukhya-Prāṇa).* Again, it means that as the thread-Self or cosmic subtle body, the Lord animates (*prāṇayati)* all beings. It is written in a Vedic text, 'I am verily Prāṇa.' As the Knower of the field (the individual Self), the Lord breathes. The Lord is also called Prāṇa due to His animating through Prāṇa. It is written in the Vishṇu Purāṇa, 'Having the nature of breathing, He sets in motion.'" See the Bhagavad Gītā IV:29; V:27; VII:5; VIII:10,12; XV:14. 3. Exhalation.

**Prāṇeśa (m)** (*prāṇa* 'vital life-force' + *īśa* 'lord') 1. The Lord of *prāṇas.* 2. A name of Lord Śiva. In the Kena Upanishad it is said: *"Sa u prāṇasya Prāṇaḥ,"* "He is the *Prāṇa* of *prāṇa.*"

**Prāṇeśwara (m)** (*prāṇa* 'vital life-force' + *īśwara* 'lord') 1. The Lord of life. 2. A name for a husband whose wife is as dear to him as his own life. 3. A name of God. In the Kaṭha Upanishad Lord Yama says to Naciketā, "No mortal lives by *prāṇa* or apāna, but all live by something else on which these two depend."

**Prāṇeśwarī (m)** (*prāṇa* 'vital life-force' + *īśwarī* 'sovereign goddess') 1. The sovereign goddess of life. 2. A name for a wife whose husband is as dear to her as her own life.

**Preman (m), Premā (f)** 1. Divine Love. 2. Supreme Love. See the Bhagavad Gītā IX:29; VIII:54.

**Premabandhu (m)** (*prema* 'divine love' + *bandhu* 'friend, relative') 1. The friend of love. 2. The loving friend.

**Premadāsa (m), Premadāsī (f)** (*prema* 'divine love' + *dās/dāsī* 'servant') 1. The servant of love. 2. The loving servant.

**Premarūpa (m), Premarūpiṇī (f)** (*prema* 'divine love' + *rūpa/rūpiṇī* 'form, image') 1. The form or embodiment of love. 2. Having a loving form or nature.

**Prithuhara (m)** (*prithu* 'great' + *hara* 'destroyer, ravisher') 1. The great destroyer, ravisher. 2. A name of Lord Śiva.

**Priyavrata (m)** (*priya* 'fond of, pleasing' + *vrata* 'vows') 1. Fond of spiritual vows. 2. One whose vows are pleasing. See the Bhagavad Gītā IV:28; VI:14; VII:28; IX:14 and the Yogasūtras II:30-1. 3. The name of a son of Manu.

**Priyā (f)** The beloved (of God). See the Bhagavad Gītā VII:17; IX:29; XII:13-20; XVIII:65,69.

**Prīta (m), Prītā (f)** The delighted or joyful.

**Prīti (f)** Delight or joy. See the Bhagavad Gītā III:17; IV:20, 22; X:10; XII:14,19.

**Pula (m)** 1. The great. 2. The name of an attendant of Lord Śiva.

**Pulaha (m)** One of the seven Ṛishis or seers, who were born from the mind of Lord Brahmā. [See **Ṛishi**]

**Pulastya (m)** Smooth-haired; one of the seven Ṛishis or seers, who were born from the mind of Lord Brahmā. [See **Ṛishi**]

**Punarvasu (m)** (*punaḥ* 'again' + *vasu* 'dweller') 1. The repeated dweller. 2. The 150th name of Lord Vishṇu as listed in the Vishṇu Sahasranāma. In his commentary, Śrī Śaṅkara states, "He who dwells (*vasati)* again and again (*punaḥ punaḥ)* in the bodies as the Knower of the field (individual Self), is called *Punarvasu*, the repeated dweller."

**Puṇḍarīka (m)** The (white) lotus. In the Chāndogya Upanishad VII, i:1 it is said:

*OM Atha Yad-Idam-Asmin-Brahma-Pure*
*Daharam Puṇḍarīkam Veśma*
*Daharo'Sminn'Antar-Ākāśas-*
*Tasmin-Yad-Antas-*
*Tad-Anveshṭavyam*
*Tad-Vāva Vijijñāsitavyam.*

OM. Now, in this city (the body) of the Absolute,
there is a mansion shaped like a small lotus.
In it is a small inner space.
What is within that, that should be sought.
That, indeed, one should desire to understand.

The following invocation taken from the Bṛihad-Āraṇyaka Upanishad is repeated while saluting the Sun after morning prayers:

*Diśām-Eka-Puṇḍarīkam-Asi,*
*Aham Manushyāṇām-Eka-Puṇḍarīkam Bhūyāsam!*

Thou art the one lotus of the quarters,
may I be the one lotus of men!

**Puṇḍarīkāksha (m)** (*puṇḍarīka* 'lotus' + *aksha* 'eye') 1. The lotus-eyed. 2. The 111th name of Lord Vishṇu as listed in the Vishṇu Sahasranāma. In his commentary Śrī Śaṅkara states, "The Lord who pervades (aśnute) the lotus (*puṇḍarīka)* known as the heart, and who is perceived within it, is called *Puṇḍarīkāksha*, the Lotus-Pervading. It is stated in a Vedic text, 'There is a lotus standing in the center of the body." This term also means the Lord's eyes (*aksha)* are shaped like lotuses (*puṇḍarīka).*'"

**Puṇḍra (m)** 1. The (white) lotus. 2. Religious marks made on the forehead.

**Puṇyabharita (m)** (*puṇya* 'virtue' + *bharita* 'full, filled with') Filled with virtue or holiness.

**Puṇyabhājin (m), Puṇyabhājinī (f)** (*puṇya* 'virtue' + *bhājin/inī* 'partaking') 1. Partaking of virtue or holiness. 2. Blissful.

**Puṇyaśīla (m), Puṇyaśīlā (f)** (*puṇya* 'virtuous' + *śīla/ā* 'character') Having a virtuous character.

**Puṇyavan (m), Puṇyavatī (f)** (*puṇya* 'virtue' + *van/vatī* 'having') The virtuous.

**Puralā (f)** A name of the Goddess Durgā or Pārvatī.

**Purandara (m)** (*puram* 'fortified city' + *dara* 'shattering') 1. The destroyer of cities or defenses. 2. A name of Lord Indra. 3. The 335th name of Lord Vishṇu as listed in the Vishṇu Sahasranāma. In his commentary, Śrī Śaṅkara states, "The Lord is called *Purandara*, 'the Destroyer of cities' because He destroys (*dāranāt*) the cities of the enemies of the gods." 4. A name of Lord Śiva. 5. The Fire-God Agni.

**Purañjana (m)** (*puram* 'full' + *jana* 'creature, person') 1. The embodiment of life. 2. A name of Lord Varuṇa.

**Purañjanī (f)** (*puram* 'full' + *janī* 'creature, person') The embodiment of life.

**Purāri (m)** (*puram* 'fortified city' + *ari* 'enemy') The enemy of (devilish) cities; a name of Lord Śiva, who destroyed the three strongholds or cities built by demons in earth, air, and heaven, representing the gross, subtle, and causal bodies.

**Purusha (m)** 1. The (original) spirit, person or being. See the *Purusha*-Sūkta, Hymn to the *Purusha*, in the Ṛig-Veda; see the Kaṭha Upanishad; and also see the Bhagavad Gītā VIII:4,8,10,22; X:12; XIII:22; XV:17-9. 2. The 14th and 406th names of Lord Vishṇu as listed in the Vishṇu Sahasranāma. In his commentary Śrī Śaṅkara states, "1) *Puram* is the body and He who reclines (śete) within it is called *Purusha*, the Body-recliner. It is written in the Mahābhārata, 'Having pervaded the nine-gated holy city (body) possessed of these sense-organs, the great Self who reclines therein is therefore called the *Purusha* or City-Recliner.' 2) According to a Vedic text, the *Purusha*-hood of the *Purusha* is thus revealed, 'I indeed existed (asam) here before (pūrvam).' 3) The Lord is called *Purusha* as He resides (sīdati) in the great (puru) who are possessed of eminence. 4) He is also thus called because He bestows (sanoti) numerous (puruṇi) fruits. 5) He is also thus called because He destroys (syati) all (purūṇi) worlds during cosmic dissolution. 6) Again, the Lord is called *Purusha* on account of pervading (pūraṇāt) and residing (sadanāt), as said in the Mahābhārata, 'Due to His pervading and residing everywhere, the Lord is named *Purushottama*, the supreme *Purusha*.' 7) In the Bṛihad-Āraṇyaka Upanishad, He is described as existing before all and burning all sins, thus,

'Because as the first (pūrvaḥ) of all, He burnt (aushat) all sins, hence He is the *Purusha.'* 8) On account of dwelling in the body, as revealed in the same Upanishad, 'He is indeed called *Purusha* who dwells in all bodies (*puriśayaḥ*).'" 3. In the Sāṅkhya and Yoga Darśanas the *purusha* refers to the individual soul as distinct from the universal one. In these schools a plurality of souls, or *purushas*, is put forward. In the Vedānta or Upanishads, however, no distinction is made between the individual Self and the supreme Self and such a plurality of selves is thus refuted. For this reason, in the Bṛihad-Āraṇyaka Upanishad, Yājñavalkya asks Śākalya about the Aupanishadam *Purusham*, or the Upanishadic *Purusha*, and not any other *Purusha* that might be imagined. In the Yogasūtras the description of Īśwara as a "distinct *Purusha*," or *Purusha-Viśesha*, does not conform with the original Brahman-Ātman non-duality of Vedānta while the description of Īśwara being untouched by affliction and action, omniscient, the primeval Guru beyond time and expressed by "OM" does. On the oneness of *Purusha* see the Bhagavad Gītā XIII: 2,22,30-2.

**Purushendra (m)** (*purusha* 'soul, person, being' + *indra* 'chief') 1. The chief of men. 2. The lord of beings. 3. A title given to kings, which means one who is among men like Indra is among the gods.

**Purushottama (m)** (*purusha* 'soul, person, being' + *uttama* 'highest') 1. The highest Soul. See the Bhagavad Gītā XV:17-19. 2. The highest of all beings. 3. The 24th name of Lord Vishṇu as listed in the Vishṇu Sahasranāma.

**Pushkala (m)** 1. The abundant or full. 2. A name of Lord Śiva.

**Pushkalā (f)** Abundant or full.

**Pushkara (m)** 1. Like the blue lotus. 2. A name of Lord Śiva.

**Pushkarī (f)** 1. Like the blue lotus. 2. A name of the Goddess Pārvatī.

**Pushpā (f)** Flower-like or blossom-like. See the Bhagavad Gītā IX:26.

**Pushpita (m), Pushpitā (f)** Flowered, blossomed.

**Pūjayitā (m), Pūjayitrī (f)** The worshipper.

**Pūjaka (m)** The worshipper. See the Bhagavad Gītā IV:25-31; VIII:22; IX:13-15,26-7, 29-34; X:9-11; XI:54-5; XII:1-20; XIII:7; XVII:14; XVIII: 46,65.

**Pūjā (f)** Worship.

**Pūjikā (f)** The worshipper. See the Bhagavad Gītā IV:25-31; VIII:22; IX:13-

15,26-7, 29-34; X:9-11; XI:54-5; XII:1-20; XIII:7; XVII:14; XVIII: 46,65.

**Pūrayitā (m)** 1. The fulfiller. 2. The 686th name of Lord Vishṇu as listed in the Vishṇu Sahasranāma. In his commentary Śrī Śaṅkara states, "Not only is the Lord verily fulfilled (pūrṇa), He is also the fulfiller (*Pūrayitā*) of all with wealth." 3. A name of Lord Śiva.

**Pūrṇa (m), Pūrṇā (f)** 1. Filled, fullness, fulfilled. 2. The 685th name of Lord Vishṇu as listed in the Vishṇu Sahasranāma. In his commentary, Śrī Śaṅkara states, "Endowed with all objects of desire and all powers, the Lord is called *Pūrṇa*, the Fulfilled." In the Brihad-Āraṇyaka Upanishad it is written:

*OM Pūrṇam-adaḥ Pūrṇam-idam.*
*Pūrṇāt Pūrṇam-udacyate.*
*Pūrṇasya Pūrṇam-ādāya,*
*Pūrṇam-evāvaśishyate.*

OM. That (unconditioned) is Full.
This (conditioned) is Full.
From That fullness, this Fullness proceeds.
Though this Fullness came from that Fullness,
Fullness alone remains.

This Upanishadic Mantra reveals the nature of the unconditioned Truth, the real nature of the conditioned universe and their non-duality or undifferentiatedness through a very skillful use of the word "*Pūrṇa.*"

**Pūrṇatā (f)** (*pūrṇa* 'full' + *tā* 'state') Fullness, the state of being full or filled.

**Pūrṇimā (f)** Pertaining to or similar to the full moon.

**Pūrya (m), Pūryā (f)** Worthy of fulfilment.

**Pūshan (m)** 1. The nourisher. 2. A name of the Sun-God Sūrya, which refers to His nourishing the whole world. It is written in the Īśā Upanishad:

*Hiraṇmayena Pātreṇa*
*Satyasyāpihitam Mukham*
*Tat-Twam Pūshann'apāvṛiṇu*
*Satya-dharmāya Dṛishṭaye.*

*Pūshann'eka'rshe Yama Sūrya Prājāpatya*
*Vyūha Raśmīn Samūha Tejaḥ*
*Yat-Te Rūpam Kalyāṇa-Tamam Tat-Te*
*Paśyāmi Yo'sāv'asau Purushas So'ham-Asmi!*

The face of Truth is concealed with a golden vessel.
O Nourisher (*Pūshan*), do Thou open it
so as to be seen by me who am of
truthful nature!

O Nourisher (*Pūshan*)! O solitary Traveller!
O Controller! O Acquirer! O Son of Prajāpati
do remove Thy rays, do gather up Thy dazzle!
I shall behold that form of Thine which is the most benign.
That Purusha who is there (behind Thy disc) I am He!

**Pūtā (f)** 1. The purified, pure. 2. A name of the Goddess Durgā.

**Pūtamati (m)** (*pūta* 'purified' + *mati* 'thought') 1. Having purified thought, pure-minded. 2. A name of Lord Śiva who is free from rajas and tamas. See the Bhagavad Gītā IV:10.

# R

**Raghu (m)** 1. The racer. 2. The name of a great king, who was an ancestor of Śrī Rāma. His lineage forms the subject of Kālidāsa's great poem entitled *Raghuvamśa.*

**Raghumaṇi (m)** (*raghu* 'name of a great king' + *maṇi* 'jewel') 1. The jewel of the *Raghus.* 2. A name of Śrī Rāma as the most illustrious among the descendants of King *Raghu.*

**Raghunātha (m)** (*raghu* 'name of a great king' + *nātha* 'lord') 1. The Lord of the *Raghus.* 2. A name of Śrī Rāma as the most illustrious among the descendants of King *Raghu.*

**Raghuvīra (m)** (*raghu* 'name of a great king' + *vīra* 'hero, valiant') 1. The hero of the *Raghus.* 2. A name of Śrī Rāma as the most illustrious among the descendants of King *Raghu.*

**Rajanī (f)** 1. The dark. 2. A name of the Goddess Durgā.

**Rakshaṇa (m)** 1. The protector. 2. The 928th name of Lord Vishṇu as listed in the Vishṇu Sahasranāma. In his commentary Śrī Śaṅkara states, "Having assumed the Sattwa Guṇa and thus protecting the three worlds, the Lord is called the protector." See the Bhagavad Gītā IV:6-8.

**Rakshākarī (f)** (*rakshā* 'protection' + *karī* 'doer') The protectress; a name of the Goddess Annapūrṇā occurring in Śrī Śaṅkara's "Annapūrṇā Stotram."

**Rakti (f)** The lovely or devoted.

**Ramaṇa (m)** [in Tamil **Ramaṇan**] 1. The delighting. 2. The name of a great Jñānī and Jīvanmukta (1879-1950). *Ramaṇa* Maharshi taught Ātma-Vicāra, (self-inquiry) to seekers approaching him. The following verses in the Bhagavad Gītā fully apply to this great sage: II:55, 69; III:17-8; IV:10,38; V:13,19,24; VI:27,45; VII:17-9; XII:3-4; XIII:30,34; XIV:1-2, 19-20; XV:5; XVIII:49-55.

**Ramaṇī (f)** The delighting or joyful.

**Ramā (f)** 1. The rejoicing. 2. The 48th of the Goddess Lakshmī's 108 names.

**Rameśa (m)** (*ramā* 'a name of the Goddess Lakshmī' + *īśa* 'lord') The Lord of Ramā (i.e. the Goddess Lakshmī); a name of Lord Vishṇu.

**Ramyā (f)** 1. The delightful or beautiful. 2. The night.

**Raṅganātha (m)** (*raṅga* 'color, theater, stage' + *nātha* 'lord') Lord of the theater; a name of Lord Vishṇu as worshipped in South India.

**Rañjanī (m)** The rejoicing.

**Rasa (m)** 1. Taste. 2. Essence. 3. Nectar. In the Taittirīya Upanishad it is written:

> *Yad-vai Tat-Sukṛitam*
> *Raso vai Saḥ*
> *Rasam hy'evāyam labdhwāānandī bhavati.*
>
> That which is the Self-Creator
> is verily Nectar (*Rasa*);
> For, having gained that very Nectar, one becomes blissful.

4. Bliss. Śrī Śaṅkara states, "The Absolute does exist and is Nectar (*Rasa*). *Rasa* stands for anything that is a means for satisfaction (i.e. a source of joy, such as sweet and sour things which are well known to be so in the world). Hence, having attained that very Bliss, one becomes blissful. A nonentity is not seen in this world to be a cause of happiness. Inasmuch as the wise knowers of the Absolute are seen to be as happy as one is from obtaining an external source of joy—though, in fact, they do not take the help of any external means of happiness, make no effort, and cherish no desire—it follows, as a matter of course, that the Absolute alone is the source of their joy. Hence there does exist that Absolute, which is full of joy and is the spring of their happiness." See also the Bhagavad Gītā VII:8. 5. The nine feelings or sentiments prevailing in poety and arts: Śṛiṅgāra (Love), Vīra (Heroism), Bībhatsa (Disgust), Raudra (Anger), Hāsya (Mirth), Bhayānaka (Fear), Karuṇā (Compassion), Adbhuta (Wonder), and Śānti (Peace).

**Rasamayī (f)** (*rasa* ' bliss, nectar' + *mayī* 'consisting of') The blissful.

**Rati (f)** 1. The pleasure of love. 2. The name of Kāmadeva's or Cupid's consort.

**Ratna (m), Ratnā (f)** The jewel-like.

**Ratninī (f)** The jeweled.

**Ravi (m)** 1. The absorber. 2. A name of the Sun-God, Sūrya. In the Vishṇudharmottara it is written:

> *Rasānam ca Tathādānād-Ravir-Ity'abhidhīyate.*

On account of taking away the juices, He is called *Ravi.*

2. The 881st name of Lord Vishṇu as listed in the Vishṇu Sahasranāma. In his commentary, Śrī Śaṅkara states, "Being the Self of the Sun, the Lord is called *Ravi*, the absorbing Sun." See also the Bhagavad Gītā V:16; VII:8; VIII:9; X:21; XI:12; XIII:33; XV:12.

**Rādhā (f)** The fortunate or successful; the name of a celebrated Gopī, beloved of Śrī Kṛishṇa, who is regarded as Goddess Lakshmī personified.

**Rādhākṛishṇa (m)** (*rādhā* 'beloved of Kṛishṇa' + *kṛishṇa* 'Incarnation of Lord Vishṇu') The Embodiment of *Rādhā* and *Kṛishṇa.*

**Rādhāvallabha (m)** (*rādhā* 'beloved of Kṛishṇa' + *vallabha* 'beloved') The beloved of Rādhā; a name of Śrī Kṛishṇa.

**Rādheśa (m)** (*rādhā* 'beloved of Kṛishṇa' + *īśa* 'lord') Lord of Rādhā; a name of Śrī Kṛishṇa.

**Rādheśwara (m)** (*rādhā* 'beloved of Kṛishṇa' + *īśwara* 'lord') Lord of Rādhā; a name of Śrī Kṛishṇa.

**Rādheśyāma (m)** (*rādhā* 'beloved of Kṛishṇa' + *śyāma* 'dark-blue') The dark-blue Lord of Rādhā (i.e. Śrī Kṛishṇa).

**Rādhikā (f)** The diminutive of Rādhā. [See **Rādhā**]

**Rāghavan (m)** The descendant of Raghu; a name of Śrī Rāma as descendant of King Raghu, the grandson of Bhagīratha.

**Rāghavendra (m)** (*rāghava* 'descendant of Raghu' + *indra* 'chief') 1. The chief or Lord of the Rāghavas. 2. A name of Śrī Rāma as descendant of King Raghu, the grandson of Bhagīratha.

**Rāja (m)** The radiant (i.e. king or sovereign). See the Bhagavad Gītā X:27.

**Rājarājeśwara (m)** (*rāja-rāja* 'king of kings, emperor' + *īśwara* 'lord, ruler') The Ruler of emperors; a name of Lord Śiva.

**Rājarājeśwarī (f)** (*rāja-rāja* 'king of kings, emperor' + *īśwarī* 'ruling goddess') The Ruler of emperors; a name of the Goddess Durgā.

**Rājeśa (m)** (*rāja* 'king' + *īśa* 'lord, ruler') The ruler of kings, emperor.

**Rājeśwara (m)** (*rāja* king' + *īśwara* 'lord, ruler') The ruler of kings, emperor.

**Rājeśwarī (f)** (*rāja* 'king' + *īśwarī* 'ruling goddess') The ruler of kings, empress.

**Rājīvāksha (m)** (*rājīva* 'blue lotus' + *aksha* 'eye') 1. Lotus-eyed. 2. A name of Śrī Rāma. 3. A name of Śrī Kṛishṇa.

**Rājnī (m)** The radiant queen.

**Rāma (m)** 1. The blissful or delightful. 2. The name of Lord Vishṇu's seventh incarnation born to King Daśaratha and his queen, Kausalyā. As an ideal king and husband, Śrī *Rāma,* is Dharma incarnate (i.e. righteousness personified). His story is told by the sage Vālmīki in the 24,000 verses of the Rāmāyaṇa. In the Mahābhārata Lord Śiva extols the greatness of Śrī *Rāma's* name by saying:

*Śrī-Rāma Rāma Rāme'ti Rame Rāme Manorame*
*Sahasra-Nāma-Tat-Tulyam Rāma-Nāma Varānane.*

O fortunate *Rāma!* O *Rāma!* O *Rāma!* Such is
the name of *Rāma* equal to the thousand names
(of Lord Vishṇu), O Beloved, O Charming,
O Mind-Enchanter, O lovely-Faced.

3. This name is the 394th name of Lord Vishṇu as listed in the Vishṇu Sahasranāma. In his commentary Śrī Śaṅkara states, "The Lord, characterized by eternal bliss, and in whom the Yogis delight *(ramante),* is called *Rāma,* the delightful. It is written in the Padma Purāṇa, 'As Yogis delight in the infinite and eternal Bliss, in the Self that is pure Consciousness, hence by the word *Rāma* the supreme Absolute is meant.' It also means Śrī *Rāma,* the son of Daśaratha, the blissful form that the Lord took of His own will." See also the Bhagavad Gītā X:31.

**Rāmabhadra (m)** (*rāma* 'blissful, delightful' + *bhadra* 'blessed, auspicious') The blessed *Rāma*; a name of Śrī *Rāma,* which is used in the following verse:

*Rāmāya Rāmacandrāya Rāmabhadrāya Vedhase,*
*Raghunāthāya Nāthāya Sītāyāḥ Pataye Namaḥ.*

Salutation to *Rāma*, to *Rāmacandra*, to *Rāmabhadra,*
the Creator, to the Lord of the Raghus, to the Lord
and Master of Sītā.

**Rāmacandra (m)** (*rāma* ' blissful, delightful' + *candra* 'moon') The moon-like *Rāma*; a name of Śrī *Rāma* that distinguishes Him from Paraśurāma and Balarāma.

**Rāmadāsa (m), Rāmdās (m)** (*rāma* 'an incarnation of Lord Vishṇu' + *dāsa* 'servant') 1. The servant of Śrī *Rāma*. 2. The name of a great saint who lived from 1884 to 1963 and whose main spiritual practice was the repetition of the thirteen-syllabled mantra revealed in the *Rāma*-Rahasya Upanishad as:

*OM Śrī Rāma! Jaya Rāma! Jaya! Jaya! Rāma!*

O fortunate *Rāma*! Victory *Rāma*! Victory! Victory! O *Rāma*!

**Rāmadeva (m), Rāmdev (m)** (*rāma* 'an incarnation of Lord Vishṇu' + *deva* 'divine') The divine *Rāma*; a name of Śrī *Rāma*.

**Rāmakṛishṇa (m)** (*rāma* 'blissful, delightful' + *kṛishṇa* 'name of an incarnation of Lord Vishṇu') 1. Śrī *Rāma* and Śrī *Kṛishṇa* joined together. The great invocation taught to Nārada by Lord Brahmā in the Kalisantaraṇa Upanishad is as follows:

*Hare Rāma Hare Rāma*
*Rāma Rāma Hare Hare,*
*Hare Kṛishṇa Hare Kṛishṇa*
*Kṛishṇa Kṛishṇa Hare Hare!*

2. The name of a great saint and renunciate of the 19th century known as Śrī *Rāmakṛishṇa* Paramahamsa.

**Rāmapriyā (f)** (*rāma* 'an incarnation of Lord Vishṇu' + *priyā* 'beloved') 1. The beloved of Śrī Rāma. 2. A name of Sītā.

**Rāmā (f)** 1. The rejoicing. 2. The consort of Śrī *Rāma*, a name of Sītā.

**Rāmeśa (m)** (*rāma* 'an incarnation of Lord Vishṇu' + *īśa* 'lord') 1. The Lord Rāma; a name of Śrī Rāma. 2. The Lord of Śrī Rāma (i.e. Lord Śiva).

**Rāmeśwara (m)** (*rāma* 'an incarnation of Lord Vishṇu' + *īśwara* lord') 1. The Lord of Śrī Rāma (i.e. Lord Śiva). 2. The name of a celebrated South Indian Śivaliṅgam worshipped by Śrī Rāma before crossing the ocean on His way to Śrī Laṅkā.

**Rāmyā (f)** 1. The delightful or beautiful. 2. The night.

**Rānī (f)** [Hindi] Queen.

**Ṛibhu (m)** Clever or skillful; the name of a semi-divine being who is associated with the Sun-God Sūrya and works in iron for the Gods.

**Ṛibhuksha (m)** Clever; a name of Lord Indra.

**Ṛibhwan (m)** 1. Clever or wise. 2. A name of Lord Indra. 3. A name of the Fire-God Agni. 4. A name of the cosmic architect Twashṭā.

**Ṛiddha (m)** The wealthy, expanded. The 278th and 351st name of Lord Vishṇu as listed in the Vishnu Sahasranāma. In his commentary Śrī Śaṅkara states, "Being endowed with virtue, knowledge, dispassion and other divine riches, the Lord is called, 'the Wealthy.' It also means He expanded (*ṛiddha*) Himself in the form of the world expansion."

**Ṛiddhi (f)** 1. Wealth or good fortune personified. 2. A name of the Goddess Pārvatī. 3. A name of the Goddess Lakshmī. See the Bhagavad Gītā X; XVI:1-3,5.

**Ṛijudāsa (m)** ( *ṛiju* 'honest, right, sincere' + *dāsa* 'servant' ) 1. The honest servant. 2. The name of a son of Vasudeva.

**Ṛijukratu (m)** (*ṛiju* 'honest, right, sincere'+ *kratu* 'power, sacrifice, intelligence') 1. Performing right sacrifices or works. 2. A name of Lord Indra who is famous for His unrivalled hundred sacrifices which entitle Him to Indrahood. See the Bhagavad Gītā X:22. 3. Sincere-minded.

**Ṛijumati (m) (f)** (*ṛiju* 'honest, right, sincere' + *mati* 'minded') The honest-minded or sincere-minded.

**Ṛishi (m)** 1. Seer. A general name for the mind-born sons of Lord Brahmā, among whom Vasishṭha is the greatest. The *Ṛishis* are the first seers of the Vedas and of the Vedic mantras. 2. Sage. A name for the Sannyāsis who have a right or integral vision of the truth. See the Bhagavad Gītā V:25.

**Ṛitadhāman (m)** (*ṛita* 'truth' + *dhāman* 'abode') 1. The abode of truth. 2. A name of Lord Vishṇu.

**Ṛitaparṇa (m)** ( *ṛita* 'truth' + *parna* 'wing, feather, leaf') Truth-winged.

**Ṛitayu (m)** Follower of the sacred law (i.e. the Vedas).

**Ṛitā (f)** The true or righteous. This name occurs in the Śānti Mantra:

*OM Śam no Mitraḥ!*
*Śam Varuṇaḥ...*
*Namaste Vāyo!*
*Twameva Pratyaksham Brahmāsi.*
*Twāmeva Pratyaksham Brahma Vadishyāmi.*
*Ṛitam Vadishyāmi.*
*Satyam Vadishyāmi...*

May Mitra be blissful to us!
May Varuṇa be blissful to us...
Salutation to You, O Vāyu!
You, indeed, are the immediate Brahman.
You alone I shall call the direct Brahman.
I shall call You righteousness.
I shall call You Truth...

It also occurs in the Aghamarshaṇa-Sūkta or Sin-effacing hymn, which begins as follows:

*Ṛitam ca Satyam Cābhīddhāt-*
*Tapaso'dhyajāyata...*

From the all-Luminous, the right and the
true were born, by His resolve...

See the Yogasūtras I:48.

**Ṛitāyin (m)** The truthful.

**Ṛitāyus (m)** (*ṛita* 'true, righteous' + *āyus* 'life') Having true life.

**Ṛitunātha (m)** (*ṛitu* 'season, fixed time, order' + *nātha* 'lord') 1. The lord of the seasons. 2. A name of spring personified. See the Bhagavad Gītā X:35.

**Ṛituparṇa (m)** (*ṛitu* 'season, fixed time, order' + *parṇa* 'wing, feather, leaf') The name of a kind of Ayodhyā.

**Rocana (m)** Glowing, radiant.

**Rohiṇī (f)** 1. Red or reddish. 2. A lunar asterism personified as Daksha's daughter and the Moon's wife. 3. A wife of Vasudeva and hence mother of Balarāma.

**Ruci (f)** Light, beauty.

**Rudra (m)** 1. The remover of pain. 2. Lord Śiva's Vedic name. 3. The 114th name of Lord Vishṇu as listed in the Vishṇu Sahasranāma. In his commentary Śrī Śaṅkara states, "1) Withdrawing all beings at the time of cosmic dissolution and causing them to cry (rodayati), the Lord is called *Rudra*. 2) It means He confers (rāti) good (rudam). 3) Again, He is thus called as He destroys (drāvayati) pain (ruḥ) and its cause. The Liṅga Purāṇa says, 'As the Lord removes (drāvayati) pain (ruḥ) and its cause, hence Śiva the supreme Cause is called *Rudra*.'" 4. pl. A group of eleven gods whom Yājñavalkya describes in the Bṛihad-Āraṇyaka Upanishad: "Which are the *Rudras*? The ten (sensory and motor) organs in the human body, with the mind as the eleventh. When they depart from this mortal body, they make one's relatives weep. Because they make them weep (rodayanti), they are called *Rudras*." See the Bhagavad Gītā X:23.

**Rudrāṇī (f)** The consort of Rudra; a name of Goddess Durgā.

**Rukmiṇī (f)** The radiant or golden. A form of the Goddess Lakshmī as the wife of Śrī Kṛishṇa.

# S

**Sabala (m)** (*sa* 'with' + *bala* 'strength') The powerful or mighty. See the Bhagavad Gītā VII:11.

**Sadāgati (f)** (*sadā* 'eternal' + *gati* 'goal') The eternal goal. See the Bhagavad Gītā XVIII:56,62.

**Sadāśiva (m)** (*sadā* 'eternally, ever' + *Śiva* 'name of God, auspicious') 1. The Ever-Auspicious. 2. A great name of Lord Śiva. 3. A name of the Self as taught to Aśwalāyana by the Lord Brahmā who expounds in the Kaivalya Upanishad the non-duality of Jīva and Īśwara thus:

*Trishu Dhāmasu Yad Bhojyam*
*Bhoktā Bhogaś-Ca Yad Bhavet,*
*Tebhyo Vilakshaṇas Sākashī*
*Cinmātro'ham Sadāśivaḥ!*

In the three abodes, what is enjoyable,
enjoyer, and enjoyment,
distinct from these, the Witness,
pure Consciousness am I, ever-auspicious!

The three abodes are the three states of waking, dream, and deep sleep, and *Sadāśivaḥ* or 'ever-auspicious' means Nitya-Kalyāṇa Kaivalyam, 'the ever-blissful Aloneness.' [See **Śiva**]

**Sadātana (m)** (*sadā* 'eternally' + *tana* 'lasting') 1. The everlasting. 2. A name of Lord Vishṇu.

**Sadguṇa (m)** (*sat* 'good' + *guṇa* 'quality of nature, virtue') Having good or holy qualities, virtuous. See the Bhagavad Gītā XVI:1-3.

**Sadratna (n or m)** (*sat* 'true' + *ratna* 'pearl, gem') Pure gem or pearl.

**Saguṇā (f)** (*sa* 'with' + *guṇā* 'quality of nature, virtue') 1. The qualified, she who is with attributes. 2. The 239th name of the Goddess Lalitā as listed in the Lalitā Triśatī in the Brahmāṇḍa-Purāṇa. In his commentary Śrī Śaṅkara states, "1) She has uniform attributes 2) She has attributes because of having the forms of the Trimūrtis (Brahmā, Vishṇu, Śiva) who are with attributes, the three guṇas of sattwa, rajas, and tamas."

**Saha (m)** 1. The enduring or mighty. 2. The 368th name of Lord Vishṇu as listed in the Vishṇu Sahasranāma. In his commentary, Śrī Śaṅkara states,

"1) The Lord forgives the lapses of His devotees. 2) He supersedes all."

**Sahaja (m), Sahajā (f)** (*saha* 'together with' + *ja* 'born') 1. The natural, original or innate. 2. One who has followed spiritual principles eagerly and constantly becomes realized and natural since no more effort is to be made and all good qualities follow him or her naturally.

**Saharsha (m)** (*sa* 'with' + *harsha* 'joy') Happy or rejoicing. See the Bhagavad Gītā II:55-7; III:17; V:20-4: VI:27-8; X:9; XII:15,17.

**Sahā (f)** 1. The enduring. 2. The Earth-Goddess, famous for Her forbearance.

**Sakalā (f)** (*sa* 'with' + *kalā* 'parts') 1. Complete. 2. A name of the Goddess Lalitā. In his commentary on Her 300 names (the Triśatī), Śrī Śaṅkara states, "1) (It means) having *Kalā* or parts. *Kalās* are artificially attributed to Her for the sake of worship. In the Chāndogya Upanishad, Jābāli describes the worship of Purusha to Satyakāma as having sixteen kalā or parts. These are attributed by the devotee to Her for the purpose of worship. They are Her limbs. She works with them. 2) It means She has the 64 *kalās*, (i.e. arts, or 16 digits of the moon). 3) *Kalā* also means the brilliance arising from happiness, etc., which She has and which She bestows upon Her devotees. Hence, *'Sakalā.'*"

**Sama (m)** 1. The same (in all). 2. The 109th name of Lord Vishṇu as listed in the Vishṇu Sahasranāma. In his commentary Śrī Śaṅkara states, "1) The Lord is called "the Same" because He is devoid of all changes at all times. 2) The name may be split as *'Sa-Ma,'*—He who is with *(sa)* Lakshmī *(ma).*" Also See the Bhagavad Gītā V:18-9; VI:29; IX:29; XIII:27-8.

**Samarasā (f)** (*sama* 'same, equal' + *rasā* 'bliss, sentiment') 1. Having equal bliss. 2. The 222nd name of the Goddess Lalitā as listed in the Brahmāṇḍa-Purāṇa. In his commentary Śrī Śaṅkara states, "1) *Sama* means eka or one. *Rasa* means taste like sweetness. Just as sweetness pervades uniformly through a lump of jaggery, She pervades uniformly through the universe of which She is the cause. 2) It also means, in the world or transmigration, God and the individual, due to their different attributes of omniscience and ignorance, appear to have different feelings and natures. But when they attain the infinite state through hearing of the Vedānta, they experience the oneness mentioned in the sentence 'Aham Brahmāsmi,' 'I am the Absolute,' and realize Her as all-pervading One in all (like the sweetness in jaggery). The Taittirīya Upanishad reveals *'Raso vai saḥ,'* 'He is verily Bliss.' *Sama* means inseparable. She is inseparable with the meaning of *'rasa'* (i.e. the Absolute, the supreme Bliss).

**Samatā (f)** (*sama* 'same, equal' + *tā* 'nominalizing suffix') Sameness or equanimity (of mind). See the Bhagavad Gītā II:15,38,48; IV:22; VI:8-9, 32;

X:5; XII:4,13,18; XIII:9; XIV:24; XVIII:54.

**Sampadin (f), Sampadinī (f)** The divinely wealthy. See the Bhagavad Gītā XVI:1-5.

**Sampat (f)** (Divine) Wealth.

**Samrāj (m), Samrājñī (f)** 1. The supreme ruler or the resplendent. 2. In the spiritual context, it refers to the Self as being supreme and all light.

**Samudra (m)** The ocean. See the Bhagavad Gītā II:70; X:24.

**Samyama (m)** (*sam* 'complete' + *yama* 'restraint') Perfect restraint or concentration. See the Bhagavad Gītā II:61, 69; III:41; IV:26-7; VI:14, 24, 26; VIII:12; XII:4: XVIII:51 and see the Yogasūtras III:1-6; 16-35; 41-48, 52.

**Samyamin (m), Samyaminī (f)** The self-restrained.

**Sanaka (m)** 1. The ancient. 2. The name of a Ṛishi, one of the four sons of Brahmā. These sons, known as the Kumāras, were born from Brahmā's mind. They took on a life of renunciation from their very youth. Seeking the Truth they went to Lord Śiva who took the form of Dakshiṇāmūrti, the Guru teaching the non-dual Truth through Jñāna-Mudrā and silence.

**Sanandana (m)** (*sa* 'with' + *nandana* 'bliss, joy') 1. The blissful. 2. One of the four Kumāras. [See **Sanaka**]

**Sanātana (m)** 1. The eternal or everlasting. See the Bhagavad Gītā II:24; VIII:20; XI:18; XV:7. 2. A name of Lord Brahmā, Lord Vishṇu, and Lord Śiva.

**Sanātanī (f)** 1. The eternal or everlasting. See the Bhagavad Gītā II:24; VIII:20; XI:18; XV:7. 2. A name of the consorts of Lord Brahmā, Lord Vishṇu and Lord Śiva.

**Sandhātā (m)** 1. The connecter or regulator. 2. The 201st name of Lord Vishṇu as listed in the Vishṇu Sahasranāma. In his commentary Śrī Śaṅkara states, "The Lord who connects *(sandhatte)* men to the results of their actions is the connecter." See also the Bhagavad Gītā VII:22; VIII:9; IX:17. 3. A name of Lord Śiva.

**Sandhyā (f)** 1. Twilight, literally "juncture." There are three such junctures at dawn, noon, and dusk for performing one's prayers. The following śloka explains the true meaning of *Sandhyā* thus:

*No'dakair-Jāyate Sandhyā*
*Na Mantro'ccāaṇena Tu*
*Sandhau Jīvātmanor-Aikyam*
*Sā Sandhyā Sadbhir-Ucyate.*

Neither by ablutions occurs the *Sandhyā,*
nor by the utterance of mantras even.
At juncture, the oneness of Jīva and Ātman
is called by saints as *Sandhyā.*

2. The name of a daughter of Lord Brahmā.

**Saṅgahīnā (f)** (*saṅga* 'attachment' + *hīnā* 'devoid of') 1. Devoid of attachment. 2. The 238th name of the Goddess Lalitā as listed in the Brahmāṇḍa-Purāṇa. In his commentary Śrī Śaṅkara states, "She is unattached because She is without parts, cause, attribute, or support and because Her nature is eternal, pure Consciousness..."

**Saṅgītā (f)** Divine music.

**Saṅkaṭaharaṇa (m)** (*saṅkaṭa* 'difficulties' + *haraṇa* 'remover') 1. The remover of difficulties. 2. A name of Lord Vishṇu.

**Santoshan (m)** 1. Contentment, which is the second of the five Niyamas listed in the Yogasūtras II:42. Commenting on this sūtra Vyāsa quotes one verse from his Mahābhārata:

*Yac'ca Kāma-sukham Loke*
*Yac'ca Divyam Mahat-sukham,*
*Tṛishṇā-kshaya-sukhasyai'te*
*Nārhataḥ Shoḍasīm Kalām.*

Whatever sensual pleasure there is in this world,
and whatever great pleasure there is in heaven,
these cannot equal a sixteenth of the happiness
derived from the cessation of desires.

Also see the Bhagavad Gītā II:55; III:17; IV:20,22; VI:8,20; X:5,9; XII:14,19. 2. The son of Dharma and Tushṭi.

**Santoshiṇī (f), Santoshī (f)** 1. Endowed with contentment. 2. Delighting in contentment.

**Sarala (m), Saralā (f)** The honest or sincere.

**Saraṇi (f)** (Spiritual) Path.

**Saraswatī (f)** (*saras* 'flowing' + *vatī* 'having') 1. Flowing (with speech and knowledge.) 2. The name of Lord Brahmā's divine consort who presides over speech, knowledge, and musical arts. She is identified with dusk, which is the last of the three Sandhyās, with the holy River *Saraswatī*, which flows underground and joins the Ganges and Yamunā at Allahābād, and with the Sushumnā Nādī within the subtle body of individuals, which is well known as the Moksha-Dwāra, the door of liberation, for departing souls. The following verse invokes the Goddess *Saraswatī*:

*Yā Kunde'ndu-Tushāra-Hāra-Dhavalā*
*Yā Śubhra-Vastrāvṛitā*
*Yā Vīnā-Varadaṇḍa-Maṇḍita-Karā*
*Yā Śweta-Padmāsanā,*
*Yā Brahmācyuta-Śaṅkara-Prabhṛitibhir-*
*Devais Sadā Vanditā*
*Sā Mām Pātu Saraswatī Bhagavatī*
*Niśśesha-Jāḍyāpahā!*

She whose complexion is white like jasmine,
moon, or snow who is enwrapped in pure
white clothes, whose hands are adorned with a
Vīṇā (lute) of choicest neck, who is seated on
a white lotus, who is always saluted by Brahmā,
Acyuta (Vishṇu), Śaṅkara (Śiva) and other Gods,
may that fortunate *Saraswatī*, the Remover of
all ignorance, protect me!

3. The name of one among the ten Sannyāsa orders traced back to Śrī Śaṅkarācārya. All Sannyāsin disciples of Śrī Swāmī Śivānanda *Saraswatī* and their renunciate disciples belong to this order.

**Sarva (m)** 1. The All. 2. The 25th name of Lord Vishṇu as listed in the Vishṇu Sahasranāma. In his commentary Śrī Śaṅkara quotes a verse by Vyāsa in the Mahābhārata, "As He is the origin and the end of all, whether existent or otherwise, and as He ever cognizes all, the Lord is called the All." The following two verses taken from the Vishṇu Purāṇa are also in praise of the All:

*Sarvasmin Sarva-Bhūtas-Twam*
*Sarvaḥ Sarva-Swarūpa-Dhṛik,*
*Sarvam Twattas-Tataś-Ca Twam-*
*Evam Sarvātmane Namaḥ.*

*Sarvātmako'si Sarve'śah*
*Sarva-Bhūta-Sthito Yataḥ*
*Kathayāmi Tataḥ Kim Te*
*Sarvam Vetti Hṛidi Sthitam.*

Thou hast become all in all.
Thou art the all, the Support of all.
All comes from Thee, hence Thou art such.
Salutations to the Self of all.

As Thou art the Self of all,
the Lord of all and present in all beings,
what shall I speak unto Thee?
Thou knowest everything in my heart.

See the Bhagavad Gītā V:29; VI:29-31; VII:7, 19; VIII:22; IX:4, 6, 29; X:8, 20, 39, 42; XI:40; XIII:2, 13-4, 17, 27-8, 30, 33; XV:15; XVIII:20, 46, 61. 3. A name of Lord Śiva.

**Sarvaga (m)** (*sarva* all' + *ga* 'go') 1. All-going, all-pervading, all-reaching, omnipresent. 2. The 123rd name of Lord Vishṇu as listed in the Vishṇu Sahasranāma. In his commentary Śrī Śaṅkara states, "The Lord who reaches *(gacchati)* everywhere *(sarvatra)* is called *Sarvaga*, the all-reaching. This is due to His having pervaded everywhere through His causality." Also see the Bhagavad Gītā IX:6; XII:3; XIII:13.

**Sarvagata (m)** (*sarva* 'all' + *gata* 'having gone') Having pervaded all, having reached everywhere. See the Bhagavad Gītā II:24; XIII:32.

**Sarvagatā (f)** (*sarva* 'all' + *gatā* 'having gone') 1. Having pervaded all, having reached everywhere. 2. A name of the Goddess Lalitā.

**Sarvagati (f)** (*sarva* 'all' + *gati* 'goal') The goal of all.

**Sarvajña (m)** (*sarva* 'all' + *jña* 'knowing') 1. The all-knowing, omniscient. See the Bhagavad Gītā IV:5; X:15; XI:38. 2. The witness of all states. See the Māṇḍūkya Upanishad 6. 3. The 453rd and 815th name of Lord Vishṇu as listed in the Vishṇu Sahasranāma. In his commentary Śrī Śaṅkara states, "1) The Lord who is all and knowing is the All-Knowing... 2) As He knows *(jānāti)* all *(sarvam)*, He is *Sarvajña*, the Omniscient, as revealed in the Muṇḍaka Upanishad, 'He (is the one) who is omniscient in general and all-knowing in detail.'"

**Sarvajñā (f)** (*sarva* 'all' + *jñā* 'knowing') 1. The all-knowing, omniscient. See the Bhagavad Gītā IV:5; X:15; XI:38. 2. The witness of all states. See the

Māṇḍūkya Upanishad 6. 3. A name of the Goddess Lalitā.

**Sarvamayī (f)** (*sarva* all' + *mayī* 'consisting of') 1. Consisting in all, the all-containing. 2. A name referring to any major manifestation of the Divine Mother.

**Sarvamātā (f)** (*sarva* 'all' + *mātā* 'mother') 1. The Mother of all. 2. The 139th name of the Goddess Lalitā as listed in the Brahmāṇḍa-Purāṇa. In his commentary Śrī Śaṅkara states, "1) (She is thus called because) She is the Creatrix of the universe. 2) Also, She is inferred by resultant act, the universe, because She, as its Cause, is not different from it. This universe, which is within Her, only manifests Her reality, being one with Her, just as a blanket is apprehended as something resulting from yarn and identical with it. 3. Also, She, being the Absolute, sees or understands one and all as non-different from Herself."

**Sarvatā (f)** (*sarva* 'all' + *tā* 'nominalizing suffix') The wholeness or totality. See the Bhagavad Gītā VII:19.

**Sarvavidyā (f)** (*sarva* 'all' + *vidyā* 'knowledge') 1. Having all-knowledge, omniscience. 2. A name of the Divine Mother.

**Sarvāṇī (f)** 1. The All. 2. The consort of the All (i.e. of Lord Śiva). 3. A name of the Goddess Pārvatī.

**Sarvātmikā (f)** (*sarva* 'all' + *ātmikā* 'Self') 1. The Self of all. 2. The all-Ātmic, that which is nothing but the Self. 3. A name of the Goddess Lalitā.

**Sarveśa (m)** (*sarva* 'all' + *īśa* 'lord') 1. The Lord of all. 2. A name of Lord Vishṇu. 3. A name of Lord Śiva.

**Sarveśī (f)** (*sarva* 'all' + *īśī* 'sovereign goddess') 1. The sovereign Goddess of all. 2. A name of the Goddess Lalitā.

**Sarveśwara (m)** (*sarva* 'all' + *īśwara* 'lord') 1. The Lord of all. See the Bhagavad Gītā XIII:27-8; XVIII:61. 2. The 96th name of Lord Vishṇu as listed in the Vishṇu Sahasranāma. In his commentary Śrī Śaṅkara states, "The Lord of all lords is called the Lord of all, as revealed in the Upanishads, 'He is the Lord of all.'" 3. A name of Lord Śiva.

**Sarveśwarī (f)** (*sarva* 'all' + *īśwarī* 'sovereign goddess') 1. The sovereign Goddess of all. 2. A name of the Divine Mother in any of Her major manifestations.

**Satī (f)** 1. The existent. 2. The good or faithful. 3. The name of Daksha's daughter who became the wife of Lord Śiva and who burnt herself to death in her father's sacrificial fire when he did not invite her Divine Husband to his sacrifice. She was later reborn as Himavan's daughter, Pārvatī, and united to Lord Śiva. 4. The 68th of the Goddess Lakshmī's 108 names. 5. A name given to women who burn themselves in the funeral pyre of their husbands.

**Satpati (m)** (*sat* 'good, genuine, existent' + *pati* 'lord') 1. The good Lord. 2. The Lord of the good ones. 3. A name of Indra.

**Sattā (f)** (*sat* 'good, genuine, existent' + *ta* 'nominalizing suffix') Pure Being or Existence. The 701st name of Lord Vishṇu as listed in the Vishṇu Sahasranāma. In his commentary Śrī Śaṅkara writes, "The state which is devoid of generic, extrinsic, and intrinsic differences is *Sattā* or pure Being, as revealed in the Chāndogya Upanishad, 'In the beginning, dear boy, this (universe) was Being alone, one only, without a second.'" In the Nṛisimhottara-Tāpinī Upanishad it is said, *"Sattāmātram Hīdam Sarvam,"* "Verily, all this (universe) is but pure Being."

**Sattwa (m)** (*sat* 'good, genuine, existent' + *twa* 'nominalizing suffix') 1. Purity or goodness. 2. The quality of nature that is characterized by purity and tranquility. 3. The name of a son of Dhṛitarāshṭra.

**Sattwavan (m)** (*sattwa* 'goodness, purity' + *van* 'having') 1. Endowing with *sattwa* (i.e. goodness, purity and tranquility). 2. A name of Lord Vishṇu.

**Satyabhāmā (f)** (*satya* 'true, truth' + *bhāmā* 'beaming') Beaming with truth; the name of a wife of Śrī Kṛishṇa.

**Satyajit (m)** (*satya* 'true, truth' + *jit* 'winner') 1. The truth-winner. In the Muṇḍaka Upanishad it is said, *"Satyam-Eva Jayate, Nānṛitam,"* "Truth alone wins, not untruth." 2. The name of a son of Śrī Kṛishṇa.

**Satyam (m)** 1. The true, truth. 2. The 106th, 212th and 869th names of Lord Vishṇu as listed in the Vishṇu Sahasranāma. In his commentary Śrī Śaṅkara states, "1) Since His nature is not unreal, the supreme Self is called truth, as revealed in the Taittirīya Upanishad, 'The Absolute is Truth, Knowledge, Infinite.' 2) The Lord is thus called because He is with and without form... 3) He is called *'Satya'* because He has the forms of *prāṇa (sat)*, food *(ti)* and sun *(yam)*. 4) He is also thus called because He is the goodness *(sādhutwa)* in holy men *(satsu)*. 5) In His nature is the virtue of truth-speaking. 6) Again, it means the Lord is the Truth of truth *(satyasya satyam)* as revealed in the Bṛihad-Āraṇyaka Upanishad, 'Prāṇas are the (relative) truth, and He is their Truth.'" In the Bṛihad-Āraṇyaka Upanishad truth is explained as follows: "This name *Satya* consists of three syllables: *'Sa,' 'Ti'* and *'Ya.'* The first and last syllables are Truth. In the middle is untruth. This untruth is enclosed on either side by truth. Hence there is a preponderance of truth. One who knows as above is never hurt by untruth." Truth is further clarified in the Chāndogya Upanishad: "These are indeed the three syllables: *'Sa,' 'ti,'* and *'Yam'*. That which is *'Sa'* is the immortal. That which is *'Ti'* is the mortal. That which is *'Yam'* holds (yacchati) the two together...Verily, he who knows thus goes daily to the heavenly world." In the Yogasūtras, truthfulness is the second among the five Yamas. See II:30,36. Also see the Bhagavad Gītā X:4; XVI:2; XVII:15.

**Satyarūpā (f)** (*satya* 'true, truth' + *rūpā* 'form, image') 1. The form or nature of truth. 2. The 233rd name of the Goddess Lalitā as listed in the Brahmāṇḍa-Purāṇa. In his commentary Śrī Śaṅkara states, "1) *Satyam* is that which is not inert or unreal. It is of the nature of *Sat-Cid-Ānanda*, Truth-Knowledge-Bliss, which is Her *Rūpam* or form. 2) *Sat* means earth, water and fire which are perceptible to the senses. *Tyat* means air and space which are to be inferred, being imperceptible as the objects of transcendental knowledge. This is revealed in the Taittirīya Upanishad, *"'ac'ca Tyac'cābhavat'* 'It became *Sat* and *Tyat.'* Her form is *Sattya."*

**Satyavan (m)** (*satya* 'truth' + *van* 'having') 1. The truthful. See the Yogasūtras II:36. 2. The name of Sāvitrī's husband.

**Satyavatī (f)** (*satya* 'truth' + *vatī* 'having') 1. The truthful. 2. The name of Vyāsa's mother.

**Satyā (f)** True, Truth.

**Savitā (m)** 1. The impeller, begetter. 2. A name of the Sun-God. Brahmacārīs meditate upon *Savitā* as Īśwara at dawn, noon and dusk while repeating the Gāyatrī Mantra, also called the Sāvitrī. *Savitā* thus becomes the impeller of their intellect. 3. A name of Lord Vishṇu. In the Vishṇu-Dharmottara it is written, *"Prajānām Tu Prasavanāt-Savite'ti Nigadyate,"* "Because He has begotten all beings, He is called *Savitā*, the Begetter."

**Sādhaka (m)** 1. Skillful, efficient. 2. A spiritual aspirant.

**Sādhana (m)** 1. (Spiritual) practice or means. 2. The name of a Ṛishi, who was one of the seers of the Rigveda.

**Sādhanā (f)** (Spiritual) practice or means.

**Sādhu (m)** 1. The righteous or holy. 2. The 243rd name of Lord Vishṇu as listed in the Vishṇu Sahasranāma. In his commentary Śrī Śaṅkara states, "1) Well-behaved, the Lord is called *'Sādhu.'* 2) He accomplishes (*sādhayati*) everything. 3) He fulfills things without the help of the usual requisites." Also see the Bhagavad Gītā IV:8; IX:30.

**Sādhwī (f)** 1. The virtuous. 2. A name of the Goddess Lalitā. In his commentary on the 300 Names of the Goddess Lalitā, Śrī Śaṅkara states, "Sādhu is one endowed with sattwaguṇa, one who is well versed in every branch of learning, of good conduct, endowed with divine attributes. He is Śiva. She, as His wife, is a traditional example of chaste or devoted wife. Hence She is '*Sādhwī*.'"

**Sādhyā (f)** 1. The attainable. 2. A name of the Goddess Lalitā. In his commentary, Śrī Śaṅkara elaborates on this name by saying, "(It indicates) the result of effort. She can be attained or realized *(Sādhyā)* as Brahman through worship, by competent seekers adept in the four disciplines (i.e. discernment, dispassion, sixfold wealth and desire of liberation) and as a result of their hearing the great Vedāntic sayings. She is thus the fruit of Sādhana or spiritual effort."

**Sāmba (m)** (*sa* 'with' + *amba* 'mother') Attended by the Divine Mother; a name of Lord Śiva as always attended by His consort, the Goddess Pārvatī who stands for Self-knowledge and whom the Lord never forgets.

**Sāmbaśiva (m)** (*sa* 'with' + *amba* 'mother' +*śiva* 'a name of God') Lord Śiva attended by the Divine Mother. [See **Śiva**]

**Sāra (m)** The Essence. In the Māṇḍūkya Upanishad expounding the transcendent state of Consciousness (Turīyāvasthā), Truth is revealed as *"Ekātma-Pratyaya-Sāram"* or "the Essence of Consciousness which is the One Self." This is explained by Śrī Śaṅkara in two ways according to the twofold meaning of *Sāra* as "traceable" and "valuable" thus: "That Turīya which is traceable *(Anusaraṇīya)* by the unfailing belief (Pratyaya) that one and the same Self (Ekātman) persists in the states of waking, dream, and deep sleep, is *Ekātma-Pratyaya-Sāram.* It also means, with regard to Its knowledge, Turīya has for Its valid proof *(Sāram)* the single (Eka) belief (Pratyaya) in the Self (Ātman), as taught in the Bṛihad-Āraṇyaka Upanishad, *'Ātme'ty'evo-'pāsīta,'* 'One should meditate upon It as the Self alone.'"

**Sārada Devī (f)** The name of the wife of Śrī Rāmakṛishṇa, who is generally referred to as the Holy Mother.

**Sāttwika (m)** 1. He who is *sattwic* (i.e. endowed with purity, goodness, and tranquility). See the Bhagavad Gītā X:36; XIV:11. 2. A name of Lord Vishṇu.

**Sāttwikī (f)** She who is *sattwic* (i.e. endowed with purity, goodness, and tranquility).

**Sāvarṇa (m), Sāvarṇi (m)** The son of Suvarṇā. The name of the next eighth Manu, whose mother will be Suvarṇā, the present seventh Manu being named Vaivaswata or the son of the Sun-God, Vivaswan.

**Sāvitra (m)** 1. The son of Savitā (i.e. of the Sun-God). 2 A name of Karṇa. 3. The name of various gods.

**Sāvitrī (f)** The consort of Savitā (i.e. of the Sun-God); a name for the Gāyatrī Mantra, which addresses Īśwara as the Sun-God "Savitā," and is thus called "*Sāvitrī*," "The sacred verse relating to Savitā." The Gāyatrī Mantra of the Ṛigveda is thus personified as the Goddess *Sāvitrī* and is identified with the midday Sandhyā or noon prayer. In praise of *Sāvitrī* as the Gāyatrī Mantra, Manu says:

*Ekāksharam Param Brahma,*
*Prāṇāyāmāhj Param Tapaḥ,*
*Sāvitryās-tu Param Nāsti*
*Maunāt-Satyam Viśishyate.*

The monosyllable (OM) is the supreme Absolute,
Prāṇāyāmas are the highest austerity,
no mantra is higher than the *Sāvitrī* (Gāyatrī)
and truth is better than (mere) silence.

Manu also says that for a boy leaving his parents during Brahmacarya, the spiritual master becomes his father and *Sāvitrī* (the Gāyatrī Mantra) his mother.

**Senāpati (m)** (*senā* 'army' + *pati* 'lord') 1. The lord of an army. 2. A name of Lord Kārttikeya.

**Seneśwara (m)** (*sena* 'army' + *īśwara* 'lord') 1. The lord of an army. 2. A name of Lord Kārttikeya.

**Sevan (m), Sevā (f)** The embodiment of service. See the Bhagavad Gītā IV:34; XIV:26.

**Sevaka (m), Sevikā (f)** The servant of God.

**Shaṇmukha (m)** (*shaṭ* 'six' + *mukha* 'face, mouth') 1. The six-faced. 2. A name of Lord Śiva's son Kumāra, also known as Skanda, Kārttikeya, Guha, Subrahmaṇya, etc. This name comes from his having taken six mouths to suck the milk of the six Pleiades or Kṛittikas.

**Siddha (m)** 1. The perfected or accomplished. 2. A class of semi-divine beings residing on higher planes. According to Śrī Saṇkara, the *Siddhas* are those who at their very birth attained a high degree of virtue, knowledge, dispassion and supremacy, including the eight powers mentioned in the Yoga Sūtras III:33,46. 3. The 97th and 819th names of Lord Vishṇu as listed in the Vishṇu Sahasranāma. In his commentary Śrī Śaṅkara states, "The Lord is called the accomplished because of His ever perfect nature. He is also thus called since His perfection (*Siddhi*) does not depend on others." See the Bhagavad Gītā IV:38; VI:45; X:26.

**Siddhārtha (m)** (*siddha* 'accomplished, perfected' + *artha* 'aim') 1. He who has accomplished his goal. 2. The 252nd name of Lord Vishṇu as listed in the Vishṇu Sahasranāma. In his commentary Śrī Śaṇkara states, "The Lord whose objects of desire are fullfilled is called *Siddhārtha*, as revealed in the Chāndogya Upaṇishad, '(This Self is) of truthful desires.'"

**Siddhi (f)** 1. Perfection, accomplishment; the 86th of the Goddess Lakshmī's 108 names. 2. The 98th name of Lord Vishṇu as listed in the Vishṇnu Sahasranāma. In his commentary Śrī Śaṅkara states, "The Lord Himself is called 'Perfection' because of His nature of Consciousness in everything or because His nature is unsurpassed. Due to their perishability, heaven and other planes are unfruitful comparatively." See the Bhagavad Gītā III:20; VIII:28; IX:20-1; XVIII:45-6, 49-50 and the Yogasūtras III: 38.

**Sītā (f)** The furrow-born; the name of Śrī Rāma's wife who is said to have sprung from a furrow made by King Janaka while ploughing the ground to prepare it for a sacrifice. The king named her *Sītā*, the "furrow," and reared her as his daughter. *Sītā* is considered the incarnation of the Goddess Lakshmī and the reincarnation of Vedavatī of the golden age. She is the model of a perfect and chaste wife.

**Sītābhirāma (m)** (*śītā* 'the wife of Śrī Rāma' + *abhirāma* 'delight') Sītā's delight; a name of Śrī Rāma.

**Skanda (m)** 1. The spurting or flowing. 2. A name of Lord Śiva's son born to destroy the demon Tāraka. He was thus called by the Gods because He flowed out of the holy Ganges at birth or because He was emitted from Lord Śiva's divine seed. Some of His other names are Kārttikeya, Subrahmaṇya, Guha, Kumāra, etc. In the Chāndogya Upanishad, *Skanda* is identified with Sanatkumāra, and both were life-long Brahmacārīs. See the Bhagavad Gītā X:24. 3. The 327th name of Lord Vishṇu as listed in the Vishṇu Sahasranāma. In his commentary Śrī Śaṅkara states, "The Lord who flows *(skandati)* in the form of the moon's nectar, or who dries up (sravati) everything in the form of the wind is called *Skanda.*"

**Smṛiti (f)** 1. Memory. In the Chāndogya Upanishad, Sanatkumāra says to

Nārada:

*Āhāra-Śuddhau Sattwa-Śuddhiḥ*
*Sattwa-Śuddhau Dhruvā Smṛitiḥ*
*Smṛiti-Lambhe Sarva-Granthīnām*
*Vipramokshaḥ.*

When sense-perception is pure (from love and hate), there is purity of mind.
When the mind is pure, memory becomes firm (in the Self).
When such memory is gained, there is release from all the knots (of ignorance).

Also see the Bhagavad Gītā VIII:14; X:34; XV:15; and the Yogasūtra I:20. 2. The body of "recalled" scriptures having a human origin, distinguished from the "Śruti" or the "revealed" Vedas of non-human origin. Examples of scriptures classified as *Smṛiti* are the Rāmāyaṇa, Mahābhārata, Purāṇas, Gītā and Sūtras. 3. Daughter of Daksha and wife of Aṅgiras. 4. Daughter of Dharma and Medhā.

**Snehan (m)** 1. Loving or affectionate. 2. Friend of all. 3. A name of Lord Śiva.

**Soma (m)** 1. The nectar of immortality. 2. A name of the Moon-God, who presides over the mind, was born from the churning of the milk ocean, and is praised in many Vedic hymns. He is the Lord of plants, especially the Soma plant giving a relative immortality, sought after by Gods and men. See the Bhagavad Gītā XV:13. 3. (*sa* 'with' + *Umā* 'name of the Goddess Pārvatī') A name of Lord Śiva meaning "He who is with Umā."

**Subhadrā (f)** (*su* 'greatly, very' + *bhadrā* 'auspicious, blessed') 1. The greatly blessed or auspicious. 2. The name of a wife of Arjuna, the younger sister of Śrī Kṛishṇa and the mother of Abhimanyu.

**Subhaga (m)** (*su* 'greatly, very' + *bhaga* 'fortunate') 1. The very fortunate. 2. A name of Lord Śiva.

**Subhagā (f)** (*su* 'greatly, very' + *bhagā* 'fortunate') The very fortunate.

**Subrahmaṇya (m)** (*su* 'greatly, very' + *brahmaṇya* 'dear to Brahmaṇas') 1. Very dear to the Brāhmaṇas or holy men. 2. A name of the son of Lord Śiva who is also known as Kārttikeya, Kumāra, Skanda, etc.

**Sudāma (m)** (*su* 'greatly, very' + *dāma* 'giving') 1. He who gives greatly, the bountiful. 2. The name of a friend and devotee of Śrī Kṛishṇa, who was poor and became wealthy through the Lord's grace.

**Sudāman (m)** (*su* 'greatly, very' + *dāman* 'giving') 1. The bountiful. 2. A name of Airāvata, the elephant of Lord Indra, who came out of the milk ocean when it was churned by gods and demons.

**Sudāminī (f)** (*su* 'greatly, highly' + *dāminī* 'giving') 1. The bountiful. 2. The name of Śamīka's wife.

**Sudarśana (m)** (*su* 'good, very' + *darśana* 'seeing, looking at, knowing') 1. The good-looking. 2. The name of the discus of Lord Vishṇu, with which He protects the worlds. It represents the mind principle (manas) and hence is swifter than the wind. 3. The 417th name of Lord Vishṇu as listed in the Vishṇu Sahasranāma. In his commentary Śrī Śaṅkara states, "1) The Lord whose vision (*darśana*) or knowledge is the excellent (*su*) fruit of salvation is called 'He who has excellent vision.' 2) It means His lovely eyes are like the lotus petals, or again, 3) that He is easily (sukhena) seen (driśyate) by His devotees."

**Sudāsa (m), Sudāsī (f)** (*su* 'good, excellent' + *dāsa/ī* 'servant') The good servant.

**Sudeva (m), Sudevī (f)** (*su* 'good, excellent' + *deva/ī* 'god/goddess') The excellent god/goddess.

**Sudhī (f)** (*su* 'good, excellent' + *dhī* 'intelligence') She who has the good intelligence that follows the revealed Vedic scriptures.

**Sudhīra (m)** (*su* 'highly, very' + *dhīra* 'intelligent, firm) 1. Very intelligent. 2. Very firm.

**Sudīti (f)** (*su* 'good, excellent' + *dīti* 'flame') The bright flame, symbolizing the Light of pure Consciousness.

**Sugandhi (m)** (*su* 'highly, very' + *gandhi* 'fragrant') 1. The very fragrant. 2. A name of Lord Śiva, meaning He is endowed with a divine fragrance and is as subtle in all beings as the fragrance in sandalwood. This name is used in the Mahā-Mṛityuṅjaya Mantra, which is as follows:

*OM Tryambakam Yajāmahe*
*Sugandhim Pushṭi-Vardhanam,*
*Urvārukam-Iva Bandhanān'*
*Mṛityor-Mukshīya Māmṛitāt!*

We worship the Three-Eyed Lord
of excellent fragrance, the Increaser of welfare.

Just as the cucumber from its binding,
may we be released from death, not from immortality!

**Sugrīva (m)** (*su* 'good, excellent' + *griva* 'neck') 1. The handsome-necked. 2. The name of Śrī Rāma's ally, an incarnation of the Sun-God and king of monkeys, whose throne was usurped by his brother Vāli. After being re-established as king, he assisted Śrī Rāma in rescuing Sītā from the hands of the demon Rāvaṇa.

**Suguṇā (f)** (*su* 'good, excellent, very' + *guṇā* 'quality, virtue') Good-natured, very virtuous, she whose mind predominates in the Sattwa *Guṇa* or purity.

**Suhartā (m)** (*su* 'good, excellent, very' + *hartā* 'seizer') 1. The good seizer. 2. A name of Garuḍa, probably referring to his having seized the moon's nectar.

**Suma (n)** Flower.

**Sumaṅgalī (f)** (*su* 'very, highly' + *maṅgalī* 'auspicious') Greatly auspicious.

**Sumanas (m)** (*su* 'good, excellent' + *manas* 'mind') Pure-minded.

**Sumati (f)** (*su* 'good, excellent' + *mati* 'thought, mind') Pure-minded.

**Sumeka (m), Sumekā (f)** (*su* 'good, excellent, very' + *meka* 'fixed') Well fixed.

**Sumeru (m)** (*su* 'good, excellent, very' + *meru* 'name of a mountain') The beautiful Mount Meru, a mythical mountain spoken of as the axis of the universe and on which the assembly of gods takes place. It stands as the backbone in the human body and is symbolized as the most prominent bead in rosaries or mālās used for doing japa.

**Sumitrā (f)** (*su* 'good, excellent' + *mitrā* 'friend') 1. The good friend. 2. The name of one of King Daśaratha's wives, who was the mother of both Lakshmaṇa and Śatrughna.

**Sumukhī (f)** (*su* 'good, excellent, very' + *mukhī* 'face') The bright-faced, a face illuminated by the inner light of wisdom.

**Sunara (m), Sunarī (f)** (*su* 'good, excellent' + *nara/ī* 'man/woman') Virtuous man or woman.

**Sunaya (m)** (*su* 'good, excellent' + *naya* 'conduct') 1. He who has good or wise conduct. 2. The good leader.

**Sunda (m)** 1. Melting, very tender. 2. The 792nd name of Lord Vishṇu as listed in the Vishṇu Sahasranāma. In his commentary Śrī Śaṅkara states, "The Lord who melts (unatti) exceedingly (sushṭhu) is called *Sunda*, that is to say the Lord is a treasure of compassion."

**Sundaram (m)** 1. The beautiful or handsome. 2. The 791st name of Lord Vishṇu as listed in the Vishṇu Sahasranāma. In his commentary Śrī Śaṅkara states, "Because He is endowed with an all-surpassing beauty, the Lord is called the Beautiful."

**Sundareśwara (m)** (*sundara* 'beautiful' + *īśwara* 'lord') 1. The beautiful Lord. 2. A name of Lord Śiva as consort of the Goddess Mīnākshī at Madurai.

**Sundarī (f)** The beautiful.

**Sunirmalā (f)** (*su* 'highly, very' + *nirmalā* 'without a blemish') The perfectly immaculate. [See **Nirmalā**]

**Sunīti (f)** (*su* 'good, excellent' + *nīti* 'conduct or behavior') She who has good conduct or behavior.

**Suparṇa (m)** (*su* 'good, excellent' + *parṇa* ' wing, leaf') 1. He who has beautiful wings. 2. A name of Lord Vishṇu's divine vehicle, the eagle Garuḍa. 3. He who has beautiful leaves. 4. The 192nd and 855th names of Lord Vishṇu as listed in the Vishṇu Sahasranāma. In his commentary, Śrī Śaṅkara states, "Due to His having beautiful wings, the Lord is called *Suparṇa*, 'He who has beautiful wings.' In the Muṇḍaka and Śwetāśwatara Upanishads the Self, in Its conditioned and unconditioned aspects, is spoken of as 'Two birds of beautiful wings.' In the Mahābhārata, the Lord says, 'I am *Suparṇa* (Garuḍa) among birds.' It also means 'having good leaves,' as stated in the Bhagavad Gītā XV:1, where the world is spoken of as an inverted tree with the Vedas as leaves and the Lord as root."

**Suparṇā (f)** (*su* 'good, excellent' + *parṇā* 'wing, leaf') She who has beautiful leaves (i.e. who is like a lotus).

**Supatha (m)** (*su* 'good, excellent' + *patha* 'path') He who follows a virtuous path.

**Suprasannā (f)** (su 'greatly, very' + prasannā 'serene') The very serene. The 54th of the Goddess Lakshmī's 108 names.

**Supriyā (f)** (*su* 'greatly, very' + *priyā* 'beloved') Greatly beloved. In the Bṛihad-Āraṇyaka Upanishad it is taught, *"Ātmānam-eva Priyam-Upāsīta,"* "One should meditate upon the Self alone as dear." See the Bhagavad Gītā VII:17; XII:20.

**Supuṇyā (f)** (*su* 'greatly, very' + *puṇyā* 'virtuous, holy') The very virtuous or holy.

**Supushpā (f)** (*su* 'good, excellent' + *pushpā* 'flower') The beautiful flower.

**Surabhāva (m)** (*sura* 'god' + *bhāva* 'existence, state, feeling') 1. The divine state. 2. The divine feeling and meditation.

**Suradeva (m)** (*sura* 'of gods' + *deva* 'god') 1. The God of gods. See the Bhagavad Gītā X:2. 2. A name of Lord Vishṇu. 3. A name of Lord Śiva.

**Suramuni (m)** (*sura* 'god' + *muni* 'thoughtful, sage') The divine sage.

**Suranadī (f)** (*sura* 'god' + *nadī* 'river') 1. The river of the gods. 2. The divine river. 3. A name of the holy Ganges.

**Suranāyaka (m)** (*sura* 'god' + *nāyaka* 'leader') 1. The leader of the gods. 2. A name of Indra.

**Surañjana (m), Surañjanī (f)** (*su* 'greatly, very' + *rañjana/ī* 'charming') Greatly or very charming.

**Surapatha (m)** (*sura* 'god' + *patha* 'path') 1. The path of the gods. 2. The milky way.

**Surapati (m)** (*sura* 'god' + *pati* 'lord') 1. The Lord or ruler of the gods. 2. A name of Indra. 3. A name of Lord Śiva.

**Surapushpā (f)** (*sura* 'god' + *pushpā* 'flower') The celestial or divine flower.

**Surasā (f)** (*su* 'good, excellent' + *rasā* 'nectar') The excellent nectar. [See **Soma**]

**Surasmi (m)** (*su* 'excellent, good' + *rasmi* 'ray') 1. He who has beautiful rays. 2. A name of the Moon-God.

**Surasundara (m), Surasundarī (f)** (*sura* 'god' + *sundara/ī* 'beautiful') Having divine beauty.

**Surādhipa (m)** (*sura* 'of god's + *adhipa* 'over-lord') 1. The Lord of the gods. 2. A name of Indra.

**Surādri (m)** (*sura* 'of gods' + *adri* 'mountain') 1. The mountain of the gods. 2. A name of Mount Sumeru.

**Surendra (m)** (*sura* 'of gods' + *indra* 'chief') 1. The chief of the gods. 2. The God Indra.

**Sureśa (m)** (*sura* 'of god's + *īśa* 'lord') 1. The Lord of the gods. 2. The 85th name of Lord Vishṇu as listed in the Vishṇu Sahasranāma. [See **Sureśwara**]

**Sureśwara (m)** (*sura* 'of god's + *īśwara* 'lord') 1. The Lord of the gods. 2. The 286th name of Lord Vishṇu as listed in the Vishṇu Sahasranāma. In his commentary Śrī Śaṅkara states, "He is the Lord (*Īśwara*) of the gods (*surāṇām)* and of the virtuous donors (*surā* )." 3. The name of one of Śrī Śaṅkara's four great disciples who was considered a partial incarnation of Lord Brahmā. While still a householder and upholder of ritualism, he entered into a long debate with Śrī Śaṅkara. When the great master won, he renounced the married life and followed the Ācārya as a Sannyāsin or renunciate. He is well known as the Vārttika-Kāra, the author of the Vārttikas or versified commentaries on some of Śrī Śaṅkara's works. His chief work is entitled the "Naishkarmya-Siddhi" or "Perfection of Actionlessness." He was reborn as Vācaspati Miśra, the reputed commentator on the six Darśanas. He was the head of the Śṛiṅgeri monastery and is thus connected with the three Sannyāsa branches known as Saraswatī, Purī, and Bhāratī.

**Sureśwarī (f)** (*sura* 'of gods' + *īswarī* 'sovereign goddess') 1. Sovereign Goddess of the gods. 2. A name for any manifestation of the Divine Mother.

**Surī (f)** The Goddess.

**Suśīlā (f)** (*su* 'very, greatly' + *śīlā* 'virtuous') The greatly virtuous.

**Sushūti (m)** (*su* 'good, excellent' + *ūti* 'birth') Of good birth.

**Suvarṇā (m)** (*su* 'good, excellent' + *varṇā* 'color') 1. Having a beautiful color. 2. Golden. 3. A name of the Goddess Lakshmī.

**Suvipra (m)** (*su* 'very, greatly' + *vipra* 'learned, inspired') 1. Very wise, learned or inspired. 2. A name used for Brahmins versed in Vedic lore.

**Sūnara (m), Sūnarī (f)** Glad or joyful.

**Sūrdās (m)** The name of a great devotee of God who lived in the 16th century A.D. and was known as the "blind bard of Agra."

**Sūrya (m)** 1. The impeller or acquirer. 2. A name of the Sun-God. The following verse is recited in honor of the Sun-God:

*Sūryam Sundara-Loka-Nātham-*
*Amṛitam Vedānta-Sāram Śivam*
*Jñānam Brahmamayam Sureśam-*
*Amalam Lokai'ka-Cittam Swayam,*

*Indrāditya-Narādhipam Sura-Gurum*
*Trailokya-Cūḍāmanim*
*Brahmā-Vishṇu-Śiva-Swarūpa-Hṛidayam*
*Vande Sadā Bhāskaram.*

I always salute to the Impeller (*Sūrya*), the beautiful Lord
of the world, the Immortal, the Essence of Vedānta,
the Auspicious, Who is Knowledge, whose very nature is
Brahman, who is the Lord of gods, the Immaculate,
the One Consciousness of the world itself, the Ruler of Indra,
of the solar deities and of men, the Master of the Gods
the Crest-Jewel of the three worlds, the very Heart of Lords
Brahmā, Vishṇu and Śiva, the Light-Maker.

3. The Begetter. The 883rd name of Lord Vishṇu as listed in the Vishṇu Sahasranāma. In his commentary Srī Śaṅkara states, "The Lord who begets (sūte) all or who brings forth splendor is called *Sūrya*, 'the Begetter.'"

**Sūryadeva (m)** (*śūrya* 'name of the Sun-God' + *deva* 'god') The God *Sūrya*.

**Sūtradhara (m), Sūtradhari (m)** (*sūtra* 'thread' + *dhara* 'holder') 1. The thread-holder. 2. The Self associated with the cosmic subtle body. 3. A name given to stage-directors.

**Swarāj (m)** (*swa* 'self' + *rāja* 'ruling, shining') Self-ruling, self-luminous. In the Mahā-Nārāyaṇa Upanishad the supreme Self is revealed as "*...So'Ksharaḥ Paramaḥ Swarāt,*" "...He is imperishable, supreme and self-sovereign." In the Chāndogya Upanishad, Sanatkumāra says to Nārada:

*...Ātmai've'dam Sarvam-Iti*
*Sa Vā Esha Evam Paśyann'*
*Evam Manvāna Evam Vijānann'*
*Ātmaratir-Ātmakrīḍa*
*Ātmamithuna Ātmānandaḥ*
*Sa Swarāḍ Bhavati.*

...The Self alone is all this.
Verily, seeing thus,
thinking thus and knowing thus,
one has pleasure in the Self, delight in the Self,
union in the Self, Joy in the Self.
He becomes Self-sovereign.

Likewise, in his Code of Law, Manu says:

*Sarva-Bhūta-Stham-Ātmānam*
*Sarva-Bhūtāni Cātmani,*
*Sampaśyann'Ātma-Yājī Vai*
*Swārājyam-Adhigacchati.*

Seeing the Self present in all beings
and all beings in the Self,
the sacrificer to the Self
verily attains self-sovereignty (or self-luminosity).

**Swarga (m)** Heaven from a Vedic perspective. There are fourteen worlds or planes, seven of which are inferior and seven superior. Among the superior planes, heaven is the third alone or it may include the other four above it also, namely, Mahaḥ, Janaḥ, Tapaḥ and Satyam. The realm of Indra is the third plane and like the other planes does not endure eternally. If one goes beyond the third plane, one may attain gradual liberation or Krama Mukti, gaining final knowledge in the seventh plane. If one cannot go higher than the third plane, one will be reborn according to his own karma, until he either attains liberation while alive (Jīvan Mukti) or goes beyond the third plane after death.

**Swarūpa (m)** (*swa* 'self, own' + *rūpa* 'form') One's own form or true nature, which in Vedānta is the true nature of the Absolute, the "Sat-Cid-Ānanda," "Truth-Knowledge-Bliss."

**Swāhā (f)** (*su* 'well' + *āhā* 'pouring') 1. Oblation. The sacrificial formula uttered while pouring oblations into the sacred fire for the gods. 2. A daughter of Daksha and the wife of the Fire-God Agni. 3. The 13th of the Goddess Lakshmī's 108 names.

# Ś

**Śabarī (f)** The name of a great woman ascetic whose story is told in the third book of the Rāmāyaṇa, chapter 74. She is said to have attained the heavenly fruit of her austerity by offering fruits to Śrī Rāma who blessed her with a visit at her Āśram. She is a manifestation of the Goddess Durgā.

**Śacī (f)** 1. The powerful or helpful. 2. A name of Indra's consort.

**Śakra (m)** 1. The strong or powerful. 2. A name of Lord Indra.

**Śakrāri (m)** (*śakra* 'a name of Indra' + *ari* 'enemy') The enemy of Śakra (i.e. of Indra); a name of Śrī Kṛishṇa who made the cowherds of Vraja stop their worship of Indra. Indra then angrily flooded their country, but Śrī Kṛishṇa lifted Govardhana Mount on His one finger for seven days to protect all. Thereafter Indra sumitted to Him. Śrī Kṛishṇa is also well known as having taken possession of Indra's celestial tree called Pārijāta.

**Śakta (m)** The able or capable.

**Śakti (f)** 1. Divine force or power, which is said to be threefold: *Icchā-Śakti* (will-power), *Jñāna-Śakti* (knowledge-power), and *Kriyā-Śakti* (action-power). It is revealed in the Śwetāśwatara Upanishad:

*Parāsya Śaktir-Vividhai'va Śrūyate*
*Swābhāvikī Jñāna-Bala-Kriyā Ca.*

His supreme power alone is heard in
the Vedas to be various and His knowledge,
strength, and action are natural to Him.

*Śakti* is also one of the six components in a mantra that is given to a disciple by the Guru at the time of initiation. 2. God's power personified as His consort and manifested as Saraswatī, Lakshmī, Pārvatī, and other goddesses.

**Śakti (m)** The fourth Guru in the traditional line of Gurus traced back to Lord Nārāyaṇa, or God Himself. He appeared after Brahmā and Vasishṭha, the Ṛishi. He was the eldest of Vasishṭha's 100 sons and the seer of a part of the Ṛigveda. He was also the father of the sage Parāśara and the grandfather of Vyāsa who came next in the line of Gurus.

**Śaktidāyaka (m)** (*śakti* 'power' + *dāyaka* 'giver') The giver of power.

**Śakuntalā (f)** She who is protected by *Śakunta* birds; the name of the mother of

Bharata, sovereign of all India. Once upon a time, Viśwāmitra was engaged in great austerity and the gods wanted to stop him lest he surpass them. They sent the nymph Menakā who charmed him away from his practices. She gave birth to a girl whom she left in a forest while Viśwāmitra returned to his austerities. The girl was protected by *Śakunta* birds till found by the sage Kaṇwa who called her *Śakuntalā* and reared her as his daughter. While in the sage's hermitage, King Dushyanta saw her and took her as his wife and they gave birth to Bharata. Her story is told in the Mahābhārata and the Padma Purāṇa and is the subject of Kālidāsa's drama, "Abhijñāna-*Śākuntalam*," the "Recognition of *Śakuntalā*."

**Śama (m)** 1. Quiet, tranquil. In a Vedāntic context this virtue comes after Viveka and Vairāgya and is the first of the "sixfold wealth" or "Shaṭ-Sampatti." In his Vivekacūḍāmani Śrī Śaṅkara explains this name,

*Virajya Vishaya-Vrātād-*
*Dosha-Dṛishṭyā Muhur-Muhuḥ,*
*Swa-Lakshye Niyatāvasthā*
*Manasaḥ Śama Ucyate.*

Detaching the mind from manifold sense-objects,
by perceiving again and again their defects,
and resting it permanently on one's objective
(i.e. God) is called *Śama* or calmness.

Also see the Bhagavad Gītā V:13; VI:3,7,27; X:4; XVIII:42,53. 2. The name of a son of Dharma and husband of Prāpti.

**Śambhava (m)** (*śam* 'happiness, bliss' + *bhava* 'origin, source') The Source of bliss; a name of Lord Śiva, also known as *Śambhu.*

**Śambhu (m)** (*śam* 'happiness, bliss' + *bhu* 'proceeding from source') 1. The source of happiness or bliss. 2. A famous name of Lord Śiva. 3. The 39th name of Lord Vishṇu as listed in the Vishṇu Sahasranāma. In his commentary Śrī Śaṅkara states, "The Lord who promotes *(bhāvayati)* happiness *(śam)* for His devotees is called the source of happiness."

**Śamyu (m)** 1. The benevolent. 2. The name of a son of Bṛihaspati.

**Śaṅkara (m)** (*śam* 'happiness, bliss' + *kara* 'maker') 1. The beneficent, the bliss-maker. 2. A famous name of Lord Śiva. 3. The name of the great Ācārya (master), also known as Śrī *Śaṅkarācārya* or Ādi *Śaṅkara*, who lived about 200 B.C. Considered a great incarnation of Lord Śiva, he stands as the ideal Sannyāsī or renunciate and jñāna-yogī. He was the disciple of Śrī Govindapāda, who was himself the incarnation of Patañjali Maharshi. His example is one of good conduct, perfect knowledge, and the highest samadhi or enlightenment. The purpose of this incarnation of Lord Śiva was to refute all wrong doctrines and to re-establish the original Vedic religion, especially that part known as Vedānta. For this reason he wrote masterly commentaries on the major Upanishads, on Vyāsa's Vedānta (or the Brahma) Sūtras and on the Bhagavad Gītā along with a number of works of his own, such as the Ātma-Bodha, Vivekacūḍāmaṇi and Upadeśa-Sāhasrī, and composed several poems to the various gods and goddesses. As the greatest exponent of Adwaita Vedānta or non-dualism, he expresses the central thought of all his teachings in the following hemistich:

*Brahma Satyam Jagan'Mithyā,*
*Jīvo Brahmai'va Nāparaḥ.*

Brahman is true, the universe illusory;
The living one is verily Brahman, not different.

His four disciples were Padmapāda, Hastāmalaka, Troṭaka and Sureśwara whom he placed as heads of the four monasteries or Maṭhas he founded at India's four quarters. He also set up the Sannyāsa order, dividing it into ten branches, among which is the renowned "Saraswatī." Śrī *Śaṅkara*, who comes as the tenth in the traditional line of Brahmavidyā-Gurus, is a Jagad-Guru or Universal Master, and the Goddess Saraswatī Herself recognized him as Sarvajña, an all-knowing sage. When his mission was fulfilled, he disappeared in a Himalayan cave at Kedarnāth, resuming his original nature as Lord Śiva. Śrī *Śaṅkara* is meditated upon with the following verse,

*Padmāsīnam Praśāntam Yama-Niratam-*
*Anaṅgāri-Tulya-Prabhāvam*
*Bhāle Bhasmāṅkitābham*
*Smita-Rucira-Mukhāmbhojam-*
*Indīvarākṣham,*
*Kambu-Grīvam Karābhyām-*
*Avihata-Vilasat-Pustakam Jñāna-Mudrām*
*Vandyam Gīrvāṇa-Mukhyair-*
*Nata-Jana-Varadam Bhāvaye*
*Śaṅkarāryam.*

I meditate upon the great *Śaṅkara* who is seated in the lotus,
Who is peaceful and given to self-restraint,
Whose glory is like that of Cupid's Enemy (i.e. Lord Śiva),
Who wears shining marks of ashes on His forehead,
Whose smiling and radiant face resembles the lotus,
Who has lotus-like eyes and a conch-like neck,
Who holds a spotless shining book and shows

the gesture of Knowledge with both His hands,
Who is worthy of salutation by the greatest gods and
Who blesses bowing devotees.

**Śaṅkarī (f)** (*śam* 'happiness, bliss' + *karī* 'maker') The beneficent; the consort of Śaṅkara (i.e. of Lord Śiva); a name of the Goddess Pārvatī.

**Śaṅkha (m)** The conch, which was produced along with other divine things during the churning of the milk ocean and which, in Lord Vishṇu's upper left hand, represents the principle of sattwic ego and the five Tanmātras or subtle elements. Its sound symbolizes the sacred syllable "OM."

**Śaṅkhadhara (m)** (*śaṅkha* 'conch' + *dhara* 'holder, bearer') The holder of the conch; a name of Lord Vishṇu, whose conch is named "Pāñcajanya."

**Śaṅkhapāṇi (m)** (*śaṅkha* 'conch' + *pāṇi* 'hand') Having the conch in hand; a name of Lord Vishṇu, whose conch is named "Pāñcajanya."

**Śaṅkhavan (m)** (*śaṅkha* 'conch' + *van* 'having') He who has the conch; a name of Lord Vishṇu, whose conch is named "Pāñcajanya."

**Śaṅkhin (m)** Possessor of the conch; a name of Lord Vishṇu, whose conch is named "Pāñcajanya."

**Śantanu (m)** (*śam* 'auspicious' + *tanu* 'form') 1. He who has an auspicious form. 2. The name of an ancient king, who was the father of Bhīshma, Citrāṅgada and Vicitravīrya.

**Śaraṇyā (f)** 1. The giver of refuge. 2. A name of Devī, the Divine Mother, which occurs in the following verse of the Devī-Māhātmya (XI:10):

*Sarva-Maṅgala-Māngalye!*
*Śive Sarvārtha-Sādhike!*
*Śaraṇye! Tryambake! Gauri!*
*Nārāyaṇi Namo'stu Te!*

O Auspicious among all auspiciousness!
O Consort of Śiva! Thou who accomplishes everything!
O Giver of refuge! O Three-eyed Goddess! O Shining!
O Consort of Nārāyaṇa, salutations be unto Thee!

**Śaravanabhava (m)** (*śara* 'reeds' + *vana* 'forest, thicket' + *bhava* 'born') He who is born in a thicket of reed; a name of Lord Śiva's son Kumāra who was born for the destruction of the demon Taraka and is also known as Kārttikeya, Subrahmaṇya, Skanda, Guha, etc. In the creation of this divine child the divine seed of Lord Śiva flowed first into the Fire-God Agni, then into the Goddess Gangā who gave birth to Him in a thicket of reeds.

**Śarmada (m)** (*śarma* 'bliss, joy' + *da* 'giver') The giver of bliss or joy.

**Śarmiṇī (f)** The blissful.

**Śarva (m)** 1. The destroyer or withdrawer. 2. The 19th of Lord Śiva's 108 names. 3. The 26th of Lord Vishṇu's 1000 names (Vishṇu Sahasranāma). In his commentary Śrī Śaṅkara states, "The Lord who withdraws (sṛiṇāti) all beings at the time of cosmic withdrawal is called the withdrawer."

**Śarvāṇī (f)** The consort of Śarva (i.e. of Lord Śiva); a name of the Goddess Pārvatī.

**Śaryāti (m)** The name of a son of Manu.

**Śaśī (m)** Hare-like or rabbit-like; a name of the Moon-God referring to the marks on the moon which resemble a hare or rabbit. See the Bhagavad Gītā X:21.

**Śatarūpā (f)** (*śata* 'a hundred' + *rūpā* 'form') She who has a hundred forms. The name of the wife of the first Manu, Swāyambhuva. In the Bṛihad-Āraṇyaka Upanishad it is revealed how the creator Virāj became as big as a man and a woman, and created men and other species through this Manu and his wife. Since she was born from him and was thus his daughter, she was afraid to unite with him and tried to hide herself by taking various forms but he himself took the corresponding masculine form each time and united with her. She is thus called *Śatarūpā*, she who has a hundred forms.

**Śauri (m)** 1. The grandson of Śūra, who was the paternal grandfather of Śrī Kṛishṇa. 2. A name of Śrī Kṛishṇa.

**Śākambharī (f)** (*śākam* 'herb' + *bharī* 'nourishing, bearing') The herb-nourishing or herb-bearing; a name of the Goddess Durgā.

**Śākinī (f)** 1. The powerful. 2. The name of a goddess identified with the Viśuddha Cakra.

**Śākta (m)** A devotee or worshipper of Śakti.

**Śākyamuni (m)** (*śākya* 'descendent from the Śakas' + *muni* 'sage') 1. The sage descendent of the Śaka tribe. 2. Name of Lord Buddha.

**Śāmbhava (m)** Devoted to Śambhu (i.e. Lord Śiva). [See **Śambhu**]

**Śāmbhavī (f)** 1. The consort of Śambhava (i.e. Lord Śiva). A name of the Goddess Pārvatī. [See **Śambhava**] 2. Name of a mudrā in which the gaze is fixed between the eyebrows.

**Śāntā (f)** 1. The appeased or pacified (i.e. whose mind is calmed down by the practice of Śama). [See **Śama**] 2. The 74th of the Goddess Lakshmī's 108 names.

**Śānti (f)** 1. Peace. Peace is invoked at the beginning and conclusion of all Upanishadic readings. Each Upanishad has its own Śānti-Pāṭha (Peace invocation). The word *Śānti* is repeated three times at the end of Śānti Mantras to remove three kinds of pain (i.e. Adhyātmic or personal, Adhibhautic or external and Adhidaivic or atmospheric). In the Yajur-Veda the following hymn is found:

*OM Dyauḥ Śāntir-Antarīksham! Śāntiḥ Pṛithivī!*
*Śāntir-āpaḥ! Śāntir-Oshadhayaḥ!*
*Śāntir-Vanaspatayaḥ Śāntiḥ!*
*Viswe Devāḥ! Śāntir-Brahma! Śāntiḥ Sarvam!*
*Śāntiḥ Śāntir-Eva! Śāntiḥ Sā Mā Śāntir-Edhi!*
*OM Śāntiḥ Śāntiḥ Śāntiḥ !*

Peace unto heaven! Peace unto the sky!
Peace unto the earth! Peace unto the waters!
Peace unto the herbs! Peace unto the trees!
Peace unto all gods! Peace unto the Absolute! Peace unto all!
Peace verily, peace! May that Peace be unto me!
OM! Peace! Peace! Peace!

Also see the Bhagavad Gītā II:70-1; IV:39; V:12, 29; VI:15; IX:31; XII:12; XVI:2; XVIII:62 and the twelfth book of the Mahābhārata entitled "*Śānti*-Parva." 2. A Peace-Goddess personified as the daughter of Śraddhā (Faith) and the friend of Karuṇā (Compassion). 3. The 584th of Lord Vishṇu's 1000 names (Vishṇu Sahasranāma). In his commentary Śrī Śaṅkara states, "The cessation of all ignorance is peace. That peace is the very Absolute."

**Śāradā (f)** The Autumnal; a name of the Goddess Saraswatī as worshipped in Kaśmīr and evoking the mildness and modesty of autumn season.

**Śāstrī (m)** Versed in the *śāstras* or scriptures in general, and the Vedas in particular. See the Bhagavad Gītā XVI:23-4.

**Śāstā (m)** 1. The teacher. 2. The 206th name of Lord Vishṇu as listed in the Vishṇu Sahasranāma. In His commentary Śrī Śaṅkara states, "The Lord who gives instructions to all by the means of revealed (Śruti) and written (Smṛiti) scriptures is called, the Teacher."

**Śāśwata (m)** [in Tamil **Śāśwatan**] 1. The permanent or perpetual. 2. The 57th name of Lord Vishṇu as listed in the Vishṇu Sahasranāma. In his commentary Śrī Śaṅkara states, "The Lord who exists at all times is called, the permanent. As revealed in the Vedas, 'He is permanent, auspicious, imperishable.'" See the Bhagavad Gītā II:20; IX:31; X:12; XIV:27; XVIII:56,62. 3. A name of Lord Śiva.

**Śāśwatī (f)** 1. The permanent or perpetual. 2. A name of the Earth-Goddess.

**Śesha (m)** The remainder; a name of Lord Vishṇu's thousand-headed serpent also known as Ananta and said to support the whole universe with its fourteen worlds. Ananta is called *Śesha* as he is the residue or remainder of the universe during cosmic dissolutions. Lord Vishṇu resting on *Śesha's* intertwined body in the milk ocean signifies the Self seated in the brain and knowable through a pure or sattwic mind. Patañjali Maharshi is an incarnation of *Śesha*. Also see the Bhagavad Gītā X:29.

**Śibi (m)** 1. The name of a Ṛishi who was one of the seers of the Ṛigveda. 2. The name of a king whose story is told in the Mahābhārata. He saved the Fire-God Agni, who had been transformed into a dove, from Indra, who had been transformed into a hawk, by offering the hawk (Indra) a quantity of his own flesh equal in weight to the dove.

**Śiva (m)** 1. The auspicious or pure. 2. The name of the third aspect of God, called Rudra in the Vedas. His glory is mainly told in the *Śiva*-Purāṇa. In the Kūrma-Purāṇa a Gītā treatise entitled "Īśwara-Gītā" embodies some of His teachings. His sacred symbol is the Liṅgam which expresses the Oneness of God and is especially worshipped during "*Śiva*-Rātri" or the "Night of *Śiva*." In the Śwetāśwatara Upanishad the Truth is referred to as *Śiva* and in the Maṇḍūkya Upanishad the true Self is referred to as *Śivam*, as in the following passage:

> *....Śāntam Śivam-Adwaitam*
> *Caturtham Manyante,*
> *Sa Ātmā Sa Vijñeyaḥ.*
>
> ...The Fourth (witnessing waking, dream,
> and deep sleep states) which they consider as
> Peaceful, Auspicious, and Non-dual is the Self,
> which should be realized.

2. Since Lord *Śiva* and Lord Vishṇu are aspects of One God, *Śiva* occurs as the 27th and 600th name of Lord Vishṇu as listed in His 1000 names (the Vishṇu

Sahasranāma). In his commentary Śrī Śaṅkara states, "Due to His purity from the three guṇas, the Lord is called *Śiva.* Also, purifying devotees through their mere remembrance of His name, He is called *Śiva.*"

**Śivabandhu (m)** (*śiva* 'a name of God' + *bandhu* 'friend') 1. A friend of Lord Śiva. 2. A name of Kubera.

**Śivadāsa (m)** (*śiva* 'a name of God' + *dāsa* 'servant') Servant of Lord Śiva.

**Śivadūtī (f)** (*śiva* 'a name of God' + *dūtī* 'messenger') 1. Messenger of Lord Śiva. 2. A name of the Goddess Durgā.

**Śivakarī (f)** (*śiva* 'auspiciousness, name of God' + *karī* 'maker, bringer') 1. The bringer or maker of auspiciousness. A name of the Goddess Annapūrṇā. 2. The 67th of the Goddess Lakshmī's 108 names.

**Śivapriyā (f)** (*śiva* 'a name of God' + *priyā* 'beloved') 1. Beloved of Lord Śiva. 2. A name of the Goddess Durgā.

**Śivarāja (m)** (*śiva* 'a name of God' + *rāja* 'king') The name of King Śivajī.

**Śivā (f)** 1. The auspicious Goddess; a name of the Goddess Pārvatī or Umā. 2. The 66th of the Goddess Lakshmī's 108 names.

**Śivānī (f)** The consort of Lord Śiva; a name of the Goddess Pārvatī or Umā.

**Śīlā (f)** The virtuous.

**Śobhanā (f)** 1. The beautiful. 2. In the Kena Upanishad, Umā Haimavatī, being the embodiment of pure Knowledge, is depicted as *Bahu-Śobhamānām* (of great beauty).

**Śraddhā (f)** 1. Faith, which is the fifth virtue of the Shaṭsampatti or the sixfold wealth. In a literal sense it is *Dhā,* 'steadiness' in *Śrat,* 'Truth' or Āstikya-Buddhi 'conviction about existence (of the Self),' without which concentration on the Self is impossible. It is also rendered as 'confidence' which implies free breathing (Viśwāsana). In his Vivekacūḍāmaṇi, Śrī Śaṅkara defines *Śraddhā* as follows:

*Śāstrasya Guru-Vākyasya*
*Satya-Buddhyāvadhāraṇā,*
*Sā Śraddhā Kathitā Sadbhir-*
*Yayā Vastūpalabhyate.*

Ascertainment of the Scripture and the

Guru's word, with conviction of their truth
is called Faith by sages,
through which the Reality is perceived.

In the Kaivalya Upanishad, the Creator Brahmā says to Aśwalāyana, *Śraddhā-Bhakti-Dhyāna-Yogād-Avaihi,* "Know (the Absolute) by faith, devotion and the Yoga of meditation!" In the Chāndogya Upanishad Sanatkumāra says to Nārada, "When one has faith, then alone does one reflect. Without faith, one does not reflect. The faithful alone reflects..." See the Bhagavad Gītā III:31; IV:39-40; VI:47; XII:2,20; XVII:3,17; XVIII:71 and the Yogasūtras I:20. 2. Faith personified as a Goddess in the Ṛigveda. 3. The 5th of the Goddess Lakshmī's 108 names.

**Śrī (f)** 1. Divine beauty, light, and wealth; a name of the Goddess Lakshmī, which occurs as the 76th of Her 108 names. Beauty or light means chiefly the light of knowledge, and wealth refers to the spiritual qualities giving rise to knowledge. 2. Illustrious, revered, when used as an honorific prefix to the names of gods, scriptures, and saints. Also see the Bhagavad Gītā X:34,41; XVIII: 78.

**Śridāman (m)** (*śrī* 'beautiful' + *dāman* 'garland') Having a beautiful garland; the name of a friend and devotee of Śrī Kṛishṇa.

**Śrīdevī (f)** (*śrī* 'a name of Lakshmī' + *devī* 'goddess') The Goddess *Śrī* (i.e. Lakshmī). [See **Śrī**]

**Śrīdhara (m)** (*śrī* 'a name of Lakshmī' + *dhara* 'bearer') The bearer of the Goddess Śrī (i.e. of the Goddess Lakshmī). The 610th name of Lord Vishṇu as listed in the Vishṇu Sahasranāma. In his commentary Śrī Śaṅkara states, "Bearing Śrī, the Mother of all beings, on His chest, the Lord is called the 'Bearer of Śrī.'"

**Śrīkaṇṭha (m)** (*śrī* 'beautiful' + *kaṇṭha* 'throat') The beautiful-throated. The 16th of Lord Śiva's 108 names, referring to the blue color on the Lord's neck, after He drank a deadly poison to save the world.

**Śrīkara (m)** (*śrī* 'beauty, light' + *kara* 'maker, doer') The maker or giver of wealth. The 611th of Lord Vishṇu's 1000 names as listed in the Vishṇu Sahasranāma. In his commentary Śrī Śaṅkara states, "The Lord who confers wealth on His devotees who remember, praise and worship Him, is called the 'Conferrer of Wealth.'"

**Śrīkarī (f)** (*śrī* 'beauty, light, wealth' + *karī* 'maker, doer') The maker or giver of wealth; a name of the Goddess Lakshmī who is Herself called Śrī. In Vedāntic context it means the Goddess Lakshmī, as symbolizing the light of Self-knowledge, gives Herself to the worshipper by revealing his/her true Self or Ātman.

**Śrīlā (f)** The fortunate or beautiful

**Śrīman (m)** (*śrī* 'beauty, light, wealth' + *man* 'having) 1. Having beauty and fortune; the beautiful. 2. The possessor of the Goddess Śrī (i.e. of the Goddess Lakshmī). The 22nd, 178th, 220th, and 613th of Lord Vishṇu's 1000 names as listed in the Vishṇu Sahasranāma. In his commentary Śrī Śaṅkara states, "1) The Lord on whose chest Śrī (Lakshmī) ever abides is called 'the Possessor of Śrī.' 2) It means He, having complete sovereignty, is the 'fortunate.' 3) It also means the 'luminous,' having an all-surpassing splendor." 3. Illustrious, revered, when used as an honorific prefix to the names of gods, scriptures, and saints. Also see the Bhagavad Gītā X:41.

**Śrīmatī (f)** (*śrī* 'beauty, light, wealth' + *matī* 'having') 1. Having beauty and fortune; the beautiful. 2. A name of Rādhā.

**Śrīnivāsa (m)** (*śrī* 'a name of Lakshmī' + *nivāsa* 'abode') The abode of the Goddess Śrī (i.e. of the Goddess Lakshmī). The 183rd and 607th of Lord Vishṇu's 1000 names (the Vishṇu Sahasranāma). In his commentary Śrī Śaṅkara states, "The Lord on whose chest abides the imperishable Goddess Śrī (Lakshmī) is called the Abode of Śrī. It also means the Lord abides in the fortunate ones."

**Śrīpati (m)** (*śrī* 'a name of Lakshmī' + *pati* 'lord') The Lord or consort of Śrī (i.e. of the Goddess Lakshmī). The 603rd of Lord Vishṇu's 1000 names as listed in the Vishṇu Sahasranāma. In his commentary Śrī Śaṅkara states, "1) Having rejected all gods, demons and others, during the churning of the milk ocean, Śrī (Lakshmī) chose Him (Vishṇu) as Her consort, and He is thus named the 'Lord of Śrī.' 2) It also means the supreme power (Parā Śakti) of which He is the Lord, as revealed in the Śwetāśwatara Upanishad, 'His supreme power alone is declared to be various.'"

**Śrī Rāma (m)** The revered or fortunate *Rāma*. [See **Rāma**]

**Śrīvatsa (m)** (*śrī* 'a name of Lakshmī' + *vatsa* 'dear') 1. Dear to Śrī (i.e. to the Goddess Lakshmī) 2. A name of Lord Vishṇu, especially of the curl of hair on His chest symbolizing Prakṛiti, the primordial matter.

**Śrīvāsa (m)** (*śrī* 'a name of Lakshmī' + *vasa* 'abode') 1. The abode of the Goddess Śrī (i.e. of the Goddess Lakshmī). 2. A name of Lord Vishṇu. 3. The lotus, since the Goddess Lakshmī is depicted seated on a lotus.

**Śruti (f)** 1. Hearing, revelation. A general name for the Vedas which were first heard by Lord Brahmā from the supreme Lord Nārāyaṇa and which are distinguished from the "Smṛiti" scriptures of human authorship. The Upanishads which form the concluding portion of the Vedas or Vedānta are included in the *Śruti*. 2. A daughter of Atri and the wife of Kardama. 3. In music, a quarter tone or microtone. [See **Veda**]

**Śubhakara (m), Śubhakarī (f)** (*śubha* 'auspiciousness' + *kara/ī* 'making, causing') Causing auspiciousness, beneficent.

**Śubhā (f)** The auspicious or beautiful. The 91st of the Goddess Lakshmī's 108 names.

**Śubhra (m)** The radiant or pure. This name is used to describe the Purusha or Self in the Muṇḍaka Upanishad, *Aprāno Hy'Amanāḥ Śubhraḥ...*" "Beyond Prāṇa and mind, pure..."

**Śubhrā (f)** 1. The radiant or pure. 2. The holy Ganges which is bright-colored and purifying. 3. Pure white; a name of the Goddess Saraswatī who is depicted seated on a white lotus or mounted on a white swan, wrapped in white clothes, adorned with white flowers and jewels, holding a white rosary—thus all white and pure.

**Śuci (m and f)** 1. The pure. 2. The 155th and 251st of Lord Vishṇu's 1000 names as listed in the Vishṇu Sahasranāma. In his commentary Śrī Śaṅkara states, "1) Due to His purifying those who remember, praise and worship Him, the Lord is called the Pure, as revealed in the Vedas, 'He is untouched, great and pure.' 2) It also means He is spotless, devoid of the taint of illusion and of its effect." 3. The 12th of the Goddess Lakshmī's 108 names. See the Bhagavad Gītā XII:16; XIII:7; XVI:3; XVII:14; XVIII:42.

**Śuddha (m)** The purified. See the Bhagavad Gītā V:7; VI:45; XVI:1; XVII:14,16; XVIII:51.

**Śuddhi (f)** 1. Purity. 2. A name of the Goddess Durgā.

**Śyāma (m)** 1. The dark. 2. A name of Śrī Kṛishṇa.

**Śyāmā (f)** 1. The dark. 2. A name of the Goddess Kālī.

# T

**Tadrūpa (m)** (*tat* 'That' + *rūpa* 'form') The form or nature of That (i.e. of the Absolute). The pronoun *Tat* or "that," pointing here to Brahman, is derived by Śrī Śaṅkara from the verbal root *Tan* meaning "to pervade" thus: *"Tanotīti Brahma Tat,"* "That which pervades *(tanoti)* is Brahman called *Tat."* In the Chāndogya Upanishad, the sage Uddālaka enlightens his son Śwetaketu nine times, through the great Vedāntic sentence *"Tat-Twam-Asi,"* "Thou art That." He says:

*Sa Ya Esho'ṇimai'tad-ātmyam-Idam*
*Sarvam,*
*Tat-Satyam, Sa Ātmā, Tat-Twam-Asi*
*Śwetaketo!*

That Being which is this subtleness
and Selfhood of all the universe, that is
the Truth, that is the Self;
That thou art, O Śwetaketu!

In the Bhagavad Gītā V:17 it is said:

*Tad-Buddhayas-Tad-ātmānas-*
*Tan'Nishṭhās-Tat-Parāyaṇāḥ,*
*Gacchanty'Apunar-āvṛittim*
*Jñāna-Nirdhūta-Kalmashāḥ.*

Their intelligence in That (Brahman),
their Self being That, established in That,
having That as their supreme goal,
sages go never again to return,
their sins shaken off by knowledge.

**Ṭakwara (m)** A name of Lord Śiva.

**Tamopaha (m)** (*tamaḥ* 'darkness' + *apaha* 'dispeller') 1. The dispeller of darkness. 2. A name of the Sun-God. 3. A name of the Moon-God. 4. A name of the Fire-God. 5. A name of Lord Vishṇu. 6. A name of Lord Śiva. 7. A name of the Guru or spiritual master. See the Bhagavad Gītā X:11.

**Taṇḍi (m)** The name of a Ṛishi who saw and praised Lord Śiva.

**Taṇḍu (m)** The name of an attendant of Lord Śiva, who was Bharata's dance teacher.

**Tanmaya (m), Tanmayī (f)** (*tat* 'That' + *maya, mayī* 'consisting') Consisting of "That" (i.e. Brahman). In the Muṇḍaka Upanishad *Tanmaya* is used in the following context:

*Praṇavo Dhanuḥ Śaro Hy'ātmā*
*Brahma Tal'Lakshyam-Ucyate,*
*Apramattena Veddhavyam*
*Śara-Vat Tanmayo Bhavet.*

The Praṇava (OM) is the bow, the (individual) self
is verily the arrow and Brahman is called its target.
It is to be hit by a careful one; like an arrow,
he should become one with It (*Tanmayaḥ*).

Likewise, in the Śwetāśwatara Upanishad it appears in the following passage:

*Ye Pūrvam Devā Ṛishayaś-Ca Tad-Vidus-*
*Te Tanmayā Amṛitā Vai Babhūvuḥ.*

Those gods and seers who realized That earlier, they
being one with That (*Tanmayāḥ*), became verily immortal.

**Tapaswī (m), Tapaswinī (f)** (*tapas* 'heat, ascetcism' + *vin/ī* 'having') 1. An ascetic, one who has "heat" or *Tapas*, which refers to Knowledge or Omniscience as the creative power of God in a divine context and to an effort to purify the mind in a human context. 2. God's divine *Tapas* is revealed in the Muṇḍaka Upanishad as, "...*Yasya Jñānamayam Tapaḥ,*" "...whose *Tapas* is constituted by Knowledge or Omniscience," and the Taittirīya Upanishad reveals God as creating the worlds through such omniscient *Tapas* thus: "*Sa Tapas-Taptwā, Idam Sarvam-Asṛijata,*" "Having exercised His *Tapas* (Omniscience), He created all this." 3. As to the human *tapas* it is enjoined in the Taittirīya Upanishad by the Water-God Varuṇa who tells his son the Maharshi Bhṛigu: "*Tapasā Brahma Vijijñāsaswa, Tapo Brahma,*" "Crave to know Brahman through *Tapas* ! *Tapas* is Brahman." As the best discipline conducive to knowledge, this *tapas* is specified in the Mahābhārata:

*Manasaś-Ce'ndriyāṇām Ca*
*Hy'Aikāgryam Paramam Tapaḥ,*
*Taj'Jyāyas Sarva-Dharmebhyaḥ*
*Sa Dharmaḥ Para Ucyate.*

One-pointedness of mind and senses
is verily the supreme *Tapas* or asceticism.
As it is higher than all virtues,

it is called the highest virtue.

4. Throughout the Rāmāyaṇa the life of ascetics in their Āśramas or Tapovanas (*Tapas* groves) is beautifully described, and its 24,000 verses opens with this very word:

*Tapas-Swādhyāya-Niratam*
*Tapaswī Vāgvidām Varam,*
*Nāradam Paripapraccha*
*Vālmīkir-Munipuṅgavam.*

The ascetic Vālmīki questioned Nārada
given to asceticism and study,
the best among speech-knowers
and the bull among sages. (I,i,1)

In this scripture, referring to both divine and human *tapas*, and using *tapas* as a central term, the Ṛishi Kaśyapa addresses Lord Vishṇu thus:

*Tapomayam Taporāśim*
*Tapo-Mūrtim Tapātmakam,*
*Tapasā Twām Sutaptena*
*Paśyāmi Purushottamam.*

Through well practised *tapas*,
I contemplate Thee, the highest Being,
Who consists in *tapas*, who art a heap of *tapas*,
the embodiment of *tapas* and whose nature is *tapas*. (I, xxix,12)

5. In his law-book Manu describes the supreme *tapas* as the breath-retention done while repeating the Gāyatrī Mantra at dawn, noon, and dusk during Sandhyā prayers. 6. It is through their power of *tapas* that the Ṛishis see the Vedic Mantras in the beginning. Great ascetics or *Tapaswins* are King Viśwāmitra, the seer of the Gāyatrī, whose unrivalled *tapas* raised him to the level of a Brahmarshi, and the Goddess Pārvatī or Umā, who practiced the utmost *tapas* for gaining Lord Śiva as her consort. 7. In the Yogasūtras, *tapas* is the first component of Kriyā-Yoga and the third of the five Niyamas. According to Vyāsa it means Dwandwa-Sahanam or bearing the pairs of opposites. It is he or she who, for the purification of the ego, willingly accepts pain that comes naturally (*not* self-inflicted) and who does not cause pain in return. See the Yogasūtras II:1,32,43 and the Bhagavad Gītā IV:10,28; V:29; VI:16-7; IX:27; X:5; XVI:1; XVIII:5; and in particular XVII:14-19.

**Tapodhana (m)** (*tapas* 'heat' + *dhana* 'rich') Rich in *tapas*. [See **Tapaswī**]

**Taponidhi (m)** (*tapas* 'heat' + *nidhi* 'treasure, abode') Treasure or abode of *tapas*. [See **Tapaswī**]

**Taponitya (m)** (*tapas* 'heat' + *nitya* 'constant') 1. Constant in *tapas*. [See **Tapaswī**] 2. Name of a teacher mentioned in the Taittirīya Upanishad.

**Tapatī (f)** 1. She who is warming. 2. The name of a daughter of the Sun-God and Chāyā, who is the wife of Samvaraṇa and the mother of Kuru.

**Taruṇa (m), Taruṇī (f)** The (ever) young.

**Tatkartā (m)** (*tat* 'that' + *kartā* 'creator') The Creator of that (universe), the Absolute or Brahman personified as the Creator Brahmā. See the Bhagavad Gītā III 27-8; IV:13-4; V:14-5; VII:6-7; IX:7-10; X:20; XI:15; XIII:29; XIV:3-4,19; XVIII:61.

**Tattwam (m)** [Tattwan in Tamil] (*tat* 'that' + *twam* 'nominizing suffix, -ness') 1. Truth, reality, essence. 2. The 963rd name of Lord Vishṇu as listed in the Vishṇu Sahasranāma. In his commentary Śrī Śaṅkara states, "Words such as Reality *(Tattwam)*, Immortality (Amṛitam), Truth (Satyam), Supreme Thing (Paramārtha) and With Reality *(Satattwam)* refer to one and the same thing, viz. the Absolute, the Truth in the highest sense and which is expressed by the word *Tattwam*, 'That-ness.'" Also see the Bhagavad Gītā II:16; III:28; IV:34; V:8. [See **Tadrūpa**] 3. In philosophy like Sāṅkhya-Darśana the name given to the different principles such as Prakṛiti and Purusha, Matter, and Spirit.

**Tavisha (m)** The strong and energetic, a name for the ocean and heaven.

**Tāṇḍava (m)** The dance of Lord Śiva.

**Tāpasa (m), Tāpasī (f)** An ascetic, one who has heat or *tapas*. [See **Tapaswī**]

**Tāraka (m)** 1. The deliverer. 2. The 105th of Lord Śiva's 108 names. 3. Knowledge born of discrimination. See the Yogasūtras III:55.

**Tāraṇa (m)** 1. Rescuing, saving. 2. The 337th name of Lord Vishṇu as listed in the Vishṇu Sahasranāma. In his commentary Śrī Śaṅkara states, "The Lord who enables one to cross (tārayati) the ocean of transmigration is called *Tāraṇa*, the Rescuing." In the Chāndogya Upanishad it is revealed, *"Tarati Śokam-Ātmavit,"* "The knower of the Self crosses over sorrow." Also see the Bhagavad Gītā XII:7; XVIII:58.

**Tārasāra (m)** (*tāra* 'saving, a name of the sacred syllable "OM"' + *tāra* 'essence') The essence of the sacred syllable "OM." This is known as *Tāra*, "the Saving." See the Tārasāra Upanishad.

**Tārā (f)** 1. Star and Savior. 2. A name of Devī, the Divine Mother, used in the Tantras.

**Tārāvatī (f)** (*tārā* 'star' + *vatī* 'having') Having stars, a name of the Goddess Durgā.

**Tāriṇī (f)** The Saving Goddess, a name of the Goddess Durgā, which refers to Her delivering Her devotees from all calamity.

**Tārendra (m)** (*tārā* 'star' + *indra* 'chief') The chief of stars; a name of the Moon-God. See the Bhagavad Gītā X:21.

**Tārikā (f)** The Savior.

**Tejas (n)** 1. Effulgence, brilliance, energy; a name of the fire element. 2. **(m)** Effulgent. This name occurs in the following verse:

*OM!*
*Namaḥ Śivāya Gurave*
*Satchidānanda-Mūrtaye,*
*Nishprapañcāya Śāntāya*
*Nirālambāya Tejase!*

OM!
Salutations to the Auspicious, to the Master,
to the Image of Truth-Knowledge-Bliss,
to the Expansionless, to the Peaceful,
to the Supportless, to the Effulgent!

Also see the Bhagavad Gītā VII:9-10; X:36,41; XV:12; XVI:3.

**Tejaswī (m), Tejaswinī (f)** (*tejas* 'effulgence' + *vin/ī* 'having') Effulgent, brilliant. This name occurs (in neuter) in the following Śānti Mantra recited at the beginning and end of some of the Upanishads:

*OM!*
*Saha Nāv'Avatu!*
*Saha Nau Bhunaktu!*
*Saha Vīryam Karavāvahai!*
*Tejaswi Nāv'Adhītam-Astu!*
*Mā Vidwishāvahai!*
*OM Śāntiḥ Śāntiḥ Śāntiḥ!*

OM!
Together, may He (God) protect us both!

Together, may He nourish us both!
Together, may we both acquire vigor!
Let our study (Adhītam) be brillant (*Tejaswi*)!
May we not hate each other!
OM! Peace, peace, peace!

Also see the Bhagavad Gītā VII:9-10; X:36,41; XV:12; XVI:3.

**Tejorāśi (m)** (*tejas* 'effulgence' + *rāśi* 'mass, heap') 1. Mass of splendor or effulgence. 2. A name of Lord Śiva. 3. A name of Mount Meru. 4. A name of Lord Vishṇu used by Arjuna in the Bhagavad Gītā XI:17.

**Tejomaya (m), Tejomayī (f)** (*tejas* 'effulgence' + *maya/ī* 'consisting of') Filled with, or consisting of effulgence, which stands for the Light of pure Consciousness.

**Tejovan (m), Tejovatī (f)** (*tejas* 'effulgence' + *van/vatī* 'having') He/she who has effulgence; the effulgent.

**Thirumal*(m)** [Tamil] The name of a South Indian sage.

**Thiruvalluvar* (m)** [Tamil] The name of a South Indian sage who was the author of the "Thirukkural."

**Tilaka (m), Tilakam (f)** 1. Sacred mark. 2. The red dot applied to the forehead, representing Lord Śiva's third eye of knowledge.

**Tishya (m)** The name of a celestial archer.

**Tishyaketu (m)** A name of Lord Śiva.

**Titikshā (f)** 1. Endurance or forbearance. In Vedānta the fourth virtue of the Shaṭsampatti, or the "Sixfold wealth." In his Vivekacūḍāmaṇi, Śrī Śaṅkara explains Titikshā in the following verse:

*Sahanam Sarva-Duhkhānām-*
*Apratīkāra-Pūrvakam*
*Cintā-Vilāpa-Rahitam*
*Sā Titikshā Nigadyate.*

The bearing of all afflictions
without caring to redress them and

---

* The **th** in Tamil transliterations is pronounced like the Sanskrit **t**.

without anxiety or lament
is called *Titikshā*, endurance.

Also see the Bhagavad Gītā II:14-5. 2. The daughter of Daksha, wife of Dharma and mother of Kshema.

**Titikshu (m)** Enduring, forbearing. He who practices *Titikshā*, endurance, which is one of the sixfold wealth (Shaṭsampatti) described in the Bṛihad-Āraṇyaka Upanishad as:

*Śānto Dānta Uparatas-Titikshuḥ*
*Samāhitaḥ Śraddhāvitto Bhūtwā,*
*Ātmany'evātmānam Paśyet.*

Becoming calm, controlled, withdrawn, enduring,
concentrated and faithful,
one sees the Self in oneself verily.

**Tīrtha (m)** 1. Holy, sacred. 2. A name given to holy waters. 3. A name given to sacred lore. 4. One of the ten Sannyāsa orders traced back to Śrī Śaṅkara, which has its seat in Dwāraka.

**Tīrthadeva (m)** (*tīrtha* 'holy' + *deva* 'god') The holy God, a name of Lord Śiva.

**Tīrthasevā (f)** (*tīrtha* 'holy, saint' + *sevā* 'service, visit') 1. Service or worship of saints. 2. Pilgrimage.

**Totilā (f)** A name of the Goddess Durgā.

**Trayī (f)** The triple. As denoting the Vidyā or sacred lore (ie. the Ṛig-Veda, Yajur-Veda, and Sāma-Veda). See the Bhagavad Gītā IX:17.

**Tribandhu (m)** (*tri* 'three' + *bandhu* 'friend') The friend of the three worlds, a name of Indra. [See **Indra** and **Swarga]**

**Trikūṭa (m)** (*tri* 'three' + *kūṭa* 'forehead, peak') 1. The name of the space between the eyebrows, also known as the Ājñā Cakra, which is considered the seat of wisdom. This name for the Ājñā Cakra refers to the meeting point of the three Nāḍīs (the Iḍā, the Piṅgalā, and the Sushumnā). See the Bhagavad Gītā V:27; VIII:10. 2. The name of several mountains, meaning "having three peaks."

**Trilocana (m)** (*tri* 'three' + *locana* 'eye') The Three-Eyed, a name of Lord Śiva referring to His having a third eye on His forehead, which symbolizes knowledge of the true Self and through which He burned the God of Desire, Kāmadeva, to ashes. See the Bhagavad Gītā XI:8; XIII:34; XV:10.

**Trimūrti (m)** (*tri* 'three' + *mūrti* 'form') 1. Having three forms; a name of God which refers to His having three principle forms, namely: Lord Brahmā (the Creator), Lord Vishṇu (the Preserver), and Lord Śiva (the Annihilator). 2. A name of Sage Dattātreya, who is considered the incarnation of the *Trimūrti.*

**Trinābha (m)** (*tri* 'three' + *nābha* 'navel') The navel or center of the three (worlds), a name of Lord Vishṇu which refers to His supporting the three worlds on the lotus of creation, which springs from His navel and on which Lord Brahmā is seated. See the Bhagavad Gītā XI: 15,18,37,43.

**Trinetra (m)** (*tri* 'three' + *netra* 'eye') The Three-Eyed, a name of Lord Śiva referring to His having a third eye on His forehead, symbolizing knowledge of the true Self and through which He burned the God of Desire, Kāmadeva, to ashes. See the Bhagavad Gītā XI:8; XIII:34; XV:10.

**Tṛipta (m)** The satisfied or contented. See the Bhagavad Gītā III:17; IV:20; VI:8. [See **Santosha**]

**Tṛipti (f)** Satisfaction, contentment. See the Bhagavad Gītā III:17; IV:20; VI:8. [See **Santosha**]

**Tripurahara (m)** (*tri* 'three' + *pura* 'city' + *hara* 'destroyer') The Destroyer of the three cities; a name of Lord Śiva, who destroyed the three cities built by demons in the three worlds. It means as the true Self the Lord is different from the three bodies and the three states.

**Tripurasundarī (f)** (*tri* 'three' + *pura* 'city' + *sundarī* 'beauty') The Beauty of the three cities; a name of Devī, the Divine Mother, which refers to Her pervading the gross, subtle, and causal bodies. Having a divine beauty She attracts the devotees to Her blissful Self and helps them to transcend the three bodies or cities.

**Tripurāri (m)** (*tri* 'three' + *pura* 'city' + *ari* 'enemy') The Enemy of the three cities; a name of Lord Śiva, who destroyed the three cities built by demons in the three worlds. It means, as the true Self the Lord is different from the three bodies and the three states.

**Triśaṅku (m)** The name of a Ṛishi in the Taittirīya Upanishad, who having realized the supreme Truth, revealed the following Mantra to be recited in Swadhyāya or Japa for the sake of mind purification and attainment of knowledge:

> *OM!*
> *Aham Vṛikshasya Rerivā.*
> *Kīrtiḥ Pṛishṭham Girer-Iva.*

*Ūrdhwa-Pavitro*
*Vājinīva Swamṛitam-Asmi.*
*Draviṇam * Savarcasam.*
*Sumedhā Amṛito'kshitaḥ.*
*Iti Triśaṅkor-Vedānuvacanam.*
*OM! Śāntiḥ Śāntiḥ Śāntiḥ!*

OM!
I am the invigorator of the (world) tree. My fame is (high) like the ridge of a mountain. My source is the Pure (Brahman). As it is in the sun, I am that pure Nectar (of the Self). I am the pure effulgent Wealth (of Truth). I am possessed of a fine intelligence, and am immortal and undecaying." Thus was the statement of *Triśaṅku* after the attainment of realisation.
OM! Peace, Peace, Peace!

**Triśūlī (m)** (*tri* 'three' + *śūlī* 'armed with a spear') The Possessor of the trident, a name of Lord Śiva which refers to His possessing the trident, a symbol of His sovereignty over the three guṇas: sattwa, rajas and tamas.

**Tryambaka (m)** (*tri* 'three' + *ambaka* 'eye') The three-eyed, a name of Lord Śiva, which occurs in the celebrated Mahā-Mṛityuñjaya Mantra, the great death-conquering mantra of the Śukla-Yajur-Veda:

*OM! Tryambakam Yajāmahe*
*Sugandhim Pushṭi-Vardhanam.*
*Urvārukam-Iva Bandhanān'*
*Mṛityor-Mukshīya Māmṛitāt!*

OM! We worship the Three-Eyed Lord (Śiva),
of excellent Fragrance, the Increaser of welfare.
Just as the cucumber from its binding,
may we be released from death, not from Immortality!

In the Liṅga-Purāṇa the word *Tryambaka* is explained thus, "He is the Lord of the three worlds, three Guṇas, three Vedas, three Devas and three castes—Brahmins, Kshatriyas and Vaiśyas. He is expressed by the three syllables 'A,' 'U,' and 'M' (constituting 'OM'). He is the Lord of the three fires, viz. the moon, sun and fire. Umā, Ambā and Mahādeva constitute the trio. So He is *Tryambaka,* the Lord of the three."

* Draviṇan is pronounced here as "Draviṇagam."

**Tukārāma (m)** The name of a celebrated and saintly devotee of God who lived in the 17th century A.D.

**Tulasī (f)** The holy basil plant, which is used for mālās (rosaries) and associated with the japa of Lord Vishṇu's names.

**Tulasīdāsa** (*tulasī* 'the holy basil plant' + *dāsa* 'servant') 1. The servant of Tulasī. 2. The name of a great devotee of Śrī Rāma who wrote a Rāmāyaṇa in Hindi and lived in the 16th century A.D.

**Tulsī (f)** See **Tulasī.**

**Tulsīdās (m)** See **Tulasīdāsa.**

**Tulya (m), Tulyā (f)** 1. The equal-minded, equanimity of mind in pleasure and pain, gain and loss, etc. See the Bhagavad Gītā XII:19; XIV:24-5. 2. God's quality of being the same in all beings. See the Bhagavad Gītā IX:29; XIII:27.

**Tura (m)** 1. The powerful; the fruitful. 2. The name of a Vedic preceptor and priest.

**Turaṇya (m)** 1. The swift. 2. One of the horses of the Moon-God.

**Turīya (m)** The Fourth. A name of the Self or Ātman as the unchanging Witness of waking, dream, and deep sleep states, and distinct from the wakeful, the dreamer, and the fast asleep. *Turīya* is synonymous with Caturtha occurring in the Māṇḍūkya Upanishad, which reveals 'OM' or the Fourth as:

*Nāntaḥ-Prajñam Na Bahish-Prajñam*
*No'Bhayataḥ-Prajñam*
*Na Prajñāna-Ghanam Na Prajñam*
*Nāprajñam/ Adṛishṭam-Avyavahāryam-Agrāhyam-*
*Alakshaṇam-Acintyam-Avyapadeśyam-*
*Ekātma-Pratyaya-Sāram Prapañco'paśamam*
*Śāntam Śivam-Adwaitam Caturtham Manyante*
*Sa Ātmā Sa Vijñeyaḥ.*

What they consider to be neither internal consciousness (dream), nor external consciousness (waking), nor (intermediate) consciousness of both, nor a mass of consciousness (deep sleep), nor consciousness (of everything), nor unconsciousness (ignorance), to be unseen, un-associable, ungraspable, without any characteristic, unthinkable, indescribable, the One-Self-Consciousness in essence, the cessation of diversity, to be peaceful, auspicious and non-dual, the Fourth; that is the Self, that is to be realized.

In commenting on this Upanishad, the illustrious Gauḍapāda states:

*Anyathā Gṛihṇataḥ Swapno*
*Nidrā Tattwam-Ajānataḥ.*
*Viparyāse Tayoḥ Kshīṇe*
*Turīyam Padam-Aśnute.*

Dream (and waking) belongs to one who sees falsely,
and sleep to one who does not know the Truth.
When their errors are removed,
One attains the Fourth state.

Śrī Śaṅkara, on his part, opens his commentary on the Māṇḍūkya Upanishad with these two verses, which are so profound and rich in meaning:

*Prajñānāṁśu-Pratānaiḥ Sthira-Cara-*
*Nikara-Vyāpibhir-Vyāpya Lokān*
*Bhuktwā Bhogān Sthavishthān Punar-Api*
*Dhishaṇo'dbhāsitān Kāma-Janyān;*

*Pītwā Sarvān Viśeshān Swapiti*
*Madhura-Bhuṅ'māyayā Bhojayan-No*
*Māyā-Saṅkhyā-Turīyam Param-Amritam-*
*Ajam Brahma Yat-Tan'Nato'smi.*

I bow to that Brahman which after having enjoyed
(in the waking state) the gross objects by pervading
all the human objectives through a diffusion of
Its rays of unchanging Consciousness that embraces all
that moves and does not move;

Which again after having drunk (in the dream state) all the
variety of objects, produced by desire (as well as action
and ignorance) and lighted up by the intellect, sleeps
while enjoying bliss and making us enjoy through illusion
(Māyā); which is counted as the Fourth from the point
of view of Māyā, and is supreme, immortal and birthless.

*Yo Viśwātmā Vidhij-Vishayān*
*Prāśya Bhogān Sthavishṭhān*
*Paścāc'cānyān Swam-Ativibhavān*
*Jyotishā Swena Sūkshmān*
*Sarvān-Etān Punar-Api Śanaiḥ*

*Swātmani Sthāpayitwā*
*Hitwā Sarvān Viśeshān Vigata-Guṇa Gaṇaḥ*
*Pātw'Asau Nas-Turīyaḥ!*

May that Fourth One protect us, which, after having identified Itself with the universe, enjoys (in the cosmic waking state) the gross objects created by virtue (and vice); which again (in the cosmic dream state) experiences through Its own light the objects of enjoyment that are called up by Its own intellect; which, further (in the cosmic sleep or dissolution), withdraws promptly all these into Itself; and which lastly becomes free from all attributes by discarding every distinction and difference!

In his Ātmajñānopadeśavidhi, Śrī Śaṅkara states:

One should give up these waking, dream and deep sleep states and should know that the Self is the Fourth. That the Self is the Fourth means that It consists of Consciousness only and nothing else, like a homogeneous piece of gold. Though It is the Fourth, It is not a state different from the three well-known ones (waking, dream and deep sleep). To be the Fourth is nothing but to be the 'Witness' of the three states as Consciousness in their proximity only.
One has inevitably to arrive at a void if the Fourth were a different state, as in that case the reality of the Self could not be known. Moreover, the doctrine of a void or vacuity (Śūnyavāda) cannot be true as it is not reasonable that things superimposed should be without a substratum.

In the Sarvasāra Upanishad the meaning of *Turīya* is revealed in the following passage:

*Avasthātraya-Bhāvābhāva-Sakshi*
*Swayam Bhāvā-Rahitam*
*Nairantaryam Caitanyam Yadā*
*Tadā Turīyam Caitanyam-Ity'Ucyate.*

When Consciousness witnesses the appearance and disappearance of the three states, being Itself devoid of appearance and without cessation, then that Consciousness is called the Fourth (*Turīya*).

In the seven states of Knowledge (Jñāna-Bhūmikās) pertaining to Jīvanmukti or liberation while alive, *Turīya* is the last one wherein there is no external or body consciousness. Beyond that is *Turīyātīta* pertaining to Videhamukti or disembodied liberation. Along these lines, the Ṛishi Vasishṭha says to Śrī Rāma in the Yoga-Vāsishṭha:

> Remaining in the certitude of Ātman or Self, without desire and with balance vision, having completely eradicated all conceptions of difference, such as "I" or "he," existence or nonexistence, is *Turīya*. That state of Jīvanmukti, free from illusions, wherein there is the supreme certainty of Ātman, is the *Turīya* state.

**Tushṭi (f)** Contentment. The 71st of Goddess Lakshmī's 108 names. See the Bhagavad Gītā X:5.

**Twashṭā (m)** 1. The builder. 2. A name of Viśwakarmā. [**See Viśwakarmā**] 3. The 53rd name of Lord Vishṇu's 1000 names as listed in the Vishṇu Sahasranāma. In his commentary Śrī Śaṅkara states, "The Lord is called *Twashṭā*, the reducer, because He reduces (tanū-karaṇāt) all beings during the cosmic withdrawal."

**Tyāga (m)** [In Tamil **Tyāgan**] Renunciation or dedication. In Karma-Yoga this refers to the renunciation of the fruits of actions; in Jñāna-Yoga it refers to the renunciation of both the fruits of actions and the actions themselves. Accordingly, Śrī Bhagavān says in the Bhagavad Gītā (XII:12):

> *Tyāgāc'Chāntir-Anantaram.*
>
> From renunciation (of fruits) peace follows immediately.

In the Kaivalya Upanishad Lord Brahmā says to Aśwalāyana:

> *Na Karmaṇā Na Prajayā Dhanena*
> *Tyāgenai'ke Amṛitatwam-Ānaśuḥ.*
>
> Not by action, not by progeny, or by wealth,
> but by (complete) renunciation, some attained Immortality.

Also see the Bhagavad Gītā XII:12; XVI:2; XVIII:2, 4-9.

**Tyāgarāja (m)** (*tyāga* 'renunciation' + *rāja* 'king') 1. The king of renunciation. 2. The name of a saintly musician who lived in the 18th century A.D. He was devoted to Śrī Rāma and composed thousands of songs in praise of the Lord. He is one of the trinity in South Indian music, along with Śyāma Śāstrī and Muthuswāmī Dīkshitar.

**Tyāgī (m), Tyāginī (f)** Endowed with renunciation; the renunciate. Śrī

Rāmakṛishṇa used to say that to get the quintessence of the Bhagavad Gītā we should reverse the two syllables in Gītā, thus obtaining "Tāgī" or "*Tyāgī*,"as renunciation is the chief message of this scripture. See the Bhagavad Gītā XII:16-17; XIV:25; XVIII:10-11.

# U

**Ucathya (m)** 1. The praiseworthy. 2. The name of a descendant or son of Ṛishi Aṅgiras and the seer of some Ṛigvedic hymns.

**Udarāja (m)** (*uda* 'water' + *rāja* 'king') The king of waters, a name of the personification of the ocean.

**Udasutā (f)** (*uda* 'water' + *sutā* 'daughter') The daughter of the ocean, a name of the Goddess Lakshmī, who was born from the churning of the milk ocean.

**Udasutānāyaka (m)** (*uda* 'water' + *sutā* 'daughter' + *nāyaka* 'lord') The Lord of the ocean's daughter, a name of Lord Vishṇu, consort of the Goddess Lakshmī.

**Udāpi (m)** A name of Vasudeva, the father of Śrī Kṛishṇa.

**Udāra (m)** The great or exalted. See the Bhagavad Gītā VII:18, *"Udārāḥ Sarva Evai'te..."* "Great indeed are all these..."

**Udāratā (f)** (*udāra* 'great' + *tā* 'nominalizing suffix') Greatness, nobleness, or generosity.

**Udāvasu (m)** The name of a son of King Janaka.

**Udāyī (m)** A name of Vasudeva, the father of Śrī Kṛishṇa.

**Udbhaṭa (m)** (*ut* 'highly, up' + *bhaṭa* 'raised') Exalted, eminent.

**Udbhāsī (m), Udbhāsinī (f)** (*ut* 'highly, forth' + *bhāsī/sinī* 'shining') Shining forth.

**Udbhāsura (m)** (*ut* 'highly, forth' + *bhāsura* 'shining, radiant') Shining forth, radiant.

**Uddānta (m)** (*ut* 'highly' + *dānta* 'controlled') The humble, subdued; he who practises *Dama*, (sense-control), the second virtue of the sixfold wealth, or Shaṭsampatti, taught in the Bṛihad-Āraṇyaka Upanishad as:

*Śānto Dānta Uparatas-Titikshuḥ*
*Samāhitaḥ Śraddhāritto Bhūtwā,*
*Ātmany'evātmānam Paśyet.*

Becoming calm, controlled, withdrawn,

enduring, concentrated and faithful,
one sees the Self in oneself verily.

**Uddhava (m)** The name of a friend and devotee of Śrī Kṛishṇa. The Lord's teachings to *Uddhava*, called the *Uddhava-Gītā*, can be found in the eleventh book of the Bhāgavata-Purāṇa.

**Uḍḍīśa (m)** (*ut* 'high' + *ḍī* 'flying' + *śa* 'reclining' or *īśa* 'lord') Reclining high or the high Lord. A name of Lord Śiva.

**Udgātā (m)** (*ut* 'Udgītha, OM, Sāmaveda' + *gātā* 'singer') The singer of *Ut*, which refers to the Udgītha or "OM" and to the Sāma-Veda; one of four priests in a Vedic sacrifice, who sings the hymns of the Sāmaveda.

**Udraka (m)** The name of a Ṛishi.

**Udwamśa (m)** (*ut* 'high' + *vamśa* 'lineage') 1. Of high lineage. 2. The name of a Ṛishi.

**Udyantā (m)** (*ut* 'highly' + *yantā* 'elevating, bestowing, ruling') 1. He who exalts or elevates. 2. The bestower. 3. The ruler.

**Ugrakālī (f)** (*ugra* 'impetuous' + *kālī* 'the dark Goddess') The impetuous Kālī, a name of the Goddess Durgā.

**Ugraśekharā (f)** (*ugra* 'impetuous, a name of Lord Śiva' + *śekharā* 'crest') The crest of the Impetuous, a name of the Goddess Gangā, the holy river Ganges, who, when falling from heaven, was restrained in Lord Śiva's hair, thus adorning Him as a crest.

**Ugrasena (m)** (*ugra* 'impetuous' + *sena* 'army') Having an impetuous army. The name of a king in the Mahābhārata.

**Ugrasenānī (m)** (*ugra* 'impetuous' + *senā* 'army' + *nī* 'leader') The leader of an impetuous army, a name of Śrī Kṛishṇa.

**Ugratārā (f)** (*ugra* 'impetuous' + *tārā* 'savioress') The impetuous Savior, the name of a Goddess in the Kālikā-Purāṇa.

**Ugreśa (m)** (*ugra* 'impetuous' + *īśa* 'lord') The impetuous or mighty Lord, a name of Lord Śiva.

**Ujjesha (m), Ujjeshā (f)** (*ut* 'highly' + *jesha/ā* 'victorious') The victorious.

**Ujjeshī (m)** (*ut* 'highly' + *jeshī* 'victorious') 1. The victorious. 2. The name of one of the forty-nine Maruts or Wind-gods.

**Ullāsa (m)** (*ut* 'highly, forth' + *lāsa* 'shining, delighting') Shining forth, delighting.

**Ullāsinī (f)** (*ut* 'highly, forth' + *lāsinī* 'shining, delighting') Shining forth, delighting.

**Ulūtī (f)** The name of a wife of Garuḍa.

**Ulūtīśa (m)** (*ulūtī* 'wife of Garuḍa' + *īśa* 'lord') The Lord of Ulūtī, a name of Garuḍa. [See **Garuḍa**]

**Umā (f)** 1. The luminous or serene. 2. A name of the Goddess Pārvatī derived from, "*U, mā!*," "O (child), do not (practice austerities)!" This was said to her by her mother Menā while she was practicing tapas to obtain Lord Śiva as her husband. [See **Haimavatī**]

**Umāguru (m)** (*umā* 'name of Goddess Pārvatī' + *guru* 'mother, father, teacher') The father of the Goddess Umā; a name of Himavan. The term *Guru*, meaning 'great' or 'respectable,' is applied to elders in general and to one's mother, father, and spiritual teacher in particular.

**Umākānta (m)** (*umā* 'name of Goddess Pārvatī' + *kānta* 'beloved') The Beloved of Umā, a name of Lord Śiva.

**Umānātha (m)** (*umā* 'name of Goddess Pārvatī' + *nātha* 'lord, husband') The Lord of Umā, a name of Lord Śiva.

**Umāpati (m)** (*umā* 'name of Goddess Pārvatī' + *pati* 'lord, husband') The Lord of Umā, a name of Lord Śiva.

**Umāsuta (m)** (*umā* 'name of Goddess Pārvatī' + *suta* 'son') The son of Umā, a name of Lord Skanda, also known as Kārttikeya, Kumāra, Guha, and Shaṇmukha.

**Umeśa (m)** (*umā* 'name of Goddess Pārvatī' + *īśa* 'lord, husband') 1. The Lord of Umā, a name of Lord Śiva. 2. Umā and the Lord, the name of a particular half-man, half-woman form of Lord Śiva.

**Uṅkāra (m)** The name of a companion of Lord Vishṇu.

**Unnati (f)** (*ut* 'upwards' + *nati* 'bending') 1. The ascending. 2. The name of the wife of Garuḍa. 3. A daughter of Daksha and the wife of Dharma.

**Unnatīśa (m)** (*unnati* 'wife of Garuḍa' + *īśa* 'lord, husband') The Lord of Unnati, a name of Garuḍa. [See **Garuḍa**]

**Upagahana (m)** (*upa* 'above' + *gahana* 'abyss, darkness') Above darkness. The name of a Ṛishi.

**Upakāśā (f), Upakāśī (f)** (*upa* 'near, almost' + *kāśā/kāśī* 'light') Aurora, dawn.

**Upanandaka (m)** (*upa* 'near' + *nandaka* 'rejoicing in') The name of an attendant of Lord Skanda.

**Upanandana (m)** (*upa* 'near, almost' + *nandana* 'delighting in') Delighting in the very hearts of beings. A name of Lord Śiva.

**Uparati (f)** (*upa* 'with, in' + *rati* 'drawing, ceasing') Cessation, withdrawal, the third virtue of the sixfold wealth or Shaṭsampatti in Vedānta. In the Bṛihad-Āraṇyaka Upanishad it occurs in the following passage:

> *Śānto Dānta Uparatas-Titikshuḥ*
> *Samāhitaḥ Śraddhāvitto Bhūtwā*
> *Ātmany'evātmānam Paśyet.*
>
> Becoming calm, controlled, withdrawn
> *(Uparataḥ),* enduring, concentrated, and faithful,
> one sees the Self in oneself verily.

In his Vivekacūḍāmaṇi Śrī Śaṅkara explains *Uparati* in the following verse:

> *Bāhyānālambanam Vṛitter-Esho'paratir-Uttamā.*
>
> The non-dependence of the mind on externalities
> is the highest *Uparati.*

In his Vedāntasāra, Śrī Sadānanda Yogīndra says:

> *Nivartinānām-Eteshām*
> *Tad-Vyatirikta-Vishayebhya Uparamaṇam-Uparatir-*
> *Athavā Vihitānām Karmaṇām Vidhinā*
> *Parityāgaḥ.*
>
> *Uparati* is the cessation of the restrained mind and senses
> from the pursuit of objects other than that (hearing,
> reflecting and meditation upon Vedāntic Truth). It may
> also mean the complete renunciation of the prescribed
> (religious) actions according to scriptural injunctions

(and not through laziness).

*Uparati*, thus, follows Śama and Dama, mind-control and sense-control, in the sixfold wealth and corresponds to Sannyāsa (i.e. entering into the life of renunciation after having ceased from worldly activities). See the Bhagavad Gītā VI:25 which says: *Śanaiḥ Śanair-Uparamet..."* "Little by little let him withdraw..."

**Upāsā (f), Upāsanā (f)** (*upa* 'near' + *āsā/āsanā* 'sitting') Worship or meditation, mainly of the Saguṇa or conditioned Brahman, but also of the Nirguṇa or unconditioned Brahman. Comparing the sacred syllable 'OM' to a bow, the individual soul to an arrow and Brahman to its target, the Muṇḍaka Upanishad says:

*Dhanur-Gṛihītwau'panishadam Mahāstram*
*Śaram Hy'Upāsā-Niśitam Sandhayīta.*

Taking hold of the bow which is a great Upanishadic weapon,
one should fix on it an arrow sharpened with meditation *(Upāsā).*

Accordingly, Śrī Śaṅkara defines *Upāsanā* as, "a continuous flow of similar thoughts with regard to some support of meditation approved by the Scriptures, to the exclusion of all other ideas." In the Bhagavad Gītā (XIII:7), worship or service of the teacher, *Ācāryo'pāsanam,* is mentioned as the sixth of the twenty means of knowledge. Also see the Bhagavad Gītā IV:25; IX:14,22; XII:1-3,6,20; XIII:25, where occurs the verb *Upās,* 'to worship.' Chapters VII to XII of the Bhagavad Gītā stand for the *Upāsanā* portion, while the first six deal with Karma and the last six with Jñāna. *Upāsanā* or worship is thus like a bridge thrown over the gulf between action and knowledge.

**Upāsaka (m), Upāsikā (f)** (*upa* 'near' + *āsaka /ikā* 'sitting') The worshipper. [See **Upāsā**]

**Upāsitā (m), Upāsitrī (f)** (*upa* 'near' + *āsitā/ trī* 'sitter') The worshipper. [See **Upāsā**]

**Upaśānta (m), Upaśāntā (f)** (*upa* 'down' + *śānta* 'calmed') The calmed down, appeased; one whose mind is controlled by the practice of Śama.

**Upāvi (m)** The name of a Ṛishi.

**Upendra (m)** (*upa* 'near, over' + *indra* 'chief, lord') 1. The overlord. 2. The 151st name of Lord Vishṇu as listed in the Vishṇu Sahasranāma. In his commentary Śrī Śaṅkara states, "In His Vāmana or Dwarf incarnation, the Lord was the younger *(upagata)* brother of Indra and is thus called *Upendra.* It also means the overlord *(upari indra)*. In the Hari-Vamśa, Indra said to Lord Kṛishṇa, 'Thou art placed by the Vedas as Lord, just as Thou art now Lord *(indra)* over *(upari)* me. So the gods praise Thee on earth, O Kṛishṇa, as *Upendra*.'"

**Upoditi (m)** The name of a Ṛishi.

**Urvarāpati (m)** (*urvarā* 'harvest' + *pati* 'lord') The lord of the harvest.

**Urvaśī (f)** 1. Thigh-born, the name of a nymph, who is said to be born from the thigh of Ṛishi Nārāyaṇa. While Nārāyaṇa was practicing austerities, Indra, fearing his divine status would be surpassed, sent nymphs to tempt him. Remaining steadfast, the Ṛishi produced a most beautiful nymph from his own thigh (Ūru) and sent her as a present to Indra. Later on through Mitra's curse, *Urvaśī* was sent to earth where she married the King Purūravas. This last story forms the theme of Kālidāsa's celebrated drama entitled "Vikramo'rva-śīyam." 2. The widely extending (i.e. *Urvaśī* as identified with the Dawn-Goddess).

**Ushaṅgu (m)** 1. The name of a Ṛishi. 2. A name of Lord Śiva.

**Ushasta (m)** The name of a Ṛishi.

**Ushā (f)** 1. Dawn, who is personified as the daughter of Heaven and the wife of the Sun-God. 2. The name of the daughter of Bāṇa and the wife of Aniruddha.

**Ushāpati (m)** (*ushā* " + *pati* 'lord, husband') The lord or husband of Ushā, a name of Aniruddha.

**Usheśa (m)** (*ushā* 'wife of Aniruddha' + *īśa* 'lord, husband') 1. The lord of the Dawn or Ushā, a name of Aniruddha. 2. The lord of the night, a name of the moon-god.

**Usrā (f)** Dawn.

**Utaṅka (m)** The name of a Ṛishi.

**Utkīla (m)** The name of a Ṛishi.

**Utpalī (m), Utpalinī (f)** Abounding in lotuses.

**Utpāra (m), Utpārā (f)** Endless, boundless.

**Uttama (m)** (*ut* 'high, excellent' + *tama* 'highly') 1. The Highest. 2. The most Excellent. 3. A name of Lord Vishṇu, generally compounded with Purusha in *Purushottama*, meaning either the highest (ūrdhwatama) or the most excellent (utkṛishṭatama) Being. See the Bhagavad Gītā VII:7; XV:17-8. 4. The name of a grandson of Manu.

**Uttara (m)** (*ut* 'over, excellent' + *tara* 'crossing, most') 1. The Redeemer. 2. The most Excellent. 3. The 494th name of Lord Vishṇu as listed in the Vishṇu Sahasranāma. In his commentary Śrī Śaṅkara states, "The Lord who redeems *(uttarati)* from the bondage of the cycle of birth is called *Uttara*, the Redeemer. As revealed in the Ṛig-Veda, it also means He is 'the most (*tara*) Excellent (*utkṛishṭa*) of all.'" Also see the Bhagavad Gītā XII:7.

**Uttāraka (m)** (*ut* 'over' + *tāraka* 'causing to cross') The deliverer from rebirth, a name of Lord Śiva.

# Ū

**Ūrja (m)** Thc strong.

**Ūrjānī (f)** Strength personified.

**Ūti (f)** Help, protection

# V

**Vadānya (m)** 1. Generous, bountiful. 2. Eloquent. 3. The name of a Ṛishi.

**Vaijayanthī (f)** Victorious, the name of Lord Vishṇu's garland of forest flowers. [See **Vanamālī**]

**Vaikuṇṭha (m)** 1. The Savior. 2. The 405th name of Lord Vishṇu as listed in the Vishṇu Sahasranāma. In his commentary Śrī Śaṅkara states, "The Lord is *Vaikuṇṭha* as He saves human beings from straying into various paths (*vividhā kuṇṭhā*). At the beginning of creation He united the five elements that were distinct from one another and thus prevented their independent course, as said in the Mahābhārata, 'I united the earth with water, space with air, and air with fire, hence my name *Vaikuṇṭha*.'" 3. The name of Lord Vishṇu's celestial abode, which is but another name for the Lord Himself, as the Lord and His abode are one and the same thing. Realizing the Lord within as the inner Self is to attain that divine Abode.

**Vairāgī (m), Vairāgiṇī (f)** The dispassionate, one who is accomplished in *Vairāgya*, dispassion. According to the traditional Yoga masters there are five degrees of *Vairāgya*: *Yatamāna-Vairāgya*, dispassion through effort, *Vyatireka-Vairāgya*, dispassion through analysis, *Ekendriya-Vairāgya*, dispassion through the single mind-sense, *Vaśīkāra-Vairāgya*, dispassion through mastery, and *Para-Vairāgya*, supreme dispassion due to Self-knowledge. See the Yogasūtras I:15-6. In Dhyāna-Yoga, the yoga of meditation, *Vairāgya* is always conjoined with Abhyāsa, repeated practice, in the development of concentration. See Yogasūtra I:12. In commenting on this sūtra Vyāsa says the flow of the mind is twofold, toward evil and good; the evil flow is arrested by *Vairāgya* and the good flow is engendered by Abhyāsa. Also see the Bhagavad Gītā VI:35-6. In Jñāna-Yoga, the Yoga of wisdom, *vairāgya* is the second of the Four Means,* the *Sādhana-Catushṭaya*. In the Vivekacūḍāmaṇi, Śri Śaṅkara defines it as:

*Tad-Vairāgyam Jugupsā Yā*
*Darśana-Śravaṇādibhiḥ,*
*Dehādi-Brahma-Paryante*
*Hy'anitye Bhoga-Vastuni.*

---

* The Four Means are 1) Viveka (discrimination) 2) Vairāgya (dispassion) 3) Shaṭsampatki (the sixfold wealth) which in turn consists of a) Śama (mind-control) b) Dama (sense-control) c) Uparati (withdrawal) d) Titikshā (endurance) e) Śraddhā (faith) and f) Samādhāna (concentration) and 4) Mumukshutwa (desire of liberation).

That is dispassion which is the disgust for all things seen here, heard about in scriptures or inferred (i.e. for all transient objects of enjoyment ranging from the body up to Brahmāhood, creatorship).

The need for *Vairāgya* is based on the authority of the Muṇḍaka Upanishad, which discusses dispassion in the following way:

*Parīkshya Lokān Karma-Citān Brāhmaṇo*
*Nirvedam-Āyān; "Nāsty'Akṛitaḥ Kṛitena?"*

Having examined the worlds acquired through action, a Brāhmaṇa should resort to dispassion (Nirvedam), thinking thus: "There is nothing that is not transient; why act?"

Accordingly in the Jabāla Upanishad, Yājñavalkya says to Janaka:

*Yad-Ahar-Eva Virajet-*
*Tad-Ahar-Eva Pravrajet.*

The very day one is dispassionate, that very day let him depart (i.e. renounce).

Dispassion thus comes from *Viveka*, discrimination between the Eternal and the non-eternal, and culminates in Sannyāsa, complete renunciation. Both *Vairāgya* and Viveka are brought about by Karma Yoga, the Yoga of selfless service, which purifies the mind and renders it fit for Jñāna Yoga. Also see the Bhagavad Gītā II:52; V:22; VIII:16; IX:20-1; XIII:8; XVIII:52; the Yogasūtras III:50; the first chapter of Vālmīki's Yoga-Vāsishṭha, entitled *Vairāgya-Prakaraṇa*, in which Śrī Rāma expresses his utter dispassion born of Viveka; and the *Vairāgya-Śatakam* "The Hundred Verses on Dispassion" by Bhartṛihari.

**Vaishṇava (m)** The devotee of Lord Vishṇu. [See **Vishṇu**]

**Vaishṇavā (f)** The consort of Lord Vishṇu, a name of the Goddess Lakshmī.

**Vajra (m), Vajriṇī (f)** [in Tamil **Vajran** (m)] The adamant, unyielding.

**Vallabhā (f)** The beloved.

**Valli (f)** [Tamil] The consort of Lord Muruga.

**Vanamālā (f)** (*vana* 'forest' + *mālā* 'garland') Garland of forest (flowers), which hanging on Lord Vishṇu's neck is named Vaijayantī, the victorious.

**Vanamālī (m)** (*vana* 'forest' + *mālī* 'wearing a garland') Wearing the *Vanamālā* garland (i.e. the garland of forest flowers). The 561st name of Lord Vishṇu as listed in the Vishṇu Sahasranāma. In his commentary Śrī Śaṅkara states, "Wearing the garland of forest flowers *(Vanamālā)* called ' Vaijayantī,' which is composed of the nature of the subtle (i.e. unmixed) elements, or Tanmātras, the Lord is *Vanamālī."*

**Vanaspati (m)** (*vanas* 'forest' + *pati* 'lord') 1. The Lord of woods or forests, a name of Lord Vishṇu. 2. A name for large trees, especially the holy fig tree.

**Vandita (m), Vanditā (f)** The saluted, worshipped.

**Vanditā (m), Vanditrī (f)** One who salutes or worships, one who performs Sandhyā-Vandanam at dawn, noon, and dusk.

**Vandya (m), Vandyā (f)** Worthy of salutation, worshipful.

**Vapusha (m), Vapushī (f)** The very beautiful.

**Varada (m)** (*vara* 'boon, blessing' + *da* 'giver') 1. The giver of boons or blessings. 2. The 330th name of Lord Vishṇu as listed in the Vishṇu Sahasranāma. In his commentary Śrī Śaṅkara states, "The Lord who gives *(dadāti)* the desired boons *(varān)* is the giver of boons. *Vara* also means the sacrificial fee, and the Lord gives it through the form of the sacrificer, as said in the text, 'Gaur-Vai Varaḥ,' 'The cow, indeed, is the sacrificial fee to give.'"

**Varuṇa (m)** 1. The withholder, withdrawer. The name of a great solar deity presiding over inhalation and night, as well as the tongue or taste, and who is thus connected with water, as the king among water deities. *Varuṇa* is invoked in the well-known Śānti-Mantra beginning with, *"OM Śam No Mitraḥ, Śam Varuṇaḥ..."* "May Mitra be blissful to us! May *Varuṇa* be blissful to us...!" and is thus often connected with Mitra, another solar deity presiding over exhalation and day. In the Taittirīya Upanishad, *Varuṇa* teaches his son Bhṛigu the knowledge of the Self as distinct from the five sheaths.* 2. The 553rd name of Lord Vishṇu as listed in the Vishṇu Sahasranāma. In his commentary, Śrī Śaṅkara states, "On account of withdrawing (samvaranāt) his rays, the setting Sun is called *Varuṇa,* the Withdrawer, as revealed in the Vedas, 'O *Varuṇa*, listen to our hymn!'" Also see the Bhagavad Gītā X:29; XI:39.

**Varūtā (m), Varūtrī (f)** The protector.

---

* The five sheaths of Kośas are 1) Annamaya (bodily) 2) Prānamaya (vital) 3) Manomaya (mental) 4) Vijñānamaya (intellectual) and Anandamaya (blissful).

**Vasanta (m)** Brilliant. Spring personified as the friend of Kāmadeva or Cupid. In the Vivekacūḍāmaṇi Śrī Śaṅkara compares wise men to spring in the following passage:

*Śāntā Mahānto Nivasanti Santo*
*Vasanta-val'loka-Hitam Carantaḥ,*
*Tīrṇāḥ Swayam Bhīma-Bhavārṇavam*
*Janān-Ahetunānyān-Api Tārayantaḥ.*

There are good souls, calm and magnanimous, who do
good to others as does the spring, and who, having
themselves crossed this dreadful ocean of birth and death,
help others also to cross the same, without
any motive whatsoever.

Also in his devotional poem "Śivānanda-Laharī," Śrī Śaṅkara compares the heart to a garden and meditation to spring:

*Śambhu-Dhyāna-Vasanta-Saṅgini*
*Hṛid-Ārāme'gha-Jīrṇa-Cchaḍāḥ*
*Srastā Bhakti-Latā-Cchatā*
*Vilasitāḥ Puṇya-Pravāla-Śritāḥ,*
*Dīpyante Guṇa-Korakā*
*Japa-Vacaḥ-Pushpāṇi Sad-Vāsanā*
*Jñānānanda-Sudhā-Maranda-Laharī*
*Samvit-Phalābhyunnatiḥ.*

In the heart garden fond of the spring season of
meditation on Śambhu (the "Blissful" Śiva), there
shines the assemblage of devotion creepers which have
shed the old leaves of sins and taken on the tender
leaves of merit, the buds of virtue, the flowers of japa
words, the pure fragrance (or mental impressions), the
flow of nectar-juice of wisdom and bliss, and the increase
of the fruit of pure Consciousness.

In the Bhagavad-Gītā X:35, Spring is considered as one of the glories of the Lord.

**Vasāti (f)** The dawn. [See **Ushā**]

**Vasishṭha (m)** The richest. The name of the foremost among the seven Ṛishis represented in the Great Bear. Born directly from Lord Brahmā's mind, he ranks as the third in the traditional line of Brahmavidyā Gurus, and he is the seer for many hymns of the Ṛig-Veda. He is called the richest because he possesses the cow of plenty. His wife is Arundhatī and among his hundred sons Śakti is his greatest successor. He is the family Guru of Śrī Rāma, and his Vedāntic teachings to the latter are embodied in Vālmīki's celebrated Yoga-*Vāsishṭha*. In the Himālayas the cave of *Vasishṭha*, named *Vasishṭha*-Guhā, where the Ṛishi is believed to have lived and meditated, is held as very sacred.

**Vasu (m)** 1. The Abode; the Dweller; wealth. 2. The 104th, 270th and 696th name of Lord Vishṇu as listed in the Vishṇu Sahasranāma. In his commentary Śrī Śaṅkara states, "1) The Lord within whom abides *(vasanti)* all beings is called *Vasu* , the Abode. 2) Also since He dwells *(vasati)* Himself in them, He is *Vasu*, the Dweller. 3) Again it means, among the eight *Vasus*, He is the Fire-God Agni (Pāvaka), as said in the Bhagavad Gītā (X:23). 4) The wealth *(Vasu)* He gives to others is Himself. 5) The Lord is called *Vasu*, as He veils *(vāsayati)* His own nature through illusion. 6) Again, it means He lives *(vasati)* in the very atmosphere, nowhere else, and is called *Vasu* or *Vāyu* (the Wind-God) due to the peculiarity of His abode, as revealed in the Kaṭha Upanishad, 'He is *Vasu (Vāyu)* dwelling in the atmosphere.'" 2 Eight of the thirty-three gods.* In the Bṛihad-Āraṇyaka Upanishad, sage Yājñavalkya says to Śākalya, "The Fire, Earth, Air, Atmosphere, Sun, Heaven, Moon and Stars, these are the (eight) *Vasus*, for in these all this is placed; therefore they are called *Vasus.*"

**Vasudhā (f)** (*vasu* 'wealth' + *dhā* 'producing') The wealth-producing; a name of the Earth-Goddess.

**Vasuki (f)** [Tamil] The wife of the great sage Thiruvalluvar.

**Vasundharā (f)** (*vasum* 'wealth' + *dharā* 'containing, supporting') 1. The wealth-containing. A name of the Earth-Goddess which occurs in a Vedic hymn recited when one is about to take a morning bath and while one puts a little earth on one's head.

*Aśwa-Krānte Ratha-Krānte*
*Vishṇu-Krānte Vasundharā,*
*Śirasā Dhārayishyāmi*
*Rakshaswa Mām Pade Pade.*

O Earth-Goddess that is traversed by a horse,
a chariot and Lord Vishṇu,**

---

* The other twenty-five gods are the eleven Rudras, the twelve Ādityas, Indra and Prajāpati.

** Riding a horse or the wheel of a chariot over a sacrificial ground renders it holy. Lord Vishṇu in His Dwarf incarnation also made the earth holy by

I shall keep Thee on my head.
Protect me at every step!

2. The 81st of the Goddess Lakshmī's 108 names.

**Vasumatī (f)** (*vasu* 'wealth' + *mati* 'having') The wealthy, a name of the Earth-Goddess.

**Vasupati (m)** (*vasu* 'wealth, vasus' + *pati* 'lord') 1. The Lord of wealth; a name of Kubera. 2. The Lord of the eight Vasus; a name of Agni and of Indra. [See **Vasu**]

**Vatsala (m)** 1. The affectionate or loving. 2. The 471st name of Lord Vishṇu as listed in the Vishṇu Sahasranāma. In his commentary Śrī Śaṅkara states, "On account of His love toward devotees, the Lord is called *Vatsala*, the Loving."

**Vatsalā (f)** She who looks upon God as her beloved Child, just as Devakī looked upon the divine infant Kṛishṇa.

**Vāgīśwara (m)** (*vāk* 'speech' + *īśwara* 'lord') 1. The Lord of (Vedic) speech. 2. A name of the Creator Brahmā, who was first given the Vedas by Lord Nārāyaṇa and who then imparted that divine speech to the Ṛishis, his mind-born sons. 3. A name of Lord Śiva, who revealed the Sanskrit alphabet to Pāṇani with His Ḍamaru.

**Vāgīśwarī (f)** (*vāk* 'speech' + *īśwarī* 'sovereign goddess') The sovereign Goddess of speech, a name of the Goddess Saraswatī (i.e. Brahmā's divine power of Vedic speech, personified as his consort).

**Vālmīki (m)** Born of an anthill. The name of the tenth son of sage Pracetas, who after leading the life of a highwayman was given the mantra Rāma to repeat. He repeated this mantra with such total one-pointedness that he lost body consciousness and stayed seated in one position so long that his body became covered by an anthill. When he regained his outer consciousness, he had been transformed into a sage. He was the Guru of Bharadwāja and is considered the first and foremost of poets, the Ādi-Kavi. He is the first to compose a thirty-two syllable verse called a śloka. At the request of Brahmā, he narrated the *Rāmāyaṇa*, (the tale of Rāma), in 24,000 verses filled with virtue and heroism. He also wrote the famous "Yoga-Vāsishṭha," which is composed of 36,000 verses and which contains the Vedāntic teachings of Ṛishi Vāsishṭha to Śrī Rāma.

---

taking three steps, one on the earth, one on the atmosphere and one on heaven.

**Vāmadeva (m)** (*vāma* 'beautiful' + *deva* 'god') 1. The beautiful God. 2. The sixth of Lord Śiva's 108 names, which refers to the fourth of his five faces* and which is connected with the element water. 3. The name of a Ṛishi who revealed the five-syllabled mantra of Lord Śiva and was one of the seers of the Ṛig-Veda. In the Bṛihad-Āraṇyaka Upanishad Vāmadeva's Self-realization is described:

> This (self) was indeed Brahman in the beginning. It knew only Itself as, 'I am Brahman.' Therefore It became all. And whoever among the gods knew It, also became That; and the same with seers and men. The seer Vāmadeva, while realizing this (self) as That, knew, 'I was Manu, and the sun.' And to this day whoever in like manner knows It as, 'I am Brahman,' becomes all this (universe).

In the Aitareya Upanishad, it is further described in the following passage:

> This fact was stated by the seer: "Even while lying in the womb, I came to know of the birth of all the gods. A hundred iron-like bodies held me down. Then, like a hawk, I forced my way through by dint of knowledge of the Self." *Vāmadeva* said this while still lying in his mother's womb. He (*Vāmadeva*) who had known thus had become identified with the Supreme, and attained all desirable things (even here); and having (then) ascended higher up after the destruction of the body, he became immortal in the world of the Self. He became immortal.

**Vāṇī (f)** 1. Eloquent in words. 2. Relating to music; sound, voice. 3. Goddess of speech; a name of Goddess Saraswatī.

**Vārāṇasī (f)** A name of the holy city of Benares, derived from the two rivers, the *Varaṇā* and the *Nāsī,* which flow into the Ganges downstream and upstream. In the Jābāla Upanishad the sage Yājñavalkya and Ṛishi Atri have the following dialogue:

> Thereafter Atri asked Yājñavalkya, "How am I to realize the Self which is infinite and unmanifested?" Yājñavalkya replied, "That Avimukta (the 'Ignorance-Freed,' Lord Śiva) is to be worshipped. The Self which is infinite and unmanifested is established (i.e. not different from) in the Lord Avimukta." Where is this Avimukta established? He is established in between the Varaṇā and the Nāsī. What is Varaṇā and what is Nāsī? The Varanā is so called as it wards off *(vārayati)* all the faults committed by the (sensory and motor) organs. The Nāsī is so named as it destroys (nāsayati) all sins committed by the organs. Which is the seat of that

---

* The other four faces or aspects of Lord Śiva are Īśāna (Lord), Tatpurusha (That Being), *Aghora* (Non-Terrifying), and Sadyojāta (the Today-Born).

(Avimukta)? That, which is the juncture of the eyebrows and the nose, is the juncture of heaven (i.e. the crown of the head) and this world (i.e. the chin). The knowers of Veda worship indeed this juncture (Sandhi) as Sandhyā (at dawn, noon and dusk). That Avimukta is to be worshipped. He who knows this (Avimukta) thus imparts the Avimukta knowledge (of non-duality to his disciples).

**Vāsava (m)** 1. The chief of the Vasus; a name of Lord Indra, who is the chief of all the gods including the Vasus. 2. A name of Lord Vishṇu. See the Bhagavad Gītā X:22.

**Vāsudeva (m)** (*vāsu* 'indwelling' + *deva* 'god') 1. The indwelling God. 2. The 332nd, 695th and 709th names of Lord Vishṇu as listed in the Vishṇu Sahasranāma. In his commentary Śrī Śaṅkara states, "The Lord who indwells *(vāsati)* or veils (*vāsayati)* all, is *Vāsu,* the indweller or the veiler. *Deva* (God) is He who sports (through creation, maintenance and dissolution), wishes to conquer (the enemies of the gods), functions ( in all beings), shines (as Selfhood), is praised (by hymns), desired (by holy men) and who pervades (everywhere). Thus, He who is *Vāsu* as well as *Deva*, is *Vāsudeva*, the indwelling God. It also means He is the son of *Vasudeva* (i.e. Lord Kṛishṇa)." See the Bhagavad Gītā VII: 19; X:37. This name occurs in Lord Kṛishṇa's twelve-syllabled mantra:

*OM! Namo Bhagavate Vāsudevāya!*

OM! Salutation to Bhagavan *Vāsudeva*!

**Veda (m)** 1. (Revealed) Knowledge. 2. The 127th name of Lord Vishṇu as listed in the Vishṇu Sahasranāma. In his commentary Śrī Śaṅkara states, "Due to His having the nature of the *Vedas,* the Lord is called *Veda* or Knowledge. This term also means He confers knowledge *(vedayati),* as said by the Lord in the Bhagavad-Gītā, 'Out of mere compassion for them, I, abiding as their Self, destroy the darkness born of ignorance, by the luminous lamp of knowledge' (X:11). It is written in the Mahābhārata, 'All the *Vedas*, all learnings along with the treatises, all sacrifices and all offerings are Kṛishṇa. Those Brāhmaṇas who know truly Kṛishṇa, have accomplished all the sacrifices.'" Also see the Bhagavad-Gītā IX:17; XV:15. 3. Ancient Śruti (i.e. the heard or revealed Vedic scriptures that are traditionally held to be Apaurusheya or non-human in their origin and thus eternal and unchanging). They are considered the Eternal Religion or the Sanātana-Dharma, which Īśwara revealed to His first-born, Brahmā, and he to his mind-born sons, the Ṛishis. The Ṛishis each saw a part of the *Vedas* through their supreme power of Tapas and in turn imparted this *Vedic* lore to the human race. Thereafter Vyāsa, a partial incarnation of Lord Vishṇu, classified the *Vedas* into branches for the benefit of humanity.

There are three *Vedas*, the *Ṛig Veda*, *Yajur Veda*, and *Sāma Veda* and a fourth one auxiliary to them, named the *Atharva Veda*. In the Bṛihad-Āraṇyaka Upanishad of the *Yajur-Veda*, sage Yājñavalkya says to his wife Maitreyī, "As from a fire kindled with wet sacrificial sticks diverse kinds of smoke issue, even so, my dear, the *Ṛig-Veda*, *Yajur-Veda*, *Sāma-Veda*, and *Atharva-Veda*...(with all their parts) are like the breath of this great Being, they are like His breath."

Each *Veda* has four parts: the Samhitās, Brāhmaṇas, Āraṇyakas and Upanishads, respectively meant for the four stages of life: the Brahmacārī (the bachelor), Gṛihastha (the householder), the Vanaprastha (the ascetic), and the Sannyāsī (the renunciate). The Samhitā and Brāhmaṇa sections make the Karma-Kāṇḍa or ritualistic portion, while the Āraṇyakas and Upanishads make the Jñāna-Kāṇḍa or knowledge portion of the *Vedas*. Again the Āraṇyakas are more rightly called the Upāsanā-Kāṇḍa, or the worship portion, and the Upanishads as the Jñāna-Kāṇḍa proper.

The *Vedas* have six limbs called the *Vedāṅgas*, dealing with phonetics, grammar, prosody, etymology, astrology, and ritual.

In addition to the three *Vedas* and their auxiliary, there are four *Upavedas* or subsidiary *Vedas*, on health, archery, music and polity.

The authority of the Vedas on all suprasensuous matters is indisputable since it precedes all human thinking. Manu says, "Not being produced by mortals, the *Vedas* cannot be measured through human reason."

**Vedavyāsa (m)** (*veda* 'the Vedas' + *vyāsa* 'compiler') The compiler of the *Vedas*, a name of *Vyāsa*, who arranged the *Vedas* in several Śākhās or branches.

**Venugopāla (m)** (*venu* 'flute' + *Gopāla* 'name of young Kṛishṇa') The flute player Gopāla, a name of Śrī Kṛishṇa. [See **Gopāla**]

**Veṇulola (m)** (*veṇu* 'flute' + *lola* 'swinging') The swinging flute player, a name of Śrī Kṛishṇa.

**Veṅkaṭaramaṇa [m]** (*veṅkaṭa* 'name of a hill' + *ramaṇa* 'charming') The charming (God) of *Veṅkaṭa* (Hill), a name of Lord Vishṇu as the presiding deity of Tirupati Temple in South India.

**Vibhu (m)** 1. The omnipresent, all-pervading, multiform. 2. The 240th and 880th names of Lord Vishṇu as listed in the Vishṇu Sahasranāma. In his commentary Śrī Śaṅkara states, "The Lord who becomes (bhavati) manifold (vividham) through the form of Brahmā and others, is called *Vibhu*, the Multiform, as revealed in the Muṇḍaka Upanishad, 'He is eternal and multiform...' He is also called *Vibhu* because He pervades everything and because He is the Lord of the three worlds." Also see the Bhagavad Gītā V:15; X:12. 3. A name of Lord Śiva.

**Vibodha (m)** Consciousness, awakening.

**Vibhūti (f)** 1. Glory, might, wealth. See the tenth chapter of the Bhagavad Gītā, entitled *Vibhūti-Yoga*, where the glory of the Lord is described, and the third chapter of the Yogasūtras, entitled *Vibhūti-Pāda*, where the sovereign might or power of Yoga is described. 2. Consecrated ash used by Lord Śiva's devotees. Smearing different parts of the body with this ash is considered the highest wealth, symbolizing purity and renunciation of desires. 3. The sixth of the Goddess Lakshmī's 108 names.

**Vicārī (m), Vicāriṇī (f)** The inquirer, one who practices Ātma-Vicāra, or Self-inquiry (ie. the inquiry into the nature of the true Self in accordance with Vedāntic teaching). In the Chāndogya Upanishad Self-inquiry is described thusly:

> OM! Now, in this city (the body) of Brahman,
> there is a mansion shaped like a small lotus.
> In it is a small inner space. What is within that,
> *that* should be sought. That, indeed, one
> should desire to understand.

In the same Upanishad the Creator Brahmā says:

> The Self which is free from sin and old
> age, deathless, sorrowless, hungerless and thirstless,
> of truthful desire and resolve, He should be sought;
> Him one should desire to understand. He who has
> found out and who understands that Self, attains all
> the worlds and all the desires.

In the Brihad-Āraṇyaka Upanishad, referring to Vicāra as Manana, the sage Yājñavalkya says to his wife Maitreyī:

> The Self, my dear Maitreyī, should be heard of, reflected
> on and deeply meditated upon. By the realization of
> the Self, my dear, through hearing (Śravaṇa), reflection
> (Manana) and deep meditation (Nididhyāsana), all this is known.

In the Yoga-Vāsishṭha *Vicāra* or inquiry is also presented as one of the four sentinels* waiting at the gates of Salvation. There the Ṛishi Vasishṭha says to Śrī Rāma:

---

* The other three sentinels waiting at the gates of Salvation are Śānti (peace), Santosha (contentment), and Satsaṅga (holy company).

If along with peace, thou shouldst develop fully Ātmic inquiry through thy subtle, pure intelligence, after a study of the holy Scriptures, then such an incomparable intelligence will reach the supreme State. It is this inquiry alone that enables one to differentiate causes from effects and constitutes the remedy for curing the disease of rebirth. Having cleared oneself of all doubts through this discriminative power which is not blurred even in the midst of the intense darkness (of ignorance), which shines with undiminished luster even in the midst of light, and through which all things are visible, one should always be engaged, even when threatened by dangers, in the inquiry of 'Whence am I? Whence came this universe of transmigration? And of whom is this universe an attribute? Such an inquiry averts the dangerous disease called ignorance.

In the Aparokshānubhūti we find these six verses describing Vicāra:

*No'tpadyate Vinā Jñānam*
*Vicāreṇānyasādhanaiḥ*
*Yathā Padārtha-Bhānam Hi*
*Prakāśena Vinā Kwacit/11*

11. Knowledge is not brought about by any other means than inquiry (*Vicāra)*, just as an object is nowhere perceived without the help of light.

*Ko'ham Katham-Idam Jātam*
*Ko Vai Kartāsya Vidyate,*
*Upādānam Kim-Astīha*
*Vicāraḥ So'yam-Īdṛiśaḥ/12*

12. "Who am I? How is this (world) created? Who indeed is its author? What is its material cause?" Such is this inquiry *(Vicāra).*

*Nāham Bhūta-Gaṇo Deho*
*Nāham Cāksha-Gaṇas-Tathā*
*Etad-Vilakshaṇaḥ Kaścid*
*Vicāraḥ So'yam-Īdṛiśaḥ/13*

13. "I am neither the body, a combination of (the five) elements, nor am I an aggregate of the senses. I am someone different from these."

Such is this inquiry (*Vicāra).*

*Ajñāna-Prabhavam Sarvam*
*Jñānena Pravilīyate*
*Saṅkalpo Vividhaḥ Kartā*
*Vicāraḥ So'yam-Īdṛiśaḥ/14*

14. Everything has its source in
ignorance and is dissolved by knowledge.
The manifold thought must be the author.
Such is this inquiry *(Vicāra).*

*Etayor-Yad-Upādānam-Ekam*
*Sūkshmam Sad-Avyayam*
*Yathai'va Mṛid-Ghaṭādīnām*
*Vicāraḥ So'yam-Īdṛiśaḥ/15*

15. The material cause of these two (ignorance and
thought) is the One, subtle, unchanging Truth, just as
earth is the material cause of a pot and the like.
Such is this inquiry *(Vicāra).*

*Aham-Eko'pi Sūkshmaś-ca*
*Jñātā Sākshī Sad-Avyayaḥ*
*Tad-Aham Nātra Sandeho*
*Vicāraḥ So'yam-Īdṛiśaḥ/16*

16. As I am also the One subtle Knower,
the Witness, true and unchanging, so there
is no doubt that I am "That"(Brahman).
Such is this inquiry *(Vicāra).*

**Vicāraṇā (f)** 1. Inquiry. In the Yoga-Vāsishṭha, Ṛishi Vāsishṭha lists *Vicāraṇā* as the second of the Seven Stages of Knowledge:*

The second stage is called *Vicāraṇā*, and is free from ignorance. In order to know about the virtues, the proper path, concentration, meditation and good actions, he who is at this stage will associate with only the wisest who have great love and can throw light upon the real significance

* The Seven Stages of Knowledge or Jñāna-Bhūmikās are *Śubhe'cchā* (desire of good), *Vicāraṇā* (inquiry), Tanumānasī (subtle mindedness), Sattwāpatti (attainment of Truth), Asamsakti (nonattachment), Padārthābhāvanā (obliviousness of objects) and Turyagā (going to the Transcendent).

of the holy Vedic sentences. He will, after discriminating between the Real and the unreal know what actions ought to be done and what not, like the master of a house acquainting himself perfectly with his domestic affairs. Pride, envy, ego, desires, delusion, etc., arising through ignorance will be easily disposed of by him like a serpent throwing off its slough. Such an intelligent person can realize truly the esoteric and mysterious significance of the Jñāna-Śāstras and of the words of an Ācārya or a wise personage.

2. A name of Vyāsa's Brahma-Sūtras, which are also known as the Vedānta-Darśana and which lead the seeker of liberation into proper inquiry of Brahman.

**Videha (m)** (*vi* 'less' + *deha* 'body') 1. The bodiless. In the Īśā Upanishad the nature of the Self is revealed in the following passage:

*Sa Paryagāc'Chukram-Akāyam...*

He is all-pervasive, pure, bodiless...

In the Praśna Upanishad, sage Pippalāda describes the fruit of realizing the bodiless Purusha as:

*Param-Evāksharam Pratipadyate Sa*
*Yo Ha Vai Tad-Acchāyam-Aśarīram-*
*Alohitam Śubhram-Aksharam Vedayate...*

He attains the supreme Immutable Itself,
he indeed who realizes that shadowless,
bodiless, colorless, and pure Immutable...

To realize the Self or Truth, which is bodiless, one should become unattached to both the gross and the subtle bodies and go beyond the ignorance pertaining to the causal body. To awaken such dispassion and put an end to identification with the body, Prajāpati addresses Indra thus in the Chāndogya Upanishad:

*Maghavan Martyam Vā Idam*
*Śarīram-Āttam Mṛityunā*
*Tad-Asyāmṛitasyāśarīra-*
*syātmano'dhishṭhānam-*
*Ātto Vai Saśarīraḥ*
*Priyāpriyābhyām*
*Na Vai Saśarīrasya Sataḥ*
*Priyāpriyayor-Apahatir-Asty'*

*Aśarīram Vāva Santam Na*
*Priyāpriye Spriśataḥ.*

O Indra, mortal indeed is this body,
held by death. But it is the support
of this deathless, bodiless Self. Verily,
the embodied is held by pleasure and pain.
Surely, there is no cessation of pleasure and
pain for one who is embodied.
But pleasure and pain do not indeed
touch one who is bodiless.

Also see the Bhagavad-Gītā V:8,9.

2. In Vedāntic terminology a *Videha-Mukta* is one who, after having been a Jīvanmukta (i.e. liberated in the body, for some time attains *Videhamukti* or disembodied liberation at the death of the body when Prārabdha-Karma is completely exhausted). 3. In Yogic terminology the *Videhas* are those who may be somewhat detached from the gross body but not so from the subtle body including the ego, and who are thus bound to be reborn, not being truly enlightened. See Yogasūtras I:19. 4. The name of King Janaka's kingdom. Being wise and enlightened and having no identification with the body, Janaka was called Janaka of *Videha* and Janaka the *Videha.*

**Vidhātā (m)** 1. The Creator, a name of Lord Brahmā. 2. The Dispenser or Supporter. The 45th and 284th names of Lord Vishṇu as listed in the Vishṇu Sahasranāma. In his commentary Śrī Śaṅkara states, "As the author of actions and of their fruits, the Lord is called *Vidhātā*, the Dispenser. It also means on account of His maintenance He particularly (viśeshena) supports (dadhāti) even the serpent Ananta, the elephants of the quarters, and the mountains who themselves bear all beings, and He is thus called *Vi-Dhātā*, the All-supporting. See the Bhagavad Gītā IX:17.

**Vidhātrī (f)** 1. The Creatress. 2. A name of the Goddess Saraswatī, consort of the Creator Brahmā.

**Vidura (m)** (*vid* 'to know' + *ura* 'adjectifying suffix') 1. The wise. 2. The name of a son of Vyāsa, half-brother of Dhṛitarāshṭra and Pāṇḍu, who was recognized as a Jīvanmukta, one liberated while alive, and who appears in the Mahābhārata as the most intelligent among the intelligent. He is said to be the God Yama, born on earth through the curse of sage Māṇḍavya.

**Vidyā (f)** 1. Knowledge, wisdom. In the Muṇḍaka Upanishad, the sage Aṅgiras addresses Śaunaka thus:

*Dwe Vidye Veditavye*
*Iti Ha Sma Yad Brahmavido Vadanti*
*Parā Cai'vāparā Ca.*
*Tatrāparā Ṛigvedo...*
*Atha Parā Yayā*
*Tad-Aksharam-Adhigamyate.*

There are two kinds of knowledge to be known—
the higher and the lower. This is what, as tradition
runs, the knowers of the Vedas say.
Of these, the lower comprises the four Vedas
and their six limbs (as mere words).

Then there is the higher (Upanishadic knowledge)
by which the Immutable is realized.

The lower form of Knowledge is said to be the Vedas, when considered as a mere assemblage of words, while the higher form is said to be the Upanishads taught by the Guru to a dispassionate seeker. As compared to that higher knowledge called Brahmavidyā Ātmavidyā, which deals with non-duality, the lower one pertaining to duality is but ignorance. Accordingly, Lord Yama says to Naciketā in the Kaṭha Upanishad:

*Dūram-Ete Viparīte Vishūcī*
*Avidyā Yā Ca Vidye'ti Jñātā.*

That which is known as ignorance (Avidyā) and that
which is known as knowledge (Vidyā) are widely
contradictory, and they follow divergent courses.

In the Sarvasāra Upanishad, knowledge is described as follows:

*So'bhimāno Yayā Nivartate Sā Vidyā.*

That by which this ego is turned back
(towards the Self) is *Vidyā* or Knowledge.

In the Kena Upanishad it is further said:

*Ātmanā Vindate Vīryam*
*Vidyayā Vindate'mṛitam.*

(Since) through the Self vigor is acquired,
(therefore) through Its knowledge, Immortality is attained.

This fact is made clear by the Ṛishi Śwetāśwatara in the Śwetāśwatara Upanishad:

*Ksharam Tw'Avidyā*
*Hy'Āmṛitam Tu Vidyā.*

Perishable indeed is ignorance.
Immortal verily is knowledge.

*Tam-Eva Viditwā Ati-Mṛityum-Eti,*
*Nānyaḥ Panthā Vidyate'yanāya.*

Knowing Him alone (the Self), one overcomes death.
There is no other path for the attainment (of liberation).

Thus, according to all the Upanishads, knowledge alone saves one from ignorance which is the root cause of all suffering. Such knowledge regarding the oneness of Brahman and Atman is also called Para Bhakti (supreme devotion). Also see the Bhagavad-Gītā IV:36-39, V:16; X:11, 32; XIII:7-11, 17; XVIII:54-5. 2. Upāsanā (worship or meditation). About thirty such *Vidyās* or Upāsanās are expounded in the Upanishads. Those on the Nirguṇa-Brahman (attributeless) bring about Sadyomukti (immediate liberation) and those on the Saguṇa-Brahman (with attribute) lead to Kramamukti (gradual liberation after death), as do those on some Pratīka (symbol). 3. Knowledge personified as the Divine Mother in the form of the Goddess Saraswatī, Lakshmī or Pārvatī. 4. The third of the Goddess Lakshmī's 108 names.

**Vidyādhara (m), Vidyādharī (f)** (*vidyā* 'knowledge' + *dhara/ī* supporter') The supporter of (magical) science. The name of a class of celestials.

**Vighneśa (m)** (*vighna* 'obstacles' + *īśa* 'lord') The Lord who removes obstacles; a name of Lord Gaṇeśa.

**Vijara (m), Vijarā (f)** The ageless, undecaying. This definition of the Self is revealed in the Chāndogya Upanishad in the following passage:

*Tam Ced Brūyur-*
*Asmimś'Ced-Idam Brahmapure Sarvam Samāhitam*
*Sarvāṇi Ca Bhūtāni Sarve Ca Kāmā*
*Yadai'taj'Jarā Vāāpnoti Pradhwamsate Vā*
*Tato'tiśishyata Iti*
*Sa Brūyān'Nāsya Jarayai'taj'Jīryati*
*Na Vadhenāsya Hanyata*
*Etat Satyam Brahmapuram-*
*Asmin Kāmāḥ Samāhitā Eva*

*Ātamāapahatapāpmā Vijaro Vimṛityur-*
*Viśoko Vijighatso'pipāsaḥ*
*Satyakāmaḥ Satyasaṅkalpaḥ...*

Should the disciples say,
"If in this city of Brahman
(the body) is contained all this, all beings and all desires, then what is left of it when old age (*jarā)* overtakes it or when it perishes?" The teacher should reply, "It (Brahman called 'inner space') does not age with the aging of the body, It is not killed by the killing of this. This (inner) space is the real city of Brahman, in It are contained the desires. This is the Self free from evil, ageless *(Vijara)*, deathless, sorrowless, hungerless and thirstless, of truthful desire and resolve..."

Likewise, in the Bṛihad-Āraṇyaka Upanishad it is revealed:

*Sa Vā Esha Mahān-Aja*
*Ātmāajaro'maro'mṛito'bhayo Brahma...*

That great, birthless Self is undecaying
(Ajara), immortal, undying, fearless and absolute...

Again in the Praśna Upanishad, sage Pippalāda says to Satyakāma:

*Tam-Omkāreṇai'vāyatanenānveti Vidwān*
*Yat Tac'Chāntam-Ajaram-Amṛitam-Abhayam*
*Param Ce'ti.*

Through "OM" as an aid, the wise one reaches
the Supreme which is peaceful, ageless (Ajara),
deathless and fearless.

In the Śwetāśwatara Upanishad, the Ṛishi Śwetāśwatara expresses his realization thus:

*Vedāham-Etam-Ajaram Purāṇam*
*Sarvātmānam Sarvagatam Vibhutwāt,*
*Janma-Nirodham Pravadanti Yasya*
*Brahmavādino Hi Pravadanti Nityam.*

I know this undecaying *(Ajara)*, primeval Self of all,
who is omnipresent because of His all-pervasiveness, of

whom the expounders of Brahman proclaim the absence
of birth and whom they verily proclaim to be eternal.

Also see the Bhagavad-Gītā VII:29; XIV:20.

**Vijaya (m)** 1. The all-excelling, all-conquering. 2. The 147th name of Lord Vishṇu as listed in the Vishṇu Sahasranāma. In his commentary Śrī Śaṅkara states, "The Lord who excels *(vijayate)* all (viśwam) in such virtues as knowledge, dispassion and sovereignty, is called *Vijaya*, the All-excelling." Also see the Bhagavad-Gītā VII:7; X:36; XI:43.

**Vijñānī (m)** 1. Having full Knowledge, realized. According to Śrī Śaṅkara, *Jñāna* is that knowledge of the Self acquired from the Scriptures and the master [i.e. an indirect knowledge (Paroksha-Jñāna), while *Vijñāna* is the personal experience (Anubhava) or direct knowledge (Aparoksha-Jñāna) of the Self]. The prefix, *Vi* here expresses distinction or excellence (Viśesha). In the Bṛihad-Āraṇyaka Upanishad it is said:

*Tam-Eva Dhīro Vijñāya,*
*Prajñām Kurvīta Brāhmaṇaḥ.*

Having known that very Self
(from the Scriptures and the Guru),
the intelligent Brāhmaṇa should strive for realization.

Similarly, in the Muṇḍaka Upanishad it is revealed:

*Tad-Vijñānena Paripaśyanti Dhīrā*
*Ānanda-Rūpam-Amṛitam Yad-Vibhāti.*

The intelligent ones see everywhere, through their distinguished knowledge *(Vijñānena)*, that (Self)
which shines distinctly as blissfulness and immortality.

Also see the Bhagavad Gītā IV:38; V:16; VI:8; VII:2, 17-19; IX:1; XVIII:42, 50-55.

**Vimalā (f)** 1. The immaculate. 2. The 69th of the Goddess Lakshmī's 108 names. See the Bhagavad Gītā XIV:14,16. [See **Amalā, Nirmalā**]

**Vimocana (m)** The Redeeming. A name of Lord Śiva, which refers to His redeeming those who salute, praise and contemplate Him.

**Vimukti (f)** Perfect liberation. [See **Moksha, Mukti**]

**Vinatā (f)** 1. The humble, inclined. 2. A name of Garuḍa's mother.

**Vinaya (m)** [in Tamil **Vinayan**] 1. The humble, modest. Placing humility at its highest level, sage Gauḍapāda says in one of his Kārikās on the Māṇḍūkya Upanishad:

*Viprāṇām Vinayo Hy'Esha*
*Śamaḥ Prākṛita Ucyate...*

This (non-dual realization) is named the
modesty of the wise and their natural tranquility... (IV:86)

2. The Subduer. The 508th name of Lord Vishṇu as listed in the Vishṇu Sahasranāma. In his commentary Śrī Śaṅkara states, "The Lord who corrects the evil-doers is called *Vinaya*, the Subduer."

**Vināyaka (m)** The remover (of obstacles); a name of Lord Gaṇeśa. [See **Gaṇeśa**]

**Vindhya (m)** The name of one of the seven main mountain-ranges in India. In the Mahābhārata there is a story in which *Vindhya* was jealous of Himavan (i.e. the Himālayas, and wished the sun to revolve around him). The Sun-God declined to do so. Thus *Vindhya* undertook to grow in height as to bar the course of both the sun and the moon. Alarmed, the gods went to Agastya for aid. The great Ṛishi approached *Vindhya* and made him bow as to open the way towards the south. He then requested that the mountain range continue bowing until he returned. Agastya however never returned and *Vindhya* could thus not surpass Himavan in height. [See **Agastya**]

**Vipinavihārī (m)** (*vipina* 'forest' + *vihārī* 'sporter') The sporter of the forests; a name of Śrī Kṛishṇa.

**Virāgī (m), Virāgiṇī (f)** The dispassionate. [See **Vairāgī, Vairāgiṇī**]

**Viraja (m)** 1. The taintless, passionless. In the Bṛihad-Āraṇyaka Upanishad the Ātman is defined thus:

*Virajaḥ Para Ākāśād-*
*Aja Ātmā Mahān Dhruvaḥ.*

The Self is taintless (*Viraja*), higher than
space, birthless, great and constant.

In the Muṇḍaka Upanishad Brahman is similarly defined:

*Hiraṇmaye Pare Kośe*

*Virajam Brahma Nishkalam,*
*Tac'chubhram Jyotishām Jyotis-*
*Tad-Yad-Ātmavido Viduḥ.*

In the supreme, golden sheath (of the heart)
is the taintless *(Viraja),* and partless
Brahman, that pure Light of lights which
the Self-knowers know.

In the Bṛihad-Āraṇyaka Upanishad one who has realized the Oneness of Brahman and Ātman is described as:

*Sarvam-Ātmānam Paśyati...*
*Vipāpo Virajo'vicikitso*
*Brāhmaṇo Bhavati.*

He who sees all as but the Self...
becomes sinless, taintless, free from doubts
and a (real) Brāhmaṇa (i.e. a knower of Brahman).

and similarly in the Kaṭha Upanishad:

*Mṛityuproktām Naciketo'tha Labdhwā*
*Vidyām-Etām Yogavidhim Ca Kṛitsnam*
*Brahmaprāpto Virajo'bhūd-Vimṛityur-*
*Anyo'py'Evam Yo Vid-Adhyātmam-Eva.*

Having obtained this knowledge expounded by the God
of Death, as also the whole process of Yoga, and being
taintless (virtueless and viceless), Naciketā realized Brahman
and became immortal. Anyone else, too, who is such a
knower of the inner Self becomes taintless and immortal.

2. The sacrificial rite performed during initiation into renunciation, Sannyāsa-Dīkshā, is called *Virajā Homa*, the taintless or passionless sacrifice, in which the following formula is repeated several times while oblations are poured into the sacred fire:

*Jyotir-Aham Virajā Vipāpmā*
*Bhūyāsam! Swāhā!*

Being passionless and sinless, may I
become the Light (of Brahman)! (For this sake)
Let this oblation be well poured!

Also see the Bhagavad Gītā VI:27.

**Virajā (f)** 1. The taintless, passionless. 2. The name of a river in Brahmaloka, the highest heaven where the Creator Brahmā lives. This river flows across the road to Brahmā's palace. Thus one has to cross it in order to reach the palace. This means one should be free from Rajoguṇa or passion and be Sattwic or pure; otherwise, one cannot reach Satyaloka, the world of Truth. This process is revealed in the Kaushītaki Upanishad:

*Sa Āgacchati Virajām Nadīm*
*Tam Manasai'vātyeti*
*Tat-Sukṛita-Dushkṛite Dhūnute*
*Tasya Priyā Jñātayaḥ Sukṛitam-*
*Upayanty'Apriyā Dushkṛitam...*

Having reached the *Virajā* River, he
crosses over it by mere thought and
shakes off his good and bad acts. His
dear ones obtain his good deeds, the
undear ones his bad deeds...

2. Accordingly, in the Muṇḍaka Upanishad the Saguṇa worshippers are referred to as taintless or passionless:

*Sūrya-Dwāreṇa Te Virajāḥ Prayānti*
*Yatrāmṛitaḥ Sa Purusho*
*Hy'Avyayātmā.*

Being taintless *(Virajāḥ)*, they go by
the path of the sun to where lives that
(relatively) immortal Being (Brahmā)
of (relative) undecaying nature.

3. In the Kshurikā Upanishad the Sushumnā Nāḍi leading to the Brahmaloka is described as:

*Sushumnā Tu Pare Līnā*
*Virajā Brahmarūpiṇī.*

The Sushumnā indeed, sticking to the Supreme,
is taintless and of the form of Brahmā.

**Virakta (m)** The dispassionate, discolored. [See **Vairāgī**]

**Virāj (m), Virāṭ (m)** The all-sovereign, all-radiant, a name of the Self as present in the gross cosmic body during the waking state. It is symbolized as the "A" in the sacred syllable "AUM." This name is explained as follows:

*Vividham Rājamānatwād- Virāṭ.*

On account of radiating diversely, He is *Virāṭ*, the All-radiant.

In the Māṇḍūkya Upanishad *Virāṭ* is called Vaiśwānara in the following passage:

*Jāgarita-Sthāno Bahish-Prajñaḥ*
*Saptāṅga Ekona-Vimśati-Mukhaḥ*
*Sthūla-Bhug Vaiśwānaraḥ*
*Prathamaḥ Pādaḥ.*

The first quarter (of "OM") is Vaiśwānara whose sphere is the waking state, whose consciousness relates to things external, who is possessed of seven limbs* and nineteen mouths,** and who enjoys gross things.

**Viriñci (m)** The Creator, a name of the God Brahmā. [See **Brahmā**]

**Virūpāksha (m)** (*virūpa* 'diverse, multiform' + *aksha* 'eye') The diversely-eyed. The seventh of Lord Śiva's 108 names, which refers to His three eyes. [See **Nitalāksha**]

**Viśaṅka (m)** The fearless.

**Viśākha (m)** A name of Lord Muruga.

**Viśālākshī (f)** (*viśāla* 'large' + *akshī* 'eye') The large-eyed, a name of the Goddess Durgā.

**Vishṇu (m)** The All-pervading. The 2nd, 258th and 657th of Lord Vishṇu's one thousand names as listed in the Vishṇu Sahasranāma. In his commentary Śrī Śaṅkara states, "The Lord who pervades (veveshṭi, vyāpnoti) or who penetrates (viśati) into all is called *Vishṇu,* the All-pervading or penetrating. It indicates that He is unlimited by space, time and substance, as revealed in the Mahā-Nārāyaṇa Upanishad, 'Having pervaded (vyāpya) everything inside and outside, the Lord Nārāyaṇa (i.e. *Vishṇu)* stands.' The *Vishṇu-Puraṇa* says, 'As

---

* The seven limbs are the heaven, sun, space, air, fire, water and earth.

** The nineteen mouths are the five sensory organs, the five motor organs, the five Prāṇas, the mind, intellect, ego and memory.

all this (universe) is penetrated (vishṭam) by the power of that great Self, hence He is called *Vishṇu*, from the root *Viś* (to penetrate). In the Mahābhārata the Lord says to Arjuna, 'O son of Pṛithā, since My radiance, standing foremost, has pervaded heaven and earth, and as I have also traversed (the three worlds), I am known as *Vishṇu*.'"

Lord *Vishṇu* is usually depicted as the Protector or Preserver of the universe, the second member of the triple Godhead. However, His keen devotees view Him as Creator, Preserver, and Destroyer of the universe and identify Him thus with the very Absolute or Brahman, for many Vedic texts refer to Lord *Vishṇu* as the highest Truth when they speak of *Tad-Vishṇoḥ Paramam Padam* (the supreme state of *Vishṇu)*.

The *Vishṇu*-Purāṇa and the Bhāgavata-Purāṇa are concerned with the glory of Lord *Vishṇu* while the Mahābhārata gives the famous One Thousand Names of the Lord, the *Vishṇu*-Sahasra-Nāma-Stotram, which are pregnant with deep spiritual meaning.

Lord *Vishṇu* is known for His numerous Avatāras or incarnations on earth, of which His ten main ones are: Matsya (Fish), Kūrma (Tortoise), Vārāha (Boar), Nṛisimha (Man-Lion), Vāmana (Dwarf), Paraśurāma (Śrī Rāma carrying an ax), Rāmacandra or Śrī Rāma, Śrī Kṛishṇa, Buddha and lastly Kalki at the end of the present Kālī (dark) age.

Lord *Vishṇu* is invoked in the well-known Śānti-Mantra in the line: *"Śam No Vishṇur-Urukramaḥ,"* "May *Vishṇu* of great strides be blissful to us!" This is because He is said to have traversed the earth, atmosphere and heaven in three steps in His Dwarf incarnation to regain the dominion of the three worlds from the Demon Bali.

Lord *Vishṇu* has two consorts, the Earth-Goddess and Lakshmī. In His four arms He holds the Śaṅkha (conch), the Cakra (discus), the Gadā (club), and the Padma (lotus), which respectively stand for the Ahaṅkāra (ego), the Manas (mind), the Buddhi (intellect), and the Citta (memory). His vehicle is Garuḍa, the divine Eagle and He rests on the divine serpent Śesha (or Ananta) on the milk ocean. His heaven is Vaikuṇṭha. [See **Vaikuṇṭha**] Also see the Bhagavad Gītā X:21.

**Vishṇupriyā (f)** (*vishṇu* 'the all-pervading' + *priyā* 'beloved') 1. The beloved of Vishṇu. A name of the Goddess Lakshmī. 2. A name of the holy basil plant. [See **Tulasi**]

**Viśoka (m), Viśokā (f)** (*vi* 'not' + *śoka* 'sorrow') The sorrowless. [See **Aśoka**]

**Viśuddhi (f)** (*vi* 'all' + *śuddhi* 'purity') 1. All purity. 2. The name of the throat cakra which is connected with the element of space and the quality of sound. Also see the Bhagavad Gītā V:11; VI:12.

**Viśwa (m), Viśwam (m)** 1. The Universe, the All. 2. The first of Lord Vishṇu's one thousand names as listed in the Vishṇu-Sahasra-Nāma. In his commentary

Śrī Śaṅkara states, "In the beginning (of Lord Vishṇu's one thousand names), the twofold Brahman (Saguṇa and Nirguṇa) is given the term *Viśwam.* 1) Being the cause of the entire universe *(viśwasya* jagataḥ), Brahman is said to be *Viśwam,* the Universe. Being the effect of a cause, the word 'Universe' is used in the beginning to show that the praise of Lord Vishṇu is possible through such names as Brahmā, etc., who are also effects. 2) This name also indicates that this universe is truly none other than the supreme Being. Thereby, Brahman is spoken of as *Viśwam,* as revealed in the Muṇḍaka Upanishad, 'This universe is nothing but Brahman...nothing but the Purusha.' In reality, there is nothing whatsoever which is different from That. 3) Again, Brahman which penetrates (viśati) is *Viśwam,* the Penetrating, as revealed in the Taittirīya Upanishad, 'Having projected the universe, He entered into it.' Moreover, that into which all beings *(viśwāni* bhūtāni) enter (viśanti) during cosmic withdrawal is *Viśwam* or Brahman, the Absolute, as revealed in the same Upanishad, 'That towards which they go and into which they enter.' So He permeates all the universe, which is His effect, and the whole universe enters into Him. Hence, either way, Brahman is *Viśwam.* 4) Lastly, *Viśwam* refers to the sacred syllable "OM," as revealed in the Māṇḍūkya Upanishad, 'The word OM, is all this universe,' which shows that the syllable OM is spoken of here through the word *Viśwam.* Due to the lack of any great difference between the named and the name itself, *Viśwam* means the very word OM (i.e. Brahman)." 3. In Vedāntic terminology *Viśwa* refers to the Self as associated with the individual gross body during the waking state, being then seated in the right eye. It is symbolized by the letter "A" of "AUM,"* and it is explained as follows:

*Sūkshma-Śarīram-Aparityajya*
*Sthūla-Śarīra-Praveshṭritwād Viśwaḥ.*

On account of pervading the gross body,
without giving up the subtle body He is *Viśwa,* the All-pervading.

**Viśwakarmā (m)** (*viśwa* 'all, universe' + *karmā* 'maker') 1. The maker of all. The name of the divine architect Twashṭā, son of the Creator Brahmā, who makes chariots and other necessities for the gods. He incarnated as Nala, a monkey who built the bridge between India and Śrī Laṅkā for Śrī Rāma to save Sītā from the grasp of the demon Rāvaṇa. 2. The 51st name of Lord Vishṇu as listed in the Vishṇu-Sahasranāma. In his commentary Śrī Śaṅkara states, "1) The Lord whose action includes all *(viśwam)* acts *(karma)* is called *Viśwakarmā,* (of all action). 2) It also means that He performs the universal action (jagat-*karma*), 3) that He has the power of variegated creation, or 4) that He resembles the god *Viśwakarmā* or Twashṭā, the divine Architect."

---

* The spelling of "OM" when it is split into "A," "U" and "M," as the diphthong "O" consists of "A" + "U."

**Viśwanātha (m)** (*viśwa* 'all, universe' + *nātha* 'lord') The Lord of the universe. A name of Lord Śiva as worshipped in Benares where He is the presiding deity. The sage Vyāsa composed eight verses in praise of *Viśwanātha*, having the following refrain:

> ... *Vārāṇasī-Pura-Patim*
> *Bhaja Viśwanātham!*
>
> ...worship the Lord of the city Vārāṇasī
> (Benares), the Lord of the universe!

**Viśwarūpa (m), Viśwarūpiṇī (f)** (*viśwa* 'all, universe' + *rūpa/iṇī* 'form') Having universal form. See the eleventh chapter of the Bhagavad Gītā, which is devoted to this concept of God.

**Viśwādhāra (m)** (*viśwa* 'all, universe' + *ādhāra* 'support') 1. The Support of the universe, a name of Lord Vishṇu. 2. A name of Lord Śiva. 3. A name of Lord Gaṇeśa.

**Viśweśa (m)** (*viśwa* 'all, universe' + *īśa* 'lord') The Lord of the universe. A name of Lord Śiva as the presiding deity of Benares. [See **Viśwanātha**]

**Viśweśwara (m)** (*viśwa* 'all, universe' + *īśwara* 'lord') The Lord of the universe. A name of Lord Śiva as the presiding deity of Benares. [See **Viśwanātha**]

**Viśweśwarī (f)** (*viśwa* 'all, universe' + *īśwarī* 'sovereign goddess') Sovereign Goddess of the universe.

**Vittakapati (m)** (*vittaka* 'wealth' + *pati* 'lord') The Lord of wealth; a name of Kubera. [See **Kubera**]

**Vittanātha (m)** (*vitta* 'wealth' + *nātha* 'lord') The Lord of wealth; a name of Kubera. [See **Kubera**]

**Vittapati (m)** (*vitta* 'wealth' + *pati* 'lord') The Lord of wealth; a name of Kubera. [See **Kubera**]

**Vitteśa (m)** (*vitta* 'wealth' + *īśa* 'lord') The Lord of wealth; a name of Kubera. [See **Kubera**]

**Viṭṭhala (m)** (*viḍ* 'brick' + *sthala* 'standing') Standing on a brick. The name of an incarnation of Śrī Kṛishṇa at Pandharpur in Deccan. There, the Lord blessed a Brāhmaṇa named Puṇḍarīka who was reputed for his filial piety. Lord *Viṭṭhala* is represented standing on a brick (*Viḍ*) with His arms akimbo.

**Vivaswan (m)** (*vi* 'forth' + *vaswat* 'shining') Brilliant, shining forth; a name of the Sun-God as father of Lord Yama and the sage Manu. See the Bhagavad Gītā IV:1.

**Viveka (m)** [in Tamil **Vivekan**] 1. (Spiritual) discrimination, discernment, which is the first among the fourfold Vedāntic Sādhana.* Śrī Śaṅkara explains *Viveka* in his celebrated "Viveka-Cūḍāmaṇi," "The Crest-jewel of Discrimination," as:

*Brahma Satyam Jagan'Mithye'ty'*
*Evam-Rūpo Viniścayaḥ,*
*So'yam Nityānitya-Vastu-*
*Vivekaḥ Samudāhṛitaḥ.*

The firm conviction of such nature as to think,
"Brahman is true, the universe is illusory,"
is called discrimination between the
Eternal and the non-eternal.

To the great Ācārya beholding the world as impermanent (Anitya) means pondering over its illusory state (Mithyātwa), because desire may arise even for impermanent things while it completely turns back if their hollowness or unreality be well-discerned. Such *Viveka* arises in a mind purified through Karma-Yoga or detachment from the fruits of action, and it generates Vairāgya or dispassion, which in turn opens the path of knowledge (Jñāna) and renunciation (Sannyāsa). 2. Discrimination personified as the son of Manas (Mind), and Nivṛitti (Renunciation).

**Vivekī (m), Vivekinī (f)** The discriminating, discerning. See the Yogasūtra 11:15.

**Vīṇā (f)** A type of Indian lute invented by Devarshi Nārada and associated with the Goddess Saraswatī, who presides over musical arts. The *Vīṇā's* neck represents Saraswatī's slender body, the two gourds Her breasts, the frets Her bangles and anklets, the strings Her hair, and the sound Her very breath or voice. The *Vīṇā's* musical sounds also represent the melodious and inspiring Vedic words imparting knowledge of the true Self. In the Chāndogya Upanishad is the following passage:

---

* The fourfold Vedāntic Sādhana consists of 1. Viveka (discrimination), 2. Vairāgya (dispassion) 3. Shaṭsampatti (the sixfold wealth) which in turn consists of a) Śama (mind-control) b) Dama (sense-control) c) Uparati (withdrawal) d) Titikshā (endurance) e) Śraddhā (faith) f) Samādhāna (concentration) 4. Mumukshutwa (desire for salvation).

*Sa Esha Ye Cai'tasmād-Arvāñco Lokās-*
*Teshām Ce'shṭe Manushya-Kāmānām Ce'ti*
*Tad Ya Ime Vīṇāyām Gāyanty,*
*Etam Te Gāyanti*
*Tasmāt Te Dhana-Sanayaḥ.*

That Person in the eye is the Lord of all the worlds that are extended below, and also the Lord of the objects desired by men. Thus, those who sing on the *Vīnā* sing of Him alone and thereby become endowed with wealth.

In the Bṛihad-Āraṇyaka Upanishad the sage Yājñavalkya addresses his wife Maitreyī, using the simile of the *Vīṇā* to show how everything is included in God:

*Sa Yathā Vīṇāyai Vādyamānāyai*
*Na Bāhyāñ'ChabdāñdChaknuyād Grahaṇāya,*
*Vīṇāyai Tu Grahaṇena*
*Vīṇā-Vādasya Vā-Śabdo Gṛihītaḥ*
*...Evam Vā Are'sya Mahato Bhūtasya*
*Niśśwasitam-Etad Yad Ṛigvedo...*
*Ayam Ca Lokaḥ, Paraś-Ca Lokaḥ,*
*Sarvāṇi Ca Bhūtāni, Asyai'vai'tāni Sarvāṇi*
*Niśśwasitāni.*

As, when a *Vīṇā* is played, one cannot distinguish its various particular notes, but only hears the general note of the *Vīṇā* or the general sound produced by different kinds of playing...even so my dear, all the Vedas...this world, the next world and all beings are all like the breath of this great Being, they are like His breath.

**Vīryavan (m)** (*vīrya* 'vigor' + *van* 'having') Vigorous.

**Vīryā (f)** (Spiritual) Vigor, strength. In the Kena Upanishad the following is revealed:

*Ātmanā Vindate Vīryam*
*Vidyayā Vindate'mṛitam.*

(Since) Through Self vigor is acquired,
(therefore) through Its knowledge Immortality is attained.

Commenting on this text, Śrī Śaṅkara states, "*Vīryam*, vigor, is balam (strength) and sāmarthyam (capacity). Vigor got by wealth, friends, incantation, herbs, austerities and Yoga cannot conquer death, being produced by impermanent things. But vigor produced by Self-knowledge is acquired through the very Self, not through anything else. Having thus no other means of acquisition, that vigor of Self-knowledge alone can conquer death. Since the vigor produced by Self-knowledge is thus obtained through the very Self, therefore through knowledge of the Self one attains Immortality."

Hence in the Muṇḍaka Upanishad it is said:

> *Nāyam-Ātmā Bala-Hīnena Labhyaḥ.*
>
> This Self is not attainable by one devoid of the
> strength (that comes from devotion to the Self).

In the Śānti-Mantra is the following prayer for the cultivation of such vigor:

> *OM !Saha Nāv'Avatu!*
> *Saha Nau Bhunaktu!*
> *Saha Vīryam Karavāvahai!*
> *Tejaswi Nāv'Adhītam-Astu!*
> *Mā Vidwishāvahai!*
> *OM! Śāntiḥ! Śāntiḥ! Śāntiḥ!*
>
> OM! Together, may He (God) protect us both!
> Together, may He nourish us both!
> Together, may we both acquire vigor (*Vīryam*)!
> Let our study be brilliant!
> May we have no ill feelings toward each other!
> OM! Peace! Peace! Peace!

In Yogasūtra II:38 it is said:

> *Brahmacarya-Pratishṭhāyām*
> *Vīrya-Lābhaḥ.*
>
> On the establishment in continence,
> (comes) the attainment of vigor.

In his commentary on the Yogasūtras, Vyāsa explains this attainment: "The Yogī firmly established in Brahmacarya increases his irresistible virtues, and being thus perfected, he becomes powerful so as to impart knowledge to the disciples." Also see the Bhagavad Gītā VII:11; XI:19.

**Vrata (m)** Observing a spiritual vow. The main spiritual vows are contained in the first limb of Yoga called Yama: non-injury, truthfulness, nonstealing, continence and non-greed. When these are fully observed, it is called the *Mahāvratam*, the Great Vow, corresponding to entry into the Sannyāsa order. See the Yogasūtras II:30-1 and the Bhagavad Gītā: IV:28; VI:14; VII:28; IX:14.

**Vratī (m), Vratinī (f)** Observing a spiritual vow. The main spiritual vows are contained in the first limb of Yoga called Yama: non-injury, truthfulness, non-stealing, continence and non-greed. When these are fully observed, it is called the *Mahāvratam*, the Great Vow, corresponding to entry into the Sannyāsa order. See the Yogasūtras II:30-1 and the Bhagavad Gītā: IV:28; VI:14; VII:28; IX:14.

**Vṛindā (f)** 1. A cluster of holy basil (Tulasī) used in worship services. [See **Tulasī**] 2. A name of Rādhā. [See **Rādhā**]

**Vyāpī (m)** (*vi* 'all' + *āpī* 'pervading') 1. The All-pervading. The 467th name of Lord Vishṇu as listed in the Vishṇu-Sahasranāma. In his commentary Śrī Śaṅkara states, "Because He is omnipresent like space the Lord is called the All-pervading, as revealed in the Vedas, 'He is omnipresent like space, and eternal.' It also means He pervades all effects as their cause." 2. A name of Brahman occuring in the following passages of the Śwetāśwatara Upanishad:

*Sarvavyāpinam-Ātmānam*
*Kshīre Sarpir-Ivārpitam,*
*Ātmavidyā-Tapo-Mūlam*
*Tad Brahmo'panishat-Param.*

The all-pervading Self which is inserted
(everywhere) like butter in milk and whose
roots are Self-knowledge and Tapas, is that Brahman
which is the supreme object of the Upanishads.

*Sarvānana-Śiro-Grīvaḥ*
*Sarvabhūta-Guhā-Śayaḥ*
*Sarvavyāpī Sa Bhagavān*
*Tasmāt Sarvagataḥ Śivaḥ.*

Possessed of all faces, heads, and necks,
He who dwells in the heart of all beings
is all-pervading and fortunate. Therefore He
is omnipresent and auspicious.

**Vyāpinī (f)** (*vi* 'all' + *āpinī* 'pervading') The All-pervading, a name of the supreme Goddess or Parameśwarī.

**Vyāsa (m)** The compiler (of the Vedas), the name of a partial incarnation of Lord Vishṇu. He is also known as *Vedavyāsa* (compiler of the Vedas), Bādarāyaṇa (dweller of Badarikāśrama) and Kṛishṇadwaipāyana (dark-complexioned Island-Dweller), as he was born on an island in the Yamunā or Jumnā River.

*Vyāsa* was the son of Parāśara and Satyavatī, half-brother of Vicitravīrya and Bhīshma, and father of Dhṛitarāshṭra, Pāṇḍu, Vidura and Śukadeva. He is the Ṛishi Apāntaratamas reborn at the behest of Lord Vishṇu. [For details of his birth see **Parāśara**] *Vyāsa* ranks as the sixth in the traditional line of Brahmavidyā Gurus.* Apart from his son Śukadeva, *Vyāsa's* disciples were Vaiśampāyana, Paila, Sumantu and Jaimini.

*Vyāsa* arranged the eternal Vedas into several branches. [See **Veda**] He composed the 100,000 verses of the Mahābhārata, including the 700 verses of the Bhagavad Gītā, which forms its core, and he wrote the eighteen Purāṇas on mythology, a noted commentary on the Yogasūtras, a law-book, and above all the Brahmasūtras (Aphorisms on Brahman) which are also known as the Vedānta-Darśana, (philosophy of Vedānta).

*Vyāsa* began writing the Brahmasūtras on the day of his enlightenment, which was the full moon of July.** He wrote them to remove the apparent contradictions found in the Upanishads and to set a logical and systematic order in their teachings, thus dispelling all wrong ideas on Brahman and bringing to light Its actual nature. The 555 sūtras of the Brahmasūtras are also known as the Bhikshu-Sūtras since they are studied by mendicant Sannyāsins (Bhikshus) during the four rainy months following Guru-Pūrṇimā. Along with the Upanishads and the Bhagavad-Gītā, they form the triple basis (Prasthānatraya) of Vedānta, in which the Upanishads are the revealed part (Śruti), the Bhagavad Gītā is the remembered or traditional part (Smṛiti) and the Brahmasūtras are the reasoning part (Nyāya).***

*Vyāsa* stands as a unique holy personage, the ideal Muni according to the Bhagavad Gītā X:37, and is considered by many still to be alive.

The following verses are in praise of *Vyāsa:*

---

* He is therefore placed after Lord Nārāyaṇa, the Creator Brahmā, the Ṛishi Vasishṭha, Śakti and Parāśara and before his own son Śukadeva, the sages Gauḍapāda, Govindapāda and Śrī Śaṅkarācārya, along with all the successors up to the living Paramahamsa Sannyāsins today.

** This day became known as Vyāsa-Pūrṇimā and later as Guru-Pūrṇimā.

*** These sūtras are condensed and profound, and should be studied with the help of an authoritative commentary such as Śrī Śaṅkara's Bhāśya, Vācaspati Miśra's Bhāmatī or Śrī Swāmī Śivānanda's commentary.

*Vyāsāya Vishṇu-Rūpāya*
*Vyāsa-Rūpāya Vishṇave!*
*Namo Vai Brahma-Nidhaye*
*Vāsishṭhāya Namo Namaḥ!*

Salutations to *Vyāsa* in the form of Lord Vishṇu
and to Lord Vishṇu in the form of Vyāsa!
Salutations to the abode of Brahman,
to the descendant of Vasishṭha!

*Acaturvadano Brahmā*
*Dwibahur-Aparo Hariḥ,*
*Aphālalocanaḥ Śambhur-*
*Bhagavān Bādarāyaṇaḥ.*

The fortunate Bādarāyaṇa *(Vyāsa)*
is Brahmā without four faces, another
Hari (Vishṇu) with (only) two arms and
Śambhu (Śiva) without a frontal eye.*

*Vyāsam Vishṇu-Swarūpam Kali-Mala-*
*Tamasaḥ Prodyad-Āditya-Dīptim*
*Vāsishṭham Vedaśākhā-Vyasanakaram-*
*Ṛishim Dharmabījam Mahāntam*
*Paurāṇa-Brahmasūtrāṇy'Aracayad-*
*Atha Yo Bhāratam Ca Smṛitim Tam*
*Kṛishṇadwaipāyanākhyam Sura-Nara-*
*Ditijaiḥ Pūjitam Pūjaye'ham.*

I worship *Vyāsa* who is Lord Vishṇu's own form, who resembles the light of the rising sun to the darkness of impurity of this Kāli (dark) age, who is the descendant of Vasishṭha, who divided the Vedas into branches, who is a seer, the seed of virtue and a great sage, who wrote the Purāṇas, the Brahmasūtras, the Mahābhārata and the Smṛiti (law-code), who is called Kṛishṇadwaipāyana and who is worshipped by gods, men and demons.

Also see the second verse in the Gītā-Dhyānam.

**Vyoman (m)** 1. The ethereal; he who is like space. 2. A name of Lord Vishṇu, which refers both to His being the cause of the space element and to His

* In these verses *Vyāsa* is identified with the Trimūrti.

similarity with space with respect to subtleness, purity and pervasiveness. 3. A name of Brahman. See the Bhagavad Gītā IX:6; XIII:32.

# Y

**Yadu (m)** The name of an ancient king and hero, who was the son of King Yayāti, the brother of Puru and the ancestor of Śrī Kṛishṇa.

**Yadunandana (m)** (*yadu* 'name of a king' + *nandana* 'joy') The joy (i.e. son) of Yadu, a name of Akrūra, Śrī Kṛishṇa's paternal uncle.

**Yadunātha (m)** (*yadu* 'name of a king' + *nātha* 'lord') The Lord of the Yadus; a name of Śrī Kṛishṇa as the pre-eminent descendant of King Yadu.

**Yadupati (m)** (*yadu* 'name of a king' + *pati* 'lord') The Lord of the Yadus; a name of Śrī Kṛishṇa as the pre-eminent descendant of King Yadu.

**Yajamāna (m)** The sacrificing (i.e. he who performs one or any of the numerous Yajñas or sacrifices). In introducing the One Thousand Names of Lord Vishṇu to King Yudhishṭhira, Bhīshma says in the Mahābhārata:

*Tam-Eva Cārcayan Nityam*
*Bhaktyā Purusham-Avyayam,*
*Dhyāyan Stuvan Namasyamś'Ca*
*Yajamānas-Tam-Eva Ca.*

Ever worshipping with devotion that
imperishable Purusha, meditating on Him,
praising and saluting Him alone,
the sacrificing one (goes beyond all pains).

Also see the Bhagavad Gītā III:9-16; IV:23-33; IX:15, 25-27, 34; XVIII:65.

**Yajña (m)** Sacrifice. The 445th and 971st of Lord Vishṇu's one thousand names as listed in the Vishṇu-Sahasranāma. In his commentary Śrī Śaṅkara states, "1) The Lord is called 'Sacrifice' because He has the form of all sacrifices. 2) It also means He exists in the form of sacrifice and thus confers satisfaction to all the gods, as revealed in the Vedas, *'Yajño Vai Vishṇuḥ,'* 'Sacrifice, indeed, is Vishṇu.'"

In the Bhagavad Gītā X:25, the Lord specifies the greatness of Japa sacrifice by saying, *"Yajñānām Japa-Yajño'smi."* "Among sacrifices, I am the Japa sacrifice."

In IV: 18, 24, 32 of the Bhagavad Gītā, the Lord expounds Jñāna-*Yajña*, (knowledge sacrifice), as seeing action as unreal and inaction as merely conditioned by that unreal action. This means realizing one's own true Self as free from both action and inaction, and unchanging. All parts of a Vedic sacrifice, like the instrument of sacrifice, the thing sacrificed, the place of sacrifice, and the sacrificer, should be seen as nothing but Brahman. The Lord then extols Jñāna-*Yajña* as better than all material sacrifices. Also see the Bhagavad Gītā VII:30; VIII:4; IX:15-6, 24; XVI:1; XVII:11-13; XVIII:5-6.

**Yajñadhara (m)** (*yajña* 'sacrifice' + *dhara* 'bearer') The sacrifice-bearer. A name of Lord Vishṇu. [See **Yajña**]

**Yajñamūrti (m)** (*yajña* 'sacrifice' + *mūrti* 'form, image') The image or embodiment of sacrifice. A name of Lord Vishṇu. [See **Yajña**]

**Yajñapati (m)** (*yajña* 'sacrifice' + *pati* 'lord') The Lord or protector of sacrifices. The 972nd of Lord Vishṇu's one thousand names as listed in the Vishṇu-Sahasranāma. In his commentary Śrī Śaṅkara states, "*Yajñapati* means the protector *(Pātā)* or master (Swāmī) of sacrifices, as said in the Bhagavad-Gītā IX:24, 'I am indeed the enjoyer as also the Lord of all sacrifices.'"

**Yajñapriya (m)** (*yajña* 'sacrifice' + *priya* 'fond of, beloved') Fond of sacrifices. A name of Śrī Kṛishṇa. See the Bhagavad-Gītā IX:24.

**Yajñatrātā (m)** (*yajña* 'sacrifice' + *trātā* 'protector') Protector of sacrifices. A name of Lord Vishṇu. [See **Yajñapati**]

**Yajñavalka (m)** (*yajña* 'sacrifice' + *valka* 'expounder') The expounder of sacrifice. [See **Devarāta**]

**Yajñāri (m)** (*yajña* 'sacrifice' + *ari* 'enemy') Foe of (Daksha's) sacrifice; a name of Lord Śiva, which refers to His having destroyed Daksha's sacrifice when Daksha did not want to invite Him, the Lord, to his sacrifice.

**Yajñeśa (m)** (*yajña* 'sacrifice' + *īśa* 'lord ') The Lord of sacrifices. A name of Lord Vishṇu. [See **Yajñapati**]

**Yajushpati (m)** (*yajuḥ* 'Yajur-Vedic Hymns' + *pati* 'lord') The Lord of Yajur-Vedic hymns; a name of Lord Vishṇu. See the Bhagavad-Gītā IX:17.

**Yaksha (m)** 1. The mysterious or supernatural. 2. The name of a class of semi-divine beings, attendants of Kubera, their king. See the Bhagavad Gītā X:23. In the Kena Upanishad, Brahman appears to the gods as one of these semi-divine beings to remove their self-conceit.

**Yakshiṇī (f)** The name of Kubera's wife.

**Yama (m)** 1. Restrainer; a name of the God of Death who is the son of the Sun-God and the brother of Manu. He lives in the South and is also known as Dharma (the God of justice), Mṛityu (Death), Antaka (Ending), Kāla (Time).

In the Kaṭha Upanishad, Lord Yama imparts knowledge of the Self to Naciketā, who was sent to him by his angry father. [See **Naciketā**] In the Bhagavad-Gītā (X:29) Yama is identified with Lord Vishṇu. 2. The 162nd and the 866th names of Lord Vishṇu as listed in the Vishṇu-Sahasranāma. In his commentary Śrī Śaṅkara states, 1) "The Lord who controls *(yamayati)* all within is called *Yama*, the Controller. 2) He is also called by this name because He is attainable through *Yama* or self-restraint, the first limb of Yoga." 3. Restraint, the first limb in Yoga. In Patañjali's Yogasūtras (II:30) *Yama* is divided into five parts: *Ahimsā* (non-injury), Satya (truthfulness), Asteya (non-stealing), Brahmacarya (continence) and Aparigraha (non-greed). According to one's position in life, these are either conditioned or unconditioned by class, place and time; see Yogasūtra II:31. Also see the Bhagavad-Gītā II:61; III:41; IV:26-7; VI:14,24,26; VIII:12; XII:4; XVIII:-51.

**Yamajit (m)** (*Yama* 'God of Death' + *jit* 'conqueror') The Conqueror of Yama (i.e. the God of Death); a name of Lord Śiva who kicked Yama when the latter came to take Sage Mārkandeya's soul to his abode. [See **Mārkandeya**]

**Yamakīla (m)** A name of Lord Vishṇu.

**Yamī (f)** Yama's twin sister, who is identified with the holy Yamunā River.

**Yamunā (f)** The name of the holy Jumnā River in India that stands for the Iḍā Nāḍī in the subtle body.

**Yaśas (m)** Glory, fame; one of the six attributes given in the definintion of Bhagavan. [See **Bhagavan**] In the Śwetāśwatara Upanishad the following is revealed:

*Na Tasya Pratimā Asti*
*Yasya Nāma Mahad-Yaśaḥ.*

There is none equal to Him
Whose name is Great Glory.

**Yaśaswī (m), Yaśaswinī (f)** (*yaśaḥ* 'glory' + *vin/vinī* 'having') 1. The glorious. 2. The 80th of the Goddess Lakshmī's 108 names.

**Yaśodā (f)** (*yaśaḥ* 'glory' + *dā* 'giver') 1. The bestower of fame. 2. The name of the cowherd Nanda's wife who was Śrī Kṛishṇa's foster-mother.

**Yaśovara (m)** (*yaśaḥ* 'glory' + *vara* 'excellent') 1. Having excellent fame. 2. The name of a son of Śrī Kṛishṇa and Rukmiṇī.

**Yati (m)** 1. The Ascetic. A name of Lord Śiva as assuming the form of an ascetic engaged in constant self-restraint and Samādhi. 2. The (spiritual) striver. A name for the Sannyāsīs who habitually strive for Moksha or liberation. In the Nārada-Parivrājaka Upanishad (IV:10-13) the Lord Brahmā expounds to Nārada the duties of the ascetics and their fruit as:

*Ahimsā Satyam-Asteya-*
*Brahmacaryāparigrahāḥ*
*Anauddhatyam-Adīnatwam*
*Prasādaḥ Sthairyam-Ārjavam,*

Non-injury, truthfulness, non-stealing,
continence and non-acquiring,
absence of haughtiness and of depression,
serenity, stability, uprightness,

*Asneho Guru-Śuśrūshā*
*Śraddhā Kshāntir-Damaḥ Śamaḥ,*
*Upekshā Dhairya-Mādhurye*
*Titikshā Karuṇā Tathā,*

Unattachment, listening to the Guru,
faith, patience, sense-control, mind-control,
indifference, boldness, and sweetness,
endurance, and also compassion,

*Hrīs-Tathā Jñāna-Vijñāne*
*Yogo Laghw'aśanam Dhṛitiḥ*
*Esha Swadharmo Vikhyāto*
*Yatīnām Niyatātmanām.*

Likewise modesty, knowledge, and realization,
meditation, eating but little, and firmness.
This is well known as the own duty
of the self-controlled ascetics *(Yatis).*

*Nirdwandwo Nityasattwasthaḥ*
*Sarvatra Samadarśanaḥ,*
*Turīyaḥ Paramo Hamsaḥ*
*Sākshān'Nārāyaṇo Yatiḥ.*

Beyond dualities, ever established in purity,
having an equal vision in everything,
the Paramahamsa in the fourth stage of life,
this ascetic is visibly the Lord Nārāyaṇa.

See the Bhagavad-Gītā IV:28; V:26; VIII: 11; XII:3-5.

**Yatirāja (m)** (*yati* 'striver' + *rāja* 'king') 1. The king of strivers or ascetics. 2. A name of Rāmānuja.

**Yādava (m)** The descendant of Yadu. A name of Śrī Kṛishṇa. [See **Yadu**]

**Yādahpati (m)** (*yādaḥ* 'water-beings' + *pati* 'lord') The Lord of the water-beings; a name of Varuṇa. In the Bhagavad Gītā X:29, the Lord says, *"Varuṇo Yādasām-Aham"* "Among water-beings, I am Varuṇa." [See **Varuṇa**]

**Yājaka (m)** The sacrificer (i.e. he who performs one or another among the numerous Yajñas or sacrifices). See the Bhagavad Gītā, III:9-16; IV:23-33; IX:15, 25-27, 34; XVIII:65.

**Yājī (m)** The sacrificing (i.e. he who performs one or another among the numerous Yajñas or sacrifices). Extolling Self-knowledge as the highest sacrifice, Manu states in his law-code (XII:91):

*Sarva-Bhūta-Stham-Ātmānam*
*Sarva-Bhūtāni Cātmani,*
*Sampaśyann'ātma-Yājī Vai*
*Swārājyam-Adhigacchati.*

Seeing the Self present in all beings
and all beings in the Self, the sacrificer
to the Self *(Ātma-Yājī)* verily attains
self-sovereignty.

See the Bhagavad Gītā III:9-16; IV:23-33; IX:15, 25-27, 34; XVIII:65.

**Yājñavalkya (m)** The son of Yajñavalka; the name of a disciple of Vyāsa's disciple Vaiśampāyana. In the Vishṇu-Purāṇa is an account of a quarrel between Vaiśampāyana and *Yājñavalkya*, in which the master asked his disciple to return the Yajur-Veda that he had taught him. *Yājñavalkya* thus disgorged his learning and other disciples, taking the form of partridges (Tittiris), swallowed the Veda upon the request of Vaiśampāyana. Thus soiled, this Veda then became known as the Kṛishṇa or Black Yajur-Veda and the Taittirīya Samhitā or the Partridges' Hymns. After this incident, *Yājñavalkya* worshipped the Sun-God and received from Him the Śukla or White Yajur-Veda, which is also known as the Vājasaneya since the Sun-God took the form of a horse (Vājī) when He revealed it to *Yājñavalkya*. One of the Upanishads from the Śukla-Yajur-Veda on renunciation bears the name *Yājñavalkya Upanishad*. His teachings, however, are mainly best embodied in the renowned Bṛihad-Āraṇyaka Upanishad of Śukla-Yajur-Veda. In one of its passages the philosopher Gārgī praises his greatness by saying, "Revered Brāhmaṇas, you should consider yourselves fortunate if you can get off from him through salutation. Never shall any of you beat him in describing Brahman." In another section of the same Upanishad *Yājñavalkya* enlightens King Janaka, making him attain the fearless Brahman. In the same Upanishad, *Yājñavalkya* teaches his wife Maitreyī the means of immortality when he is about to enter into the Sannyāsa order:

*Na Vā Arc Sarvasya Kāmāya*
*Sarvam Priyam Bhavati,*
*Ātmanas-Tu Kāmāya*
*Sarvam Priyam Bhavati.*
*Ātmā Vā Are Drashṭavyaḥ - Śrotavyo*
*Mantavyo Nididhyāsitavyo Maitreyī,*
*...Idam Sarvam Viditam.*
*Yatra Tw'Asya Sarvam-Ātmai'vābhūt...*
*Tat-Kena Kam Paśyet...*
*Tat-Kena Kam-Abhivadet...*
*Tat-Kena Kam Vijānīyāt*
*Yene'dam Sarvam Vijānāti*
*Tam Kena Vijānīyāt...*
*Vijñātāram-Are Kena Vijānīyāt...*
*Etāvad-Are Khalw'Amṛitatwam.*

It is not for the sake of all, my dear Maitreyī, that all is loved, but it is for the sake of oneself. (Therefore) the Self should be realized—It should be heard of (Śravaṇa), reflected on (Manana) and deeply meditated upon (Nididhyāsana), then all is known...When, to the knower of Brahman, everything has become the Self, then what should one see and through what? What should one speak and through what?...What should one know and through what? Through what should one know That owing to which all this is known?...Through what, O Maitreyī, should one know the Knower?...This much indeed, my dear, is the means of immortality.

*Yājñavalkya's* teaching thus culminates in complete renunciation of the non-Self and perfect realization of the non-dual Self. *Yājñavalkya* is the example of the Vidwat-Sannyāsī (knowing renunciate) (i.e. one who embraces the Sannyasa order after the attainment of Self knowledge for the fruition of his knowledge into Jīvanmukti—liberation while living—and to impress on others that real Self-knowledge mean complete renunciation of the non-Self).

**Yogeśa (m)** (*yoga* 'oneness, of Ātman and Brahman' + *īśa* 'lord') 1. The Lord of Yoga. A name of Śrī Kṛishṇa. See the Bhagavad-Gītā III:3; IV:1-3; IX:5, X:7,10; XVIII:75-78. 2. A name of Lord Vishṇu. 3. A name of Lord Śiva. 4. A name of Yājñavalkya.

**Yogeśwara (m)** (*yoga* 'oneness, of Ātman and Brahman' + *īśwara* 'lord') 1. The Lord of Yoga. A name of Śrī Kṛishṇa. See the Bhagavad-Gītā III:3; IV:1-3; IX:5, X:7,10; XVIII:75,78. 2. A name of Lord Vishṇu. In the Mahābhārata the omniscient Bhīshma says:

*Yogo Jñānam Tathā Sāṅkhyam*
*Vidyāḥ Śilpādi Karma Ca,*
*Vedāḥ Śāstrāṇi Vijñānam-*
*Etat-Sarvam Janārdanāt.*

Yoga, knowledge, as well as Sāṅkhya,
sciences and the fine arts,
The Vedas, treatises and all learning -
all this sprung from Janārdana (i.e. Lord Vishṇu).

**Yogeśwarī (f)** (*yoga* 'oneness, of Ātman and Brahman' + *īśwarī* 'ruling goddess') The sovereign Goddess of Yoga. A name of the Goddess Durgā.

**Yogī (m)** 1. Possessed of *Yoga*; one who follows the teachings of *Yoga*. 2. The 849th of Lord Vishṇu's one thousand names as listed in the Vishṇu Sahasranāma. In his commentary Śrī Śaṅkara states, "*Yoga* is knowledge, and the Lord is called *Yogī* due to His accessibleness through that very Jñāna-*Yoga*. Also, since *Yoga* means Samādhi (Perfect Steadiness) and the Lord ever steadies perfectly (samādhatte) His Self within His Self, He is thus called *Yogī*." See the Bhagavad-Gītā VI:2,4,8,18,27-8,46-7; VIII:28; X:15.

**Yoginī (f)** 1. Possessed of Yoga; one who follows the teachings of Yoga. 2. A name of the Goddess Durgā.

**Yogya (m), Yogyā (f)** Fit for Yoga; the capable or qualified for Self-Realization. See the Yogasūtras II:41, where the Ātma-Darśana-*Yogyatwa*, (fitness for Self-Realization) is said to be the outcome of Śauca, or purity.

**Yudhishṭhira (m)** (*yudhi* 'in battle' + *sthira* 'firm') Firm in battle. The name of the eldest of the five Pāṇḍava brothers, who succeeded Pāṇḍu as king and is considered an incarnation of the God Dharma (i.e. the God of Justice or Righteousness also known as Yama or the Death-God). His story and entry into heaven is told in the celebrated Mahābhārata.

**Yukta (m)** Concentrated; one whose mind is intent on the Self alone. See the Bhagavad Gītā IV:18; V:23; VI:7-8,14,18; VII:17-18.

**Yukteśwara (m)** (*yukta* 'concentrated' + *īśwara* 'lord') Concentrated on the Lord as being one's own true Self or Ātman. See the Bhagavad Gītā IV:18; V:23; VI:7-8,14,18; VII:17-18; XIII:2,10; XV:19.

**Yukti (f)** 1. Oneness of Ātman and Brahman. 2. Reasoning in the light of Vedāntic Scripture which leads to Oneness or realization of the Self as Brahman alone.

**Yuvan (m)** 1. The youthful. 2. A name given to several Vedic Gods such as Agni, Indra and the Maruts. 3. A name of Lord Śiva as Dakshiṇāmūrti, the young Guru, who is praised in the following verse:

*Mauna-Vyākhyā-Prakaṭita-*
*Parabrahma-Tattwam Yuvānam*
*Varshishṭhāntevasad-Ṛishigaṇair-*
*Āvṛitam Brahmanishṭhaiḥ,*
*Ācāryendram Karakalita-*
*Cinmudram-Ānandamūrtim*
*Swātmārāmam Muditavadanam*
*Dakshiṇāmūrtim-Īḍe.*

I praise the youthful Dakshiṇāmūrti who revealed
the Truth of the supreme Brahman through a silent
exposition, who is surrounded by groups of aged
disciples, sages devoted to Brahman, who is the
best of teachers, whose (right) hand
shows the gesture of Knowledge, who is the
embodiment of bliss, who delights in His own
Self and whose face is rejoicing.

[See **Dakshiṇāmūrti**]

**Yuvati (f)** 1. The youthful. 2. A name of several Goddesses such as Durgā and Ushā.

"Ekam Sad-Vipra Bahuda Vadanti."
(Truth is One, sages call It variously.)
-Ṛig-Veda

"The Name that can be named is not the constant Name."
-Tao Te Ching

"'Tell me I pray, Your Name.'
'Why do you ask My Name. It is Mysterious.'
Then Manoah and his wife understood; they fell on their faces and worshipped."
-Judges 13: 17-21

"The Mysterious Name is 'hidden in the secret.'"
-Mahānārayaṇa Upanishad

"Bearer of all names, how shall I name You—You alone the Unnameable?"
-Gregory of Nazianzen

# PART II:

# CROSS-REFERENCE

# *How to Use the Cross-Reference and the Guide to the Cross-Reference*

The Cross-Reference is divided into two sections. "Section I: God" contains meanings that relate to attributes, qualities, and names of God. "Section II: Other Aspects" contains more general meanings relating to numerous virtues, saintly beings, light, nature, holy places, and so on.

For example: "God as Light" would appear in "Section I: God" under the heading "Attributes: God as Light." Under this heading you would find seven different categories of God as Light such as: Bright, Brilliant, Effulgent, Glittering, Glowing, Light and Luminous. Under each category you will find a choice of anywhere from one to fifteen or more different names.

Another example would be the meaning "Nature: Flora" which would appear in "Section II: Other Aspects." Here you will see eight categories of Nature: Flora, including: Flower, Forest, Fragrant, Garland, Jasmine, Lotus, Plant/Grass, Tree. As in "Section I: God" there will be a selection of names to choose from under each category.

The Guide to the Cross-Reference provides an alphabetical listing of subjects. This gives a quick overview of all the subjects in the Cross-Reference, with page numbers for each.

The Guide is the same in order and listing as subjects in the Cross-Reference, but without the names.

For example: you may wish to choose a name that has some relation to the meaning "Light." You can refer to the Guide and you will find the subject "Attributes: God as Light" with the categories: Bright, Brilliant, Effulgent, and so on, listed underneath it. You will also find page numbers after each category which will refer you to the Cross-Reference. You may perhaps select the category "Brilliant." By turning to the page given for "Brilliant," you will find all the names with that meaning. Each name with its full meaning is found in Part I, the Dictionary portion of the book.

# *Guide to the Cross-Reference*

## *Section 1: God*

### *Attributes: God as the Absolute*

Absolute, 247
Highest, 247
Omniscient, 247
Supreme, 247

### *Attributes: God as Glorious*

Auspicious, 247
Blessed/Bestowing Blessing, 248
Fortunate, 248
Glorious, 248
Grace filled, 248
Graceful, 248
Great, 248
Prosperous, 248

### *Attributes: God as Infinte*

All-Encompassing, 248
All-Pervasive, 248, 249
Attributeless, 249
Birthless, 249
Complete, 249
Eternal, 249
Full, 249
Immortal, 249
Infinite, 249
Omnipresent, 249
Unchanging, 249
Whole, 249

### *Attributes: God as Light*

Bright, 250
Brilliant, 250
Effulgent, 250

## *Attributes: God as Powerful*



## *Attributes: Physical Attributes of God*



## *God: Lord of*

## *God: Names of*



## *God: Symbols of*



## *Goddess: Names of*

## *Personality: God as Destroyer*



## *Personality: God as Ruler*



## *Personality: God as Savior*



## *Personality: God as Supporter*



## *Personality: God in Various Roles*

# *Guide to the Cross-Reference*

## *Section II: Other Aspects*

## *Nature: Celestial Bodies*



## *Nature: the Elements*



## *Nature: Flora*



## *Nature: Mountain*

## *Nature: Time/Seasons*

Dawn, 287
Night, 287
Seasons, 287
Spring, 287
Time, 287
Twilight, 287

## *Relatives of*

Arjuna, 287
Aruṇa, 287
Atri, 287
Bhagīratha, 287
Bṛihaspati, 287
Devahūti, 287, 288
Dhṛitarāshṭra, 288
Drupada, 288
Hanuman, 288
Indra, 288
Jahnu, 288
Janaka, 288
Kṛishṇa, 288
Kubera, 288
Kuntī, 288
Manu, 288
Pāṇḍu, 288
Rāma, 288
Sumitrā, 288
Śantanu, 289
Viśwamitra, 289
Vyāsa, 289

## *Ṛishis/Saints/Gurus*

Ṛishis/Saints, 289, 290
Gurus, 290

## *Royalty*

King, 290
Prince, 290
Princess, 291
Queen, 291

# CROSS-REFERENCE
# *SECTION I: GOD*

## *Attributes: God as the Absolute*

### *Absolute*
Absolute
Brahman
Brahmamayī
Brahmarūpa, Brahmarūpiṇī
Kakuda
Kevala
Nirantara, Nirantarā
Parātpara
Pareshṭi
Tanmaya, Tanmayī
Uttama

### *Highest*
Kakuda
Parama, Paramā
Parameshṭhin
Paramikā

### *Omniscient*
Sarvajña, Sarvajñā
Sarvavidyā

### *Supreme*
Adhyātman
Para, Parā
Parama, Paramā
Paramikā
Paramātman
Parameshṭhin
Parameśa
Parameśwara, Parameśwarī
Pareśa

## *Attributes: God as Glorious*

### *Auspicious*
Anāpadā
Badrīnāth
Bhadra, Bhadrā
Bhadramūrti
Bhāvyā
Bhūti
Kalyāṇa, Kalyāṇī
Maṅgalā
Subhadrā
Sumaṅgalī
Śantanu
Śiva
Śivakarī
Śubhakara, Śubhakarī
Śubhā

### *Blessed/Bestowing Blessing*
Devāśis
Kalyāṇa, Kalyāṇī
Kalyāṇasundara

### *Fortunate*
Bhagavan
Bhagavatī
Rādhā
Subhaga, Subhagā
Śrī
Śrīlā

### *Glorious*
Bhagin, Bhagī
Kīrti
Mahanīya
Pratāp
Yaśas
Yaśaswī, Yaśaswin

### *Grace Filled*
Arula
Kṛipā
Prasād

### *Graceful*
Latā
Latikā

### *Great*
Aryaman
Ārya, Āryā
Āryaka, Āryakā
Āryamārga
Āryamiśra
Āryavan
Āryavatī
Mahatī
Mahādeva, Mahādevī
Mahālakshmī
Mahāpūjya
Mahātman
Mahendra
Mahendrāṇī
Maheśwara, Maheśwarī
Mahī
Mahodāra
Paramodāra
Pula
Udāra
Yaśovara

### *Prosperous*
Bhūti

## *Attributes: God as Infinite*

### *All-Encompassing*
Sarva
Sarvaga
Sarvagata, Sarvagatā, Sarvagati
Sarvamayī
Sarvāṇī
Sarvavidyā
Viśwa

### *All-Pervasive*
Sarvaga
Sarvagata, Sarvagatā

Vishṇu
Vyāpī
Vyāpinī
Vyoman

*Attributeless*
Nirguṇā

*Birthless*
Abhū
Aja
Guha
Nirbhava

*Complete*
Sakalā

*Eternal*
Nitya, Nityā
Śāśwata, Śaśwatī
Vijara, Vijarā

*Full*
Annapūrṇā
Pūrṇa, Pūrṇā
Pūrṇatā
Pushkala, Pushkalā
Sudāma
Sudāman
Sudāminī
Vadānya

*Immortal*
Acyuta
Akshara
Akshaya, Akshayā
Amaran, Amarā
Amaraja
Amararatna, Amararatnā
Amararāja
Amaraprabhu
Amareśa
Amṛita, Amṛitā
Amṛitavapu
Amṛiteśa
Dhruva
Nirapāya
Nirnāśa, Nirnāśinī
Nitya, Nityā
Sadātana
Sanātana, Sanātanī
Śaśwata, Śāśwatī
Vijara, Vijarā

*Infinite*
Aditi
Akhaṇḍa, Akhaṇḍā
Amiti
Ameyan, Ameyā
Amitābha
Anala
Ananta, Anantā
Anyā
Bhūman
Niravadhi
Nishpāra
Utpāra, Utpārā

*Omnipresent*
Sarvaga
Sarvagata, Sarvagatā
Vibhu
Vishṇu

*Unchanging*
Avikārī, Avikāriṇī
Nirvikāra
Sama

*Whole*
Sarvatā

# *Attributes: God as Light*

### *Bright*
Citran
Citrā
Citrāvasu
Citrāvaswī
Sumukhī

### *Brilliant*
Tejas
Ullāsa, Ullāsinī

### *Effulgent*
Bharga
Tejas
Tejaswī, Tejaswinī
Tejomaya, Tejomayī
Tejorāśi
Tejovan, Tejovatī

### *Glittering*
Bhṛigu

### *Glowing*
Rocana

### *Light*
Antarjyoti
Ābhāti
Ātmajyoti
Bhāskara
Devajyoti
Devaśrī
Divyajyoti
Dīpa
Dīpikā
Ekajyoti
Jagatprakāś
Jñānaprabhā
Jyoti
Prabhā
Prabhāvan
Prabhāvatī
Ruci
Ullāsa, Ullāsinī

### *Luminous*
Atideva
Ābhā
Bhānu
Bhānumatī
Candrabhūti
Dyuti, Dyutiman
Kāntā
Pradīp
Prakāśa, Prakāśinī
Swarāj
Umā

# *Attributes: God as Powerful*

### *Indestructible*
Avināśī, Avināśinī

### *Invincible*
Ajaya, Ajayā
Aparājita

Ashāḍha
Nirargala, Nirargalā

### *Powerful*

Aindrī
Ajaya, Ajayā
Ambhrina
Anāśī, Anāśinī
Aparājita
Baladeva
Balarūpa
Devaśakti
Dharmaśakti
Divyaśakti
Indra
Irya
Mahābala
Mahāśakti
Mahendra
Paraśakti
Sabala
Saha
Sahā
Śacī
Śakti
Śākinī
Tura

### *Victorious*

Jaya, Jayā
Jayadeva, Jayadevī
Jayaśrī
Jayeśwara, Jayeśwarī
Jetā, Jetrī
Jina
Jishṇu
Jiti
Ujjesha, Ujjeshā
Ujjeshī
Vijay

## *Attributes: Physical Attributes of God*

### *Armored*

Kavacin

### *Beautiful*

Ahalyā
Cāru, Carvī
Cāruhāsa, Cāruhāsinī
Cāruman, Cārumatī
Cārurūpa, Cārurūpiṇī
Cāruśīla, Cāruśīlā
Hariṇi
Indirā
Kalyāṇa, Kalyāṇī
Kalyāṇasundara
Kānti
Kāntimatī
Keśava
Lakshmī
Lalitā
Lalitāmbikā
Lāvaṇyā
Līlāmayī
Līlāvatī
Mañju
Mañjula, Mañjulā
Mañjuman
Mañjumatī
Padmaśrī
Rakti
Ramyā
Sudarśan
Sundara, Sundarī
Sundareśwara
Supushpā
Surasundara, Surasundarī

Śobhanā
Śrī
Śrīdevī
Śrīman
Śrīmatī
Śubhā
Tripurasundarī
Vāmadeva
Vapusha, Vapushī

## *Clad in Animal Skin*
Kṛittivāsa

## *Colored: Black/Dark*
Kālī
Kṛishṇa
Kṛishṇā
Mahākālī
Rajanī
Śyāma
Śyāmā

## *Colored: Blue*
Indīvarinī
Kālakaṇṭha
Kālakaṇṭhī
Nīlagala
Nīlagrīva
Nīlakaṇṭha

## *Colored: Golden*
Āditya
Haima
Haimavatī
Hariṇī
Hariścandra
Hiraṇya
Hiraṇyagarbha
Kakanda
Pītavāsas
Pītāmbara
Rukmiṇī
Suvarṇā

## *Colored: Red/Rosy*
Aruṇa
Aruṇā
Pāṭalā
Rohiṇī

## *Colored: Silver*
Candrabhūti

## *Colored: Tawny*
Kapila
Kapiladeva
Kapilarudra

## *Colored: White*
Arjuna
Arjunī
Kumuda
Kumudinī
Pāṇḍuranga

## *Colored: Yellow*
Pītavāsas
Pītāmbara

## *Colorless*
Avarṇa, Avarṇā

## *Discus-Bearing*
Cakrabhṛit
Cakrin

## *Eyed, Fawn-*
Kuraṅgākshī

## *Eyed, Lotus-*
Kamalalocana, Kamalalocanā
Kamalanayana, Kamalanayanā
Kamalanetra
Kamalāksha, Kamalākshī
Kamalekshaṇa, Kamalekshaṇā

Nīrajāksha, Nīrajākshī
Paṅkajāksha, Paṅkajākshī
Puṇḍarīkāksha

### *Eyed, Three-*

Trilocana
Trinetra

### *Eyes*

Ekadṛiś
Ekalocana
Ekanayana
Ekāksha
Kāmākshī
Kṛishṇanetra
Mīnākshī
Netra
Niṭalāksha
Trilocana
Trinetra
Tryambaka
Virūpāksha
Viśālākshī

### *Face*

Candramukha, Candramukhī
Candravadana, Candravadanā

### *Forehead*

Niṭalāksha
Niṭalekshaṇa

### *Hair*

Keśava
Khakuntala
Pulastya

### *Marked*

Lakshmaṇa
Puṇḍra
Śrīvatsa
Tilaka
Trikūṭa

### *Matted Locks*

Kapardin, Kapardinī
Jaṭādhara
Jaṭin

### *Navel*

Kamalanābha

### *Ten-Armed*

Daśabhūjā

### *Throat*

Kālakaṇṭha, Kālakaṇṭhī
Nīlagala
Nīlagrīva
Nīlakaṇṭha
Śrīkaṇṭha

### *Youthful*

Ajara, Ajarā
Āryakumāra
Bāla, Bālā
Bāladeva
Bālikā
Kana
Kanyā
Kiśora, Kiśorī
Kumāra, Kumārī
Navīna, Navīnā
Taruṇa, Taruṇī
Yuvan
Yuvati

# *God: Lord of*

## *King of Gods*

Devarāj
Aiśwara, Aiśwarī
Bhagavān
Bhaktidāyaka
Bharu
Bhūteśwara
Devaja, Devajā
Ekanātha
Gaurīnātha
Gaurīśa
Īśa
Īśwara
Maheśa
Maheśwara
Pati
Prabhu
Rājeśa
Rājeśwara
Sarveśa
Sarveśwara
Satpati
Surādhipa
Ugreśa

## *Lord of Beings*

Bhūtanātha
Bhūtapati
Bhūteśa
Bhūteśwara
Purushendra

## *Lord of Creatures*

Paśupati
Prajāpati
Prajeśa

## *Lord of the Earth*

Avanīśa
Avanīśwara
Bhūdeva
Bhūpati
Mahīnātha
Narendra
Nareśa
Nareśwara
Prāṇeśwara

## *Lord of Gods*

Devapati
Devendra
Deveśa
Rājarājeśwara, Rājarājeśwarī
Suradeva
Suranāyaka
Surapati
Surādhipa
Sureśa
Sureśwara, Sureśwarī

## *Lord of Heaven*

Nākanāth
Nākapati
Nākādhipa
Nākeśa
Nākeśwara

## *Lord of the Mountain*

Adripati
Adrirāja
Girirāja
Girīndra
Himavan
Himādri
Himālaya
Menādhava
Nagapati
Nagarāja
Nagādhipa
Nagādhirāja
Nageśwara

Umāguru

## Lord of Rivers
Nadīnātha
Nadīpati
Nadīśa

## Lord of the Universe
Viśwanāth
Viśweśwara, Viśweśwarī
Viśweśa

## Lord of Waters
Ambupati
Purañjana
Varuṇa

Yādaḥpati

## Lord of the World
Bhava
Bhaveśa
Bhuvanapati
Bhuvaneśwara
Bhūtanātha
Bhūtapati
Bhūteśa
Jagadīśa
Jagadīśitā
Jagadīśwara
Jagannātha
Jagatpati
Jagatprabhu

# God: Names of

## Brahmā
Ireśa
Jagatkartā
Kamalodbhava
Kañjara, Kañjāra
Kapila
Padmaja
Padmālaya
Parameshṭin
Prajāpati
Prajeśa
Prajeśwara
Sanātana
Trimūrti
Vāgīśwara
Vidhātā
Viriñci

## Buddha
Arhat
Gautama
Jina
Khajit
Ojobalā
Ojopati
Śākyamuni

## Indra
Amarabhartā
Amararāja
Devapati
Devarāja
Devendra
Jishṇu
Mahendra
Nakeśwara
Nākanātha
Nākapati
Nākādhipa
Nākeśa

Parjanya
Ṛibhuksha
Ṛibhwa
Ṛijukratu
Satpati
Suranāyaka
Surapati
Surādhipa
Surendra
Śakra
Tribandhu
Vasupati
Vāsava
Yuvan

## *Kṛishṇa*

Bhūdhara
Dāmodara
Devakīnandana
Gayati
Girdhara
Gokuleśa
Gopāl
Gopiśwara
Gopījana
Jagadvandya
Kannan
Kuñjavihārin
Lola
Mṛigīpati
Muktida
Muktidāyaka
Muralī
Muralīdhara
Murāri
Pāṇḍuraṅga
Prajāpāla
Rādhākṛishṇa
Rādhāvallabha
Rādheśa
Rādheśwara
Rādheśyām
Rājīvāksha
Rāmakṛishṇa
Śakrāri
Śauri
Śyām
Ugrasenānī
Veṇugopāla
Veṇulola
Vipinavihārī
Viṭṭhala
Yadunātha
Yadupati
Yajñapriya
Yādava

## *Kubera*

Dhanada
Dhanapati
Dhanapāla
Dhanādhipa
Dhaneśa
Dhaneśwara
Harasakha
Śivabandhu
Vittakapati
Vittanātha
Vittapati
Vitteśa

## *Rāma*

Avanipāla
Candramukha
Candravadana
Kapiprabhu
Kapiratha
Kauśikapriya
Kodaṇḍa
Kodaṇḍin
Patitapāvana
Raghumaṇi
Raghunātha
Raghuvīra
Rāghava
Rāghavendra
Rājīvāksha
Rāmabhadra
Rāmacandra
Rāmadeva

Rāmakṛishṇa
Rāmeśa
Rāmeśwara
Sītābhirāma
Śri Rāma

## *Rudra*

Candila
Candrila
Kapilarudra
Krivi
Nandirudra

## *Subrahmaṇya*

Ārumugan
Devasena
Gaṅgāsuta
Guha
Kārtika
Kārttikeya
Kumāra
Muruga
Senāpati
Seneśwara
Shaṇmukha
Skanda
Śaravanabhava
Umāsuta
Viśakhan

## *Śiva*

Adambha
Amarādhipa
Amareśa
Amṛiteśa
Andhakāri
Aniruddha
Ādinātha
Ānandabhairava
Balarūpa
Bhairava
Bharga
Bharu
Bhava
Bhaveśa
Bhayāpaha
Bhānu
Bhārgava
Bhikshu
Bhīma
Bholānātha
Bhūdeva
Bhūdhara
Bimbadhara
Candila
Caṇḍīpati
Candramauli
Candramukuṭa
Candranātha
Candraśekhara
Candreśwara
Candrila
Cidambara
Deveśa
Durāsada
Durvāsa
Ekadṛiś
Ekajyoti
Ekalochana
Ekanayana
Ekanetra
Ekāksha
Gaṇanātha
Gaṇapati
Gandhadhāra
Gaṅgābhrit
Gaṅgādhara
Gaurīnātha
Gaurīpati
Gaurīśa
Giribandhu
Giribāndava
Giridhava
Girijādhava
Giripati
Girīśa
Girīśwara
Guṇanidhi
Guṇarāśi
Guṇākara

Haima
Hara
Indubhṛit
Indukirīṭa
Īśa
Iśāna
Īśwara
Jagaddhara
Jagadīśa
Jagadīśitā
Jagadīśwara
Jagatpati
Jagatprabhu
Jagatprīti
Janapriya
Jaṭādhara
Jaṭin
Jayeśwara
Jīvana
Joṭin
Kandarpamathana
Kapardin
Kavachin
Kālabhairava
Kālabhaksha
Kalādhara
Kalāvan
Kālaghāta
Kālakaṇṭha
Kālanātha
Kālīvilāsin
Kāmāri
Kāmeśa
Kāmeśwara
Kāśīnātha
Kāśiśa
Kāśiśwara
Khakuntala
Kilakila
Kodaṇḍa
Kodaṇḍin
Koṇavādin
Kṛishkara
Kṛishṇanetra
Kṛitakara
Kṛittivāsa
Kṛivi
Kuberabāndhava
Kuberabandhu
Lambana
Mahādeva
Mahākāla
Mahākānta
Mahān
Mahānaṭa
Mahārūpa
Maheśa
Maheśwara
Mahinasa
Manthāna
Milīmilin
Mohan
Mṛiḍa
Munīndra
Muñjakeśa
Nakula
Nandirudra
Nandīśwara
Narādhara
Narmadeśwara
Naṭana
Naṭarāja
Naṭavara
Naṭeśa
Naṭeśwara
Nābha
Nāgarāja
Nātha
Nāṭyapriya
Nīlagala
Nīlagrīva
Nīlakantha
Nirañjan
Nirdosha
Nirlepa
Nirmoha
Nishkalaṅka
Niṭalāksha
Ojasvin
Pakshin
Parameshṭhin
Parameśwara

Paśupati
Pāmsula
Pāpaharaṇa, Pāpahara
Pinākī
Prajāpati
Prajeśa
Prajeśwara
Prāneśa
Pṛithuhara
Purandara
Purāri
Pushkala
Pushkara
Pūrayitā
Pūtamati
Rājarājeśwara
Rudra
Sadāśiva
Sanātana
Sarveśa
Sarveśwara
Sāmba
Sāmbaśiva
Śambhava
Śambu
Śaṅkara
Śaruha
Śivakāmī
Śivarāja
Snehan
Soma
Śrīkaṇṭha
Subhaga
Sugandhi
Sundareśwara
Surapati
Ṭakwara
Tamopaha
Tāraka
Tejorāśi
Tishyaketu
Tīrthadeva
Trilochana
Trimūrti
Trinetra
Tripurāri
Triśūlī
Tryambaka
Uḍḍīśa
Ugreśa
Umākānta
Umānātha
Umāpati
Umeśa
Upanandana
Ushaṅgu
Uttāraka
Vāmadeva
Vibhu
Vimocana
Vīrabhadra
Virūpāksha
Viśwanāth
Viśwādhāra
Viśweśa
Viśweśwara
Yajñāri
Yamajit
Yati
Yuvan

### *Vishṇu*

Abhū
Acalan
Acintya
Acyuta
Aja
Akrūra
Akshara
Amaraprabhu
Amogha
Amṛita
Amṛitavapu
Anagha
Anala
Anādi
Anila
Aniruddha
Aparājita
Aravindāksha
Arha

Arka
Aśoka
Ādideva
Āditya
Babhru
Bhagavan
Bhartā
Bharu
Bhayāpaha
Bhānu
Bhīma
Brahman
Brahmaṇya
Brahmā
Cakrabhṛit
Cakrin
Candrāmśu
Daksha
Dāmodara
Deva
Devakīnandana
Deveśa
Dhaneśwara
Dharma
Dhṛitātman
Dhruva
Durlabha
Eka
Ekātman
Goptā
Govinda
Guha
Hamsa
Hari
Hayagrīva
Hiraṇyagarbha
Indaspati
Indrāvaraja
Ireśa
Ishṭa
Īśa
Īśwara
Jagaddhara
Jagadīśa
Jagadīśwara
Jagannātha
Jagatpati
Jagatprabhu
Jahnu
Janārdana
Jaya
Jayanta
Jetā
Jishṇu
Jīvana
Kālakunja
Kamalākānta
Kamalanābha
Kañjanābha
Kavi
Kāma
Kāmadeva
Kāmapāla
Kānta
Keśava
Kṛishṇa
Kṛitajña
Kumuda
Kundara
Madhusūdana
Mahābala
Mahādeva
Mahān
Mahāśakti
Mahāvīra
Mahendra
Maheśwara
Mahīdhara
Mahīnātha
Manohara
Mantra
Manu
Marīci
Mādhava
Māyāpati
Māyāvin
Medhāvin
Mukunda
Munīśwara
Muñjakeśa
Nanda
Nara

Narahari
Narasimha
Nārāyaṇa
Neta
Nirguṇa
Nirvāṇa
Nishṭhā
Padmanābha
Paṅkajanetra
Paṅkajāksha
Paramātman
Parameshṭhin
Parameśa
Parameśwara
Parandhāman
Paraśurāma
Pavitra
Payaspati
Pāṇḍuraṅga
Pītavās
Pītāmbara
Prabhava
Prabhu
Prajāpati
Pramoda
Pranava
Prāṇa
Punarvasu
Puṇḍarīkāksha
Purandara
Purusha
Purushottama
Pūrayitā
Pūrṇa
Rakshaṇa
Rameśa
Ravi
Rāma
Riddha
Ṛitadhāman
Sadhu
Saha
Sama
Sanātana
Sandhātā
Saṅkataharaṇa
Sarva
Sarvaga
Sarvajña
Sarveśa
Sarveśwara
Satyam
Siddha
Siddhārtha
Sunda
Sundara
Sureśwara
Śambhu
Śankhadhar
Śaṅkhapāṇi
Śaṅkhavan
Śaṅkhin
Śarva
Śāśwatan
Śuci
Śrīdhara
Śrīkara
Śrīman
Śrīnivāsa
Śrīpati
Śrīvatsa
Śrīvāsa
Tamopaha
Tattwa
Tāraṇa
Trimūrti
Trinābha
Twashṭā
Udasutānāyaka
Upendra
Uttara
Vaikuṇṭha
Vanamālī
Varada
Varuṇa
Vasu
Vatsala
Vāsudeva
Veda
Veṅkataramaṇa
Vibhu
Vidhātā

Vijay
Vinaya
Viśwa
Viśwakarmā
Vishwādhara
Vyāpī
Vyoman
Yajña
Yajñadhara
Yajñamūrti
Yajñapati
Yajñatrātā
Yajñeśa
Yajushpati
Yamakīla
Yogeśwara
Yogī

*Vishṇu/Śiva*
Dattātreya
Trimūrti

## God: Symbols of

*Bow*
Gāndīva
Kodaṇḍa
Kodaṇḍin

*Chariot*
Bhagīratha

*Conch*
Devadatta
Śaṅkha

*Discus*
Cakrin
Sudarśan

*Musical Instruments*
Kolambī
Vīnā

*Staff*
Pāmsula

*Vehicles*
Garuḍa
Hamsa, Hamsā
Nandi, Nandī

## Goddess: Names of

*Devī*
Aiśwarī
Akhilāṇḍeśwarī
Amaleśwarī
Bhaktidāyinī
Bhedanāśinī

Devāṅganā
Devī
Devīka
Jagadīśwarī
Jagajjananī
Jaganmātā
Jananī
Jayā
Jayeśwarī
Jīvanī
Madānaśinī
Mahādevī
Mahāśakti
Maheśwarī
Mādhavī
Muktidāyinī
Nikhileśwarī
Patnī
Rakshākarī
Surī
Śaraṇyā
Tripurasundarī

## *Durgā*

Amṛitamālinī
Ādyā
Bābhravī
Bhadrakālī
Bhairavī
Bhāvyā
Bhīmā
Bhuvanamātā
Caṇḍālikā
Caṇḍikā
Caṇḍī
Cāmuṇā, Cāmuṇḍī
Daśabhujā
Daśaharā
Īśā
Īśānī
Jagadambā
Jagadambikā
Kanyā
Karvarī
Kauśikī
Kālabhairavī
Kālī
Kāntāravāsinī
Kānti
Kātyāyanī
Khakāminī
Kriyā
Kuhāvatī
Kumārī
Kumbharī
Lalitā
Lalitāmbikā
Maheśwarī
Mahishamardinī
Mandayantī
Mardinī
Nandinī
Nirañjanā
Nityā
Pāṭalā
Puralā
Pūtā
Rajanī
Rājarājeśwarī
Rudrāṇī
Śākambharī
Śivadūtī
Śivapriyā
Śuddhi
Tārāvatī
Tāriṇī
Totilā
Ugrakālī
Viśalākshī
Yoginī
Yuvati

### *Kālī*

Ānandabhairavī
Bhadrakālī
Bhavāśinī
Caṇḍālikā
Cāmuṇḍā, Cāmuṇḍī
Daśabhujā
Kapardinī
Kṛishṇā
Kṛiśodarī
Mahākālī
Śyāmā

### *Lakshmī*

Amalā
Bhagavatī
Bhagavatpriyā
Bhārgavī
Bhūdevī
Bhūti
Dhanadā
Dhanadāyinī
Dhanalakshmī
Dhananetrī
Dhaneśwarī
Indirā
Īśwarī
Jayalakshmī
Jayaśrī
Kamalā
Kamalālayā
Kālakarnī
Kānti
Mahādevi
Mahālakshmī
Maṅgalā
Mukundapriyā
Nārāṇī
Nārāyaṇī
Netrī
Padmahāriṇī
Padmamukhī
Padmaśrī
Padmā
Padmākshī
Padmālayā
Padmāvatī
Ramā
Rādhā
Ṛiddhi
Rukmiṇī
Sanātanī
Sītā
Suvarṇā
Śrī
Śrīdevī
Śrīkarī
Udasutā
Vaishṇavī

### *Pārvatī*

Adrijā
Ambikā
Anantā
Annadā
Annapūrṇā
Aparṇā
Āryā, Āryakā
Bhagavatī
Bhārgavī
Bhavānī
Bhavaprītā
Cintāmāṇī
Gaurī
Giribhū
Giriduhitā
Girijā
Girinandinī
Girisutā
Haimavatī
Īśwarī
Kālakaṇṭhī

Kāmākshī
Kāśīśwarī
Mahādevī
Maṅgalā
Mānasā
Menājā
Mīnākshī
Mṛiḍapriyā
Mṛiḍā, Mṛiḍī
Mṛiḍānī
Mūkāmbikā
Nārāyaṇī
Naṭeśwarī
Parameśwarī
Pūrani
Pushkarī
Ṛiddhi
Sanātānī
Sarvāṇī
Śāmbavī
Śaṅkarī
Śarvāṇī
Śivā
Śivānī
Umā

### *Rādhā*

Mṛigī
Śrīmatī

### *Saraswatī*

Bhagavatī
Bhāratī
Brahmāṇī
Brāhmī
Gīrdevī
Haṁsavāhanā
Irā
Īśwarī
Medhāvatī
Medhāvinī
Prajñā
Sanātanī
Śārada
Vāgīśwarī
Vāṇī

### *Sītā*

Jānakī
Maithilī
Rāmapriyā
Rāmā

### *Śakti*

Bhūdhātrī
Divyaśakti
Kuṇḍalinī

## *Goddess of: Beings, the Earth, the World*

### *Goddess of Beings*

Sarveśwarī

### *Goddess of the Earth*

Avanīśwarī
Bhūdevī
Mahī

### *Goddess of the World*

Bhavatārinī

Bhavānī
Bhuvanamātā
Bhuvaneśwarī
Jagadambā
Jagadambikā
Jagadīśwarī
Jagajjananī

# *Goddess: Mother/Mother of Gods*

## *Lalitā*

Ekarasā
Hākinī
Hamsavāhanā
Harapriyā
Harshaṇī
Īḍitā
Īkshitrī
Īśitrī
Kalāvatī
Kalyā
Kalyāṇī
Kamalākshi
Kamanīyā
Kañjalocanā
Kālahantrī
Kāmākśī
Kāmeśī
Kāmeśwarī
Kāntā
Kārayitrī
Kāvyalolā
Labhyā
Saguṇā
Sakalā
Samarasā
Saṅgahīnā
Sarvagatā
Sarvajñā
Sarvamātā
Sarvātmikā
Sarveśī
Satyarūpā
Sādhwī
Sādhyā

## *Mother*

Ambā
Ambālā
Ambālī
Ambālikā
Ambayā
Ambikā
Ammā
Bhartrī
Gāyatrī
Irā
Jagadambā
Jagadambikā
Jaganmātā
Jananī
Mājī
Mātā
Mātājī
Prasavitrī
Sarvamātā

## *Mother of Gods*

Aditi

# God: Transcendental

Dehātīta

Turīya

# God: True Nature

Swarūpa

# God: With Form

## *Image/Form*

Amṛitavapu
Balarūpa
Bhadramūrti
Brahmarūpa, Brahmarūpiṇī
Cārurūpa, Cārurūpiṇī
Devamūrti
Devarūpa, Devarūpā, Devarūpiṇī
Mahārūpa
Mūrti
Premarūpa, Premarūpiṇī
Śatarūpa
Tadrūpa
Trimūrti
Viśwarūpa
Yajñamūrti

## *Incarnation*

Avatāra, Avatāriṇī
Devāmśa

## *Symbol*

Ādarśa
Ekaliṅga
Pratīka
Pratimā

# God: With Non-Human Form

## *Bull*

Nandi
Nandinī

## *Deer*

Hariṇī

*Eagle*
Garuḍa
Kāmavīrya
Khaga
Mahājit
Mahāvīra
Nāgāri
Suhartā
Suparṇa
Ulūtīśa
Unnatīśa

*Elephant*
Bhuvanadhara
Ekadanta
Ekarada
Gajamukha
Gajavadana
Gajavaktra
Gajānana
Gajendra
Gaṇanātha
Gaṇapati
Gaṇeśa
Gaurītanaya
Heramba
Heruka

*Horse*
Amṛitabandhu
Turaṇya

*Lion*
Narahari
Narasimhan

*Serpent*
Ananta
Bhūdhara
Nāgarāja
Nāgendra
Nāgeśa
Nāgeśwara, Nāgeśwarī
Śesha

*Swan*
Hamsa, Hamsā
Hamsavāhanā

# *God: Within*

Antaryāmī
Antaryāminī
Vāsudeva

# *Personality: God as Benefactor*

*Fulfiller*
Pūrayitā

*Giver*
Balaprada, Balapradā
Bhaga

Bhaktidāyaka
Bhaktidāyinī
Bhuktida, Bhuktidā
Bhuktidātā
Bhuktidātrī
Bhuktidāyaka
Dātā, Dātrī
Kāmapāla
Kundara
Śaktidāyaka
Śrīkara, Śrīkarī
Varada
Yaśodā

# *Personality: God as Creator*

### *Cause*
Kārayitrī

### *Creator*
Anādi
Anila
Ādyā
Bimba
Brahmā
Jagatkartā
Prabhāvana
Tatkartā
Viriñci

### *Life-Giver*
Jīvada
Jīvadātā
Jīvadātrī
Jīvana, Jīvanī

### *Mover*
Hamsa, Hamsā

### *Primeval*
Ādi
Ādideva
Ādinātha

# *Personality: God as Destroyer*

### *Chastiser*
Janārdana

### *Conquerer*
Khajit
Mahājit

### *Destroyer*
Bhedanāśinī
Daśaharā
Hara
Kandarpamathana
Kālahantrī
Madanāśinī

Madhusūdana
Mahākāla
Mahishamardinī
Mohanāśin, Mohanāśinī
Pāśahantā, Pāśahantrī
Pṛithuhara
Purandara
Śarva
Tripurahara
Tripurāri

### *Devourer*

Andhakāri
Ānandabhairava, Ānandabhairavī
Bhavāśinī
Bhayāpaha
Bhīma
Bhīmā
Cāmuṇḍā, Cāmuṇḍī
Damayantī
Gaṇeśa
Hākinī
Janārdana
Kālabhaksha
Kālaghāta
Kāmāri
Khajit

### *Dispeller*

Kalmali
Tamopaha

### *Enemy of Evil*

Murāri
Purāri
Śakrāri

### *Fierce*

Bhairava, Bhairavī
Caṇḍikā
Caṇḍī
Kālabhairava, Kālabhairavī

### *Remover*

Gaṇeśa
Hari
Pāpahara, Pāpaharaṇa
Rudra
Saṅkataharaṇa
Vighneśa
Vināyaka

## *Personality: God as Ruler*

### *Commander*

Devasena

### *Leader*

Nara
Netā
Netra, Netrī

### *Ruler*

Bhūteśwara
Ekanāyaka
Īśa, Īśā
Īśāna
Īśānī
Maheśwara, Maheśwarī
Nātha
Pati
Patnī

Rajeśwara, Rajeśwarī
Samrāj
Samrājñī
Sandhātā
Udyantā

# Personality: God as Savior

## *Guardian*
Pāla
Pālaka
Pālita
Prajāpalā

## *Preserver*
Bartrī
Bhartā
Gupti

## *Protector*
Amarādhipa
Bharaṇyu
Bhuvanapati
Gopāla
Goptā
Gupti
Mārgapālī
Mārgavaṭī
Pāla
Pālaka
Pālita
Prajāpāla
Rakshaṇa
Rakshākarī
Ūti
Varūtā, Varutrī

## *Purifier*
Patitapāvana
Pavana
Pavitra

## *Redeemer*
Uttara

## *Refuge*
Śaraṇyā

## *Savior*
Bhavatāriṇī
Patitapāvana
Tāraka
Tāraṇa
Tārasāra
Tārā
Tārikā
Tāriṇī
Ugratārā
Uttāraka
Vaikuṇṭha

# *Personality: God as Supporter*

### *Bearer*
Baladhara
Bhūdhara
Bhuvanadhara
Jagadvahā
Lambana

### *Nourisher*
Annam
Annapūrṇā
Śākambharī

### *Supporter*
Amarabhartā
Babhru
Bharaṇyu
Bharata
Bhartā
Bhartṛihari
Bhūdhātrī
Dharā
Dharaṇī
Dharaṇīśwara
Dharitrī
Gaṅgādhara
Jagaddhātā, Jagaddhātrī
Mahīdhara
Narādhāra
Trinābha
Vidhātā
Vidhātrī
Viśwādhāra

# *Personality: God in Various Roles*

### *Architect*
Kārū
Ṛibhwa
Viśwakarmā

### *Hunter*
Kannapan

### *Lawyer/Law-Giver*
Ādirāja
Jābāli
Manu
Sāvarṇa, Sāvarṇi

### *Physician*
Caraka
Dhanwantari
Jīvada
Jīvadātā
Jīvadātrī

### *Speech*
Bhāratī
Gīrdevī
Saraswatī
Vāgīśwara, Vāgīśwarī
Vāṇī

# CROSS-REFERENCE
# *SECTION II: OTHER ASPECTS*

## *Accomplishments*

### *Accomplished One*
Kṛitakara
Siddha
Siddhārtha
Siddhi

### *Consciousness*
Caitanya, Caitanyā
Cidghana
Sudīti

### *Culmination*
Kāshṭhā
Lakshya

### *Enlightenment*
Buddha
Dyotana, Dyotanī
Jatavedas
Kaivalya, Kaivalyā
Nirvikalpa
Vibodha
Vijñānī

### *Excellence*
Īśwarakoṭi
Kakubha

### *Goal*
Lakshya
Sadāgati
Sarvagati

### *Intelligence*
Ekabuddhi
Medhā
Sudhī
Sudhīra

### *Knowledge*
Bhārgavī
Cidambara
Cidambareśa
Cinmaya, Cinmayī
Devabodha
Jñānadeva
Jñānaketu
Jñānam
Jñānamūrti
Jñānaprabhā
Jñānarūpa, Jñānarūpiṇī
Kṛitajña
Mādhava
Veda
Vicāraṇā

### *Liberation*
Kaivalya, Kaivalyā
Moksha
Mokshapriya, Mokshapriyā
Mukta
Muktā
Muktādevī
Mukti
Muktida
Muktidāyaka

Muktidāyinī
Muktīdevī
Mukunda
Mumukshā
Mumukshu
Nirvāṇa
Vimukti
Videha

## *Oneness*
Adwaita
Aikyan, Aikyā
Eka
Ekabuddhi
Ekadṛiś
Ekajyoti
Ekaliṅga
Ekanātha
Ekapurusha
Ekarasā
Ekarata
Ekarshi
Ekasatī
Ekatā
Ekāgratā
Ekānta, Ekāntinī
Ekārāma
Ekātman
Ekāśraya, Ekāśrayā
Kevala
Nirbheda, Nirbhedā, Nirbhedinī
Yukta
Yukti

## *Scholarship*
Paṇḍit, Paṇḍita
Śāstrī
Suvipra

## *Vision*
Darśana

## *Wisdom*
Bodhidharma
Bodhin, Bodhinī, Bodhī
Bodhisattwa
Dhīman
Dhīmatī
Maidhāva
Manīshā
Manīshin, Manīshinī
Manu
Mantrī, Mantrīṇī
Medhā
Medhāvatī
Medhāvin
Medhāvinī
Medhira
Nīti
Nītiman
Prajña
Prajñā
Suvipra
Śāstrī
Vibodha
Vidura
Vidyā

# *Arts*

## *Acting*
Mahānaṭa
Raṅganātha

## *Art*

Citraka
Kalā
Kalāmālā
Kalāvan
Kalāvatī

## *Dance*

Mahānaṭa
Naṭana
Naṭarāja
Naṭavara
Naṭeśa
Naṭeśwara
Nāṭyapriya
Taṇḍu
Tāṇḍava

## *Music*

Gandharva
Gāthaka
Gītā
Lola
Mīrā
Mīrābai
Muralī
Muralīdhara
Sangītā
Tyāgarāja
Vāṇī

## *Musical Instruments*

Kolambī
Muralī
Muralīdhara
Veṇugopāla
Veṇulola
Vīṇā

## *Poetry*

Ādikavi
Bhartṛihari
Kamalākānta
Kapilarudra
Kavi
Kavīndra
Kavīndu
Kavīśwara
Kavitā
Kālidāsa
Kāru
Kāvyalolā
Kīri
Mārulā

## *Scripture*

Bṛihaspati
Caṇḍī
Gītā
Jaya
Śāstrī
Trayī
Veda
Vyāsa

## *Writing*

Bādarāyaṇa
Bādari
Bhojarāja
Dattātreya
Jābāli
Jayadeva
Kapila
Kapiladeva
Karmanda
Nārada
Thiruvalluvar
Vālmīki
Vedavyāsa
Vyāsa

# *Benevolence*

*Benefactor*
Brahmaṇya

*Beneficient*
Śaṅkara, Śaṅkarī

*Benevolent*
Śamyu
Śankara, Śankarī

*Charitable*
Dānavan, Dānavatī

*Giving*
Datta, Dattā
Dattātreya
Dātā, Dātrī

# *Celestial Beings*

Nābhasa, Nābhasī
Tishya
Urvaśī
Vidyādhara, Vidyādharī

# *Devotee/Messenger/Servant of God*

*Devotee of God*
Ajamīl
Gauraṅga
Gopī
Gopīkā
Hanuman
Kannapan
Kucela
Mīrā
Mīrābai
Śāmbhava
Śrīdāman
Sudāma
Sūrdās
Tukārām
Tulasīdāsa
Uddhava
Vaishṇava

*Messenger of God*
Devadūta, Devadūtī
Śivadūtī

## *Servant of God*

Dāsa, Dāsī
Devadāsa, Devadāsī
Gurudās, Gurudāsa, Gurudāsī
Gurusevaka, Gurusevinī
Kālidāsa
Kāmbojinī
Kanakapīda
Kaṇḍānaka
Kuñjala
Mukundadās
Premadās, Premadāsī
Pula
Rāmdās
Rijudās
Sevak, Sevikā
Sevan, Sevā
Sudāsa, Sudāsī
Śivadās
Tulasīdāsa
Upanandaka

# *Divine Play*

Devamāyā
Kālīvilāsin
Kuñjavihārin
Līlā
Līlāmayī
Līlāvatī
Lola
Māyā
Māyāpati
Māyāvin
Mohan
Mohinī
Vipinavihārī

# *Divinity*

Daiva, Daivī
Deva
Devaja, Devajā
Devajyoti
Devalīlā
Devamaṇi
Devamuni
Devamūrti
Devarshi
Devarūpa, Devarūpā, Devarūpiṇī
Devaśakti
Devaśrī
Devatā
Devānīka
Devātman
Divyajyoti
Divyamati
Divyā
Surabhāva

# Food/Nectar

### Food
Annadā
Annadāyini
Annam
Annapati
Annapūrṇā

### Honey/Sweets
Mādhavī
Madhura
Mādhurī
Mañju
Mañjula, Mañjulā

### Nectar
Amṛita, Amṛitā
Ānandāmṛita
Kīlāla
Rasa
Rasamayī
Soma
Surasā

# Friend

### Friend
Amṛitabandhu
Bandhu
Devabandhu
Dharmabandhu
Dīnabandhu
Giribandhu
Giribāndhava
Harasakha
Kamalabandhu
Kamalabāndhava
Kṛishṇabandhu
Kuberabandhu
Kuberabāndhava
Maitreya, Maitreyī
Maitrī
Mārgabandhu
Mitra
Oman, Omā
Omātrā
Premabandhu
Snehan
Sumitrā
Śivabandhu
Tribandhu
Uddhava

### Friendliness
Maitrī
Maitreya, Maitreyī

# Happiness

## *Bliss*

Ānanda,
Ānandabhairava
Ānandabhairavī
Anandamaya
Ānandamayī
Ānandana
Ānandaprem, Ānandapremā
Ānandāmṛita
Ānandī, Ānandinī
Balarāma
Kṛishṇa
Nandinī
Nirvāṇa
Rāma
Samarasā
Sanandana
Śaṅkara
Śarmada
Śarmiṇī

## *Delight*

Ānandita, Ānanditā
Devarata, Devarati
Dharmarata
Ekarata
Ekarati
Mahākānta
Mandayantī
Ramaṇa

## *Happiness*

Aśoka
Aśokā
Kārpaṇī
Kuśalin, Kuśalinī
Nandi, Nandī
Rāmā
Śambhu
Śāradā
Viśoka, Viśokā

## *Joy*

Āprīta, Āprītā
Devakīnandana
Girinandinī
Harshaṇī
Hṛishṭi
Jagatprīti
Mahīyā
Mandayantī
Mandu
Nanda
Nandi, Nandī
Nandirudra
Prahlāda
Pramodan
Pramodinī
Prīta, Prītā
Prīti
Ramaṇī
Saharsha
Sūnara, Sūnari
Yadunandana

## *Rejoicing*

Mandayantī
Rañjanī

# *Health/Life-Force*

### *Health*
Anāmaya, Anāmayā
Kalya
Niruja
Yuvan

### *Life-Force*
Ojasika
Ojasīna, Ojasīnā
Ojaswan, Ojaswatī
Ojaswin, Ojaswinī
Ojasya, Ojasyā
Ojās
Ojman
Prāṇa
Prāṇeśa
Prāṇeśwara, Prāṇeśwarī
Śākti
Śākta,
Vīryā

# *Holiness*

Sādhu
Tīrtha
Tīrthadeva

# *Holy Places*

### *Ganges*
Amarasarit
Bhāgīrathī
Gaṇgā
Gaṇgābhṛit
Gaṇgādhara
Gaṇgāsuta
Jāhnavī
Kapiladhārā
Khāpagā
Kirātī
Mandākinī
Nandinī
Nākanadī
Suranadī
Śubhrā
Ugraśekharā

### *Holy Places*
Amarāvatī
Badrīnāth
Dhūmāvatī
Gayā
Govardhana

Guṇārāma
Harādri
Kailāsa
Kāñcī
Kāśī
Paradhāman
Ṛituparṇa
Vārāṇasī

### *Holy Rivers*

Amarasarit
Gaṇgā
Godāvarī
Kāverī
Mandākinī
Narmadā
Nākanadī
Saraswatī
Suranadī
Yamunā

## *Jewels*

Amalaratnā
Amararatna, Amararatnā
Candramaṇi
Cintāmaṇi, Cintāmaṇī
Devamaṇi
Dinamaṇi
Dyumaṇi
Guṇaratnā
Indumaṇi
Kanyāratnā
Kaustubha
Maṇi, Maṇī
Mānikya
Muktā
Raghumaṇi
Ratna, Ratnā
Ratninī
Sadratna

## *Love*

### *Beloved One*

Bhadrapriya, Bhadrapriyā
Bhagavatpriya, Bhagavatpriyā
Devapriya, Devapriyā
Gītāpriyā
Guhapriyā
Gurupriyā
Harapriyā
Ishṭa, Ishṭan
Ishṭā
Janapriya
Kamalākānta
Kamanīyā
Kānta
Kauśikapriya
Mānasaprema
Mṛiḍapriyā
Mukundapriyā
Narapriya
Priyā
Rāmapriyā
Supriyā

Śivapriyā
Vallabhā
Vishṇupriyā

### *Devotion*
Aramati
Bhaktan, Bhaktā
Bhakti
Bhaktidāyaka, Bhaktidāyinī
Ekabhakta
Ekabhakti
Ekapara, Ekaparā
Manāyu
Nishṭhā
Prapatti
Rakti

### *Heart*
Guheśwara
Hridaya
Hṛidya, Hṛidyā
Nābha

### *Love*
Ānandaprema, Ānandapremā
Guruprem, Gurupremā
Joshṭā
Joshṭrī
Prem, Premā
Premabandhu
Premadās, Premadāsī
Premarūpa, Premarūpiṇī
Snehan
Vatsala, Vatsalā

## *Nature: Celestial Bodies*

### *Constellation*
Ashāḍha

### *Heaven*
Nākin, Nākinī
Swarga

### *Mercury*
Induja

### *Milky Way*
Mandākinī
Nākanadī
Surapatha

### *Moon*
Candran, Candrā
Candraśekhara
Candrasūrya
Candravadana, Candravadanā
Candravimala, Candravimalā
Candreśwara
Indubhṛit
Indujanaka
Indukirīṭa
Kairavī
Kalā
Kalādhara
Kalānidhi
Kalāvan
Kalāvatī
Pūṛnimā

### *Moon God*
Candradeva
Candran, Candrā
Oshadipati
Rāmacandra
Śaśī
Soma

Suraśmi
Tamopaha
Tārendra
Usheśa

## *Moon-Related*

Amṛitāmśu
Bharaṇyu
Bimbadhara
Candrabhānu
Candraka
Candrakanti
Candrakānta, Candrakāntā
Candramālikā
Candramaṇi
Candramauli
Candramukha, Candramukhī
Candramukuṭa
Candrāmśu
Candranātha
Candraratna, Candraratnā
Candrikā

## *Planet*

Induja

## *Sky/Space*

Ākāśa, Ākāśā
Khadyotana
Khaga
Khakuntala

## *Star*

Arundhatī
Nakshatra
Tārā
Tārāvatī
Tārendra

## *Sun/Sun God*

Āditya
Amśuman
Amśumatī
Amśumālī
Annapati
Arka
Bhaga
Bhānu
Bharaṇyu
Bhāskara
Bhāsu
Dinabhartā
Dinakara
Dinakartā, Dinakartrī
Dinamaṇi
Dinanātha
Dinapati
Dinarāja
Dinādhīśa
Dineśa
Dineśwara
Divākara
Divāmaṇi
Dyumaṇi
Ekarshi
Irya
Jishṇu
Jivana
Kamalabandhu
Kamalabāndhava
Kaṃapitā
Khadyotana
Mārtaṇḍa
Mitra
Prabhākara
Pūshan
Ravi
Savitā
Sūrya
Sūryadeva
Tamopaha
Ushāpati
Varuṇa
Vivaswan

## *Sun-Related*

Aryaman
Candrasūrya

Citrabhānu

# Nature: the Elements

## *Earth*
Ādyā
Dharaṇī
Dharā
Dharitrī
Irā
Jagadvahā
Kshamā
Mahī
Mādhavī
Saha
Śāśwatī
Vasudhā
Vasumatī
Vasundarā

## *Fire*
Agni
Anala
Annapati
Arka
Bharaṇyu
Bharata
Citrabhānu
Jātavedas
Jātavedasī
Pāvaka
Purandara
Ṛibhwa
Tamopaha
Vasupati
Yuvan

## *Ocean*
Jaladhi
Kadhi
Lavaṇa
Nadīnātha
Nadīpati
Nadīśa
Payaspati
Samudra
Tavisha
Udarāja
Udasutā

## *Rain*
Parjanya

## *Stream*
Khāpagā

## *Waters*
Candrasara
Samudra
Tīrtha

## *Wind*
Īra
Jīvana
Maruta
Pavana
Ujjeshī
Vāyu

# Nature: Flora

## Flower
Kadamba, Kadambī
Kundinī
Kusuma, Kusumā
Manjarī
Mādhavī
Mālatī
Mālikā
Mālinī
Pushpā
Pushpita, Pushpitā
Suma
Supushpā
Surapushpā

## Forest
Araṇyadevī
Vanaspati

## Fragrant
Gandhadhāra
Gandhakālī
Gandharva
Gandhasāra
Gandhi, Gandhinī
Mṛitsnā
Sugandhi

## Garland
Amṛitamālinī
Candramālikā
Kalāmālā
Mālā
Mālinī
Mālya
Vaijayanthī
Vanamālā
Vanamālī

## Jasmine
Kundara
Kundinī
Mālatī
Mālikā

## Lotus
Aravinda
Aravindāksha
Indīvariṇī
Kairava
Kamala, Kamalā
Kamalabandhu
Kamalabāndhava
Kamalanayana, Kamalanayanā
Kamalanābha
Kamalanetra
Kamalākānta
Kamalāksha, Kamalākshī
Kamalālayā
Kamalinī
Kamalīkā
Kamalodbhava
Kañja
Kañjanābha
Kañjavadana, Kañjavadanā
Kavela
Kumuda
Kumudinī
Nalinī
Padmahāriṇī
Padmaja
Padmamukhī
Padmanābha
Padmapāda
Padmaśrī

Padmavatī
Padmā
Padmākshī
Padmālaya
Padmālayā
Padmāvatī
Padminī
Paṅkaja
Paṅkajāksha, Paṅkajākshī
Puṇḍarīka
Puṇḍarīkāksha
Puṇḍra
Pushkara, Pushkarī
Suparṇā
Utpalī, Utpalinī

### *Plant/Grass*

Tulasī,Tulsī
Vishṇupriyā
Vṛindā

### *Tree*

Mandāra
Pārijāta

# *Nature: Mountain*

## *Mountain-related*

Adrijā
Agastya
Amarādri
Giri
Giribandhu
Giribāndhava
Giribhū
Giridhara
Giridhava
Giriduhitā
Girijā
Girijādhava
Girinandinī
Giripati
Girīśa
Girisutā
Girīśwara
Govardhana
Harādri
Kailāsa
Karṇikācala
Kuberagiri
Kuberāchala
Pārvatī
Sumeru
Surādri
Trikūṭa
Vindhya

# Nature: Time/Seasons

### Dawn
Aruś
Upakāśā, Upakāshī
Urvaśī
Ushā
Usheśa
Usrā
Vasati

### Night
Rāmyā

### Seasons
Ṛitunātha

### Spring
Ishma
Ishya
Vasanta

### Time
Kālabhaksha
Kālaghāta
Kālahantrī
Kālanātha
Mahākāla

### Twilight
Sandhyā

# Relatives of

### Arjuna
Bhīma (brother)
Citrā (wife)
Draupadī (wife)
Kuntī (mother)
Nakula (brother)
Sahadeva (brother)
Subhadrā (wife)
Yudhishṭhira (brother)

### Aruṇa
Śwetaketu (grandson)
Uddālaka (son)

### Atri
Anasūyā (wife)
Ātreya (descendant)
Dattātreya (son)
Durvāsa (son)
Śruti (daughter)

### Bhagīratha
Bhāgīrathī (daughter)
Dilīpa (father)
Raghu (grandson)

### Bṛihaspati
Śaṁyu (son)

### Devahūti
Kapila (son)
Kardama (husband)

Manu (father)

### *Dhṛitarāshṭra*
Ambikā (mother)
Duryodhana (son)
Gāndhārī (wife)
Vidura (brother)
Vyāsa (father)

### *Drupada*
Draupadī (daughter)
Dhṛishṭadyumna (son)

### *Hanuman*
Añjanā (mother)
Vāyu (father)

### *Indra*
Aindrī (wife)
Guhapriyā (daughter)
Indrāṇī (wife)

### *Jahnu*
Jāhnavī (daughter)

### *Janaka*
Sītā (daughter)
Udāvasu (son)

### *Kṛishṇa*
Akrura (uncle)
Aniruddha (son)
Baladeva (brother)
Candrabhānu (son)
Cārumatī (daughter)
Devakī (mother)
Gopī (devotee)
Kālindī (wife)
Kārshṇi (descendant)
Mādrī (wife)
Rādhā (consort)
Rukmiṇī (wife)
Satyabhāmā (wife)
Satyajit (son)
Vasudeva (father)
Yaśodā (foster mother)
Yaśovara (son)

### *Kubera*
Yakshiṇi (wife)

### *Kuntī*
Arjuna (son)
Bhīma (son)
Karṇa (son)
Yudhishṭhira (son)

### *Manu*
Ākūti (daughter)
Devahūti (daughter)
Dhruva (grandson)
Manāvī (wife)
Priyavrata (son)
Śaryāti (son)

### *Pāṇḍu*
Ambālikā (mother)
Dhṛitarāshṭra (brother)
Kuntī (wife)
Mādrī (wife)

### *Rāma*
Bhagīratha (ancestor)
Bharata (brother)
Daśaratha (father)
Kausalyā (mother)
Lakshmaṇa (brother)
Raghu (ancestor)
Sītā (wife)
Śatrughana (brother)

### *Sumitrā*
Lakshmaṇa (son)
Śatrughana (son)

### *Śantanu*
Bhīshma (son)
Gaṅgā (wife)
Satyavatī (wife)

### *Viśwamitra*
Bharata (son)

Śakuntalā (daughter of Menakā)

### *Vyāsa*
Dhṛitarāshṭra (son)
Satyavatī (mother)
Vasishṭha (ancestor)

# *Ṛishis/Saints/Gurus*

## *Ṛishis/Saints*
Agastya
Ambarīsha
Ambhrina
Aṅgira
Apnavāna
Arga
Aruṇa
Ativiśwa
Atkila
Atri
Āndāl
Āruṇi
Bādarāyaṇa
Bādari
Bhagīratha
Bhṛigu
Cyavana
Devamuni
Devarshi
Devaśrī
Dṛiśāna
Durvāsa
Ekalū
Ekarshi
Gandhi
Garga
Gārgī
Gautama
Irimbithi
Jābāli
Jñānadeva
Kakshīvat
Kandalāyana
Kanva
Kaśyapa
Kata
Kauśika
Kavīndra
Kavīśwara
Kāmanda
Kuruṇḍi
Kuśīvaśa
Maharshi
Mahīsura
Mārkaṇḍeya
Muni
Munīndra
Munīśa
Munīśwara
Muñjakeśa
Nārada
Nidhruvi
Pulaha
Pulastya
Rājarshi
Ṛishi
Sanaka
Sādhana
Suramuni

Śibi
Taṇḍi
Thirumal
Thiruvalluvar
Ucathya
Udraka
Udwaṁśa
Upagahana
Upāvi
Upoditi
Ushaṅgu
Ushasta
Utaṅka
Utkīla
Vadānya
Vālmīki
Vyāsa
Yājñavalkya

### *Gurus*
Bṛihaspati
Dakshiṇāmūrti
Droṇa
Gurubhāva
Gurudāsa, Gurudāsī
Guruprem, Gurupremā
Gurupriyā
Gurusevaka, Gurusevinī
Hiraṇyagarbha
Īshwa
Nāyaka
Netā
Netra
Netrī
Śakti
Śaṅkarācārya
Śāstā
Śāstrī
Tamopaha

## *Royalty*

### *King*
Ādirāja
Amararāja
Ambarīsha
Atirāja
Avanipāla
Bhagīratha
Bharata
Bhojarāja
Daśaratha
Dhananetā
Dhṛitarāshṭra
Dilīpa
Drupada
Hariścandra
Jahnu
Janaka
Kalyāṇavartman
Kauśika
Mahārāja
Mahīpāla
Raghu
Rāja
Ṛituparṇa
Śantanu
Śibi
Śivarāja
Triśaṅku
Tyāgarāja
Ugrasena
Yadu

### *Prince*
Āryakumāra

*Princess*
Gāndhārī
Maithilī
Mānyavatī
Mīrā
Mīrābai

*Queen*
Cuḍālā
Līlā
Mahārājñī
Mahārānī
Rānī

# *Self/Soul*

Adhyātman
Akartā
Akhilātman
Atmajyoti
Ātman
Devātman
Dharmātman
Dhṛitātman
Ekapurusha
Ekātman
Hiraṇyagarbha
Jīvakan, Jīvikā
Mahātman
Nishkāraṇa
Paramātman
Paramātmikā
Sarvātmikā
Sāra
Sūtradhāra
Swarāj
Virāj
Virāṭ

# *Spiritual Path*

*Ascetic/Renunciate*
Bhikshu, Bhikshukī, Bhikshuṇī
Caraka
Jaṭin
Joṭin
Khidira
Muñjakeśa
Nara
Nārāyaṇa
Parivrājaka
Piṇḍāra
Pravrāj, Pravrājaka
Śabarī
Tapaswī, Tapaswinī
Tapodhana
Taponidhi
Taponitya
Tāpasā, Tāpasī
Yājñavalkya

*Goal*
Lakshya
Sadāgati
Sarvagati

### *Initiation*
Dīkshā
Dīkshiṇī, Dīkshita

### *Path*
Āryamārga
Dharmapatha
Kalyāṇavartman
Saraṇi
Supatha
Surapatha

### *Pilgrimage*
Kṛitatīrtha
Tīrthasevā

### *Seeker*
Arjuna
Cārin, Cāriṇī
Ishṭi
Mumukshu
Naciketā
Sādhaka
Sādhu
Vicārī, Vicāriṇī
Yati
Yatirāja

## *Spouses*

### *Gods*
Lakshmī/Nārāyaṇa
Lakshmī/Vishṇu
Padmāvatī/Venkateśwara
Pārvatī/Śiva
Rādhā/Kṛishṇa
Rukmiṇī/Kṛishṇa
Saraswatī/Brahmā
Sītā/Rāma
Vallabhā/Gaṇeśa
Valli/Muruga

### *Heroes/Sages*
Aditi/Kaśyapa
Ahalyā/Gautama
Ahimsā/Dharma
Aindrī/Indra
Ambālikā/Vicitravīrya
Anasūyā/Atri
Arundhatī/Vasishṭha
Citrā/Arjuna
Dakshiṇa/Yajña
Devahūti/Kardama
Devakī/Vasudeva
Dhṛiti/Dharma
Gandhārī/Dhṛitarāshṭra
Gaṅgā/Śantanu
Indrāṇī/Indra
Jātavedasī/Agni
Kardama/Devahūti
Kātyāyanī/Yajñavalkya
Kīrti/Dharma
Lajjā/Dharma
Maitreyī/Yājñavalkya
Manāvī/Manu
Mati/Viveka
Menā/Himavan
Menakā/Himavan
Śacī/Indra
Sāvitrī/Satyavan
Yakshiṇī/Kubera
Vasuki/Thiruvalluvar

# *Virtues*

## *Boldness*
Dhairyan
Dhairyavan, Dhairyavatī

## *Compassion*
Dayā
Dayālan
Dayāvan, Dayāvati
Karuṇā
Karunāvatī
Kṛipā
Kripādharā
Kṛipālu
Kṛipāmayī
Kṛipāparā
Kṛipāsāgara
Mṛiḍa,
Mṛiḍapriyā
Mṛiḍā, Mṛiḍī
Mridānī

## *Contentment*
Santosha
Santoshī
Tṛipta
Tṛipti
Tushṭi

## *Courage*
Abhaya, Abhayā
Nirbhaya
Titikshā
Viśaṅka
Viśākha
Yudhishṭhira

## *Desirelessness*
Akāma, Akāmā
Nirmada
Nishkāma
Nishkāmukā

## *Detachment*
Anahaṅkāri, Anahaṅkārinī
Asakti
Asaṅga, Asaṅginī
Avadhūta
Guṇātīta
Nirlepa
Nirmama
Saṅgahīnā

## *Dharma*
Bodhidharma
Dharmabandhu
Dharmacakra
Dharmacāriṇi
Dharmadeva
Dharmanātha
Dharmanitya, Dharmanityā
Dharmapara
Dharmapatha
Dharmaputra
Dharmarata
Dharmaśakti
Dharmātman
Dharmiṇī
Dharmishṭha, Dharmishhā
Dhārmika, Dhārmikī
Kṛitadharma
Niti
Nītiman
Ṛītā

## *Discrimination*
Nirmoha
Nirmohinī
Viveka
Vivekī, Vivekinī

*Dispassion*
Vairāgī
Vairāginī
Viraja, Virajā
Virakta
Virāgī, Virāgiṇī

*Faith*
Nidhruvi
Satī
Śraddhā

*Freedom*
Aklishṭa, Aklishṭā
Akopa
Akrodha
Akrūra
Anasūya
Anāpadā
Aśoka
Aśokā

*Gentleness*
Lalitā
Lalitāmbikā
Nalinī

*Goodness*
Satī
Satpati
Sudeva, Sudevī

*Heroism*
Mahāvīra
Naravīra
Nārya
Yadu

*Honesty*
Ṛijumati
Sarala, Saralā

*Hope*
Āśā

*Humility*
Adambha, Adambhā
Nati
Uddānta
Vinatā
Vinaya

*Innocence*
Lalitā
Lalitāmbikā

*Mercy*
Dayā
Dayālan
Dayāvan, Dayāvatī
Kṛipā
Kṛipādharā
Kṛipālu, Kṛipāmayī
Kṛipāparā
Kṛipāsāgara
Mṛiḍa
Mṛiḍi, Mṛiḍā

*Mind Control*
Nirahaṅkāra
Nirmada
Nirmoha
Nirodha
Niruddha
Nivṛitti

*Modesty*
Hrīmatī, Hrīman
Lajjā

*Non-Injury*
Ahimsā

*Patience*
Kshamā
Titikshu

*Peace*
Praśānt
Praśāntī
Śānta
Śānti

*Renunciation*
Tyāga
Tyāgī, Tyāginī

*Righteousness*
Dhārmika, Dharmikī

*Sacrificing*
Hotā
Ishṭin, Ishṭinī
Ṛijukratu
Swāhā
Yajamāna
Yajña
Yajñadhara
Yajñamūrti
Yajñapati
Yajñapriya
Yajñatrātā
Yajñeśa
Yājaka
Yājī
Yājnavalkya

*Sense Control*
Dāmodara
Indra
Jitendriya
Samyama
Samyamin, Samyaminī
Uparati
Upaśānta, Upaśāntā

*Skillful*
Daksha
Dakshiṇa
Dakshiṇā
Kṛitnu
Kuśala, Kuśalā
Kuśalin, Kuśalinī
Ṛibhu
Ṛibhuksha
Ṛibhwa
Sādhaka
Yogya, Yogyā

*Surrender*
Prapatti

*Tranquility*
Suprasannā
Śama
Umā
Upaśānta, Upaśāntā

*Truthful*
Ārjava, Ārjavā
Kṛishṇa
Ṛitādhāman
Ṛitāyin
Ṛiyāyus
Satyabhāmā
Satyajit
Satyam, Satyā
Satyarūpā
Satyavan
Satyavati
Tattwa

*Vow*
Devavrata
Dhyānavrata
Ekavrata
Priyavrata
Vrata
Vratī, Vratinī

### *Worthiness*
Arha
Pūrya, Pūryā
Ucathya

## *Wealth*

Dhanada
Dhanadāyinī
Dhanalakshmī
Dhananetā
Dhananetrī
Dhanapatī
Dhanapāla
Dhanādhipa
Dhaneśa
Dhaneśwara
Dhaneśwarī
Jayalakshmī
Kubera
Lakshmī
Mahālakshmī
Ṛiddha
Ṛiddhi
Sampadin, Sampadinī
Sampat
Vasumatī
Vasupati
Vittakapati
Vittanātha
Vittapati
Vitteśa

## *Worship*

### *Items of Worship*
Vibhūti

### *Offerings*
Dakshiṇa, Dakshiṇā

### *Sacrificer*
Yājaka
Yājī

### *Worship*
Arcanā
Arka
Arkī, Arkinī
Āratī
Bhajana, Bhajanā
Devahūti
Ishtā
Ishṭi, Ishṭinī
Īḍitā, Īḍitrī
Jagadvandya
Kṛipaṇyu
Mahāpūjya
Mūrti
Namasya, Namasyā

Pareshṭī
Pūjaka
Pūjayitā, Pūjayitrī
Pūjā
Pūjikā
Tīrthasevā
Upāsaka, Upāsikā
Upāsā, Upāsanā
Upāsitā, Upāsitrī
Vanditā, Vanditrī
Vandya, Vandyā

# *Yoga: Meditation and Mind*

## *Mantra*

Akshara
Bindu
Hari Om
Mantra
Mantrī, Mantriṇī
Nādabindu
Omkāra
Praṇava
Sāvitrī

## *Meditation*

Devamuni
Dhyānapara
Dhyānarata
Dhyānavan, Dhyānavatī
Dhyānavrata
Dhyāyinī

## *Mind and its Qualities*

Divyamati
Ekamati
Mati
Pūtamati
Mahāsattwa
Manoramā
Samatā
Sumati
Tulya, Tulyā

## *Yoga*

Yogeśa
Yogeśwara, Yogeśwarī
Yogī, Yoginī
Yogya, Yogyā

# *Index to the Cross-Reference*

The Cross-Reference has its own index—a complete alphabetical list of meanings, which can be used in a similar way.

For example: you may wish to select a name that means "lotus." By turning to the Index, you will find "lotus" listed alphabetically along with the page number upon which it appears in the Cross-Reference. Now that you are in the Cross-Reference you can review all the names with the meaning "lotus." Then you may select a name and look up its specific meaning in the Dictionary.

## A



## B

# C



# D

# E



# F

flower, 285
food, 278
forehead, 253
forest, 285
form, 267
form, non-human, 267, 268
fortunate, 248
fragrant, 285
freedom, 294
friend, 278
friendliness, 278
fulfiller, 268
full, 249

# G

Ganges, 280
garland, 285
gentleness, 294
giver, 268, 269
giver, law-, 272
giver, life-, 269
giving, 276
glittering, 250
glorious, 248
glowing, 250
goal, 273, 291
God (all of Section I), 247-272
Goddess, 262-266
gods, king of, 254
gods, lord of, 254
gods, mother of, 266
gods, spouses of, 292
golden, 252
goodness, 294
grace filled, 248
graceful, 248
grass, 286
great, 248
guardian, 271
gurus, 290

# H

hair (see also: locks, matted), 253

# L



# M

# N



# O



# P

## Q



## R



## S

# Ś

# T



# U



# V



# W

# Y

# *About the Editors*

*Prem Anjali, Ph.D.*, earned her doctorate in counseling psychology from The Union Institute Graduate School. She is currently writing a book on Yoga psychotherapy. Since 1975, she has been a member of the staff of Integral Yoga Publications (IYP), and also has been a Contributing Editor for the *Integral Yoga* Magazine, as well as a number of other IYP publications, including, *The Healthy Vegetarian, The Master's Touch, Gems of Wisdom, How To Find Happiness,* and *Pathways to Peace*. She has produced numerous audio tapes, including, *The Sacred Mantram* series, *Guided Meditation*, and *The Breath of Life* series. She also has served as the personal assistant to Sri Swami Satchidananda (Sri Gurudev) since 1979. She has had the privilege of seeing Sri Gurudev bless devotees with spiritual names and explain their meanings. It was this profound experience that inspired this book.

*Sri Swami Yogananda* is Founder-Director of the Kaivalya Ashrama in France. An eminent Sanskrit scholar, well-versed in the scriptures of Vedanta, Sri Swamiji is highly qualified as a teacher of the science of Yoga. His knowledge of Sanskrit and his clear intellectual insight greatly enhances this work. Swami Yogananda was the first Western disciple initiated by his revered Master, Sri Swami Satchidanandaji Maharaj, into the Holy Order of Sannyas. Attainment of that great spiritual blessing, early in 1971, crowned the keen interest Swamiji had taken in Yoga since adolescence, and he was given the name Yogananda, Bliss of Yoga. Filled with faith and devotion, Sri Swamiji lives what he professes.

*Lakshmi Barsel, Ph.D.*, received her doctorate in linguistic anthropology from Columbia University. She has been a student of Swami Satchidananda since 1979 and presently lives at Satchidananda Ashram-Yogaville. She was previously an instructor at the Yogaville Vidyalayam, a private, non-profit school developed to be a *Vidyalayam*, Temple of Learning, where students can benefit from incorporating the precepts and practices of Integral Yoga into the classroom. The Sanskrit language holds a special interest for Dr. Barsel, who also serves as a linguistic consultant for Integral Yoga Publications.

# *About Sri Swami Satchidananda and the Integral Yoga Institute*

The Reverend Sri Swami Satchidananda (Sri Gurudev) is a world-renowned spiritual teacher and Yoga Master. He is a living example of both the teachings of Integral Yoga and its goal. Not limited to any one organization, religion or country, Sri Gurudev receives invitations from around the world to speak about the way to peace—both individual and universal—and to bring people together in ecumenical gatherings. He is the author of *Integral Yoga Hatha* (in French and English editions), *To Know Your Self, Integral Yoga: The Yoga Sutras of Patanjali,* and other books, and is the subject of the biography, *Sri Swami Satchidananda: Apostle of Peace.* Sri Gurudev also serves as Advisor to the International Yoga Teachers Association, European Union of National Yoga Federations, and the California Yoga Teachers Association, and is Honorary President of the British Wheel of Yoga. He is the recipient of the Martin Buber Award for Outstanding Service to Humanity, and the Humanitarian Award of the Anti-Defamation League of B'nai B'rith as well as two Honorary Doctorates.

The Integral Yoga Institute/Integral Yoga International was founded in the United States in 1966 and functions under the guidance of Sri Gurudev. Today, over 40 Integral Yoga Institutes (IYIs) and Integral Yoga Teaching Centers (IYTCs) throughout the United States and abroad offer classes and workshops in postures, meditation, nutrition and stress reduction, as well as all of the branches of Yoga. Daily classes, evening programs and longer courses are all available to the public. Teacher Training courses, seminars and silent retreats are also held regularly. Integral Yoga Publications disseminates the teachings of Sri Gurudev through books, audio cassettes, video tapes and a bimonthly magazine. Integral Yoga Distribution also makes available books, tapes and items from a wide variety of spiritual paths and disciplines.

*The Goal of Integral Yoga, and the birthright of every individual, is to realize the spiritual unity behind all the diversities of the entire creation and to live harmoniously as members of one universal family. This goal is achieved by maintaining our natural condition of: a body of optimum health and strength, senses under total control, a mind well-disciplined, clear and calm, an intellect as sharp as a razor, a will as strong and pliable as steel, a heart full of unconditional love and compassion, an ego as pure as crystal, and a life filled with Supreme Peace and Joy.*

-Sri Swami Satchidananda